Philip Seymour Hoffman

ALSO BY PETER SHELLEY
AND FROM McFARLAND

*Neil Simon on Screen: Adaptations
and Original Scripts for Film
and Television* (2015)

*Gwen Verdon: A Life on Stage
and Screen* (2015)

Sandy Dennis: The Life and Films (2014)

Australian Horror Films, 1973–2010 (2012)

Jules Dassin: The Life and Films (2011)

*Frances Farmer: The Life and Films
of a Troubled Star* (2011)

*Grande Dame Guignol Cinema: A History
of Hag Horror from* Baby Jane *to* Mother (2009)

Philip Seymour Hoffman
The Life and Work

PETER SHELLEY

McFarland & Company, Inc., Publishers
Jefferson, North Carolina

Special thanks to Barry Lowe and Kath Perry, with additional thanks given to Candy Honore and Stewart South.

LIBRARY OF CONGRESS CATALOGUING-IN-PUBLICATION DATA

Names: Shelley, Peter, 1962– author.
Title: Philip Seymour Hoffman : the life and work / Peter Shelley.
Description: Jefferson, North Carolina : McFarland & Company, Inc., Publishers, 2017. | Includes bibliographical references and index.
Identifiers: LCCN 2016056251 | ISBN 9781476662435 (softcover : acid free paper) ∞
Subjects: LCSH: Hoffman, Philip Seymour, 1967–2014. | Actors—United States—Biography. | Motion picture producers and directors—United States—Biography.
Classification: LCC PN2287.H565 S54 2017 | DDC 791.4302/8092 [B] —dc23
LC record available at https://lccn.loc.gov/2016056251

BRITISH LIBRARY CATALOGUING DATA ARE AVAILABLE

ISBN (print) 978-1-4766-6243-5
ISBN (ebook) 978-1-4766-2572-0

© 2017 Peter Shelley. All rights reserved

No part of this book may be reproduced or transmitted in any form or by any means, electronic or mechanical, including photocopying or recording, or by any information storage and retrieval system, without permission in writing from the publisher.

On the cover Philip Seymour Hoffman as Truman Capote in *Capote*, 2005 (Sony Pictures Classics/Photofest)

Printed in the United States of America

*McFarland & Company, Inc., Publishers
Box 611, Jefferson, North Carolina 28640
www.mcfarlandpub.com*

Table of Contents

Preface ... 1

1. The Beginning ... 5
2. *Boogie Nights* ... 23
3. *True West* ... 43
4. *Love Liza* ... 53
5. A Son, *Capote* ... 71
6. Oscar ... 87
7. *Synecdoche, New York* and *Doubt* ... 102
8. *Mary and Max, Jack Goes Boating* ... 117
9. *A Late Quartet, The Master* ... 134
10. *The Hunger Games: Catching Fire, A Most Wanted Man* ... 151
11. The End ... 167

Appendix: Appearances on Film, Television and in Theater ... 185
Bibliography ... 191
Index ... 217

Preface

When the news came that Philip Seymour Hoffman had died on February 2, 2014, it was shocking. It wasn't just that we had lost another movie star to a drug overdose. The actor's history of addiction was known and there had been reports that he had slipped back in the months prior to his death, which made the cause of his demise less surprising. The shock of it was more that Hoffman had suddenly left us, since he had been visible in movies and on the stage for more than two decades.

In commercial films and art house fare, Hoffman was always there, but now he was gone. He left behind a body of work that *Rolling Stone* said was a tribute to his struggle for excellence and a restless need to create and work. He had 55 theatrical and television movies to his credit. The word "genius" was used by some to describe him. One of his friends called him a genius because he committed without prejudice, believed wholeheartedly and toiled tirelessly and without restraint, and was always pushing, pushing, pushing toward the edge, wherever that was.

If the actor's death at age 46 lacked the mythic resonance of others like James Dean, Marilyn Monroe and River Phoenix who had also died too young, the reason might have been that Hoffman was not a traditional movie star. His career trajectory may have been a sign of the new era in movies where stars moved between leading roles and supporting roles, and also worked in television. But Hoffman did not present as a movie star. He didn't have the same glamour appeal as contemporaries Brad Pitt and George Clooney, two actors he had played in support of. Hoffman was known more as an actor's actor, who could steal scenes from anyone without showboating because he was just so good. He was often described as one of the best of his generation.

Hoffman could play tragedy and farce, do period and contemporary parts, do accents, cut and dye his hair, and gain and lose weight. He even danced and sang in *Along Came Polly* and *The Master*. But as no actor can play everything, he also had limitations. These involved his portly physicality and an emotional restriction where he could play anger and rage well but tears were more difficult to produce. Hoffman's appetites seemed to make it hard for him to stay fit, particularly as he aged. His blonde hair turned white, not gray, with age, which was an advantage. But while Hoffman could be a mannered performer, overusing hand gestures and self-conscious touching and a raucous laugh for enthusiasm, he always seemed truthful. You were aware that he was acting but you didn't mind so much because you believed him. He had technique but unlike, say, Meryl Streep, another star he supported, you didn't resent it.

French movie card showing Hoffman's different looks in, from left top, *Flawless* (1999), *Magnolia* (1999), *Along Came Polly* (2003) and *Capote* (2005).

Hoffman was brave. He had no movie star vanity and was prepared to look silly and be humiliated. Think of how he "sharted" himself in *Along Came Polly*. This may have endeared him forever to teenage boys but might otherwise have haunted the reputation of someone who wanted to be perceived as a serious actor. His apparent affinity for outsiders provided him with parts that few movie stars would have attempted. He played gay men more than once, as well as a transgender person, a chronic masturbator and obscene telephone caller, gamblers, substance abusers and alcoholics. Perhaps what helped the actor was that he had an Everyman quality that allowed audiences to access characters that could be unattractive. Hoffman was known to be generous and unassuming about his own talent in real life that helped, even when he was playing unattractive people.

As an actor he could be sensitive but also loutish. His best roles were a combination of the two, where he had both introverted and extroverted characteristics. The actor was smart enough to pick roles that had dimension, even when the dimension may have appeared to be slim, as in *Mission: Impossible III*. That film demonstrated that Hoffman could do villains, but it also showed how he had the business savvy to alternate between commercial and art house projects. One might question some of his commercial choices; his appearances in the *Hunger Games* movies towards the end of his career are suspect since they offer such unchallenging work. However, apart from the continued visibility they gave Hoffman, they also no doubt helped him to maintain a box office cache for other projects and also perhaps supported the work of his film company, Cooper's Town.

Hoffman wasn't a traditional leading man. His one attempt at playing one, in *State and Main*, was unsuccessful. If he had a romance on screen, it was not a traditional romance, and if he was shown to have sex, he was not a Don Juan. When Hoffman was naked on screen, it wasn't so we could ogle his body. His leading man roles were more character parts where he was preoccupied with his work or recreation rather than his leading lady, if he had one. And if he did, she was either a marginal character, or as in *Jack Goes Boating* she was as untraditional as he.

Ethan Hawke said that Hoffman was an unconventional movie star in an era where there was no such thing as unconventionality. According to Hawke, nowadays everyone was gorgeous and had abs, and you had Hoffman standing saying, "Hey, I've got something to say, too! It may not be pretty, but it's true." Hawke added that was why the world needed the actor so badly. Hawke would also comment on Hoffman's ascendance to leading man roles with *Capote* (2005), saying he graduated from being promising and interesting to being in complete control of a very complicated part. He had "grown up."

I first noticed Hoffman in his heartbreaking breakout role in *Boogie Nights* (1997). His Scotty was vulnerable and self-conscious but self-aware enough to know how he had miscalculated in making a pass at a heterosexual man and regretting it. It was a supporting part but it made an impact and led to better things. Hoffman's *Capote* won him the Best Actor Academy Award and if his achievement is somewhat diminished by Toby Jones essaying the role better in *Infamous*, it still assured him a permanent place in Hollywood's history. My favorite Hoffman performance is probably in *Happiness* (1998). Despite playing what could have been a loathsome pervert who is obsessed with a woman he could never get, it was Hoffman's character's reaction to another woman that seemed to be as socially awkward as his character that was surprising and ultimately very touching. This was the kind of role the actor excelled at and, though it was a supporting one, it gave him a range of emotions to express.

The existing books on Hoffman include a 2014 one in Italian by Marco Bolsi; several that are collections of Wikipedia entries; and an illustrated one by the Editors of Plexus, published in 2016. There are chapters on the actor in Rosemarie Tichler and Barry Jay Kaplan's *Actors at Work* and Murray Pomerance's *Shining in Shadows: Movie Stars of the 2000s*. But none of them provides a satisfactory look at Hoffman's life and career. This book attempts to do so, although since some of his work in film and television is unavailable for viewing, it regrettably cannot be considered a definitive study. Notably missing are in-depth analyses of the Polish *Szuler* (aka *Cheat*, 1994), which is said to have been the first film he made but not the first released, and the never-aired pilot of the television comedy series *Happyish* (2014). In these and other cases, as much information as possible has been provided. Accessing sources and any associated biographies and books on Hoffman's co-workers allowed me to consider differing views of some of the events in his life and to highlight any apparent inaccuracies. I also reviewed newspaper and magazine interviews that the actor gave, with the *New York Times* archives and the Internet Movie Database's Related News being particularly helpful. YouTube.com was also invaluable.

The book presents Hoffman's career in the context of his life. For all the movie and TV work I have viewed, I have positioned Hoffman's place in the project, commented on his look and performance, provided notes on the character's importance to the narrative, and included any comments I have found *by* the actor as well as comments *on* him by his co-workers.

1

Beginning

Philip Seymour Hoffman was born on July 23, 1967, in Fairport, a suburb of Rochester, New York. He described the place as being much like Kansas, but in the past it had been known for its industry. After the building of the Erie Canal, Fairport had been an active port and thrived through its selling of baking soda, pectin and the original open-top sanitary can, a breakthrough in the safe use of factory-canned goods.

It was rural conservative and far from cosmopolitan but the Hoffmans were relatively well-to-do and geared towards a cultured life. The family had German, English, Irish and Dutch ancestry. His father Gordon Stowell Hoffman, a native of Geneva, New York, worked for the Xerox Corporation, one of the region's major employers, travelling the country to update systems in the early days of computers (the 1970s and '80s). Hoffman seemed not to know exactly what his father did, and preferred to say it was something "spooky with computers," and also "old-school-meets-new-school-type stuff." His mother Marilyn O'Connor (*née* Loucks) came from nearby Waterloo. She worked as an elementary schoolteacher, then became a civil rights activist, lawyer and eventually a family court judge in 2000.

The Hoffmans had four children: Gordon Jr. a.k.a. Gordy, Jill, Emily and Philip. Hoffman said that they would have been upper-middle-class if their parents had stayed together but since they divorced, the family was basically middle-class. His parents were not especially religious, though Gordon was said to be German Protestant and Marilyn Irish Catholic. Philip went to Sunday school. He was baptized as a Catholic and confirmed, but although he attended mass, he considered it more a chore than a blessing. He was turned off by the church's boring rote repetition, and he found the scriptures "sometimes really brutal."

The Hoffmans divorced when Philip was nine. Marilyn had custody of the children. Gordon moved out and was from then on an absent father. Hoffman believed that his mother was a special woman, the most positive can-do person he knew and the most fun, incredibly intelligent and optimistic. She'd always look at a situation and say, "Right, what do I want to do now?" Hoffman's father was one of the brightest men he ever met, but in contrast, a more brooding intellectual guy and more a slave to his emotions than his mother.

The biggest influence on Hoffman's youth was Gordy, who was two years older and very energetic, creative and smart. Something of an entrepreneur, Gordy would be forever finding money-making schemes, taking his brother to cut down trees in someone's yard, or picking strawberries to sell on the street corner. Hoffman idolized him and wanted to emulate him. But he also made efforts to surpass him. To live up to the status as the charismatic Gordy's brother, Hoffman chose sports, which would see him rise above his brother and his peers. Sports became his childhood passion and this was a part of himself that he never lost. Hoffman's friends would joke that he was the only person in the world who got stronger from eating ice cream. By the time he'd reached Fairport High School, he'd revealed a talent for tennis, basketball, baseball, football and, understandably given his stocky build, wrestling. Hoffman would also smack a few golf balls around the grounds of the Martha Brown Middle School.

Hoffman said that before a wrestling match he would start yawning and doze off in front of the people. He attributed this to the anxiety and stress of the moment. Hoffman added that he would later have the same experience before performing on stage: He would doze off in his dressing room. Gordy described his brother as a jock and a natural athlete. Gordy added that Philip was a vulnerable, open, heart-on-his-sleeve kid, and that the emotional vocabulary that Philip would later access was already there as a boy. Being a gifted athlete gave Hoffman a better-than-average control over his body. At this time, the boy was not dreaming of a life on the stage but he made a screen debut of sorts at age nine, playing a prison guard in Gordy's Super-8 suspense movie *The Last Escape*.

Marilyn approved the idea of her son loving sports because she was a big sports fan. She also took him to the theater. When Hoffman was 11 or 12 she took him to see his first play, at the Geneva Theatre regional house in Rochester, where a lot of new plays were performed by actors brought in from New York. The play was Arthur Miller's *All My Sons* and the boy sat in the front row. He said that it was like a miracle to him and it permanently changed him. When he was in junior high school, he and his mother went back to the theater regularly. He said he loved it but he never thought he'd ever do it. Some of the productions he saw were *Quilters* and *Alms for the Middle Class* starring a teenage Robert Downey, Jr., which was particularly inspirational. Hoffman also recalled being moved by the made-for-TV movie *The Jericho Mile* (1979). However as a jock he could also be dismissive of the local arts scene, such as when he sabotaged neighborhood plays involving his sister Emily. By the time Hoffman was in high school, Gordy had already graduated so the boy became closer to Emily, who was a year younger.

In his sophomore year of high school he suffered a neck injury during wrestling practice. Sources differ as to whether this occurred when the boy was 14 or 15. It resulted in his having to wear a neck brace. A doctor advised him that the injury meant his career in contact sports was over. Wearing the brace, he would play baseball. Hoffman was a freckle-faced kid who perceived himself as unattractive and the brace didn't help his self-image. When his doctor asked him if he still had pain, he lied.

Hoffman made a pact with God that he would no longer play sports. So instead of trying out for baseball, he auditioned for a play. There was a beautiful high school girl he had a huge crush on. He reported that she walked by him one day and when he asked where she was going, she told him she was going to audition for a play. It seemed like something worth giving up baseball for. He auditioned for and won the part of Becky Thatcher's brother in a musical production of *Tom Sawyer*. He got to be with the girl every day, although she did not return his feelings. But suddenly the crush gave way to the realization that he was doing theater and being an actor and hanging out with people who had the same interest.

Hoffman eventually enjoyed the experience, applying the same competitive drive he had with wrestling to grappling with roles on the stage. Doing the show gave him an upset stomach from nerves but he carried on and learned how being on stage provided a release from the pain. Hoffman felt that acting required concentration and he considered it walking into the fire with his fear.

He wasn't about to also sacrifice his love of sports, however, even for acting— at least not yet. When his mother said it was okay to be a theater person who also liked to watch baseball, he joined the drama club. Hoffman felt acting and sports were similar because both demanded discipline, creativity and visualization. In wrestling, if he was on top, he could strategize a move and see himself do it, much like acting. Both had a goal he could go after, and from this activity, character was revealed. This character showed what the person was made of—whether they went for broke and put everything on the line. Acting was another high-stakes game for Hoffman, and after he stopped playing sports, one passion replaced another.

He got a small part in a play and came to appreciate the camaraderie of the participants. He also benefited from the support he received from teachers who approached their work from a very creative standpoint and saw his interest in the theater. This resulted in Hoffman excelling educationally in high school. His drama teacher, Midge (sometimes called Marjory) Marshall, kept the kids away from the standard musicals in favor of Shakespeare and "serious" material. Hoffman auditioned for and was cast as Radar in a production of *M*A*S*H*. But when he stole a big scene from "Hotlips," he was told he would never be given a lead until he learned to work within the troupe. Hoffman researched and analyzed his characters and used his imagination to bring them to life. These methods helped him stand out but it was perceived as attention-seeking.

In Arthur Miller's *The Crucible*, he played the minor role of John Proctor's jailer, depressed and drunk. Impressed, Marshall said he radiated pathos in every droop and slurred word. She advised him that could hold the stage, and he was so truthful that she promoted him.

Hoffman also took a class called "The Novel" where he read what he considered really great stuff like *The Stranger* and *The Great Train Robbery*. In high school it was felt that if you remembered what you learned you were good and if you didn't you were bad. The actual interpretation of what you had learned was never encouraged. Hoffman said the class opened up a whole new world of reading *and* having an opinion, deciphering, identifying and personalizing what he had read. He said was a great course because it led to who he later became.

In his senior year at Fairport High School, 17-year-old Hoffman played Willy Loman in *Death of a Salesman*, a role he would reprise later in life. The English department had wanted to stage the play for years, since it was being studied in junior high. Marshall always refused because she said there was never a high school boy who could play Willy. But then she had Hoffman. He knew it was way beyond him, but he asked himself what the sense was in doing something he knew he could do. Hoffman said it was the law of nature that the higher, the risk the more you were compelled to succeed. Later he would say that he looked for something that took him to a scary place, something unknown, that would take up all his time, all his head—his everything.

During rehearsals the young actor went to New York and saw Dustin Hoffman's 1984 Broadway performance of Loman. He attended a matinee on the last day of the play's run and sat in a box seat with three friends. After the show they talked about it and Hoffman was still talking about it when he got home. He was taken by the sense of theater as a community that he was a part of, and couldn't wait to tell his schoolmates about it. He admitted that he blatantly stole Dustin Hoffman's emotional ideas for the part, which made the young actor's performance crude but impassioned.

Before he went on stage, his mother had asked him what he expected from the experience, and he told her he wanted a standing ovation. Hoffman wanted the audience to know how hard he had worked to deliver. He wore horn-rimmed spectacles to attempt to pass as the 57-year-old Loman. Sources differ as to the size of the audience—between 600 and 700 11th graders at one performance. Marshall said that she was nervous because juniors could be so unruly. She said that from the moment Hoffman ambled on stage with the salesman's two sample suitcases, the audience was silent. They reportedly gave polite applause to each actor as they took their curtain call, but when it was Hoffman's turn, he got his standing ovation. The audience was said to have been stunned by his risk-taking. His sister Emily commented that seeing him in the play made her know her brother was destined for a life as an actor. Whether or not he became famous, she knew that he was going to do theater.

Hoffman read Lee Strasberg's book *A Dream of Passion*, which told of calling yourself not an actor but an artist. This opened Hoffman's eyes. He started learning and absorbing in a fuller, quicker way, by looking at himself through an artist's eyes. Hoffman said everything became more interesting because everything became part of how he was going to create something. He didn't know what that was going to be but he wanted to be free to explore all avenues and not just be told that something was his niche and that was what he was going to do successfully. Hoffman felt the sense of possibility was not encouraged enough in education, and later he would get involved in education in public schools.

He was accepted for a Saratoga Springs high school program run by New York State's Circle in the Square Summer School of the Arts. Thirty-two kids from all over the state participated. Hoffman said that summer had a lot to do with his decision to study theater in college. He credited two teachers for two different approaches: one action-oriented "high stakes, life and death stuff," and the other more internal and classically Method. It seemed to him that one without the other meant bad acting, but the two together meant you had a shot at doing well. Hoffman commented that a lot of acting teachers would say, "Don't think, just do" but he had a teacher say, "No, no, no. Be a thinking actor." The boy felt that they advised students not to think they were going to fail, and that thinking didn't have to make you self-conscious. He related it to a ballgame where you could watch the ball and think about how it how it was going to curve and then you might actually hit it.

At the school, Hoffman met future collaborators Bennett Miller and Dan Futterman. Futterman would also go to the same college as the actor, and they lived in the same dorm two floors away from each other. Futterman knew New York and showed Hoffman around. Miller commented that when he first met Hoffman he saw that everybody else liked him. Then, and later in life, Miller said that he couldn't think of anybody ever saying a bad word about him, although personally he found him to be a pain in the ass. Hoffman became very popular, not because he was a social animal, but more because he was genuinely serious about what he was doing. He was passionate and also fun. He drank a lot of beer, and he could tell a story and light up a room. You wanted to be around him. Hoffman was even then like Truman Capote in that you wanted to sit at his table. When the summer ended, Hoffman flew from Rochester twice to visit Miller at his Westchester County home. That same year he scored his first professional acting job with the local Shipping Dock Theatre, having been plucked from school by director Barbara Biddy for a part in *A Breeze in the Gulf*.

Graduating from school in 1985, Hoffman auditioned to study theater at Syracuse University, Carnegie Mellon and New York University and was accepted into the latter's Tisch School of the Arts. Between starting on the program and graduating from high school, he continued training at the summer program. To support himself while at university, Hoffman worked as an usher because his parents did not have the means to help him financially. With friends, he co-founded his own experimental acting company, the Bullstoi Ensemble (sometimes spelled Bolstoy), while still on campus. However, after reading through one Eugene O'Neill play, they decided they were too hung over to rehearse in the mornings, the only suitable time for such extracurricular work.

Hoffman began to have a problem with partying, indulging in "advanced" drinking and drugging. He would do anything he could get his hands on and he liked it all. Hoffman claimed he did so because he panicked over whether he was going to get to do the kind of things he wanted to do in his life. He admitted he put himself into situations and predicaments that were dangerous and he realized that he wouldn't be able to do the things he wanted to if he kept on in the same way. He tried to quit on his own for a couple of years but he eventually realized that he couldn't do it alone so he checked himself into rehab at the age of 22.

Hoffman said he might have died from drug abuse early if his success in acting had come at a younger age and he always thanked God it didn't. He had so much empathy for those young actors who were 19 and were rich, famous and troubled. The actor said that rehab gave him a renewed outlook on life, and he told himself that he could do the things he wanted to get done. In a 2011 interview Hoffman said that he knew deep down that he still looked at the idea of drinking with the same ferocity that he did back then. It was still pretty tangible. He advised that just because all that time had passed didn't mean maybe it was just a phase. Hoffman said that was who he was.

He studied at the Circle in the Square Theatre School and graduated with a Bachelor of Fine Arts drama degree in 1989. He still didn't know he would have a career but at the end of his tenure he started to think it was the only thing he wanted to do. But something happened that changed his mind. Hoffman was in love and seriously considered dropping out of acting. He and his girlfriend planned to avoid the conservative traps of jobs and responsibilities and simply be together. When Hoffman learned that she was going to audition for the 1989 Williamstown Theatre Festival in Massachusetts, he auditioned too, in front of Austin Pendleton. The director liked Hoffman immediately, later recalling that he came in straight out of college and was exceptionally far along in his work. He was hired by Pendleton, who became something of a mentor for the young actor. Later the director would say that some people you take credit for discovering, but with Hoffman anyone in the room would have hired him.

At Williamstown, Pendleton directed *Henry IV Parts I and II* which ran from July 4 to 15, 1989, with the actor credited as Philip Hoffman. He appeared in *Part I* as a member of the funeral procession and in *Part II* as Peter Bullcalf. In August 1989 Hoffman acted with Pendleton on Bertold Brecht's *Mother Courage* with Olympia Dukakis in the title role; he played a Peasant Son. Pendleton then cast him as Edgar in his production of *King Lear* at the Hole Theatre in New Jersey. Hoffman recalled that his pants ripped and he wasn't wearing any underwear; he slipped on stage when he came on, the rip went from his "ball sack to the top of the crack of his ass" and he said his "ass was hanging out in the breeze." He would later use this story as an improvisation for a scene in *Capote* and in the DVD audio commentary gave more detail about it. He was not wearing underwear because he had to be naked late in the play.

In New York he went for the usual Off-Broadway acting jobs but was unsuccessful. When he wasn't bumming around, drinking coffee with his friends, he supported himself by working as a waiter, a children's caregiver, a swimming pool lifeguard at a high-rise gym, and a cashier at the trendy restaurant Indochine. The lifeguard job gave him the opportunity to meet one of his heroes, Miles Davis. His jobs were short-lived; he was always fired for incompetence brought on by lack of motivation. What Hoffman really wanted to do was act, and though he had set his heart on a stage career, he was up for screen work. Despite the fact that the stocky strawberry blond with everyday looks seemed to be nobody's idea of a leading man, he decided to try Hollywood.

Ironically, the first job Hoffman landed was filmed in New York: a supporting part in the NBC crime drama *Law & Order* episode "The Violence of Summer," broadcast on February 5, 1991. It was written by Michael Duggan and directed by Don Scardino. Billed as Philip Hoffman, he played drug runner Steven B. Hanauer, one of four young men accused of the gang rape of TV reporter Monica Devries (Megan Gallagher). The actor appears in four scenes and he has two strong moments. In the first, in a courtroom scene, he yells at the co-defendant Ryan M. Cutrona (Ken Johnston)—Hoffman's face turns red as he yells "We know what you did!" at Johnston. In the second scene, the actor does a strange covering of his eyes with his hands when he hears that the rape case against him has been dismissed. The rape is not shown so we don't know if Steven participated, but the narrative has him recharged and convicted of attempted rape in the second degree.

Some sources claim that Hoffman made his film debut, as Phil Hoffman, in the Polish period drama *Szuler a.k.a. Cheat* (1994). This was said to have been filmed on location in Poland in 1991. Written and directed by Adek Drabinski, it centered on gamblers Victor Moritz (Jerzy Zelnik) and Baron Rufolf de Sevre (Justin Deas) in 1750 Europe. Hoffman played the supporting part of Martin, a coachman. *Szuler* was first screened at the 1992 Polish Film Festival and released in Poland on March 10, 1994. Dubbed-into-Russian excerpts can be seen on YouTube. Hoffman is in two scenes in the footage, the second one showing him laughing, over-gesturing and squeezing his hat self-consciously as he speaks to his master. The actor later advised that to prepare for the part he read James Michener's book *Poland* because for a while he was fascinated by the history of Poland.

He was again billed as Phil Hoffman in his American film debut, the black-and-white indie *Triple Bogey on a Par 5 Hole* (1991). It was written and directed by Amos Poe and filmed in New York. In this crime comedy, French screenwriter Remy Gravelle (Eric Mitchell) interviews the orphaned Levy children, who live on a luxury yacht moored in New York Harbor, and others about the deaths of their parents. The golf reference in the title comes from the fact that the parents made money robbing golfers, but had been killed in a failed attempt on a Maine course. The yacht is also named *Triple Bogey*. Hoffman played Klutch, a friend of Satch Levy (Jesse McBride), and appeared in a one-minute scene in the poolroom on the yacht. He wears a bandana, a dark sleeveless shirt and dark gloves. After losing a game to Satch, he gives him $20. He also laughs throughout the scene, as Klutch speaks to Remy and Satch, then exits. Poe provides one medium shot of Hoffman alone, his figure surrounded by darkness. The film was first screened at the Berlin International Film Festival on February 17, 1991, and released in New York on March 21. It was praised by *New York Times* reviewer Vincent Canby, who made no mention of Hoffman.

Poe had met the actor through his actor-manager friend Davian Littlefield, who took him to the Home Theatre in New York in the spring of 1990. Hoffman was doing a one-act play there and Littlefield considered signing him. The actor was in an ensemble for pieces about racism, in a play that he had written. His play had a couple coming out of a movie theater after seeing an Eddie Murphy film, and had Hoffman do an insane monologue where his character claimed that she only liked Murphy because she thought black men had big penises. Impressed by Hoffman, Poe offered to write a scene for him in the film. The director's advice to Hoffman when they shot the scene was for him to mimic Jack Nicholson, though what he does is not an obvious impersonation. Poe also recommended Hoffman to writer-director Steven Starr for his film *Joey Breaker* (1993). After Hoffman's death, Poe commented that he had a passion for acting that was palpable. He said you couldn't help but just go, "This guy has got all the talent in the world." Poe added that Hoffman had so much in him that it was almost like he had too much for one person.

The actor appeared in the Jane Anderson play *Food and Shelter* at New York's Vineyard Theatre from May to June 1991. Directed by Andre Ernotte, it told the story of a young American homeless family that wins $100 in a lottery and splurges on a day at Disneyland. Hoffman played the part of the father, Earl. Mel Gussow in the *New York Times* wrote that Hoffman gave a vibrant performance.

In his next film, writer-director Stacy Cochran's comedy *My New Gun* (1992), New Jersey housewife Debbie Bender (Diane Lane) is given a gun by her radiologist husband Gerald (Stephen Collins) for protection. It is stolen by their neighbor, Skippy (James LeGros), whom Debbie also has an affair with. The film was shot on location in Teaneck, New Jersey. Hoffman played the supporting role of Chris, Skippy's co-worker at the Red Chimney restaurant. He appears in one scene. We don't know how Chris comes to be shot by the gun by Skippy's father Andrew (Bill Raymond) when Chris goes to Skippy's car. Chris' behavior of yelling for joy at rain and invading people's personal space when he speaks to them can be interpreted as that of someone who is an innocent or a lout. Also, being unshaven at work is another ambiguous character trait. However Chris is observant enough to comment on how Skippy should fill a glass with ice before soda water. Hoffman's performance features his mannerisms of over-gesturing and self-conscious touching, as Chris touches his chin as he speaks.

The film was first screened at the Toronto Film Festival on September 13, 1992, and then released on October 26[2]. The feature tagline was "A comedy about the American dream," and the DVD tagline was "A man, a woman, and the gun that keeps them together." It was praised by Janet Maslin in the *New York Times* and Emanuel Levy in the book *Cinema of Outsiders: The Rise of American Independent Film*. It got a mixed review from *Variety*'s Todd McCarthy who, while not naming Hoffman, claimed that the supporting performances were on the broad side. The film was a box office failure. Diane Lane said that Hoffman seemed so fragile that the cast almost tiptoed around him.

For his next film he was billed as Philip Seymour Hoffman. The actor said that his reasoning for using the middle name was not romantic or special or obnoxious. When he started acting there was another Philip Hoffman, spelled exactly like his, who was successful in musical theater on Broadway. He and the other Philip Hoffman were getting each other's checks. In two-actor one-name situations, the union asked the newcomer to change their name. Hoffman thought to add his middle initial but felt that wasn't enough, so he decided to add his grandfather's name Seymour.

He played a supporting role in Paramount's romantic comedy *Leap of Faith* (1992). It was written by Janus Cercone and said to be based on the book *The Faith Healers* by James Randi, though the source is uncredited in the film. It was directed by Richard Pearce and shot from June 21 to September 1, 1992, on locations in Texas and at a studio at Las Colinas in Irving, Texas. Fraudulent Christian faith healer Jonas Nightengale (Steve Martin) uses his revival meetings in the rural town of Rustwater, Kansas, to bilk believers. Hoffman played the supporting role of Matt, one of Jonas' crew. His shoulder-length hair, parted on the left side, falls over his face though it is often covered in bandanas. Matt also has a beard and chews gum, which suggests his contempt for the shows and the way they exploit people. This contempt is leavened by his enjoyment of the gospel choir and the music used in the show since we see him dancing to them. Matt's wardrobe alternates between shorts and big boots, and then wearing a white jacket over them at the first meeting and then a black jacket and black pants at the second and third meetings. He is seen handing out flyers for the show, and flirting with a teenage girl in a car, behavior that is repeated when he flirts with the girl before Jonas' show. Matt's duties include signaling audience shills, handing out collection buckets, helping people to go to Jonas on stage, catching the ones that Jonas has placed hands on, taking the microphone away from Jonas who no longer needs it, and holding back the crowd when they head for Jonas.

Hoffman appears in seven scenes (including dancing with the crowd to the choir under the closing credits) and has few lines. His best scene is after the crippled boy Boyd (Lukas Haas) is seemingly cured: Matt yells and laughs in enthusiasm over the money the company can make from using his miracle as part of their show. As with his bandanas, Matt is suggested to be a type of stoner as he calls Jonas "man."

The film was released on December 18, 1992, with the taglines "Real miracles, sensibly priced" and "Are you ready for a miracle?" It was praised by Janet Maslin in the

New York Times, but received mixed reviews by *Variety*, Roger Ebert in the *Chicago Sun-Times* and Peter Travers in *Rolling Stone*.

After Hoffman died, Steve Martin said that if you missed Hoffman as Willy Loman, you missed a Willy Loman for all time. Hoffman returned to New York and now lived in in Brooklyn with just a futon bed and worked at a deli. Later he would say that the Brooklyn apartment had two bedrooms and he shared it with a roommate, splitting $750 a month in rent.

He was next cast in Universal's *Scent of a Woman* (1992) where he was billed as Philip S. Hoffman. The film was a remake of an Italian comedy with the same title; that older film was directed by Dino Risi, scripted by Ruggero Maccari and Risi, and based on the Giovanni Arpino novel *The Dark and Honey*. The remake had a screenplay by Bo Goldman and was directed by Martin Brest. It was filmed from December 3, 1991, to April 6, 1992, on location in New York and New Jersey and at the Kaufman Astoria Studios. The plot concerned 17-year-old Charlie Simms (Chris O'Donnell), a Boston Baird Preparatory School student who gets a weekend job caring for blind retired army lieutenant colonel Frank Slade (Al Pacino) at Thanksgiving.

Hoffman played the supporting part of George Willis, Jr., another student. Both boys watch as three other students prepare a prank against the headmaster, Mr. Trask (James Rebhorn), that results in damage to his new Jaguar. They are called to give testimony at a special session of the student faculty disciplinary committee in front of the student body. George reluctantly names the three boys, presumably persuaded to do so by his father (an alumni and a major fundraiser for the school). George's testimony is guarded, since he claims that he could not see without his contact lenses, although this is the only time in the narrative that his eyesight is mentioned. Because George's

Hoffman at left, with Chris O'Donnell in *Scent of a Woman* (1992).

testimony is vague, the moral burden falls on Charlie, who by refusing to identify the three boys risks expulsion.

Hoffman appears in eight scenes and is also heard twice on the telephone with Charlie. Despite the fact that the actor is technically too old to be playing a teenage schoolboy, he gets away with it, and he adds dimension to what could have been an unlikable character. George is a smarmy rich kid with a sense of entitlement, which he demonstrates by being arrogant and rebellious. He laughs and smiles inappropriately, smokes, mocks Trask, spits on the ground, roughhouses with other boys, and wears what appears to be a green leaf in his hair. George also has an overfamiliar manner, especially with Charlie (whom he calls "Chaz") by invading his personal space and touching him. He asks Charlie, who works in the library, to let him take a book that is supposed to be held in reserve. He distracts the librarian Mrs. Hunsaker (June Squibb) so she won't see the three boys pull their prank, and boldly offers his hand to Trask to wish him a nice Thanksgiving after having lied about being able to identify the boys.

Hoffman makes George funny when he shakes his head to say "Quite a piece of machinery" in reference to Trask's Jaguar. In the climactic scene, he makes us sympathize with George's predicament: His anger is shown by a sharp and violent move away from his father (Baxter Harris) who sits with him on the stage for the committee session. George may remain unlikable and his testimony compromised in order to protect himself, but the label of snitch is applied to him. Trask's decision to not expel him is qualified by the committee to say that he receive neither recognition nor commendation for his cooperation. We do not see George after the session so we do not know his fate. However, it is assumed that his relationship with the three boys has been damaged, since they are all suspended. Closeups of Hoffman when the committee members make their determination and when the student body applauds Charlie, who is not punished for his testimony, also suggest that George is aware of what he has lost.

The film had a limited release beginning on December 23, 1992, and then a wide release on January 8, 1993, with the tagline "Col. Frank Slade has a very special plan for the weekend. It involves travel, women, good food, fine wine, the tango, chauffeured limousines and a loaded .45. And he's bringing Charlie along for the ride." It was praised by the *Chicago Sun-Times'* Roger Ebert but received mixed review from *Variety* and Janet Maslin in the *New York Times*. It was a box office success. Al Pacino won the Best Actor Academy Award; there were also nominations for Best Picture, Best Director and Best Screenplay Based on Material Previously Produced or Published.

Hoffman supposedly had to audition five times to get the part and then helped audition other actors for the film by working as a line reader. One of those actors was Ethan Hawke, with whom he would later co-star in *Before the Devil Knows You're Dead* (2007). Hoffman told Hawke that he wouldn't get the *Scent of a Woman* part because he was too interesting.

Hoffman later said that when he saw the film on television, he was a bit mortified by parts of his performance, saying to himself onscreen, "Do less, Phil, less, less!" He Mike Nichols, who later directed the actor in *Charlie Wilson's War* (2007) and in *Death of a Salesman* on stage in 2012, said that *Scent of a Woman* was when he first noticed him. Nichols felt Hoffman summed up all the ways those boarding-school bullies were

In still for *Joey Breaker* (1993).

scary, and there was something deeply ethical about him as an actor that was apparent even then. He said Hoffman had the integrity and commitment to represent his characters without any judgment.

The actor next played a supporting role in the Skouras Pictures/Starr Pictures/Poe Production independent romantic comedy *Joey Breaker*, shot in New York and on location in St. Lucia, West Indies. The material was autobiographical since writer-director Steven Starr was a former agent at William Morris. The title character, essayed by Richard Edson, was an agent for the New York firm of Morgan Creative and the plot concerns his various clients and his romance with Jamaican waitress and nursing student Cyan Worthington (Cedella Marley). Hoffman played Joey's assistant Wiley McCall, who has a hippy-lout element to his character since he repeatedly uses the phrase "rock and roll." During the narrative Wiley is promoted to agent, thanks to Joey. The act is presented as one of generosity and later when Joey tells the agency boss that a mail room boy has been promoted to take Wiley's position, it is apparent that Joey has the power to do so.

Hoffman appeared in 13 scenes, as well as being heard and seen in the reflection of a computer screen. All but one of his scenes were in the agency's office, the exception being when Wiley goes to a club to see one of Joey's clients do his comedy routine. In the office he wore business attire although without a jacket and with different ties, a telephone headset and sometimes a baseball cap. Hoffman employs his mannerisms of over-gesturing and laughing, but enthusiastic yelling is given context since it is used when Wiley learns he is to be promoted. Perhaps the hand-gesturing can also have a context as the behavior of a phony, which Wiley's subservient posture (and eating an apple as he speaks on the telephone) suggests he is. Hoffman's best moment is perhaps his silent unspoken thanks to Joey for the new job, where he touches Joey's arm and then looks down after his boss exits.

The film debuted on March 5, 1993, at the Santa Barbara International Film Festival, and then released in New York on May 14, 1993, with the tagline "There's more to life than making a deal." It was praised by Stephen Holden in the *New York Times* but lambasted by Lawrence Cohn in *Variety*. Cohn wrote that Hoffman consistently upstaged the star with bravura thesping, building on the strong impression he made as the weak-willed preppy in *Scent of a Woman*.

He was billed as Philip Hoffman for his next film, the Touchstone Pictures comic horror *My Boyfriend's Back* (1993), written by Dean Lorey and directed by Bob Balaban. It was filmed from November 2 to December 19, 1992, on Texas locations. Small town high school senior Johnny Dingle (Andrew Lowery) is killed in a convenience store robbery gone wrong and returns as a zombie to romantically pursue 18-year-old Missy McCloud (Traci Linds). Hoffman played Chuck Bronski, muscle for Missy's rejected boyfriend Buck Van Patten (Matthew Fox) and eventually one of Johnny's victims.

The actor appeared in four scenes. Chuck is another of Hoffman's louts, here recalling some of Brando's Stanley Kowalski from *A Streetcar Named Desire* (1951). Chuck walks like a gorilla, with a hunched back and a protruding jaw. He is presumably a football player, since he wears a letter jacket and a baseball cap backwards. His aggressiveness is demonstrated when he yells at people to get out of the way when Buck walks down a school hallway, and his hostility to Johnny as a romantic threat to Buck. He hits a locker next to Johnny before asking him what he is looking at, and his epithets range from "dirtbag" to "dead little snot" to "stinky dead yahoo toucher." In his second scene Hoffman is funny when he tells Johnny, "We're watching you, dead boy. We don't like your kind. You're stinking up the whole school." Hoffman's third scene has a shock cut to Buck swinging a baseball bat after Missy is seen attempting to kiss Johnny in the library. The actor gets a little laugh when Buck sees that he has Johnny cornered and uses a delicate gesture to remove the last piece of glass from a case that covered a fire axe. However Chuck hitting himself in the head when he raises the axe to strike Johnny shows that he is not particularly bright. The narrative has Johnny supposedly eating Buck's stomach, although Balaban doesn't let us see this, only suggesting the action with Johnny's bloodied mouth and the reaction of others.

The film was released on August 6, 1993, with the taglines "A comedy that proves true love never dies" and "Johnny would give an arm and a leg to date Missy. Well, maybe just an arm." A box office failure, it was lambasted by *Variety* and received a mixed review from the *New York Times'* Stephen Holden.

Bob Balaban said that Hoffman was delightful and sweet and wonderful. He went up to the director at one point in a break in the shooting and said, "Bob, I want you to know, I don't always play football heroes who get eaten by zombies. I can basically do anything." Balaban said that Hoffman made the comment in the simplest way, and it made him think he was an endearing person who really knew what he could do. The actor told him, "I can be romantic, I can be adventurous, I can be the bad guy, I can be the good guy. I really can do anything, so please remember that." Balaban had never been spoken to that way by anybody, and he felt that Hoffman didn't have an ounce of

From left, Traci Lind, Andrew Lowery, Danny Zorn, Matthew Fox and Hoffman on far right in front of unidentified band members in *My Boyfriend's Back* **(1993).**

ego in it. The director would later appear on-camera with Hoffman in one scene in *Capote* (2005).

Hoffman next appeared in the independent comic crime drama *Money for Nothing* (1993), written by Ramón Menéndez, Tom Musca and Carol Sobieksi and based on "The Joey Coyle Story," an article by Mark Bowden. The film was directed by Menéndez from February 1 to March 30, 1993, on location in Philadelphia and Pittsburgh. Set in South Philadelphia, it told the true story of unemployed dockworker Joey Coyle (John Cusack) who found $1.2 million that fell out of an armored delivery car. After having the money laundered and attempting to flee the country, Coyle is caught after a five-day hunt but acquitted of charges on the grounds of temporary insanity. Hoffman played the supporting role of Cochran, another unemployed dockworker who hangs around at the local bar, drinking, smoking and playing darts. The actor is in four scenes, with his hair cut short and parted in the middle, and sporting a moustache. He uses a regional accent, laughs and overdoes the gesturing. In his best scene, he hears on television about the reward being offered for Joey's capture. Cochran tries to use the telephone in a back room to report him; his buddy Dunleavy (Currie Graham) pulls out the phone cord to stop Cochran from finishing the call, and the men scuffle. Hoffman's aggression in attacking Dunleavy is disappointingly mild, perhaps because it is mixed with the shame of being a snitch.

The film debuted on August 20, 1993, in Toledo, Ohio, and then given a wide release on September 10, with the taglines "There were a million reasons to give the money back. But Joey Coyle couldn't think of one," and "What would you do if you found a million bucks?" The film was praised by Kevin Thomas in the *Los Angeles Times* and received a mixed reaction from Megan Rosenfeld in *The Washington Post*. It was not a hit.

As Philip Hoffman, his next film role was in the Largo International N.V./JVC Entertainment crime actioner *The Getaway* (1994), a remake of the 1972 Sam Peckinpah film of the same title. The new film, directed by Roger Donaldson from a screenplay by Walter Hill and Amy Jones (based on the novel by Jim Thompson), was filmed from April 5 to June 26, 1993, on location in Arizona and Mexico. The plot concerned professional safecracker Carter "Doc" McCoy (Alec Baldwin) and his wife Carol (Kim Basinger), who are hired by businessman Jack Benyon (James Woods) to steal money from a Phoenix dog track safe. Hoffman played the supporting part of Frank Hansen, one of Benyon's crew supplied for the theft. The actor appears in four scenes, including the set piece robbery. He wears earrings and is unshaven, and his hair is gelled back. Frank's wardrobe is flannel shirts, a leather jacket and jeans; like Doc and their accomplice Rudy Travis (Michael Madsen), he wears a tan jumpsuit and white mask for the robbery. Hoffman makes Frank a variation on his previous louts by using a soft nasal voice and self-conscious physicality, touching his face and laughing when he speaks. The actor yells when Frank brandishes a gun; tells the driver of a hijacked tanker truck to get out of the cab; and breathes heavily when he tells Rudy that he has set the bomb on the truck. In the vault room after Frank shoots the guard, he repeatedly calls Rudy "man" and uses "fucking" in his anxious state. The plot point of Rudy and Frank declining to use bullet-proof vests for the robbery gets a payoff when Rudy shoots Frank afterwards. Frank's dead body rolls down an embankment in slow motion after he is pushed out of a car.

The film was released on February 11, 1994, with the taglines "Choosing between love and money is one thing. Getting away with both is something else" and "A dangerous deal. A double cross. And the ultimate set up is yet to come." It was praised by Todd McCarthy in *Variety* but received a mixed reaction from Caryn James in the *New York Times* and Roger Ebert in the *Chicago Sun-Times*. Kim Basinger's performance was nominated for the Worst Actress Razzie Award.

Hoffman next appeared on the RHI Entertainment made-for-TV family adventure *The Yearling* (1994), broadcast on CBS on April 24, 1994, and based on Marjorie Kinnan Rawlings' Pulitzer Prize-winning novel. It was directed by Rod Hardy and scripted by Joe Wiesenfeld. The plot told the story of 12-year-old Jody Baxter (Wil Horneff), whose family farms a swampy patch of scrub forest in the Florida Everglades in the 1920s. He brings a buck fawn home after its mother is killed but learns a life lesson when the animal becomes a yearling and eats the family crop. Hoffman played the supporting part of Buck, a member of the neighboring Forrester family. This part was played by Chill Wills in an earlier (1946) movie version. The character appears to be less a brute than his brothers, since he volunteers to help the Baxter family with chores when the father (Peter Strauss) is bedridden after a rattlesnake bite. Buck is also loutish, perhaps when under the influence of moonshine, and he interrupts a Christmas dance by entering and dancing with the corpse of a grizzly bear. This dancing also gets a funny but perverse payoff when he is seen slow-dancing with it.

The actor presents Buck as a hillbilly who smokes, with dirty clothes and a thick, sometimes impenetrable Southern accent. Hoffman wears a beard and his long hair often hangs in his face. He uses his mannerism of over-gesturing less here, and also employs some enthusiastic yelling. Hoffman gets a laugh out of Buck's line about going to the Christmas party: "If they don't want us, they can throw us out—if'n they can." His best moment comes when he yells at his brother Lem (Brad Greenquist), calling him a coward for sabotaging the Baxter wagon. Hoffman regrettably mugs in reaction to the fistfight between Lem and Pinny at the dance.

The film was praised by Ray Loynd in the *Los Angeles Times*. *Variety*'s Drew Voros wrote that Hoffman (and two of the other actors playing Forresters) provided a *Deliverance*-style tension.

Hoffman next played a supporting role in the Touchstone Pictures romance *When a Man Loves a Woman* (1994), directed by Luis Mandoki from a screenplay by Ronald Bass and Al Franken. It was shot from May 17 to August 8, 1993, on location in Mexico, San Francisco and Hollywood. Set in San Francisco, it centered on the marriage between airline pilot Michael Green (Andy Garcia) and school counselor Alice (Meg Ryan), an alcoholic. Hoffman played Gary, a man who Alice meets at the Devon Clinic rehabilitation center. Hoffman has few lines but presents his character as self-consciously nervous, which perhaps gives context to Hoffman's mannered use of gestures and laughing. Gary is briefly suspected of having an affair with Alice by Michael, since he sees they have a physical intimacy which the married couple have lost. Hoffman scores a laugh when he "dashes off" after Michael catches him and Alice talking in the Green house. Gary's comfort with her is conveyed by the way he has his legs up on a seat, and his apparent guilt is also conveyed by the fact that he cannot look Michael in the eye. Alice tells her husband that Gary only needs her as a friend.

The film was released on April 29, 1994, with the taglines "Through the good times. Through the bad times. When a Man Loves a Woman it's for all times" and "What Love Built a Secret Could Destroy...." It was praised by Leonard Klady in *Variety* and Roger Ebert but was lambasted by Janet Maslin in the *New York Times*.

Hoffman's next film role was in the Paramount Pictures-Capella International comedy *Nobody's Fool* (1994). It was directed and written by Robert Benton, based on a novel by Richard Russo. The film was shot from November 19, 1993, to March 8, 1994, in New York State. It centered on 60-year-old Donald "Sully" Sullivan (Paul Newman) in the rural town of North Bath, New York, and takes place between Thanksgiving and New Year's. A laborer for the Tip Top Construction company, he is reunited with his estranged son and family.

In the supporting role of Raymer, the town's police officer, Hoffman has three scenes: giving Sully a ticket for the broken tail light on his truck, confronting and shooting at Sully for driving on the sidewalk, and a scene with Sully and Judge Flatt (Philip Bosco) after Raymer has jailed Sully for assault. Hoffman wears a policeman's uniform and has short hair, and a black eye after Sully strikes him. In Raymer's confrontation with Sully, Hoffman presents the character in a comic way. He slips on ice on the sidewalk as he approaches, is nervous when he aims his gun and reacts in surprise when he shoots it. Raymer's lack of confidence is perhaps later rationalized when he is described as a "moron" by Judge Pratt and we learn that he has been suspended for his inappropriate behavior.

The film began a limited release on December 23, 1994, and then a wide release on January 13, 1995, with the taglines "In a town where nothing ever happens ... everything is about to happen to Sully" and "Worn to perfection." It was praised by Todd McCarthy in *Variety*, Caryn James in the *New York Times* and Roger Ebert. The film was a hit. Oscar nominations were received by Newman for Best Actor and Benton for Best Writing: Screenplay Based on Material from Another Medium.

Hoffman returned to the stage at Chicago's Goodman Theatre for a production of William Shakespeare's *The Merchant of Venice*. Directed by Peter Sellars, it was produced as part of what was called the Shakespeare Laboratory, where "a new generation approaches Shakespeare." After previews that began September 30, 1994, the show ran from October 12 to November 5, and was then scheduled to play engagements in London, Hamburg and Paris. Hoffman played the clown Launcelot Gobbo. David Richards in the *New York Times* lambasted the actor's performance as "all shouted rancor and not funny in the least." Hoffman was later asked if it was harrowing for him as a young actor to have audiences walk out during a performance, as they reportedly did at this show. He replied that that was just theater, where people walk out, stand up, yell things and eat candy in the front row. Hoffman said what was harrowing about theater was actually doing it.

An excerpt from the production can be seen on YouTube, as well as a 1994 BBC documentary about the pre-rehearsal workshop held in New York in the summer of 1994. Hoffman is seen in the documentary several times. He is unshaven with messy hair and a beard and wears a white t-shirt, gray shorts and runners. The film alternates between scenes showing the actors reading from their scripts and performing to camera. Hoffman is given some long closeups, more than he'd had to date in his feature film and television roles. Launcelot's actions here include lying on the ground at the feet of his father, Old Gobbo (Del Close), which has unintentional humor from the fact of the actor simultaneously reading his lines from his script. Hoffman's performance is otherwise large, using over-gesturing and yelling, which may be acceptable in the context of theater. However in a montage of characters who repeat the phrase "Mislike me not for my complexion" to camera, he provides a mannered pause in the middle of the sentence.

Hoffman was reportedly a real contender for the part of Waingro in writer-director Michael Mann's crime drama *Heat* (1995) but Kevin Gage got the part. The film was a hit.

After returning from the tour in 1995, Hoffman joined the LAByrinth Theatre Company, a group founded by John Ortiz (who had appeared with Hoffman in *The Merchant of Venice*), Paul Calderon, Gary Perez and David Deblinger. Hoffman had informed Ortiz that he was tired of Los Angeles and thinking of moving back to New York. Ortiz told him about his Little Rascals theater group and said he was welcome to hang out with them. Hoffman described the company as multicultural and diverse, the way New York City was. He said it was really quite an eclectic group of people. The actor's long-term commitment to the company would see him act, produce and direct and he could even be seen selling sodas in the lobby of their base at Chelsea's Center Stage on 21st Street.

Hoffman made his debut for the company performing in *Divine Horsemen*, written and directed by Calderon. Running from December 13 to 16, 1995, it was about a hitman, a pickpocket and a tired old man who find themselves amidst a robbery gone bad. Rehearsals had been in the apartments of the company or, when the performers were lucky, in a rat-infested, semi-abandoned theater on the West Side. Hoffman also produced the company's *Shmoo*, a serio-comic piece combining videos and monologues to give voice to often ignored groups like the young, the old and the mentally impaired. It starred David Deblinger.

The actor next appeared in the Rysher Entertainment-Green Parrot-Trinity crime drama *Hard Eight* (1996), an expansion of writer-director Paul Thomas Anderson's 24-minute short *Cigarettes & Coffee* (1993). *Hard Eight* was reportedly shot (under the title *Sydney*) in Reno, Nevada, two years prior to its release. Written and directed by Anderson, it explored the new friendship between down-on-his-luck John Finnegan (John C. Reilly) and wealthy professional gambler and hood Sydney (Philip Baker Hall). Hoffman played the supporting role of Young Craps Player in the first of five collaborations with Anderson. The actor has what amounts to a three-minute cameo. The character is another obnoxious lout who taunts Sydney when he plays a game of craps by repeatedly calling him an old man. Hoffman wears his long hair combed off his forehead and an undone shirt over a t-shirt. He gives the character a Southern accent and smokes, and provides laughter by yelling, swearing, etc. According to Hall, Hoffman's lines were all improvised, but Anderson said that the part was written.

The director said that he first saw Hoffman in *Scent of a Woman* and felt that he gave such an incredible performance that he fell in love with him. He thought whoever this guy was, he had to know him. Anderson wrote the film with Hoffman in mind. He wanted to be the kind of writer-director that gave actors the opportunity to do something they had not done before. Anderson admitted that the role was in the tradition of characters that Hoffman had played but he didn't feel bad about it because he really wanted it to be the best of its kind. The director said he was really blown away by what the actor did in the film. The day that Anderson met Hoffman was the day they shot the scene.

The film was screened at the Sundance Film Festival on January 20, 1996. It was given a wide American release on February 28, 1997, with the taglines "When good luck is a long shot, you have to hedge your bets" and "If you stay in the game long enough, you'll see everything, win everything, and lose everything." It was praised by Stephen Holden in the *New York Times* and Roger Ebert but was not a hit.

Hoffman played a supporting role in the Warner Bros.-Universal-Amblin Entertainment action adventure *Twister* (1996), shot on location in Oklahoma and Iowa and at the Warner Bros. studios from May 1 to August 21, 1995. Scripted by Michael Crichton and Anne-Marie Martin and directed by Jan De Bont, it depicted a group of storm chasers led by meteorologists Dr. Jo Harding (Helen Hunt) and her husband, weatherman Bill (Bill Paxton). They had invented a machine with sensors to take measurements from inside a tornado. Hoffman played the part of Dusty (which was reportedly first offered to Garth Brooks who turned it down). Dusty is a member of the team who drives the "Barn Burner," monitors television and radio reports and sometimes films the group's actions. The character was a variation on one of the actor's louts, using words like "dude," "man" and "awesome" to indicate a hippy sensibility. Playing loud rock music, drinking as he drives, poking his head into the car window of rival tornado team driver Eddie (Zach Grenier) to try and kiss him, and eating with his mouth open are other indications of his rebelliousness.

As Dusty, Hoffman wears his hair long and is unshaven. Dusty's wardrobe included a jacket worn on his head, baggy pants and baseball cap, and he sometimes wears headphones. Hoffman's performance includes laughing, yelling and over-use of hand gestures. However the character allowed him to demonstrate some range, from comic to serious. Dusty mostly presents as a comic figure mixed with aggressive obnoxiousness, but additionally he shows compassion over the fate of Jo's Aunt Meg (Lois Smith) who gets injured in a tornado; bravery in being the first of the crew to go to her damaged house; and concern for Jo during another tornado. Dusty also has an awareness of Jo's mixed agendas when he tells her about another tornado that the group could pursue when she is with Meg. Hoffman's lines are limited to exclamations like "It's the wonder of nature, baby" describing the tornados, though he gets to deliver part of an anecdote about why Bill is known as "The Extreme."

The film was released on May 10, 1996, with the taglines "The Dark Side of Nature," "Don't Breathe. Don't Look Back," "Go for a ride you'll never forget!," and "The Beautiful yet Destructive side to life." It received a mixed review from Todd McCarthy in *Variety* but was praised by Janet Maslin in the *New York Times* and Roger Ebert. A hit, it was nominated for the Best Sound and Best Visual Effects Academy Awards. The film supposedly included a shot of Hoffman's genitals, unintentionally exposed in a scene where he lifted his leg while sitting on a lawn chair. It was said to be edited out for the DVD and VHS releases. Hoffman is only seen wearing long pants in the film so this may be a myth.

Hoffman said that he did the film because he had never been in an action movie, and there were no guns in it. In his 2010 interview with Craig Ferguson he said he took the job partly to finance moving from L.A. back to New York. Hoffman was also interesting in working with director De Bont because he had heard so many crazy stories about him. Hoffman said he got along with him well but De Bont was driven. De Bont said that he thought the actor was brilliant. He also said the scene where Dusty tries to kiss Eddie was improvised by him after De Bont had told him to do something to chase the car away.

From February 9 to 25, 1996, Hoffman appeared in a stage production of Emily Mann's drama *Greensboro: A Requiem* at the McCarter Theater in Princeton, New Jersey. It was directed by Mark Wing-Davey and its subject was the attack by Ku Klux Klan members and self-styled American Nazis on an anti–Klan rally in a black Greensboro, North Carolina, neighborhood on the morning of November 3, 1979. Hoffman played various parts including Klansman David Matthews and an F.B.I. Agent. The production received a mixed review from Vincent Canby in the *New York Times*.

From April 23 to May 26, 1996, Hoffman appeared in a stage production of Caryl Churchill's *The Skriker* at the Off-Broadway Joseph Papp Public Theatre. Directed by Mark Wing-Davey, it was set in a London haunted by unhappy gremlins. Hoffman played the part of Raw Head and Bloody Bones. The play was praised by Ben Brantley in the *New York Times*, who wrote that the actor was excellent, giving bracingly unsentimental life to a wounded prototype.

2

Boogie Nights

Hoffman next played a supporting role in writer-director Paul Thomas Anderson's follow-up to *Hard Eight*. The film was an extension of Anderson's 32-minute short, *The Dirk Diggler Story* (1988), which had been inspired by John Holmes and others in the adult film industry. The New Line Cinema-Lawrence Gordon Productions-Ghoulardi Film Company drama *Boogie Nights* (1997) was filmed from July 10 to October 4, 1996, in Los Angeles.

Seventeen-year-old nightclub dishwasher Eddie Adams (Mark Wahlberg) is discovered by adult film director Jack Horner (Burt Reynolds) and becomes the 1970s porn star Dirk Diggler. Hoffman played the part of Scotty J., Horner's sound man and one of the film crew that forms a surrogate family around the director. This extends to Scotty later attending the wedding of actress Becky (Nicole Ari Parker) and Jerome (Michael Jace), cleaning the apartment of Dirk, filming the birth of the baby of actress Jessie (Melora Walters) and actor Buck (Don Cheadle), and holding reading cards at Buck's television commercial filmed by Amber (Julianne Moore).

The actor appears in 20 scenes, including three montages. He wears his hair long and parted on the side and is unshaven, and his tight clothes at Jack's pool party reveal Scotty's chubbiness. The clothes issue is also addressed when Scotty buys the same shirt as Dirk and Reed (John C. Reilly); the latter two wear it attractively and on Scotty it's ill-fitting. Hoffman speaks in a Valley boy accent and has an effeminate manner to suggest the character's gayness. The issue of Scotty being gay is a variation on the original short, where Dirk was gay but there is no Scotty character. Dirk in the feature is straight and only later participates in gay sex when he is in need of money for his drug habit. Scotty's hesitance to express his desire for Dirk is paralleled with the suggested interest of Todd (Thomas Jane) who blatantly ogles Dirk when they meet.

Hoffman employs his over-gesturing mannerism and laughing but here they share context with Scotty's other self-conscious tics like touching himself and nervously chewing on a pen attached to a clipboard. The self-touching is most effectively shown when he stands behind Dirk as Dirk has his drugged-tirade at Jack; Scotty holds his arms as he watches, looking frightened. Scotty breathes heavily when he holds the boom and watches Dirk's first filmed sex scene, which indicates his desire. Hoffman is funny showing Scotty's panicked reaction to Dirk attacking a recording studio executive, but his best scene is Scotty's advance on Dirk at the 1979 New Year's Eve party. He suddenly kisses Dirk after the pretext of showing him his new car, which is a duplicate of Dirk's red Corvette. Scotty then apologizes, trying to save face by claiming to be drunk. He begs Dirk to kiss him again and then repeatedly calls himself an idiot and cries after Dirk has left. Hoffman adds to the scene by also making it funny and it stands as perhaps his most effective and poignant acting in film.

The film was first screened on September 11, 1997, at the Toronto International Film Festival. It played on October 8 at the New York Film Festival, began its limited release on October 10 and went into wide release on October 31. The taglines were "Everyone has one special thing" and "The life of a dreamer, the days of a business, and the nights in between." A hit, it was praised by Emanuel Levy in *Variety*, Janet Maslin in the *New York Times*, Roger Ebert, Peter Travers in *Rolling Stone et al.* Anderson was Oscar-nominated for Original Screenplay and Burt Reynolds and Julianne Moore were nominated for the Best Supporting Actor and Actress.

The *Boogie Nights* DVD includes deleted scenes, some featuring Hoffman. These include an extended version of one of Dirk's films where Scotty slates the mark twice, Scotty applauding and whistling at the first award ceremony, Scotty telling Amber about an incident at a bar where he wanted to fight a man, and Scotty offering snowballs to Dirk, Todd, Reed and Nick (Michael Penn) at the music recording studio. Another deleted scene has Scotty outside Dirk's home when he brings his smashed Corvette home; Scotty offers to sell his car in order for Dirk to have the money to pay for the repairs. The Platinum Series DVD supplies a biography for Scotty which states that he has worked for Jack for four years doing sound and props, and then lives with Dirk in his mansion with Reed; Scotty works as Dirk's personal assistant. On the DVD's cast member audio commentary, John C. Reilly said the center of Scotty's character was the way the actor holds his arms, how he puts one hand on his elbow trying to hide his body. Mark Wahlberg commented that he felt Dirk might have kissed Scotty back in the car park scene. This would have been to give Scotty what he wanted since that is Dirk's character, but his judgment was altered by his cocaine use. Paul Thomas Anderson also describes a moment that was cut from the scene where Dirk is in the bathroom trying to get an erection for a shoot but fails because of the cocaine. Apparently Scotty unknowingly walked in on Dirk, wanting to use the bathroom, but Dirk ordered him out.

Hoffman's idea was that Scotty was a young man basically living a very adolescent life. He was obviously a gay man who hadn't really accepted himself and in the narrative never felt quite safe enough to come out. As part of his research, he and some of the cast visited a porn set. Hoffman said that he was proud of the choices he made for the film and that Anderson was very helpful. Interviewed by David Kamp for *GQ* in 2001, the actor commented that it was a really great party movie and one of the few he had made that he could say he had fun on. On *CBS Sunday Morning* (May 27, 2012) he said he had the best time in the world on the film. Hoffman was one of the actors interviewed for the article "Livin' Thing: An Oral History of *Boogie Nights*" by Alex French and Howie Kahn. In it he revealed that Anderson had written the role with him in mind. Hoffman said he didn't have the first idea how to go about doing it, but he was excited about trying to figure that out.

Thomas Jane said that when he auditioned for the part of Todd Parker, Hoffman and John C. Reilly were brought in and they would do scenes where they would just start riffing, acting like they'd been on coke for 48 hours straight. Jane said Hoffman was great at improv, and Jane just kind of slipped right into it and they all clicked. Costume designer Mark Bridges said Hoffman wanted to wear clothes that were really tight—as if he was still wearing stuff that he wore when he was a teenager. He kept trying on garments that was smaller and smaller, and Bridges had to go get clothes from the rack of William Macy who played Little Bill. After Hoffman's death, Mark Wahlberg remembered him as generous, fearless and selfless, and made him feel comfortable about the kissing scene. Wahlberg said the two of them spent a bit of time together, having a barbecue at Wahlberg's apartment in Los Angeles, where Hoffman and he were running around having beers and lighting fireworks. Perhaps because of the fracas, the next day Wahlberg got an eviction notice.

For the LAByrinth Theatre Company, Hoffman next appeared in the comic-bookish musical comedy *Queen Latina and her Power Posse Versus the Evils of Society* (October 26, 1996, to March 1, 1997), was directed by Gary Perez. He then played a supporting role in the Robbins Entertainment romantic comedy *Next Stop Wonderland* (1998), shot in Boston, Massachusetts, from October 16 to December 6, 1996. The film had a screenplay by Brad Anderson and Lyn Vaus and was directed by Anderson. The plot depicted the romantic lives of 29-year-old nurse Erin Castleton (Hope Davis) and 35-year-old marine biology student and volunteer aquarium diver Alan Monteiro (Alan Gelfant), who are meant for each other. Hoffman played Sean, Erin's activist boyfriend; he leaves at the beginning of the narrative to stop the building of a dam on sacred Indian ground in Tantooni, Arizona. The actor appears in four scenes including one with Sean on TV at the protest where he is chained to a rock and repeats the cry "I don't give a damn" as he points to the camera, and one of his videotaped message to Erin to explain why he has left her. Sean temporarily stops being an activist after he becomes disillusioned with the Tantooni Indians who now decide to build a casino on the site. However he goes back to activism after driving a pizza delivery car in Boston. A photograph of Hoffman is also seen in a newspaper with him described as a gadfly disrupting the building of a prison on the waterfront.

As Sean, Hoffman wears glasses, long hair and is unshaven, although when he returns to Boston he has cut his hair and shaved. The character also wears a series of hats—beanies, a beaver hat with ear flaps, and a baseball cap. He is funny when he yells "Violence is not the answer" when Erin attacks him upon learning that he is leaving her. In Sean's videotaped message Hoffman has a moment where he picks his ear and looks at what he has taken out. Anderson favors Davis in Sean's scene where he returns to Erin, so that we see more of her listening than Hoffman telling her that he needs to change and implying that he wants to come back to her. Despite the limited coverage in the scene, and Anderson's use of music over the dialogue, the actor manages to convey Sean's touching sincerity.

The film was screened on January 17, 1998, at the Sundance Film Festival, and on May 13 at the Seattle International Film Festival on May 31, 1998, before receiving a wide release on August 21, 1998. The taglines were "Being alone is fine. Being alone together is perfect," "Love is the Destination," "A new comedy for the incurable romantic in all of us," "Dating is like a box of chocolates … you never know what you're going to get. Some are sweet, some are nuts and some are truly wonderful" and "Romance is her destination." It was praised by Todd McCarthy in *Variety* and Stephen Holden in the *New York Times* and was a hit.

Hoffman appeared in the 22-minute comic short *The Fifteen Minute Hamlet* (1996), written by Tom Louiso, Ethan Tucker and Michael Goldberg and based on a Tom Stoppard play. This in turn was based on William Shakespeare's play *The Tragedy of Hamlet, Prince of Denmark*. The short was also directed by Louiso, who had appeared with Hoffman in *Scent of a Woman* where they had spent a lot of time waiting around together and playing the "Pole Position" video game. (The men had also shared a flat in their early days as actors but they moved out when the place kept flooding.) Hoffman played the parts of Bernardo, Horatio and Laertes in the short, which utilizes the conceit of being done in one continuous take. Wearing his hair longer, he alternates between being clean-shaven and sporting a beard. He also uses a range of English accents to differentiate the characters. He is first seen asleep in the opening sequence which acts as a making-of section before the play starts, and Hoffman uses the mannerisms of heaving breathing, over-gesturing, laughing and yelling. The latter have context in the general stylized pitch of performance of all the cast. Hoffman's best moment is perhaps his death scene which he makes funny.

He next appeared in a supporting role in the Polygram Filmed Entertainment-Working Title Production crime comedy, *The Big Lebowski* (1998). Filmed around Los Angeles from January 27 to April 25, 1997, it was written by Ethan Coen and Joel Coen and directed by Joel Coen. Set in the early 1990s, it involves an unemployed, aging pothead and avid bowler, The Dude (Jeff Bridges). His real name is Jeffrey Lebowski and he gets entangled with a wheelchair-bound Pasadena tycoon with the same name (David Huddleston) when his wife Bunny (Tara Reid) appears to be kidnapped for a ransom of $1 million. Hoffman played the part of Brandt, the tycoon's nerdish assistant. The actor wears his hair short and glasses and a series of dark suits and colored ties. His over-familiar touching of The Dude shows both Brandt's vanity and supercilious condescension. The actor speaks with a pronounced intonation and is funny in his embarrassed laughter at Bunny's crudity, and when affecting empathic sadness to match Lebowski's supposed sadness when telling The Dude of Bunny's kidnapping.

The film was first screened on February 15, 1998, at the Berlin International Film Festival and released on March 6, 1998, with the taglines "They figured he was a lazy time-wasting slacker. They were right," "Her life was in their hands. Now her toe is in the mail," "Times like these call for a Big Lebowski," "It takes guys as simple as the Dude and Walter to make a story this complicated ... and they'd really rather be bowling" and "Lebowski: Not a man, a way of life." Todd McCarthy in *Variety* wrote that Hoffman milks surplus laughs out of his part. The film was praised by Janet Maslin in the *New York Times*, Roger Ebert, and *Rolling Stone*'s Peter Travers, the latter describing Hoffman as invaluable.

Hoffman is seen photographed by Jeff Bridges in the collection of photographs presented as a bonus feature on the Collector's Edition DVD of the film. He is shown twice in a black and white photograph wearing the faces of tragedy and comedy, which Bridges calls "Tragedia/Comedia."

Hoffman said the film was another one that was truly fun to make. He said the Coens were a great audience because they laughed a lot, and though he would only make one film with them, they later reunited in the theater. Hoffman said he laughed out loud the first time he read the script, finding it hysterical, and really loved the brothers' movies going back to *Blood Simple* (1984). He knew they were really talented guys, having a rare gift to go from serious drama to hysterical comedy and mixing up those two things, and he felt they could do anything. Hoffman reported that although Joel got credit as the director, the brothers pretty much co-directed. On the set he got notes from both of them, but they never clashed or got in each other's way.

Hoffman appeared in Michael Penn's three-minute music video for the song "Try." Directed by Paul Thomas Anderson, it was shot in Los Angeles and released on April 7, 1997. Hoffman appears twice in the video, sporting long hair and a full beard, and wearing a dark-colored baseball cap with a dark-colored jacket over a white t-shirt with a *Planet of the Apes* image and dark-colored shorts. He runs down a hallway next to Penn singing, holding a long-stemmed microphone, and hands Penn a guitar. Later he holds the microphone to Penn's mouth as he sings.

Hoffman next appeared in the LAByrinth Theatre Company production of *Race, Religion, Politics*, written by Stephen Adly Guirgis and directed by Charles Goforth. It ran from April 9 to 27, 1997, and explored the prejudice and bonding as construction workers relaxed in a bar.

He appeared in False Alarms Pictures' 29-minute short comedy *Culture* (1997), written and directed by Will Speck and Josh Gordon. He played the supporting part of Bill in a story about a young newspaper editor undermined and ruined by his nasty old biddy of a secretary. It was screened in October 1997 at the Chicago International Film Festival where it won the Best Narrative Short Film Award and was nominated for the Best Live Action Short Academy Award.

Hoffman participated in the KTCA-TV–Middlemarch Films–Twin Cities Public Television miniseries *Liberty! The American Revolution* (1997), broadcast on PBS on November 23, 1997. A nearly six-hour documentary on the events in the 18th century that led to the American Revolution, written by Ronald Blumer and directed by Ellen Hovde and Muffie Meyer, it included analysis from historians, re-enactments and excerpts from letters, diaries and other documents of the period spoken by actors in period costume. The actors, filmed at New York City's City Stage studios, appeared in medium closeup and spoke directly to the camera. Wearing his hair long, Hoffman appeared in two episodes as Joseph Plumb Martin, a Connecticut farmer who served in the American Continental Army and kept a diary for the seven years of the war. In episode 3, "The Times That Try Men's Souls," Martin appears five times and is also heard under recreated footage. He begins in a white jacket and tie as he speaks about his enlistment, the regional antipathy among the recruits from different provinces, and the 1776 battle of Long Island. His hair is messy and he has a blanket around him when he tells of marching through New York swamps at night. He wears a blue-black and red jacket and headscarf when speaking of winter in New Jersey. In episode 5, "The World Turned Upside Down," he appears three times and is also heard under reenactment footage. He wears the dark uniform with white strips of the American soldier and speaks about the 1781 siege of Yorktown, Virginia; about getting his discharge papers after the treaty of independence had been signed and the war ended; and the suffering he had endured in the war.

From November 2, 1997, to January 4, 1998, Hoffman appeared in the Jane Anderson one-act play *Defying Gravity* at the American Place Theatre. Directed by Michael Wilson, the Off-Broadway play was a fantasy about space travel, spirituality and the *Challenger* disaster. Hoffman played NASA crewman C.B., one of four characters who go to the Florida coast to watch the space shot. *Defying Gravity* received a mixed reaction from Charles Isherwood in *Variety* but was praised by Peter Marks in the *New York Times*, who wrote that Hoffman was honest and unpretentious.

He next appeared in another supporting role in Initial Entertainment–Zesta Entertainment–No Bones Productions' *Montana* (1998). Shot on location in New Jersey and New York in 1997, the crime/action comedy was directed by Jennifer Leitzes from a screenplay by Erich and Joe Hoeber. It centered on a New York gang led by The Boss (Robbie Coltrane); the gang includes his lead hitters, Claire Kelski (Kyra Sedgwick) and Nick Roth (Stanley Tucci). The gang's sense of loyalty is tested when money is stolen by the MBA bookkeeper Duncan (Hoffman), and when The Boss' girlfriend Kitty (Robin Tunney) runs away. The obsequious Duncan dresses in suits and ties with suspenders, with Hoffman wearing glasses and his hair slicked back. He only gets to wear two suits in the narrative, which appears to cover two days. One suit is brown with a red tie and the other blue with a blue tie; there is also a gray trenchcoat for his climactic scene. Duncan is mostly seen at the gang's house except for the climax when he goes to a park planning to kill and bury Claire. She kills him by stabbing him with a shovel.

Hoffman suggests Duncan's duplicity by using a soft voice, smiling and smirking. His patronizing manner toward Claire earns him a slap in the face from her. Hoffman again over-uses hand gestures, and breathes heavily when Duncan goes to shoot Kitty and when he is called in to see The Boss, thinking that he has been found out. In the latter scene, director Leitzes give the actor a long reaction to The Boss' news that his son Jimmy (Ethan Embry) has been killed by Kitty. Hoffman shows Duncan's transition from fear to understanding that The Boss has not discovered his betrayal yet. He also is impressive in his monologue to Kitty about her entrapment in the gang.

The film premiered at the Sundance Film Festival on January 16, 1998, was screened at the Athens Film Festival on September 13, and then appeared to go straight to video without receiving a theatrical release. Its taglines were "Sicker than most" and "Never underestimate the power of a woman." It received a mixed review from *Variety*'s Todd McCarthy, who wrote that Hoffman was memorable as a toady turncoat.

The January 25, 1998, *New York Times* reported that Hoffman was to appear in the New York Theatre Workshop production of the Mark Ravenhill play *Shopping and Fucking*. The Off-Broadway production was then in previews and set to run from February 2 till March 8. The director of the original London production, Max Stafford-Clark, was sharing duties with Gemma Bodinetz. Hoffman was to play the part of Mark, a former stockbroker, now a heroin addict nominally on the mend. The new production was lambasted by Ben Brantley in the *New York Times* who wrote that Hoffman wore Mark's desperation and English accent like a fancy, ill-fitting overcoat. Vincent Canby also wrote about the production in the *Times* and praised it and the actors in it. Sources indicate that the season was extended to April 11, 1998.

Hoffman next appeared in the ensemble cast of the Good Machine-Killer Films comedy *Happiness* (1998), written and directed by Todd Solondz and shot on location in New Jersey and Florida. Reportedly Jack Black and Jon Lovitz were considered for the part of Allen (ultimately played by Hoffman) and James Urbaniak auditioned for it. The characters included the Jordan family of three sisters, poet Helen (Lara Flynn Boyle), housewife and mother Trish (Cynthia Stevenson) and teacher and musician Joy (Jane Adams), and the people around them; all seem to suffer from sexual dysfunction and loneliness. Allen is a

In still for *Happiness* (1998).

chronic masturbator and obscene phone caller obsessed with Helen, his next-door neighbor in their New Jersey apartment building. He works in an office in Data Resources and lives alone, but also consults Trish's husband, psychiatrist Dr. Maplewood (Dylan Baker). The doctor is heard thinking to himself during the session that Allen is boring; his patient also believes this about himself. Allen is the object of desire of another neighbor, Kristina (Camryn Manheim), although he is initially uninterested in her. She is presented as being as sexually undesirable as he is, but the narrative has him turn to her because he is too afraid to pursue Helen, and after Helen rejects him. However it is implied that there can be no future for the new couple, who are seen dancing together and sleeping clothed back to back in her bed, since we hear later that Kristina's murder of the building doorman, Pedro (Jose Rabelo) is discovered.

Allen's anger about his situation is expressed by his throwing the telephone after Helen calls him back, presumably because she has taken the control he feels with his obscene calls away from him. It is also expressed in his drunken abuse of Kristina when he finds her in his apartment and yells at her to get out. We forgive the latter cruelty in light of his drunkenness and because of his later kindness towards her. He offers her a tissue when she cries, slow dances with her, and takes her to dinner at a restaurant and tells her that he likes her. Kristina's stated aversion to sex, amplified after she has been raped by Pedro, implies that any relationship she is to have with Allen will be nonsexual. Allen is seen in bed with her, which suggests that he is okay with it, since this would seem to be preferable to the misery of his masturbation. Allen's relationship with Helen is a series of misunderstandings. It is apparent when we see them together in the building foyer that she has no interest in him, and he is too shy to say anything to her other than hello and goodbye. Allen going through the telephone book to find victims for his phone calls appears to be random, so his calling Joy can be read as a coincidence. However, Helen will tell Joy that she thinks he is a good match for her, so we assume that Helen is unaware of the incident. Allen finally calls Helen and abuses her, but perversely this turns her on, and she then pursues him. He drops his sexual aggression when he admits that he cannot make love to her the way she wants, and the way he has claimed he could. When Allen goes to her apartment to admit his identity, Helen lets him in. Perhaps she is willing to see if he can be who she wants him to be. However when he reaches for her as they sit on the couch, she rejects him by telling him that he is not her type. Allen's relationship with Kristina, however, is more real. She has an unrequited love for him that turns into a relationship of companionship.

Allen mostly wears business clothes. He wears only boxers in one scene when he is on the telephone at home and we also see him in the shower though his body is obscured by the curtain. The character also has glasses and short hair. The part allows the actor to play a nerd who breathes heavily, touches himself self-consciously, and slurs and stutters his words. Hoffman again uses his over-gesturing mannerism but not as excessively as in other films. Allen is heard before he is seen in his first scene; this device is repeated when he telephones Joy. Director Solondz perversely uses a choral version of Mozart's "Requiem" under Allen's obscene phone call and when Allen is in Helen's apartment, and the Air Supply song "All Out of Love" when Allen and Kristina slow dance at Joe and Mary's bar. The surprise is that the actor can make Allen equally pathetic and funny. He is too shy to speak to Helen in the elevator and looks up at the ceiling. His slow dancing with Kristina is both sad and sweet. Allen is also pathetic when he drives home, drinking and sobbing in fear of being pursued by Helen. Hoffman is funny in the way he asks for Claire on the telephone in an obscene phone call attempt, in his swearing abuse at Helen and when he uses laughter in answering his co-worker who nearly catches him on the phone. He also has a physical grace in Allen's slow walk to the door when he is drunk, the slow reaching of his hand for Helen when they sit apart on the same couch, and when lying on Kristina's bed in a fetal position.

The film was first screened at the Cannes Film Festival on May 15, 1998, then at the Deauville Film Festival on September 11, the Toronto International Film Festival on September 15, the Chicago International Film Festival on in October and the New York Film Festival on October 9. It then opened in New York on October 11 and began its wide release on October 16. It received a mixed reaction from *Variety*'s Todd McCarthy who wrote that Hoffman again proved himself one of the sharpest young character actors around, and was praised by Janet Maslin in the *New York Times* and Roger Ebert. The film had won the Fipresci Prize at Cannes for its "bold tracking of controversial contemporary themes, richly-layered subtext, and remarkable fluidity of visual style." It was not a box office success. In the loose sequel *Life During Wartime* (2009) Solondz featured the Jordan sisters (played by different actors). The character of Allen also appeared, now known as Allen Mellencamp, and was played by Michael Kenneth Williams.

Asked about working with Solondz, Hoffman said he would follow people like him into a fire because they were so assured of where they were going and because they were so passionate about it, and those were the directors that he wanted to work with. In an interview with the *New York Times*' Jonah Weiner (July 16, 2010), he recalled the discomfort he felt on the set playing the character and feared that people were going to laugh at him since it involved exposing such vulnerability. Solondz told him that he thought people were going to feel for him; Hoffman believed he was telling him he wanted him to find a way to feel for the character. What also made it easier was that the actor said the writer-director had great empathy for the characters and wasn't judging them. When Hoffman was interviewed by David Kamp for *GQ* in 2001 he said that doing the film made him anxious, having to sit in his boxers for three hours and jerk off, but ultimately it was a great piece of filmmaking.

Hoffman next played a supporting role in the Universal Pictures—Farrell-Minoff—Blue Wolf—Bungalow 78 Productions biographical comedy *Patch Adams* (1998), shot from February 9 to June 26, 1998, on location in San Francisco and in Asheville and Chapel Hill, North Carolina. Tom Shadyac directed from a screenplay by Steve Oedekerk based on the book *Gesundheit: Good Health Is a Laughing Matter* by Hunter Doherty Adams and Maureen Mylander. It told the true story of Hunter "Patch" Adams, a student in 1971 at the Virginia Medical University, who defied convention by treating patients with humor. Hoffman played Adams' dorm roommate and group study partner Mitch Vroman, another medical student. Mitch created an obstacle for Patch by reporting him to Dean Walcott (Bob Gunton) for allegedly cheating. Mitch is shown to be as unpopular as Patch is popular. Mitch asks Patch for help with a patient not responding to his treatment and tells him that he wants to learn Patch's ways, although the complaint that she refuses to eat is not shown to be overcome when Patch takes her into a blow-up pool of noodles. Later Mitch gives Patch advice to appeal to the State Medical Board after he is dismissed by Walcott, although we see that Mitch applauds but does not stand with other attendees of the hearing when the decision is overturned.

Hoffman appears in 13 scenes, and wears glasses and short hair. Mitch is shown to be uptight by his wearing of a sweater (buttoned all the way up) and ties, unlike the other students, and particularly in contrast to the counter-culture wardrobe of Patch. He also wears the white coat and green scrubs of a doctor. Hoffman makes Mitch a humorless prig (Patch describes him as arrogant and pompous) and he uses an upper-class accent. Hoffman suggests that Mitch is upset by the fact that his patient refuses to eat, trying but failing to cry. His best scene is when Patch calls him a prick. Mitch defends being a prick when he replies, "Maybe I am. But you ask the average person when death comes knocking at their door whether they want a prick on their side or some kindergarten teacher who's gonna kiss their ass. When that day comes, I want the prick." Hoffman yells to show the character's self-righteous anger.

The film used the taglines "Based on a True Story" and "Laughter is contagious." It was lambasted by *Variety*'s Joe Leydon, who wrote that Hoffman was a standout as he struggled mightily—and, to his credit, successfully—to flesh out a tissue-thin character. A box office success, *Patch Adams* earned Marc Shaiman a Best Music Score Academy Award nomination. The DVD features outtakes, one of them a scene between Patch and Mitch where Hoffman repeatedly blows his lines, and alternate takes of the morgue scene.

Tom Shadyac described Hoffman as a wonderful actor. He said that the character of Mitch was written as a tall, classic, square-jawed blueblood but Shadyac was impressed with the actor's chameleon-like quality. He reported that he had an "insane" chemistry with Robin Williams (who played Patch) and both actors enjoyed riffing together. The director said that the "prick" scene was played on different levels, some with more subtlety by Hoffman, but Shadyac decided to go with the "hotter" take. He also commented that on the day the scene where Patch asks for Mitch's advice, Hoffman was having a personal crisis which he did not let stop his work. Apparently his grandfather was gravely ill, and he would die soon after. For his 2001 interview by David Kamp for *GQ* Hoffman said that obviously it wasn't the most artistic film he had ever done but that was really beside the point. For him it was a chance to play an upper-class persona which he felt he hadn't done in the past. And Hoffman got to sit in the makeup trailer day in and day out and listen to Williams make him "laugh his fuckin' ass off."

In September 1998 Hoffman played a supporting role in the MGM-Tribeca Productions comedy crime drama *Flawless* (1999), shot in New York and written and directed by Joel Schumacher. Robert De Niro stars as retired New York City police officer Walt Koontz, who suffers a debilitating stroke and gets singing lessons as speech rehabilitation with Russell "Rusty" Zimmerman (Hoffman), his nightclub piano player and drag queen neighbor in the Brooklyn El Palacio Hotel and Apartments building. Rusty finds the money that Raymond Camacho (Vincent Laresca) has stolen from Mr. Z (Luis Saguer) and plans to use it to have an operation so he can become a woman as he believes he is a woman trapped inside a man's body.

Aside from dressing like a woman offstage and performing in drag, Rusty indulges in other unconventional behavior like using drugs, and he is defensive, brave, generous, sensitive, funny and pathetic. He is caustic in response to Walt's homophobic slurs but nevertheless gives him singing lessons, admitting to doing it because he needs the money. He is generous with helping his drag queen friends and neighbor Amber (Karina Arroyave) whose ashes he collects after she is murdered. He plans to use some of the money to give Amber a funeral and throw Walt a surprise graduation party. Rusty is brave when he tells Mr. Z that he will give back the money if he spares the wounded Walt who has come to save him, when he fights back Mr. Z's thugs, and climbs the

Hoffman on left with Robert De Niro at right for *Flawless* (1999).

building's exterior to try and save Walt. While it is good to see the suggestion that Rusty has a sex life, he is pathetic in having a married boyfriend, Sonny (John Enos), who is abusive and uses him for money to pay gambling debts. Although Rusty chastises Walt for being self-pitying, he can be the same. This is demonstrated when he returns from his mother's funeral and admits to Walt that he is not a singer and a female impressionist, but a lonely and fat and ugly drag queen.

Director Joel Schumacher lets us see the character from Walt's point of view, as a grotesque, with extreme closeups of Rusty's mouth and eyes as he applies makeup. His screenplay juggles bad lines with good. Some of Rusty's good lines are when he tells Z's thugs, "You homicidal maniacs are so sensitive"; when he replies to Walt telling him he can't do the lessons with "Can't lives on won't street"; when he tells Walt. "There is no romance without finance"; and when he quips, "Life's a bitch so I became one." The bad lines include "I left sensitivity back in the sand pile" and "I'm more man than you'll ever be and more woman that you'll ever get"—a line recycled from the comedy *Car Wash* (1976), which Schumacher also wrote.

Hoffman usually wears his hair held back from his forehead behind a headband. Only at his mother's funeral does he wear male clothes (a suit and tie); otherwise he's seen in female-style clothes and drag outfits by Daniel Orlandi. The actor gets above-the-title billing after De Niro. Hoffman's part is perhaps the most substantial he'd had to date. His willingness to play gay characters before perhaps created a precedent for Rusty, although this is a more extreme part. Hoffman avoids some pitfalls—Rusty could have been an embarrassing or offensive stereotype, but Hoffman plays him funny, tender and likable. His mannerisms (overuse of hand gestures, laughing, self-touching) all have a context for the character, whom he also gives a whispering voice as if it is the one he will use later as a woman. Otherwise Hoffman gives Rusty the nasal affection of a gay man but doesn't overdo it. The role also shows his singing ability.

The film was released on November 24, 1999, with the taglines "Nobody's Perfect. Everybody's Flawless" and "They couldn't like each other less or need each other more." Roger Ebert wrote that Hoffman showed he was one of the best new character actors, able to take a flamboyant role and find the quiet details in it. Emanuel Levy in *Variety* said that Hoffman had many marvelous moments but ultimately his performance lacked depth. Stephen Holden in the *New York Times* wrote that Hoffman brought an angry heat to a stunt role and made you aware every second that he was giving a carefully shaped, larger-than-life performance. The film was not a box office success.

Hoffman said Rusty was just a person who wanted to be loved and feel safe and to be free to do what he wanted, and anybody could relate to that. He was attracted to the role because he liked the unexpected directions in which the script went and because the idea of portraying a drag queen seemed especially challenging. To prepare for the role, Hoffman immersed himself in Drag and Transsexual studies 101. He visited Manhattan drag show establishments, chatted with several queens and studied the documentaries *Paris Is Burning* (1990) and Lee Grant's *What Sex Am I?* (1985). On the set, Hoffman received guidance from drag artists Nashom Benjamin, Scott Allen Cooper, Joey Arias, Raven O. and Jackie Beat. The actor also learned the keyboard to play a singing coach. The film's music producer Bruce Roberts assigned arranger Billy Stritch to teach Hoffman how to play and his live performance was used for shooting.

For the scenes where Rusty was on stage in full regalia, the actor wore a padded bodysuit that snapped in an uncomfortable spot. Hoffman said it was tough getting around in it. He had a lot of anxieties about getting the part right but he felt Schumacher and De Niro were really very indulgent of him. Hoffman commented that there were scenes that seemed very tricky when you first read them but he felt a part wasn't interesting unless it was challenging. There was a moment when Walt yelled at Rusty that he takes it in the ass and Rusty had to acknowledge that he had a point. Hoffman said that the film wasn't always politically correct but if people got up in arms about it, that was their problem.

Interviewed by Gregg Kilday for *The Advocate* (November 23, 1999), Hoffman said that for the majority of the film he tried to play Rusty as feminine as possible without being outrageous. He felt he looked outrageous at 5'10" and 200 pounds underneath all those clothes but he wanted to make the character look as attractive as possible. Hoffman figured this was because Rusty had this big straight man visiting him and he didn't want to scare him away. The actor also spoke about the role in his June 4, 2000, *Inside the Actors Studio* appearance. Hoffman reported that he was in Italy filming *The Talented Mr. Ripley* when he prepared for *Flawless*. He said Schumacher sent him videotapes on transgender people and the drag world and the director scheduled the shooting dates around the actor's work on *Mr. Ripley* so he could do both parts, which meant that Hoffman was traveling back and forth. It didn't confuse him but the actor said it was really nice to be able to lay down one and pick up the other. He did the film for scale because it had a low budget, and it was shot in eight weeks. Hoffman spoke about how uncomfortable his body suit was and how one time he had so much trouble getting it on that he almost broke into tears, thinking they got the wrong guy and that he was never going to be able to do it. He eventually did get the suit on but he remembered thinking that was the day he was going to quit. Hoffman was afraid that when people saw him in the dress and makeup they would laugh but what helped was that there was one drag queen who was physically as large as him and he was an inspiration. The actor reported that De Niro was amazingly nice and respectful of him and Hoffman considered him to be one of the world's greatest actors.

Schumacher said that the project was originally inspired by a friend of his who had suffered several strokes and regained his speech with the help of a music teacher. The teacher impressed Schumacher as a strong and patient man and after meeting him he realized how music was such a great vehicle that there was an interesting movie there. He sketched out the stroke victim as a tough guy who had shut down emotionally and experimented with several combinations for the second half of the equation. These included a May-December male-female couple, a white-black teaming, and a male-male tango team before deciding on the straight guy-transsexual combo after seeing *What Sex Am I?*

Schumacher said he wanted to make a film about what it means to be a man, but in a non-preachy way. The drag queens he had known in the Village since he was a teenager were real tough guys, because they had to be to survive. Schumacher auditioned hundreds of drag queens, including Charles Busch and John Epperson, but couldn't find one that had the acting chops to play opposite De Niro.

The director chose Hoffman because he felt a drag queen fell in nicely with the quirky characters the actor seemed to thrive on. Schumacher said that the actor was the only one he met he thought really understood the role. He knew immediately that Rusty was not a drag queen or a gay man but a transgender person, someone who thinks he has been born into the wrong body. Schumacher claimed that the actor brought a lot of humanity to the role, and his casting came after a long discussion with Hoffman. He didn't ask him to screen test in drag before awarding him the part. The director supported the way the actor looked in drag because he said in his mind Rusty was never the prettiest girl on the block. He said Hoffman was ferocious about detail and had a passion for perfection when filming. He would do a great take, and when they looked at the scene on video playback, the actor would say he didn't like he was holding his pinkie when he was smoking, and would ask for another take.

The actor next played a small supporting part in the Mirimax International—Paramount Pictures—Mirage Enterprise—Timnick Films thriller *The Talented Mr. Ripley* (1999). It was shot from August 10 to December 7, 1998, in Italy and New York by director Anthony Minghella. Minghella also wrote the screenplay which was based on the Patricia Highsmith novel. The novel had previously been made into a 1960 French-Italian film by Rene Clement called *Plein soleil* (aka *Full Son* and *Purple Noon*).

Matt Damon stars as Tom Ripley, a young underachiever in 1950s New York. He is sent by shipping magnate Herbert Greenleaf (James Rebhorn) to Italy to retrieve his spoiled playboy son Richard "Dickie" Greenleaf (Jude Law). Dickie's friend Freddie Miles (Hoffman) describes him as the perfect example of the cream of America—rich and thick and has no taste. The point about taste is highlighted in the scene where Tom kills Freddie after he describes the "horrible" furnishings of Tom's Rome apartment as "bourgeois." It is therefore fitting that Tom should use one of his aesthetic touches—a bust of the Roman emperor Hadrian—to kill Freddie. Freddie being rich gives him a sense of entitlement, which is demonstrated in the way he parks his car on the sidewalk rather than on the street. He also has a sense of exclusion since it warns him about those that do not fit in, like Tom. Both Tom and Freddie are in love with Dickie, Tom in a sexual way and Freddie in a non-sexual way. Freddie loves the idea of Dickie being his best friend

In still for *The Talented Mr. Ripley* (1999).

and he can't bear the fact that this role has been usurped by this cuckoo. Freddie exists as the nemesis to Tom because he is jealous of Tom's new closeness to his best friend, and while he is normally fun, he now feels estranged from Dickie. His entry into the narrative is the catalyst for the drama since there is such resentment and hostility on both sides. It is a contest for Dickie and Freddie initially wins in making Dickie question Tom's friendship, since it is apparent that Freddie does not like him. Dickie suspects that Tom is gay and attracted to him, a suspicion that Freddie makes more overt in the scene where he is killed.

Hoffman wears his hair in a short style with a fringe flip. Although Freddie is said to be heterosexual, the actor gives him gay affections, like speaking in a nasal voice, sitting with his legs crossed in a feminine way, and being limp-wristed. The latter is a variation on Hoffman's over-gesturing mannerism that actually has a context here, as does his self-touching which fits Freddie's narcissism. Another mannerism that he uses for the character is his enthusiastic laugh, which fits since Freddie both laughs arrogantly to himself and sardonically at Tom. We see Hoffman dancing when Freddie listens to music at a record shop, and swimming when Freddie plays with Dickie in the ocean. Apart from his laughter, the actor also uses a glare, a grimace and repetition to express Freddie's disdain for Tom. Hoffman snorts in exasperation when Freddie sees Tom peeping at Dickie having sex with Marge (Gwyneth Paltrow) on his boat and repeats his name, relishing the pinning of Tom's embarrassment. In the Rome apartment, Freddie repeats a one-note playing of Tom's piano, as a taunt, and adds an odd throwing back of his eyes. Hoffman is also funny in the scene when Freddie imitates Tom.

The film premiered on December 12, 1999, and released on December 25, with the taglines "How far would you go to become someone else," "Everybody should have one talent ... what's yours?" and "It's better to be a fake somebody than a real nobody." It was praised by Janet Maslin in the *New York Times*, who said that Hoffman was scene-stealingly wonderful, and by Roger Ebert. Todd McCarthy (*Variety*) wrote that Hoffman was superb and exact in his portrait of a bright but boorish snob. It was a hit and received Academy Award nominations for Best Adapted Screenplay, Best Art Direction-Set Decoration, Best Costume Design, Best Musical Score and Best Supporting Actor (Jude Law).

Hoffman said that Freddie had that old-school New York upper-crust way, but at the end of the day, he was just a good-time guy. He was honest and boisterous, but he came across as not that great a guy. The actor liked him because what he said was right and he was the only person immediately onto Ripley's duplicity. Because of that, Freddie was perceived as a jerk, and got killed, so it made the audience question who they had sympathy for. Interviewed in the September 1999 edition of *Out Magazine*, Hoffman commented on how the film dealt with the novel's controversial homosexual content, saying it was as edgy as you could get for a Hollywood movie. He felt that Minghella had approached it in a way that the book could only hint at, since it was published in 1955. In his interview in the book *Actors at Work* by Rosemarie Tichler and Barry Jay Kaplan, the actor commented on Freddie's playing of the piano in the Roman apartment scene. He said that the action was not scripted. He was supposed to play something to show Freddie had skills at the piano, although at the time Hoffman was still learning how to look like he knew how to play for *Flawless*. He decided that Freddie could not play and that the action was done to ridicule Tom's bourgeois taste. It was also designed on a psychological level to show that Freddie had this ability to size up someone and to identify Tom immediately as a fraud. Hoffman believed that Freddie was smart and loyal to his friends and he was angry that Dickie had been taken away from him, which made Freddie determined to get to the bottom of what had happened. In his June 4, 2000, *Inside the Actors Studio* interview, Hoffman said Freddie was not a stretch for him because he had played upper-class parts before. Hoffman remembered how it was such a joy and so freeing to be somebody like that, and he also enjoyed having the great death scene. In his 2001 *GQ* interview by David Kamp, Hoffman said that he worked one day a week for six weeks and that he and Cate Blanchett and her husband ate in good restaurants and visited all the museums.

Minghella commented that Hoffman was a wonderful actor who had demonstrated versatility and range in his performances. He thought the actor was in his element as Freddie, though as a person he couldn't have been further from the part, and he had the ability to conjure this drawling, gross—but *human*—person. Minghella felt that Hoffman was at his best in the Roman apartment scene, and that Matt Damon imitated Hoffman's voice for real, rather than relying upon dubbing, when Tom imitates Freddie. Hoffman later appeared in the biographical documentary *The Directors: The Films of Anthony Minghella* (1999).

After Hoffman's death, Damon commented that he was one of the best actors that ever lived and a beautiful person, and said that his death was horrible. Damon reported that he last saw him at the 2013 premiere of *The Hunger Games: Catching Fire* in Los Angeles, and he had dinner with him in Berlin where Hoffman was visiting at the same time Damon was shooting *The Monuments Men* (2014). The dinner was said to have happened a month before the actor went into rehab, though Damon said he was as shocked as anybody to read about his death, because Hoffman's problem wasn't something Damon could see. The young actor said his friend's body of work didn't suggest he had any substance abuse issues, and his struggle with addiction wasn't apparent in their private encounters. Gwyneth Paltrow said that Hoffman was a true genius.

Meryl Streep would work with the actor in 2001 on stage in *The Seagull* and in the film *Doubt* (2008). She said that when she saw him in *The Talented Mr. Ripley* she sat up straight in her seat and said, "Who is that?" She thought to herself that he was fearless and Hoffman had done what all actors strived to do: give an awful character the respect he deserved, and he made him fascinating. John C. Reilly commented that the film was an example of how his friend was unafraid to play an unsympathetic part, being unconcerned about his image.

From January 12 to June 24, 1999, Hoffman appeared in his next Paul Thomas Anderson film, the New Line Cinema–Ghoulardi Film Company drama *Magnolia* (1999), shot in locations around California and in Reno, Nevada. The film presented a mosaic of interrelated characters in the San Fernando Valley who are victims of chance and strange times.

Hoffman played Phil Parma, a nurse for Earl Partridge (Jason Robards) who is dying of brain and lung cancer. Phil telephones the Seduce and Destroy motivational speaker Frank T.J. Mackey (Tom Cruise), Earl's estranged son, so that he may visit before Earl dies. Phil also interacts with Earl's wife Linda (Julianne Moore) and the family's pack of dogs. His nursing skills are shown as he listens to Earl and gives him morphine.

Phil's dedication is shown when he refuses to let the replacement nurse take over, perhaps because he is aware that Earl does not have much time left. He comes across as not too bright since when he speaks to Frank's call center he talks of doing the movie scene "where the guy's trying to get ahold of the long-lost son and this being the scene in the movie where you help me out." Linda makes Phil hang up the phone before he can speak to Frank, but Frank later comes to the house and sees him and Earl.

Hoffman's hair is worn short and he only has one costume, a blue short-sleeved smock over a long-sleeved white sweater and dark pants. Hoffman uses fey mannerisms for Phil. The character has few active moments; he's a passive character who watches and listens. Hoffman brings emotion to scenes, with tears in his eyes, particularly when listening to Linda's apology to him. We see and hear him singing the Aimee Mann song "Wise Up" in the montage where all the characters sing, and he has a closeup shocked reaction to the sound of frogs falling from the sky onto the Partridge property.

The film premiered on December 8, 1999, then released on December 17, 1999, with the tagline "Things fall down. People look up. And when it rains, it pours." It was praised by Emanuel Levy in *Variety*, Janet Maslin in the *New York Times* (she called Hoffman extremely memorable), Roger Ebert in the *Chicago Sun-Times* and Peter Travers in *Rolling Stone*. The film was a hit and received Academy Award nominations for Best Original Screenplay, Best Song and Best Supporting Actor (Tom Cruise).

Anderson said he really didn't want Hoffman to play another "character-character," but rather a really simple, uncomplicated, caring character. Anderson said he wrote the part of the saintly nurse for him because he was that good—committed to art and not in a phony, grandstanding way. That's why Hoffman felt it was not a coincidence that his character was also named Phil. The actor described his character as someone who took pride in the fact that every day he was dealing with life-and-death circumstances. Hoffman said that Phil had a strong understanding of the importance of helping someone die, even though he knows that every time he goes through it, it's going to be painful. Hoffman described the film as opera without the music and said that it was an advantage to work with someone you had a history with and who wrote for you. Hoffman found the film one of the easiest he ever had to do because, knowing the environment, it created a feeling of how Anderson felt when he directed—that he was there to make sure the others did the best they could. So Hoffman would show up and he was there for Anderson. The actor said Jason Robards was an extraordinary actor who had what separated the men from the boys. Robards had a 17-page speech to which Hoffman had to listen, which was hard for the younger actor but in his opinion it was some of the best work he had ever done. Because listening was so hard to do, Hoffman said he was usually not very interested in tackling it, but with Robards it was simple because every word and thought and idea was so well done.

In his June 4, 2000, appearance on *Inside the Actors Studio* Hoffman said that playing a character in that type of film, one with the morals and the principles that this one had, was something that overjoyed him. In his 2001 *GQ* interview, Hoffman commented that it was kind of an honor that Anderson entrusted him with a caretaker part after he had played two character parts for him. He said Anderson wrote a part as a friendly, loving gesture and it was exhilarating to work with Robards. But Hoffman said the nature of the acting was so sad that it felt sad to work on it.

2. Boogie Nights 39

From May 11 to May 29, 1999, he appeared in the Off-Broadway production of the Richard Greenberg comedy *The Author's Voice* at Greenwich House. The play was on a double-bill with Peter Hedges' play *Imagining Brad*, and the director was Evan Yionoulis. Hoffman played the part of Gene the Gnome, a semi-paralyzed novelist who has another man pose as its author for the world. Charles McNulty of *Variety* wrote that Hoffman made a vividly creepy impression. Ben Brantley in the *New York Times* said that Hoffman simply wasn't repellent enough, suggesting nothing more threatening than Truman Capote in a hooded sweatshirt.

Actor James Urbaniak auditioned for the part of the Gnome and wrote about Hoffman in it. He described his silent entrance where the actor was on the floor, slowly crawling Army style and pulling his big man's weight towards a desk. Urbaniak wrote that the physical intensity and emotional depth was nowhere near what he had himself done in his audition, and he realized it was unlikely that he would have ever achieved it. Urbaniak said that Hoffman's entrance would remain a touchstone, a lesson, a perfect distillation of his acting. It was a mix of bold theatricality and naked vulnerability that reminded Urbaniak of Charles Laughton, with his West End bravura married to pre–Actors Studio emotional realism. For him, the entrance was a 30-second master class in committing, digging deep, raising the stakes, going further.

Hoffman played a supporting role in the Columbia Pictures/Dreamworks Pictures/Vinyl Films musical romance *Almost Famous* (2000), shot from May 24 to October 6, 1999, in Tuscon, New York, Los Angeles, San Diego and Santa Monica. It was semi-autobiographical for writer-director Cameron Crowe and concerned his alter ego William Miller (Patrick Fugit). As a 15-year-old high-schooler in 1973 he was hired by *Rolling Stone* magazine to write a story about the rock band Stillwater's "Almost Famous" 1973 bus road tour of America. Hoffman played Lester Bangs, a rock critic and editor of *Creem* magazine, who gives William his first job as a writer for his magazine and gives advises William when he telephones. Lester is part-hippie since he addresses William as "man" and smokes and swears, but also admits to being an "uncool" guy, like William. He identifies them as being artists who are smarter than good-looking people. William writes in his notes when he talks with Lester that he is "righteously dumb" but this is untrue, since his advice is sound and he speaks eloquently.

Hoffman here has dark brown hair (worn in a longish style) and a brown moustache, replicating the look of the real-life Lester Bangs who died in 1982 at an early age of a drug overdose. He can be seen in the HBO Making Of featurette on the film's DVD. Hoffman employs the mannerisms of the over-use of hand gestures, laughing to himself, and yelling for enthusiasm. We also get to see the actor doing a funny dance when he is being interviewed at a radio station. Lester is also funny when he hangs up the telephone in disgust when William tells him the music he is listening to is Stillwater. Hoffman's best scene is perhaps his telephone scene with William when he talks about being an "uncool" guy.

The film was first screened on September 8, 2000, at the Toronto International Film Festival, then given a limited release beginning on September 13 and a wide release on September 22. The tagline was "Experience it. Enjoy it. Just don't fall for it." A.O. Scott in the *New York Times* said that Hoffman played with guile and gusto. Peter Travers in *Rolling Stone* wrote that Hoffman made acerbic comic magic out of a sliver of screen time. The film was not a hit but it won the Academy Award for Best Original Screenplay and there were nominations for Best Film Editing and Best Supporting Actress for Frances McDormand and Kate Hudson.

Cameron Crowe said that Lester in real life was a mentor to him and he wanted to celebrate the man and write about how he would call in him late at night and sometimes ask for help and advice. He wanted to capture the soul of the rock critic who Crowe felt was probably happiest alone, surrounded by records and takeout food. The director said that Hoffman "found" Lester and it was a beautiful thing. The actor commented that Crowe had been quite successful at films he had told from his heart and he thought Lester saw that heart in him as a boy. Hoffman felt that the character had the idea that rock was dead but he still wanted to be around something that was alive and breathing and pumping and moving and new. One of the things that excited him about playing the part was Crowe's love for the man, who was described as a crazy, brilliant fan of music. It was reported that Hoffman's schedule only permitted him to be on the set for four days and he had the flu the whole time. Jon Favreau and Jack Black both auditioned for the part of Lester. In the film's production notes, Hoffman was quoted as saying that Crowe talked to him about Lester and what he meant to him and then the actor read the script. Hoffman felt it was one of those times when he knew the part was something he had to do.

After Hoffman died, Crowe spoke about him in a *Rolling Stone* interview by David Browne (February 14, 2014). He said that what both men had in common was a forceful presence with a big heart. Crowe knew Hoffman from *Twister* and *Boogie Nights* where he was he amazing because you saw him melt into this compassionate figure you just ached for. And that was part of Lester. Crowe checked out some other actors, and some were really good, but he knew it had to be Hoffman. Speaking to Hoffman on the telephone, Crowe sensed that he loved music and understood Lester. Crowe thought Hoffman had already been reading Lester's 1971 essay "Psychotic Reactions and Carburetor Dung." He told the actor that they were going to have two days of rehearsal and Hoffman paused and then said he may only have needed a couple of hours. But Crowe insisted on the two days.

Not long after, Hoffman came to Los Angeles to see him, dressed kind of like Lester in a leather jacket. Crowe could see had had a glint in his eye, as if Hoffman already knew the character. In the jacket he looked more like a rock critic than an actor. To Crowe, he was instantly a huge presence, not unlike Lester. They talked about the meaning of the script and the commercialization of music and movies, and the director and the actor bonded. They watched Lester on a BBC interview and Crowe thought the actor was putting the pieces together, studying Lester's movements in his process. When Lester was talking about Bryan Ferry, Crowe saw Hoffman soaking up the mannerisms and the gregarious sharpness of Lester's wit. They went over the scenes and Crowe felt that the actor was ready. Crowe joked that if he had a camera, he could have filmed Hoffman then and there. When the director saw that their meeting had lasted for two hours, the actor laughed and said, "Told ya," because he was right about the amount of time he needed.

Crowe said that Hoffman would listen to Lester on headphones between takes, and then pull off the headset right before he was ready to go. Crowe spoke about the uncool scene where he wanted to capture the ache and private glory of those two guys and the fact that Lester was going to give this kid some advice and yet they were brothers. It wasn't just a mentor and his student, it was two guys alone in the world sharing their deepest feelings. Hoffman refused to let his flu stop him from working, particularly since this was the last scene he shot for the film, though he commented that his face was going to be a little red. The actor gave Crowe what he wanted and the director was pleased that the scene showed a side of Lester he couldn't believe he was seeing. On the audio commentary of the Bootleg Edition DVD Crowe said that the scene originally had Lester storming through the apartment shouting his advice like a warrior king. After discussion and rehearsal, Hoffman thought it would work better if it was quieter, as if the two were the only ones in the world still up at that hour of the night. The actor also decided that Lester should expose his loneliness, a quality of the man that Crowe had forgotten, but that he felt Hoffman was channeling. In New York, Hoffman invited Crowe to see him in *True West* on stage and the director thought he gave a blazing performance. He went backstage where there was a small throng to see Hoffman, and Crowe said that Hoffman seemed energized. The actor looked through the crowd, crooked his finger and called the director to him. Hoffman pulled him back into his dressing room and told him he had made a really good movie. The two would talk on the telephone a few times after that night, but it was the last time Crowe ever saw him.

Patrick Fugit was interviewed by Jeff Labrecque for *Entertainment Weekly* (January 18, 2015) about his memories of Hoffman. The actor was only 16 at the time he made the film and he did not know who Hoffman was, but he would make a lasting impact on him. Fugit was fresh out of a Salt Lake City theater school and he had done some television work but nobody had taught him how to act on film. Because of Hoffman's limited availability there would be no time for him to rehearse with the actor, and Crowe had warned him that Hoffman would probably be in character the whole time. This proved to be true. Fugit said the actor wasn't Lester all day long but he was still very intense. Although others would tell Fugit how well he was doing because they knew as the film's lead his confidence had to be kept up, Hoffman was not like that at all. He was there to do his job and it was like he wanted Fugit to keep up with him. Crowe had told him that the actor had the flu and Hoffman would waddle on set, mumbly and eyes half-closed. He would sit down and close his eyes, as if he was psyching himself up. When action would be called Fugit said Hoffman was "as intense as sh—!" Other actors would paraphrase Crowe's lines, but Hoffman would say everything as it was written. He was like a surgeon—exact and he fit everything about the character and what he needed to communicate to the audience and what he needed to communicate about Lester and also make it feel natural. Basically, Hoffman had thought about the character, he had prepared, and he came to set ready.

On Hoffman's second day they shot the scene where Lester walked up the street with William. Hoffman embodied the character as a pretty cynical, dark guy and he asked Fugit how old he was. When Fugit said 16, Hoffman replied, "You little f—ing sh—. What have you done before?" The actor did break character on the day when he started talking about the film industry and acting and how the art of both was dying. Of course this paralleled with Lester's idea that rock and roll was dying. Hoffman compared the beginning of Fugit's career to William's career, and he told him that he should have come along 10 or 15 years earlier, just as Lester told William.

The diner scene had been lit quite brightly from the outside and the light was behind Hoffman so every time Fugit would look at him, he would start squinting and his eyes would start watering. To combat this, the young actor looked down at the paper pad to pretend he was writing, since William did write in the scene. Fugit was told he had to look at Hoffman when he read his lines, but he couldn't do so because of the light. Hoffman saw this and asked that the light be moved, and he and the cinematographer John Toll argued about it. He told Hoffman that he could make an adjustment but the light was there for a reason and the actor replied, "F—k lighting! Do you want it to look f—king good or do you want the kid to be able to act?" Fugit felt the tension of the moment. The young actor didn't feel he could say anything and Hoffman stepped up and did it for him. The light was moved and the scene was shot, and afterwards the actor smiled at Fugit and told him, "Dude, if something's bothering you, you have to speak up."

The last telephone scene between Lester and William was shot at the end of the schedule. The actors spoke for real on the telephone. They did a lot of takes, but the last take was the one that was used. Crowe had Hoffman talk about how much fun he'd had on the film. He said he didn't want Fugit to worry even though he probably wasn't going to see a lot of the same people again. This made the younger actor cry, which was needed for the scene, and Hoffman then did his lines, and it was all there. They did the rest of the scene twice and that was it. Fugit said he watched the film again when he turned 30 in 2012, and it struck him just how special it was that he got to do those scenes with Hoffman. And every time he would see Hoffman in something else, Fugit would say that, down the line, they *could* work together again. But it never happened.

Hoffman next directed Stephen Adly Guirgis' play *In Arabia, We'd All Be Kings* for the LAByrinth. He had mentioned he wanted to direct and when Guirgis began writing the play he asked the actor if he wanted to direct it. Hoffman read five scenes and found them great, and he said he had a real feeling for how he could help the writer finish the play. Running at the Center Stage from June 23 to July 17, 1999, it concerned a group of modern-day losers living in the Times Square area. Wilborn Hampton in the *New York Times* wrote that Hoffman mounted a crisp and taut production and molded his good cast into a strong ensemble that never seemed to pause to catch its breath. Hoffman and the show's costume designer Mimi O'Donnell began a relationship.

Around this time it was reported that the actor was offered a supporting part in the crime comedy *Lucky Numbers* (2000). He turned it down and the part of Walter was played by Michael Moore. Moore, interviewed by Hoffman for the documentary *Last Party 2000*, spoke about this to him though the actor made no comment about it.

3

True West

On November 12, 1999, the *New York Times* reported that Hoffman would co-star with John C. Reilly in a revival of Sam Shepard's play *True West*, which would run from February 15, 2000, at the Circle in the Square. The play showed the reunion of two estranged brothers, one a burglar, the other a Hollywood screenwriter; they try to teach each other the tricks of their respective trades. The actors had previously appeared in the Paul Thomas Anderson films *Hard Eight, Boogie Nights* and the forthcoming *Magnolia* (1999). Reilly reported that he had been instrumental in getting Hoffman hired, suggesting his friend when director Matthew Warchus asked who should play the part. Reilly had been told by Anderson, before he met Hoffman, that he (Hoffman) was the next John C. Reilly. Reilly asked Anderson why he would say something like that but then, doing the play, he found that things had come full circle, because when he was asked for someone to play his brother, it made total sense. Both actors were known as character actors but their names would be listed above the title for the production, which would be Hoffman's Broadway debut.

In Hoffman's June 4, 2000, *Inside the Actors Studio* interview he said that he was filming *State and Main* in the fall of 1999 when Reilly telephoned him about doing the play. Hoffman said that his first reaction to the offer was that it was nice but he didn't know if he could do it. When Reilly told him they would be able to switch parts, Hoffman said that was kind of strange and kind of a gimmick, and he didn't know if he was interested in that. His friend told him how good he thought Warchus was and that Hoffman should read the play again. So he did and realized he'd forgotten how good it was.

The *New York Times*' Jamie Malanowski wrote on November 21, 1999, that, with Hoffman's recent film performances and his upcoming Broadway show, he seemed a candidate to become the last hot actor of the 20th century. Malanowski conceded that Hoffman was not likely to cop a *People* magazine cover, but he predicted that, soon, an awful lot of people were going to know who he was. The actor was reportedly bleary-eyed and sleep-deprived the day he was interviewed by Malanowski and seemed hesitant to embrace the possibility of becoming the next big thing. "I don't know, we'll see," he said dubiously. "I don't want to assume anything. I don't even want to assume that people will like what I've done."

At the time of the interview, Hoffman was in Massachusetts making *State and Main* (2000), a comedy by writer-director David Mamet that began shooting on September 21, 1999, on location in Massachusetts. In the movie, a Hollywood cast and crew are shooting the film *The Old Mill* on location in the small rural town of Waterford, Vermont. Hoffman played Joseph Turner White, a playwright who has just written his first screenplay (*The Old Mill*)—and needs to *re*write it when the company learns that the old mill has burned down, as well as to accommodate the lead actors. He is a witness when Bob Barrenger (Alec Baldwin) is involved in a car accident and has a minor with him, Carla Taylor (Julia Styles). Joseph must choose between telling the truth and perjuring himself in court; telling the truth will cost him his Hollywood career. He initially chooses to lie, but the deposition is told to townspeople pretending to be court officers, at the request of local drama society and book shop manager Annie Black (Rebecca Pidgeon). When Joseph learns of this, he decides he will tell the truth at the real hearing, following the code "You shall not bear false witness." This proves to be unnecessary after the prosecuting lawyer, Doug McKenzie (Clark Gregg), is bribed by the film company. Joseph is also given a romantic subplot: Annie sells him a typewriter he needs to work on the script, works as his typist after he injures his hands, and assists him with the script revisions. His decision to eventually tell the truth is done presumably because he is prepared to choose a new life with Annie over his Hollywood career.

The role is Hoffman's first romantic one but it is an unconventional leading role, given the ensemble nature of the cast. The romantic subplot is the only one in the narrative, and we see the actor kiss his romantic interest only near the conclusion. Hoffman appears in 26 scenes, some of them continuous since the narrative only covers three days. The closest another actor has to this is William H. Macy who plays Walt Price, the film's director, who appears in 20 scenes, some of *them* continuous. Mamet uses a lot of closeups for the actor's coverage but they have a counterproductive effect since they are unflattering. Hoffman wears glasses and speaks in a soft voice except when he yells after getting a fishhook in his finger, and when announcing that he has come to give his deposition. Hoffman overuses hand gestures and self-conscious touching, sits in a cross-legged feminine way in one scene, and also fiddles with something in his hand when he tries to interrupt Walt to tell him he has lost his typewriter. He has an effective closeup expressing Joseph's anguish when he approaches the court to give his deposition, but Hoffman's best scene is perhaps the farcical one when he juggles the advance of the film company's leading actress Claire Wellesley (Sarah Jessica Parker) when Annie simultaneously arrives in his hotel room to type.

In still for *State and Main* (2000).

3. True West

State and Main was screened on August 26, 2000, at the Montreal Film Festival, on September 8 at the Toronto International Film Festival, on October 12 at the Austin Film Festival, and November 3 at the Savannah Film and Video Festival. It was given a limited release on December 22, 2000, and then a wide release on January 12, 2001, with the taglines "When a film crew came to Waterford, Vermont—They Shot First and Asked Questions Later" and "Big movie. Small town. Huge trouble." It was praised by Eddie Cockrell in *Variety*, Roger Ebert in the *Chicago Sun-Times* and Peter Travers in *Rolling Stone*. Stephen Holden in the *New York Times* wrote that Hoffman was just about perfect.

David Mamet said that he had admired of Hoffman's bizarre and magnificent work in *Boogie Nights*, *Happiness* and *Patch Adams*. After the actor died, Mamet said he had no idea at the time they made the film that Hoffman had any problem, addiction or otherwise, and he was shocked by his death.

Hoffman said that his character, a new screenwriter, wasn't used to the film world, and that *State and Main* showed his struggle to compromise and change and problem-solve just to get his movie done. Hoffman claimed that the film was perfectly drawn because if Joseph doesn't tell the truth, he not only loses his sense of morality, he also loses the woman—and *that* raises the stakes. Hoffman considered the best line in the script to be "The only second chance is a chance to make the same mistake twice," because he thought that was true. He considered the part his first romantic lead and part of the challenge was to lose weight for it. Another challenge was working with Mamet, whom he said was a really smart guy, and if you disagreed he always had an answer for you. In his 2001 *GQ* interview by David Kamp Hoffman reported that Mamet had to keep telling him to keep his mouth closed, but the actor defended this trait by saying that's how he was. Hoffman advised that when he was really listening to someone, he started turning into this Labrador retriever.

On the DVD cast audio commentary David Paymer said that Hoffman was obviously one of the most gifted actors there was and that he was versatile. Paymer said it was the first time Hoffman had played the ingénue and he did a great job, though it wasn't your typical ingénue because it was quirky, sweet, vulnerable and very funny. Paymer added that Hoffman was a great guy, and quite serious about his work. The two actors went to the dailies and they would compare notes afterwards. Sarah Jessica Parker commented that Hoffman gave a wonderfully powerful, insightful, lovely performance. She also reported that they were both serious New York Yankees fans. Parker purchased tickets for the cast to attend a game at Fenway Park, which Hoffman also attended.

For LAByrinth the actor co-produced *Dreaming in Tongues*, a piece using comedy, music and dance to explore language and communication. This was performed on December 20, 1999, compiled and written by the cast but conceived, co-created and directed by John Gould Rubin. For the company he also co-produced *Stopless*, a David Deblinger play directed by Gould Rabin; it ran at the Center Stage in New York from January 5 to 29, 2000. The play had gotten its start at the LAByrinth 1999 Summer Intensive, a yearly retreat where actors created new works. Hoffman challenged Deblinger to write a new play after working with him on *Shmoo* because he thought it was time to link the journeys of the characters he created.

The play was about two brothers, each obsessed and seeking ecstasy, one through religion and the other via sex. The cast of four also included their mother and the stripper-girlfriend of the sex-obsessed brother. The title echoed the brothers' inability to escape from their respective addictions. After 14 pages of the play were staged at the retreat, the company committed to the project and there was a four-day workshop in October 1999. On January 25, 2000, Hoffman made the first of two appearances on Warner Bros. comedy talk show *The Rosie O'Donnell Show*. She said that he was one of the best actors working.

For *True West*, Hoffman and Reilly switched roles every three performances, flipping a coin the day of the play to determine that night's casting, and this demand became more daunting than was expected. The production was scheduled to open on February 24, 2000, but then had to be postponed for a week. Previews began on February 17. In late February, on the last performance during the show's first week of previews, Hoffman sustained an injury. He was playing the writer Austin and Reilly the burglar Lee and Lee smashed Austin's typewriter with a nine iron. Reilly sent Hoffman flying into the typewriter. This caused a gash to the actor's elbow, but Hoffman carried on, choosing to ignore the blood running from his wound.

The show ran from March 2 till July 29, 2000. Ben Brantley of the *New York Times* wrote that Hoffman's performance style had an undulating pattern of eruptions. He also commented on the ploy of having the actors rotate in the leading roles. Brantley said that if you had followed their work on film, you probably would have your own ideas of who was meant for which part. But, "forget it. Whichever way you've sliced it, you're right."

Hoffman was interviewed by Jancee Dunn for the February 17–24, 2000, *Time Out New York* magazine. The interview took place in a West Village tavern, with Hoffman in glasses and a two-day stubble and appearing rumpled; Dunn reported that the actor was more handsome in person than on screen. Hoffman said that if you really want to get him riled you should call him Hollywood's character actor *du jour*, as one reporter did. He didn't want to be talked about like that because he didn't want to be the soup of the day. The actor told Dunn he had quit smoking three months prior and this perhaps made his hands restless. He had been smoking a pack and a half a day, and now he admitted to waking up in the middle of the night and eating. Hoffman said sugar was a guilty pleasure because it was easy and it made him feel smart. Speaking about his acting past, he commented that even in his leanest years he had never done commercials or any project just for the money. The actor had only done stuff he wanted to do and he guessed he was lucky that way. As opposed to when he split $750 a month to share a two-bedroom Brooklyn apartment, the actor said if he spent money it was now at Nobu. He would splurge $300 in a restaurant before buying a stereo system or a Vespa. He also commented on *Twister* and *The Talented Mr. Ripley*.

The actor advised that unlike some, once he was done playing a character in a movie he shook him off, and the minute he didn't have to do them any more he felt such joy. Hoffman said he liked being himself and didn't like carrying around some character's baggage that he had been creating and building. Speaking about *True West*, Hoffman said that getting both of the characters down was like doing two plays. What Hoffman thought was difficult about it was what was really great about it: Playing both parts felt like he was exploring nooks and crannies he never would have otherwise.

At this time Hoffman hadn't committed to do anything else yet but he was sure that he wouldn't do something just for the Benjamins no matter how popular he became. He felt you would only do that when you had two kids to support, and not when you were a single guy thinking you need 300 grand and you better do this shitty-ass job. Hoffman also commented on the ever-increasing buzz about him as an actor. His recent award nominations had also increased his wattage. The actor commented on how hard he thought acting was and the constant effort it took, on and off the set. Hoffman said acting was not easy, ever, and when you start thinking it was easy, all of a sudden you suck.

Reilly spoke about Hoffman's fearlessness as an actor, being unafraid to show all the sides of his character, and how close he got with him by doing *True West*. He thought of Hoffman as a real contemporary and said he was a transformer.

Reilly, interviewed by Tobias Perse for the same edition of *Time Out New York*, talked more about Hoffman. He said his friendship helped doing the play because he knew going into it that it had to be with someone who he could feel vulnerable around. He also spoke about the videotapes he made with Paul Thomas Anderson between *Hard Eight* and *Boogie Nights*, where he played a cop. Hoffman appeared in one where he played the perp after it was reported that someone had been throwing rocks at the back of a house. Reilly drove up in the car and saw Hoffman down at the other end of an alley, acting like he wasn't doing anything wrong. Then Reilly gunned the engine and Hoffman started running. He fell over fences and was tackled and then Hoffman would get away. Reilly said it was hilarious, and went on for an hour, with Anderson filming the whole time.

Jessie McKinley reported for the *New York Times* on the production's opening night party at the Laura Belle venue. Hoffman sat in a corner booth with Reilly and friends Will Farrell, Jimmy Fallon, Paul Thomas Anderson and Don Cheadle. The actor reportedly stayed late, looking relaxed and remaining cordial, shaking hands, sipping bottled water and sodas, and taking care of his mom. He was said to look humbled by the good reviews the play received and the attention. He kept a cigarette in hand most of the night and commented that this is what you studied for and people were excited because of what happened on stage. Hoffman said that it was unlike a party for a film because people were not there just to see who else was there.

The actor was mentioned in a *New York Times* article by Bruce Wagner on February 20, 2000. It was reported that a talent agent manqué who claimed to be the Dalai Lama's West Coast personal assistant, was prosecuted in November 1999 in connection with her persistent and unwelcome public groveling before Hoffman and others and she was now at the Frontera correctional facility for women.

On March 9, 2000, he made his second appearance on *The Rosie O'Donnell Show* with John C. Reilly to promote *True West*. The actor was interviewed in the green room on the Circle in the Square for a *New York Times* article by Robin Pogrebin that was published March 28, 2000. He said the point of playing two roles in *True West* was to explore the fact that the characters could inhabit two different bodies and still be the same person. He said the play was one person and the battle of two parts of everybody. Hoffman used the word osmosis in describing how he incorporated Reilly's work into his own performance. Because of the intense interdependence the play demanded, he said it was important to trust each other and to be generous about sharing ideas. Even though they were going to interpret everything differently, they were both responsible for the same part. It helped that the actors were already friends, and apparently Reilly's suggestion that Hoffman play his brother was an idea that Matthew Warchus already had.

The director had asked Reilly to suggest a possible partner because he felt a foundation of mutual respect was essential for the piece. Warchus said that if an actor is asked to share his territory with another actor, it could be a real strain and if there was any kind of competitiveness, it could get very ugly. Neither Hoffman nor Reilly initially liked Warchus' idea that they alternate roles, since they would be required to memorize the entire play as the brothers almost never leave the stage. But the director made a compelling argument and the actors were sold. Hoffman said they had four and a half weeks to put up two shows and there had been a point in rehearsals that was characterized as a crisis. The actors were finding it difficult to learn the lines, and said they couldn't do it since they had half of one brother in them and half of the other, and they didn't know who they were as individuals. The work was grueling but they discovered that changing roles actually turned out to be a luxury. It became a relief to move from one character to another, particularly since each part had different vocal and physical demands. The actors also drew upon their relationships with their brothers (Reilly had three and Hoffman one).

In his *Inside the Actors Studio* interview, conducted on November 26, 2006, at the 92nd Street Y, Hoffman spoke about doing the play. He commented that watching another person do the part was an ego challenge, particularly when he could see that Reilly was figuring it out quicker than he was. But Hoffman didn't think he would have found the character of Lee if he hadn't rehearsed the play in that manner. The actor said that even when he alternated roles, the blocking was pretty much the same. Hoffman had great admiration for Reilly and loved doing the play with him. The actor said Reilly was extraordinary because he never knew what his co-star was going to do, which would make Hoffman have to consider what he would do in response.

Hoffman said that despite his recent success in films, the play was in another category because it meant more to him. For him the theater was more real and it allowed him to be part of something that was the event itself, something that was bigger than himself. He hoped that it would be one of the experiences people would remember, much like the experience of seeing *All My Sons* was for him. Hoffman reported that people would come to the actors after the show and say it was just like a rock concert. He said that he had panic attacks doing the show because it got under his skin like no other play, and he literally had to cling on to Reilly because it did something to him that he couldn't put into words. Hoffman told how at one rehearsal where the playwright attended, after the actors had been battling with the script, Reilly got his attention to show him that Sam Shepard was asleep. The actors felt that was bad and then he woke up and told them that he was going to leave to let them figure it out. That told Hoffman that Shepard trusted that they were going to find their way and their finding their way was much more important than him dictating to them at the time. And that he felt comfortable enough to fall asleep. The interview also revealed that Hoffman's father had retired from his job at Xerox and was now pursuing a degree in social work.

In his 2001 *GQ* interview with David Kamp, Hoffman described how in the early months of 2000 Manhattan was papered with posters of the two actors in the play. They looked out at the world in a cavalier way as if to say they ruled and that you would no doubt emerge from the theater gobsmacked at what they had done. However Hoffman admitted that they both had moments in rehearsal being very scared about the fact that what they were attempting could blow up in their faces. He considered the play tricky and felt that in the wrong hands it could easily degenerate into histrionics.

On April 14, 2000, the *New York Times* reported that the Tony Administrative Committee denied a request from the producers that Hoffman and Reilly, who switched roles every third performance, be considered as a single entity, rather than as individual performers. The idea behind the request was so that the actors would not compete against each other or cancel each other out. That decision forced the awards' nominating committee to decide whether to nominate either of the actors or both on May 8, 2000. It was announced that it had been decided to nominate both actors for the Best Actor award. On May 9, 2000, Hoffman appeared at the Blockbuster Entertainment Awards show, held at L.A.'s Shrine Auditorium.

Hoffman told Charlie Rose on his WNET New York show on May 30, 2000, that if Reilly wasn't attached, he wouldn't have done *True West* and after having done the play with him, Hoffman couldn't imagine doing it with anybody else. Asked if he preferred one role over the other, the actor replied there was a time when he felt more confident about one part but it changed for him so eventually he had no preference. Reilly said that Sam Shepard was at rehearsals for a week and for a week of performance, and Hoffman said the playwright added lines here and there where felt he needed a little something extra. According to Hoffman, Shepard was supportive and helpful in telling some personal anecdotes about himself in connection with the play.

Commenting on success, the actor said he and Paul Thomas Anderson joked all the time about why he couldn't cast him in leading roles since Hoffman was not the kind of star that Hollywood demanded. Reilly said he had asked Anderson if he would write a play for the two actors but the director decided that he didn't want to because then they would do it the way they wanted on stage with the implication that Anderson would lose control. Rose commented that 1999 was Hoffman's best year in terms of acting. Hoffman said that acting was a weird thing in terms of what could be defined as the best, and he truly believed that you were only as good as what you were doing right then. Hoffman said he could have four shows in a row where you thought he was just kicking it and then at the next performance it was like a car crash happened on the stage. It would make him revert to the embryo of acting and force him to re-examine and re-ask all the questions and that was what made him a better actor. Hoffman said if he just kept thinking how great his last work was, he wouldn't get any better and would probably slowly get worse, so the theater reminded him that he didn't know everything and had to stay on top of his game. The actor told a story of a recent performance when they were 90 minutes into the play and he suddenly remembered that a friend of his was in the audience that night. The thought had not occurred to him until that time and Hoffman felt that was a beautiful experience because he didn't even think about the fact that there were people watching him. The theater gave him that experience and it really was a magical thing.

On the same *Charlie Rose* show, the *New York Times*' chief drama critic Ben Brantley commented on Hoffman and Reilly getting individual Best Actor Tony Award nominations. He said that giving the award to one of them and not the other was unfair and would cancel out both from winning. Brantley agreed that the fair thing to do would have had them nominated as one, as the producers lobbied for. A May 21, 2000, *New York Times* article reported that some of the Tony nominators expressed frustration that they were unable to award something special to the two actors. Even though they had taken the trouble to see both versions of the production, they said they were forced to vote for best actor based only on the play's opening night casting. Actress Frances Sternhagen, who served on the committee, said they were both superb and they both shared the play and she questioned why the committee had such a rule which made it hard to give credit where credit was due.

Both actors were scheduled to appear on the Tony award show which took place at Radio City Music Hall. Hoffman was shown in the audience when his nomination was announced, with Reilly sitting in front of him. The award was given to Stephen Dillane for *The Real Thing*. Hoffman was photographed by Patrick McMullen at the afterparty at the Marriott Marquis with Eartha Kitt. He and Reilly were replaced by Josh Brolin and Elias Koteas in the play from June 21, 2000.

The actor was profiled by Mary E. McCrank in an article in the May–June 2000 edition of *Rochester Magazine*. Accompanying it were photographs by Antonino Barbagallo of Hoffman in what was said to be his standard trendy garb—green khaki jacket and pants, black shoes and black chunky glasses. He had come to Rochester for a *Flawless* screening which was also a benefit for Shipping Dock Theatre and the LAByrinth Theatre Company. Hoffman stayed at his mother's home in Penfield and he commented on getting the magazine cover, which he claimed was his first, saying he had never expected anyone to see him in that light. The actor spoke about his childhood, saying he never thought he would ever work with anybody and didn't know if he would get out of Rochester. Not that he disliked his home town, which he described as a groovy city.

On June 4, 2000, Hoffman was interviewed in New York by James Lipton for TV's *Inside the Actors Studio*. He covered *Flawless*, *Magnolia*, *The Talented Mr. Ripley*, *True West* and the LAByrinth Theatre Company. It is interesting to see that as himself he employs his acting mannerisms of over-gesturing, laughing and self-conscious touching. Lipton asks Hoffman his regular ten questions originated by French television personality Bernard Pivot on his show *Apostrophes*. The actor advises that his favorite word is okay, and his least favorite is relax. What turns him on is a beautiful woman but also when he runs into somebody who is nice because they want to be. What turns him off is when people think they have the right to somehow let their baggage be your news. The sounds or noise Hoffman likes is humming to himself and the ones he hates are car alarms. His favorite curse word is "Fucking motherfucking stupid fucking cocksucker, shut the fuck up." Hoffman says he likes to keep it going "until they're like 'I'm gonna ask you to leave!' So, oh, *you're* gonna ask me to leave! So, the curse word is really about a whole fight, it's gotta be a conversation." The profession other than his that he would like to attempt is teaching, and the one he wouldn't like to participate in is being a critic. Asked if Heaven exists, what he would like to hear God say when he arrives at the pearly gates, he answered, "All right, let's do it again."

He was next the director of the Stephen Adly Guirgis play *Jesus Hopped the "A"*

Train, produced by LAByrinth at the Center Stage from July 18 to August 12, 2000. The prison drama concerned two Rikers Island inmates facing murder charges. It was workshopped in June 2000. In a *Time Out New York* magazine interview by Mike Batistick (August 3–10, 2000), Hoffman said that Guirgis was a really good actor and that is what made his writing so good. Hoffman also commented about LAByrinth. The previous year he and John Ortiz and David Deblinger negotiated with Eric and Jill DeArmon to obtain the Center Stage space as a permanent home for the company.

The play was restaged by Hoffman at the Off-Broadway East 13th Street/CSC Theatre from November 29 to December 31, 2000. Previews began from November 21, 2000. In a September 15, 2000, *New York Times* article, Hoffman commented on the playwright and the company. This production was lambasted by *Variety*'s Pamela Renner, who wrote that Hoffman's direction was sledgehammer. But Ben Brantley in the *New York Times* wrote that Hoffman provided a visceral energy and sustained a harsh current of physicality in which you could feel the violence of thoughts in conflict. The director took the play to London's Donmar Warehouse where it ran from March 6, 2002, as part of the three-month festival "American Imports," and then the West End's Arts Theatre. One of the actor's *Talented Mr. Ripley* co-stars Gwyneth Paltrow was in London to star in a production of the David Auburn play *Proof* at the Donmar Warehouse. She reportedly saw Hoffman's production with him and commented after the performance that the play was so fantastic that she was almost speechless. Paltrow said it was profoundly moving and well acted. She had missed the New York production but thought this one was wonderful.

Hoffman narrated and was featured in the Steinlee Buchthal-Palisades Pictures-Indelible documentary *The Last Party 2000 a.k.a. The Party's Over*, filmed from June 2000 to January 20, 2001. Directed by Rebecca Chaiklin and Donovan Leitch, it is considered a sequel to the 1993 documentary *The Last Party*, about the 1992 Democratic National Convention.

The new film covered the 2000 presidential election campaign: the Republican State Convention in Texas, the Republican National Convention in Philadelphia, the Democratic National Convention in Los Angeles, the presidential debates in St. Louis and Boston, Election Day in New York City, the Supreme Court decision and George W. Bush's Inauguration Day. Hoffman and the production team did their own campaign trail following these events as well as visiting the World Trade Organization protests in Seattle; the Ruckus Democracy Action Camp in Malibu, California; the NRA Gun Show in Maryland; the Million Mom March in Washington, D.C.; the Christian Coalition Luncheon; the Kensington Welfare Rights Union in North Philadelphia; the Farm Aid Benefit Concert in Virginia; the Shadow Convention in Los Angeles; the Green Party Rally in New York City; and protests outside the party conventions like the March For Economic Human Rights.

The actor also spoke to Prof. Noam Chomsky, Green Party presidential candidate Ralph Nader and other actors, musicians, politicians, activists, religious leaders, people on the street, schoolchildren, the elderly, newspaper reporters and journalists. Hoffman states in the narration that he wanted to host the documentary because he felt ill-informed and always had an aversion to politics, although he could not say why. He and the team wanted to see what issues people were concerned with and learned that these issues were not being discussed at either of the main conventions. The team were unable to enter the Republican National Convention until they brokered a deal to supply them with a rock band in exchange for access. The documentary covered an election that became controversial because of the count in Florida, where it was alleged that the Republicans employed dirty tricks to sway the result and also that the Supreme Court decision had two of the justices having a conflict of interest favoring Bush.

The film was released in New York on November 21, 2001, with the tagline "America, this is your wake up call." Joe Leydon in *Variety* wrote that Hoffman was a genial host, and Dave Kerr in the *New York Times* said that Hoffman was good at listening intently, then nodding in furious agreement as pundits offered their assessments of the current state of democracy.

In the DVD audio commentary by Rebecca Chaiklin and Hoffman, he says he wanted to stay as neutral as possible in the film so as not to make it his experience but rather everybody's, and you were just along the trip with him. He said what was important was the people he met and talked to and that approach, he felt, helped make the film more moving. Hoffman said another reason to make the film was to get more people to vote. An interesting moment in the commentary is when the actor remarks on the drug addiction of Scott Weiland, the lead singer of the Stone Temple Pilots. Hoffman says addiction is a tough disease, a comment that becomes more resonant given his later death. Chaiklin reports that she hopes to make another similar film for the 2004 presidential election; this did not occur.

The *New York Times* wrote on August 17, 2000, that Hoffman interviewed Susan Sarandon at the Patriotic Hall for the film in Los Angeles on August 16, 2000. They talked about President Clinton's address to the convention and especially the very theatrical lead-in during which he was seen making his way through the strangely empty corridors of the Staples Center. Hoffman said when he was watching it he could feel a tear in his eye. He had to stop himself and say, "Oh no, I'm getting moved, I'm getting manipulated." Donovan Leitch compared Hoffman to Robert Downey, Jr., who hosted *The Last Party*. He said Downey was like Puck, frolicking through the convention. Hoffman was always aware of what was going on around him, and he was very intellectual and very much wanted to know what was going on. His mantra was: "Why should I care? Why is this important to me?" The actor said one of the main reasons that he decided to do the film was because he really didn't know all that much about the political process, outside of the basics. In the 2001 *GQ* article on Hoffman, David Kamp wrote that he had attended an advance screening of the film and commented that the actor trundled through the political theater as an earnest naif, growing ever more queasy as the vacuity of Campaign 2000 sunk in. Kamp quoted Donovan Leitch, who said that he had been with celebrities who get recognized before but he felt Hoffman really touched people on a deeper level.

The December 22, 2000, *New York Times* revealed that Hoffman would be part of an all-star production of *The Sea Gull*, Anton Chekhov's darkly funny play about actors, depressives and star-crossed lovers. It was to be directed by Mike Nichols and produced by the Joseph Papp Public Theater and would also feature Meryl Streep, Kevin Kline, Natalie Portman, Christopher Walken and Allison Janney. Performances were planned to begin in July or August 2001.

4

Love Liza

Hoffman next played his first leading role in the Kinowelt Filmproduktion–GmbH–Wild Bunch–StudioCanal–Muse–Blacklist comedy *Love Liza* (2002), filmed on location in New York, Los Angeles, Mobile, Alabama and New Orleans, Louisiana. The screenplay was by Hoffman's brother Gordy and it was directed by Todd Louiso. It reportedly took five years to get funding to make the film. Hoffman played website designer Wilson Joel, whose wife Liza (Ann Morgan) recently committed suicide. It is not stated how she did it but it is suggested that she gassed herself in the garage with her car's fumes. This links to Wilson's newfound habit of "huffing" gasoline and the fuel, which runs a radio-control model plane, which he flies. Another narrative point is the letter Liza has written to Wilson which he refuses to open. Liza's mother Mary Ann Bankhead (Kathy Bates) is curious about it and this leads her to steal it. Wilson uses the gas to relieve his grief and depression, which has made an insomniac and prompted him to quit his job. It also gives him a hallucination about seeing Liza naked in the bathroom. The character's disconnect from the world is accentuated by his bad luck with objects, like the drink that falls over into the sand at the beach, the vase of flowers that won't sit at the cemetery and his car's glove compartment which won't close. Wilson's huffing is paralleled with two teenagers who do the same. After Wilson helps them get more gas, he is caught by his new boss Tom Bailey (Stephen Tobolowsky) and loses that job. The plot points join in the climax when Wilson reads the letter, which comes with a match. Striking it to burn the letter also ignites the gas in his house, which leaves him homeless.

Hoffman gets above-the-title billing for the first time in his career, and though this is a leading role, there are scenes without him. Hoffman wears his hair long, and dons glasses when he is at work. His wardrobe favors a yellow-golden jacket over a blue sweater and dark pants and sneakers. We also see Hoffman bare-chested and in trunks at the beach and at the Sidell Roundup in the pond when he swims, and at the film's end when he apparently only wears boxers and socks and walks on the highway. We also see Wilson playing basketball, which recalls the actor's childhood history as a jock. Director Louiso's coverage of Hoffman is better than that of David Mamet in *State and Main* so we don't retreat from him, despite the almost grotesque out-of-focus closeups he uses for Wilson's huffed episodes.

The role is not the romantic one that Mamet provided since Wilson is an abandoned protagonist and the potential new romantic interest from his boss Maura (Sarah

Koskoff) is rejected. The idea that he is a substance abuser also works against the idea of Wilson as a romantic figure, since he is shown to be addicted and self-destructive. To Hoffman's credit, he manages to keep the character likable. Another factor that might have worked against his likability is Wilson's expressed anger which Hoffman mostly makes funny. Examples of this are when Wilson yells at Mary Ann about how he doesn't want a letter from Liza and his yelling at the Pancake House Cashier (Cullen Douglas). Wilson's yelling at Denny (Jack Kehler) for entering his house without being invited and his yelling at the gas station attendant (Wayne Duvall) are both unfunny and the scene where Wilson laughs excessively at his office and causes his co-workers to exit also fails.

Hoffman has some other interesting moments. These include Wilson's fear when Denny sees he keeps his gas and fuel in the fridge, the odd way he holds up his hand when watching the Roundup boat race, his shocked reaction to Mary Ann yelling "You had everything!" to him, his silent reaction to seeing she has the stolen letter, and his tears when he reads it.

The film was first screened on January 14, 2002, at the Sundance Film Festival, then on September 18, 2002, at the Toronto International Film Festival; November 10, 2002, at the London Film Festival; November 15, 2002, at the AFI Film Festival; and given a limited release in the United States on December 30, 2002, with the tagline "A Comic Tragedy." It did not receive a wide release. It was praised by *Variety*'s Todd McCarthy who wrote that Hoffman displayed a live wire personality that made him a magnetic figure and he achingly put across the solitary despair of the man's crack-up. A.O. Scott in the *New York Times* said that Hoffman's omnipresence was something of a mixed blessing. His skill for precision and understatement, and for unexpectedly allowing a gleeful energy to burst out in otherwise somber circumstances, were impressively evident, but the movie was so small and emotionally constricted that it gave him too little room to explore his range. Roger Ebert in the *Chicago Sun-Times* wrote that Hoffman was a teacher who brought attentive concern to his characters, as if he has been giving them private lessons and now it was time for their first public recital. The film was a box office success.

The DVD audio commentary provides information about deleted scenes and scenes that were written and not shot. These include a second scene of Wilson huffing the gas of a taxi at the airport, one where Wilson attempts to huff at night at the Roundup and is caught by Denny, and a scene where Wilson is on the telephone with his buddy whom he played basketball and had dinner with. Hoffman said that the scene where Wilson first attempts to break into Mary Ann's house was supposed to feature policemen but for budget reasons this was scaled down to just one observing neighbor. Gordy said he enlarged the part of Mary Ann in order to attract a name actress, and added the scenes where Wilson explains his situation to the truck driver and the girls at the Roundup. Another change was Mary Ann in her bathroom with the reveal that she had the letter; originally Wilson was to have found her dead in the bath. As Mary Ann is not seen after this scene, it is possible that she still also committed suicide. Gordy also originally had Wilson reading Liza's letter twice out loud, and Louiso shot this and then reduced the reading to one time in editing but kept the last line being said twice. The actor had the idea that Wilson's odd behavior including his huffing was not generally commented on by others since they had an awareness of his situation and therefore allowed it. Hoffman also said that Wilson having his things stolen suggested the poetic nature of the film since it was not always literal in its storytelling. He said it took a certain poetic license that allowed you to experience basically this state of human nature, which was grief and loss, and the shock of it. He saw Wilson's reaction to his grief as action, trying to get through the feeling.

Hoffman in an interview spoke of another scene that was not filmed. When Wilson jumped into the pond to swim with all the boats, he went underwater. You saw underwater and you heard the boats buzzing above, and it felt very insulated. But they didn't have money for an underwater camera.

He said the point of the film was to deal with Wilson's three or four months of grief and his addiction to huffing straight on, but it was not a metaphor for recent world events like 9/11. Gordy advised that he wrote the first draft in August 1996 in 18 days. He and his brother both happened to be in Rochester ten days after Gordy had finished it and Hoffman read it over the Labor Day weekend. Gordy hadn't written it for his brother or anybody in particular and Gordy let his brother read it because he (Philip) had a great eye for material. Gordy just wanted to get some feedback from Philip, but his brother told Gordy he wanted to play the guy. Hoffman gave the screenplay to Paul Thomas Anderson, who showed it to the people at Sundance. It was a finalist in their Screenwriters' Lab but wasn't chosen for development. About a year later, Hoffman talked to his friend Todd Louiso who he thought should make the film. The long time it took to get financing coincided with Hoffman's profile getting higher, and after Kathy Bates accepted the role of Mary Ann, they had a package. He originally agreed to play Denny but his clout and name allowed him to move into the leading role.

In the February 27, 2014, *Rolling Stone,* Louiso said that backers felt they were insane to think Hoffman could be a leading man. He admitted that it was Bates' casting that enabled the budget to be raised. Now that Philip had played a leading role, Gordy could not see him going back to playing small parts. Hoffman disagreed. He said he had not huffed any gas to play the part because he had heard that doing so dumbs you down, so instead Hoffman just created what it might have been like to do so. Gordy said that one perk about working together was that at a Rochester film festival, the deputy mayor declared a Hoffman Brothers Day.

On the December 16, 2002, *Charlie Rose Show,* the actor said he had always looked up to Gordy as the brightest and most creative person he had ever known and someone he had always been a bit intimidated by. He said that Gordy's mind didn't work like other people's and that the film he wrote was a great testament to that. Gordy decided to tell a story about a grieving man and it was unlike any other Hoffman had seen, which was why he wanted to do it. He recalled that two years previously he went back home to help his mother run for family court. When they went to Hoffman's former high school to speak, several teachers asked where Gordy was, saying that he was a real talent. The actor laughed that the memory of his brother would upstage himself and his mother. The actor said he also attended auditions and in particular fought to cast Jack Kehler, who he thought was fantastic, as Denny.

After Hoffman's death, Louiso said that the actor overflowed with love and affection for his friends and family. Louiso also said he was just a regular guy, even boring! They would watch football together and go out and have meals silently like an old married couple. Louiso knew the last two years of his life had been really rough for the actor. It just showed how strong the disease of addiction was. The director also explained Hoffman's astonishing output by saying that he channeled his addictive personality into his work.

For the January 2001 *GQ* magazine, Hoffman was interviewed by David Kamp and photographed by Michael Thompson. The interview took place in a restaurant in Manhattan's West Village, where Hoffman had lived for the last few years. Kamp wrote that in person the actor was a resolutely ordinary presence, almost janitorial. His grandiose formulated professional three names seemed ill-suited to someone so unassuming, someone who wanted to be called Phil. Hoffman had a week's worth of beard growth and was layered in the drab utility wear of someone who made oil deliveries on a cold morning in his native Rochester. Kamp said you had to squint real hard to recognize the movie actor underneath all the visual interference, which included a pair of McGeorge Bundy glasses, and the actor liked it that way. When Kamp told Hoffman that he was a beloved person, the actor blushed (or so Kamp thought, since given his coloring, it was hard to tell). Hoffman said he was still unused to people recognizing him and he didn't particularly relish the experience. Kamp wrote that Hoffman was an "actorly" kind of actor who professed to being more comfortable in the theater than he was on films, and he had a theater person's seminarian gravity. He smiled and was affable but he was not a barrel of laughs. The writer told the actor it must have been fun to play the roles he had played but Hoffman seemed mildly peeved as if fun was too trivial a word to describe his work. He wanted the audience to have fun but working hard as an actor was not necessarily fun all the time. He gave as an example how during *True West* John C. Reilly screamed right into Hoffman's ear that he was a "fucking asshole and a loser." But the actor classified the play as the highlight of his career to date.

Hoffman next played a supporting role in the Revolution Studios–Joanne Sellar–Ghoulardi Film Company Paul Thomas Anderson romantic comedy *Punch-Drunk Love* (2002). Filmed in Hawaii and in California from February 1 to March 19, 2001, it had the working titles *Punchdrunk Knuckle Love, Just Desserts* and *The X-4 Project.* Adam Sandler starred as self-employed wholesale bathroom supply salesman Barry Egan, who has a romance with an English field consultant, Lena (Emily Watson), while being extorted by a phone-sex line run by a furniture and mattress salesman, Dean Trumbell (Hoffman). Sean Penn was originally going to play Dean but had to drop out.

Dean orders two brothers of Phone Sex Sister Georgia/Latisha (Ashley Clark) to go to Los Angeles to visit Barry after he cancels his credit card and refuses to give Latisha the $750 she requests. Four brothers go, force Barry to withdraw $500 from his bank account and then attack him. The brothers continue their harassment of Barry, crashing into his car and injuring passenger Lena, before he considers contacting the police. Dean may initially appear to be reasonable, despite the fact that he is blackmailing Barry, but he gets indignant with Barry on the telephone and swears at him. This response motivates Barry to go to Utah and confront Dean.

Hoffman, unshaven and long-haired, appeared in three scenes; his wardrobe includes a necklace. It is to Hoffman's credit that his performance manages to block out the overbearing soundtrack that upstages the other actors and blights the film.

Hoffman's best scene is perhaps Dean's telephone conversation with Barry where he plays a lout by swearing, and physically expresses arrogance by having his hand on his hip. The actor gestures when he speaks on the phone, and slams it down twice in anger. Anderson supplies a nice moment for the face-off between Dean and Barry, which he holds for longer than expected, with Hoffman heard breathing in contrast to Sandler's silence.

On May 19, 2002, the film premiered at the Cannes Film Festival. Anderson won the Best Director award in a tie. It was then screened on September 13 at the Toronto International Film Festival, October 2 at the New York Film Festival, October 8 at the Chicago International Film Festival, and then received a wide release on October 11. Peter Travers in *Rolling Stone* wrote that Hoffman was in in his own fine, raging form. The film was not a box office success.

A deleted scene that appears on the Special Edition DVD has a 53-second Mattress Man commercial. In it Hoffman wears a black leather jacket, white t-shirt and blue jeans and holds a guitar which he silently plays as he stands on the roof of the store. He then jumps onto five mattresses, which are attached to the top of a car and bounces off them onto the ground in front of the store. When this happens, the crew runs to see if he is okay and he says the only injury is to the guitar, which broke in the fall.

Hoffman next appeared in the Alliance Atlantis–Andras Hamori Productions–Natural Nylon Entertainment crime drama *Owning Mahowny* (2003). Shot in New Jersey and Ontario from March 25, 2001. The Maurice Chauvet screenplay was based on the book *No Limit* (aka *Stung: The Incredible Obsession of Brian Molony*) by Gary Stephen Ross. The story was based on real events that had already inspired a Canadian made-for-TV movie, *The Highroller* (1984). Dan Mahowny (Hoffman), the Canadian Imperial Bank of Commerce's new assistant manager, uses bank funds to pay for his gambling habit. He goes to Atlantic City to gamble at the casino run by Victor Foss (John Hurt). He is eventually caught for stealing $10.2 million and sentenced to prison for six years for fraud. Dan has a moment of awareness of his addiction when in one scene he has a vision of himself watching his own craps game, but this does not stop his playing. He seems less of an addict loser because he has a live-in girlfriend, his co-worker Belinda (Minnie Driver), whom Dan calls Blin. She initially rationalizes his habit by saying that he works hard so he is allowed to play hard, but later becomes aware of the problem after he refuses to leave the Las Vegas gambling table to spend time with her. Belinda's realization comes after she had assumed that Dan had taken her to Vegas to marry her. Hoffman gets some funny lines which he delivers in an understated way. When Frank Perlin (Maury Chaykin) says he won't take any more of his horse race bets, Dan replies, "What am I supposed to do? Go to the racetrack and watch?" Dan asks Doug (Vincent Corazza) to mind $40,000 he wins at cards and then asks for it back, telling him, "You brought a curse to that table." We are told that Dan rejects a prostitute by telling her he is "only interested in lady luck."

Hoffman is credited with his name above the title and the role is another rare lead for him. Hoffman wears glasses and a moustache and his combed-down hair is slightly long. His wardrobe includes suits of dark blue and brown colors with ties, and he also wears mismatched jacket and pants with no tie when he gambles. He plays a variation on one of his nerds who keeps his head down and has his hands in his pockets, so that his mannerisms of self-conscious touching and over-gesturing and his breathing heavily when excited about his gambling have a context. Director Richard Kwietniowski gives Hoffman some unflattering extreme closeups. He has a good scene when Driver confronts him about his addiction and he apologizes for Vegas and tries to defend his behavior. The actor's best scene is perhaps when he panics in a car in a trip to Philadelphia. Afraid he will be robbed, he empties his pockets of the rolls of cash he carries and hides under the car's front seat. It turns out that Dan is not robbed but Hoffman conveys the character's emotion, which is in contrast to his otherwise unemotional and modest demeanor.

The film premiered at the Sundance Film Festival on January 23, 2003. It then opened on May 2, 2003, with the taglines "To some it's a game. To others it's a habit. But to Dan Mahowny—beating the odds is everything" and "The true story of a mild mannered banker and his magnificent obsession." Roger Ebert of the *Chicago Sun-Times* wrote that Hoffman's performance was a masterpiece of discipline and precision. Ebert called the actor that fearless poet of implosion and said that he played the role with a fierce integrity, never sending out signals for our sympathy because he knew that Mahowny was oblivious to our presence. The film was lambasted by Elvis Mitchell in the *New York Times* who wrote that Hoffman shaded his whining with more variety than you might have expected. He said that the actor assumed the role completely and so convincingly that you would think he was a victim of the Slinky disease: He was born without a neck. The film was not a box office success.

Hoffman commented that all people had secret lives and when they were exposed they were forced to re-examine who they were. He had a feeling about the film that he was going to be shocked by what he saw and he meant that in a positive way. Hoffman said what he went through shooting it was what the movie was about, which was an excruciating tension. He hoped everyone experienced that addiction and madness that compulsion created.

Kwietniowski said there was a kind of Everyman quality to Hoffman, and even in in his pervy parts his performances were touching. His presence was rather magnetic because he wasn't conventionally good-looking. Since the actor didn't normally play leading men, the director thought he might have had a bit of a fight on his hands with the people financing the picture, but this was not so. Interviewed for *The Advocate* on June 10, 2003, the director said he needed an extraordinary actor and he had revered and admired Hoffman for so long he thought he was the only one to play it. Kwietniowski said that some people had commented that Hoffman didn't play leading roles for good reasons, that he was too good, intense and supersaturated to be a leading man. The director questioned why the actor shouldn't be a lead.

Producer Seaton McLean reported he had sent the script to Hoffman and then happened to see him at the 2001 Toronto Film Festival where *State and Main* had a September 8, 2000, screening. McLean told Hoffman that he was a partner in the company and that they had a project he felt would be perfect for him. Hoffman said he had just finished reading the book two days prior after his manager had sent it to him, and he was halfway through the script and felt that the story was fantastic. McLean said that after having a two-minute script conversation, Hoffman stopped himself, smiled and said "I've said waaaaay too much." Presumably the actor overcame his caution when he later agreed to do the film. Asked whether Hoffman's portrayal matched with the real Brian Molony, Gary Ross said they had the same stocky build, bushy moustache, glasses, slightly unkempt look and earnestness. He also reported that the actor somehow managed to assimilate the psychic essence of Molony—a yawning emptiness that nothing except gambling was able to fill.

On May 6, 2001, the *New York Times* included the New York Shakespeare Festival production of *The Seagull* in its guide to the Summer Festivals. The show was to be staged at the Delacorte Theater from July 24 to August 19. On July 23 it was reported that now the show was to begin previews from July 24 and to open on August 12. The play had a new adaptation by Tom Stoppard. On July 30 it was reported that the show was only to run until August 19, 2001. On August 1, it was announced that due to ticket demand the show's run had been extended until August 26. On August 3 it was reported there was talk of a Broadway run of the show. Kenneth B. Lerer, chairman of the Public Theater, advised that it was very complicated when you talked about moving it and he said it was a question of the actors and director Mike Nichols. A *New York Times* article by Peter Marks (August 5, 2001) revealed that Hoffman was to play the part of Konstantin and that the cast had rehearsed for five weeks. Hoffman said that he was cast after Nichols visited him backstage after seeing him in *True West* and told him he had a job for him. When Allison Janney became unavailable, Marcia Gay Harden replaced her.

Charles Isherwood in *Variety* said that Hoffman was an unusual choice for the role and pride and passion were notably absent from his somewhat too lachrymose performance. However his pained bleat of a voice brought a certain slacker-era irony to the role. Ben Brantley of the *New York Times* wrote that Hoffman was closer to third-generation Actors Studio. He said that the immensely gifted performer gave off real emotional ferocity and sorrow but he was still all feelings in search of a concretely defined character. The *New York Times* reported on August 18, 2001, that despite speculation and negotiations to move the play to Broadway, officials at the Public said that a transfer would not be possible because of scheduling conflicts among the cast.

During the production Mike Nichols gave Hoffman a gift of a black and white photograph of Anton Chekhov in a trenchcoat with an upturned collar and a Bolshevik-looking hat. Ian McKellen said the open-air venue was not conducive to the delicacy and intimacy of the play and yet Hoffman amazingly shrank the space between him and the audience and made you feel you were spying on his insides. After the actor's death, McKellen added that Hoffman's work survived his death, which was the only consolation in people's grief and regret.

On May 25, 2001, the *New York Times* reported that Hoffman was to direct for the Manhattan Class Company a play by Rebecca Gilman entitled *Glory of Living*. The dates and casting had yet to be announced but it was expected to have a midfall opening. From October 1, 2001, Hoffman began rehearsals for the play. It starred Anna Paquin, who had also appeared in *Almost Famous* but had no scenes with Hoffman. The play was scheduled to open on October 30, 2001, at the Manhattan Class Company Theater. Paquin played Lisa, an abused teenager who helps abduct a hitchhiker and ends up on death row. The production would run until December 1, 2001. Charles Isherwood in *Variety* wrote that Hoffman's direction exacerbated the play's chilly, clinical tone. Ben

Brantley in the *New York Times* said that Hoffman's work was astute because he went out of his way to avoid the thunder of melodrama, and that he showed increasing evidence of becoming a first-rate director. Hoffman said that working with Paquin was fantastic. Paquin said that Hoffman had extraordinarily high standards for himself and expected that from everyone else. He was tough and she responded well to that.

On November 19, 2001, Hoffman was one of many actors performing a concert version of *The World of Nick Adams* at Avery Fisher Hall. The show was an adaptation by A.E. Hotchner of a series of Ernest Hemingway short stories, with music by Aaron Copeland. The event was organized by Paul Newman to benefit the Association of Hole in the Wall Gang Camps, which provided outdoor experiences for children with cancer and other life-threatening diseases.

In 2001 the actor did a favor for Tina Fallon, with whom he had attended high school, and was part of the celebrity cast in a benefit for her 24 Hour Play Company. Its mission was implicit in its name: It threw some writers, directors and actors into a room, concocted a half-dozen short plays and, 23 hours later, performed an hour of same for a paying audience. In the *New York Times* (September 10, 2003), Fallon reported on the benefit, saying only the fearless signed up and she nearly scared them away with a pre-show announcement that she'd intended as a joke. She promised the cast that doing the show wouldn't actually damage their careers. Fallon said nobody laughed but no one fled, either because she felt nobody wanted to wimp out on what she described as the theatrical equivalent of bungee-jumping.

He next appeared in a supporting role in the Universal Pictures–Dino De Laurentiis–MGM crime thriller *Red Dragon* (2002), shot from January 7, 2002, on location in Florida, Maryland and at Universal in Hollywood. It was a remake of the film *Manhunter* (1986), which introduced the character of Hannibal Lecter to cinema; Lecter was also featured in *The Silence of the Lambs* (1990), *Hannibal* (2001), *Hannibal Rising* (2007) and the NBC-TV series *Hannibal* (2013–15). Considered a prequel to *Silence of the Lambs*, *Red Dragon* had a screenplay by Ted Tally based on the novel by Thomas Harris. The head of tech services of the Chicago Chromalux Video and Tape Services company, Francis Dolarhyde (Ralph Fiennes), is a serial killer known as the Tooth Fairy, being pursued by FBI investigator Will Graham (Edward Norton). The Lecter connection comes from the fact that Graham was the fed who captured him, and also that Dolarhyde is an avid Lecter fan and writes to him. Dolarhyde also collects the tabloid newspaper *The National Tattler* columns of Freddy Lounds for his

In German lobby card for *Red Dragon* (2002).

scrapbook, and his marking out the photograph of Freddy (Hoffman) and the nickname "Tooth Fairy" prefigures his later attack on Freddy. Freddy writes his weekly column "Take It from Teddy" and he has also written a paperback about Lecter. We learn that he is unscrupulous in getting material for the paper, since he reportedly sneaked into Graham's hospital room after he was stabbed by Lecter and photographed him. Freddy also photographs Graham at the Baltimore State Forensic Hospital where he visits Lecter and is caught with a fake FBI identification trying to obtain autopsy photographs of one of Dolarhyde's victims. To avoid prosecution for his felony, Freddy agrees to provoke Dolarhyde, and this decision leads to Freddy's murder. The worst that Freddy says about the police is to call them chumps (their description of him is much worse) and he only swears when he finds Dolarhyde's truck in his parking space. Freddy's habit of smoking gets an ironic narrative payoff when he is burned to death.

Hoffman wore his hair in a shorter cut, with a wardrobe of business shirts and a casual gray jacket and dark pants. Freddy's tactics pale in comparison to the behavior of the serial killers in the narrative, and Hoffman succeeds in making him sympathetic when he becomes Dolarhyde's victim (he has his lips bitten off). This is perhaps Hoffman's best scene in the film. Freddy cries when he tells Dolarhyde he is afraid to look at him but the actor does not supply tears. However he does convince in his earnest, childlike responses in the situation, without making it apparent that Freddy is only telling the killer what he wants to hear so that he can survive. Director Brett Ratner presumably uses a stuntman for Freddy's last scene where the burning figure rolls down the street in a wheelchair to his death, which is covered by a long shot with our view of the man obscured by the flames; regrettably, the arms are shown to be loosened from the chair.

The film was released on September 30, 2002, with the taglines "Before the Silence," "Meet Hannibal Lecter for the First Time," "How It All Began!," "FBI Agent Will Graham Is About to Enter the Mind of a Killer. He Must First Let Hannibal Lecter Inside His Head," "Before the Silence, there was the Dragon" and "To understand the origin of evil, you must go back to the beginning." Todd McCarthy in *Variety* wrote that Hoffman socked over his showy role. The film was a hit.

The Collector's Edition DVD includes deleted scenes, alternative versions of scenes and extended scenes. Hoffman appears in some of these. There is a deleted scene of Freddy reading a Dolarhyde letter into a tape recorder, which allows us to hear more of the letter than is heard in the film. In the movie, Freddy can be heard screaming on the tape; an alternative version of the scene did not feature the screaming. Editor Mark Helfrich preferred this version; Ratner and screenwriter Ted Tally preferred to have the screaming, particularly because Ratner felt it was the emotional center of the FBI room scene. After the scream was included, a new line was inserted: Jack Crawford's (Harvey Keitel) "Well, we can't get hung up on this," which added to the impact of the scream on the FBI officers. In another alternative version scene, Freddy (flaming in the wheelchair) came directly to the garage attendant and to camera.

Hoffman said he liked the character of Freddy and he was happy that he got to be in what he considered a classic horror movie. The actor said the scene with Fiennes was one of his favorite.

Brett Ratner reported that Hoffman wanted to play Dolarhyde but his schedule didn't permit him to take such a big part, so he accepted Freddy instead. The director said that he had to beg Hoffman to do the film and he thought he ultimately agreed because of the assembled cast since he was a huge fan of actors. Ratner said Hoffman was probably the most committed actor he had ever worked with. Ratner advised that Hoffman did this thing in the film where he kept sucking on a pen, which the director found to be brilliant and so subtle because it was such a smarmy kind of nuance. For the scene where Freddy is given the story to publish in *The Tattler*, Ratner advised that Anthony Hopkins came to watch because he was a big fan of Hoffman's. Hopkins wanted to see how Hoffman worked since he had no scenes in the film with him. Ratner told Hoffman about this after filming and Hoffman was very flattered. Ratner also reported that Hoffman insisted on actually being glued to the chair during his encounter with Dolarhyde. Ratner believed he was right in his request because it was impossible to fake the glued effect where Freddy was yanking on his skin to try and get free.

After Hoffman's death, Ratner reported that he and the actor had gone to NYU film school together and that there was a certain buzz while he was there that he was the one to watch. The director said that the role of Scotty in *Boogie Nights* is what really did it for Ratner. He felt every actor wanted to be Mark Wahlberg's character, the guy with the big package, the cool guy. But Hoffman was okay with being the weak guy. Ratner said the subtlety in his acting and his emotional depth made audiences fall for his characters. He felt Hoffman wasn't afraid to show the vulnerability and pain that was in him as a man and that was incredibly cool to Ratner. After the actor's death, Ratner watched *The Talented Mr. Ripley* and thought Hoffman stole every scene he was in. He also thought there wasn't a scene in any film Hoffman was in where he didn't do that.

On April 8, 2002, Hoffman appeared in the musical revue *Miscast* at the Supper Club as a benefit for the Manhattan Class Company Theater. From May 13 to July 3 he played a supporting role in the Touchstone Pictures-40 Acres and a Mule Filmworks-Industry Entertainment-Gamut Films crime drama *25th Hour* (2002). Shot on location in New York and Texas over 37 days, it was a historical time capsule of the pit clean-up of Ground Zero after the 9/11 attacks. It had a screenplay by David Benioff based on his novel and was directed by Spike Lee. The plot concerned the last 24 hours of 31-year-old Brooklyn drug dealer Monty Brogan (Edward Norton) as he re-evaluates his life before facing a seven-year jail term. This was Norton's second time with Hoffman after *Red Dragon*.

Hoffman played the part of 31-year-old Jacob "Jake" Elinsky, an English teacher at the Coventry Prepatory School and one of Montgomery's two best friends from childhood, the other being stockbroker Frank Xavier Slattery (Barry Pepper). Jacob is described by Montgomery as a whining malcontent and by Frank as a rich Jew from the Upper East Side who walks around unhappy because he was born privileged, and that he has chronic bad breath. Monty states that Jake is an honest man and he chooses him to mind his dog Doyle while he is in prison. Perhaps Monty does this because he knows Jake needs the affection and companionship since we see him hug the dog twice. Jake's honesty initially has him resist the temptation of Mary (Anna Paquin) despite his admission to Frank that he has a crush on her. It is presumably his drunken state at the Bridge Club that makes him pursue her and kiss her, which he quickly realizes is inappropriate. Jake is also honorable in his resistance to Monty's asking Frank to make him ugly so that Monty will be a less desirable object in prison, and it seems Monty uses this against him when he strikes Jake to motivate Frank to hit him back. Despite Jake being hit, he eventually pulls Frank off Monty to stop him from hitting him further and tenderly helps the battered Monty up from the ground. After Monty goes to jail we see Jake walking Doyle in the street so we see how he has followed up on the commitment.

Hoffman wears glasses and his hair short, slicked back when he teaches, but unslicked otherwise, with a mismatched-color suit and tie at work and a casual jacket and pants and a baseball cap when he goes to the club at night. The pale jacket that Jake wears to the club appears to be the same one Hoffman wore as Freddy Lounds in *Red Dragon*. Jake is another nerdish character for the actor and he conveys his shyness by looking down repeatedly in class and at the club. He also sits in a feminine way with one leg crossed over the other in the teacher's lounge. Hoffman makes Jake's discomfort in the club funny with his body language and the shock he expresses in reaction to Mary's drunken advance, mixed with the expression of his desire for her in the way he looks at her exposed body. The actor's best scene is perhaps the extended scene between Jake and Mary alone in the club's VIP room that leads to the bathroom kiss and the aftermath. Director Lee shoots the scene in the bathroom with a red filter and narratively it is more effective because of Mary's lack of reaction to the kiss. Lee then has then has Hoffman in a long closeup after he leaves the bathroom, looking directly into the camera as he rides the dolly.

The film was released on December 16, 2002, with the taglines "This life was so close to never happening," "Can you change your whole life in a day?" and "One wrong choice ... one last night ... 24 hours to live a lifetime." A hit, it was praised in *Variety*, *The Chicago Sun-Times* and *Rolling Stone*.

The DVD has deleted scenes in which Hoffman appears. He is in a montage about the meaning of the word sway, where Jake explains it to a class where the actor is in again in closeup riding the dolly camera; he is in a scene in the hallway of the club with Monty and Mary where Hoffman breathes heavily, perhaps from the effort of climbing the stairs; and there is an extended club scene where Mary does her death scenes from the school production of *Hamlet* as Laertes and Jake laughs.

Hoffman said that he told Lee after finishing the film that he ran the set probably better than most people he had worked with. The actor also spoke about how he felt the characters were multi-facetted and had a lot of depth and a lot of color. Hoffman said working with Paquin as an actor was like seeing something through to its fruition after having directed her, and he loved doing it. He commented that he sympathized with his character completely, and believed that Jake was attracted to Mary because she stood for everything that he would never be: brave.

The actor told Charlie Rose in his December 16, 2002, interview that the film was another he could not turn down because it was Spike Lee. He found the script very moving and cried by the end of it because it was so wonderful. Hoffman admitted that because he had been so busy in the last couple of years, he was a little tired and distracted when he was making it. He wanted to do the best he could and found doing the work effortless because the way Lee controlled the set made the actor feel relieved.

Spike Lee said he had long been a fan of Hoffman, and knew he wanted to work with him, but he had to be right for the role. Lee cast the actor after discussing the idea with Norton. Lee considered him a great actor but found him impatient, and reported that Hoffman was a good softball player in the squad that the company formed during production for recreation. Screenwriter David Benioff said the actor was physically different from the character in the novel who was written as small and very wiry (people said he looked like a ferret). However he felt Hoffman was so good that it made Benioff forget the discrepancy. The writer reported that his adaptation lost the character point of Jake being the greatest pedestrian in New York's history who took pride in the way he walked to get from point A to point B in the shortest possible time, and how he timed traffic lights and dodged crowds.

Hoffman was asked whether the fact that directors wanted to work with him over and over was a bit of a safety net for him. He replied that there were only a couple of directors he had worked with more than once, Paul Thomas Anderson and Anthony Minghella. He said he thought he was like any actor, thinking he was never going to work again even if he was working a lot. With regards to Anderson, Hoffman felt if the director didn't use him in another film for the rest of his life, it wouldn't matter. He thought that they were so close and that they had done a lot of work together that he didn't owe Hoffman anything.

On July 15, 2002, WENN reported that the actor was possibly to be involved in a new film about Robin Hood. Screenwriters Gregg Chabot and Kevin Peterka had prepared a new biography of the heroic outlaw, set ten years after his story traditionally ended. Hoffman was sought for the title role as an overweight version, with Russell Crowe rumored to play the villainous Sheriff of Nottingham. This film was never made. Crowe later played Robin Hood in a 2010 film directed by Ridley Scott.

Hoffman next played a supporting role in the Miramax Films-Mirage Enterprises/Bone Fide Productions historical romance *Cold Mountain* (2003), filmed on location in Romania, in Virginia and in North and South Carolina from July 15 to December 2002. Hoffman's scenes were shot in South Carolina in September 2002 and in Romania in October 2002. Anthony Minghella's screenplay was based on the Charles Frazier novel and was it directed by Minghella. During the waning days of the American Civil War, a wounded Confederate soldier W.P. Inman (Jude Law) embarks on a perilous journey back home to Cold Mountain, North Carolina, to reunite with sweetheart Ada Monroe (Nicole Kidman).

Inman meets the Reverend Veasey (Hoffman) in his travels. The reverend is first caught by Inman trying to throw the drugged Negro slave Rebecca (Rasoo J'han) down a gorge because he has impregnated her, which he calls a grievous wrong. Inman saves Rebecca and ties the reverend to a pole in his town with a note saying what he has done as a gag in his mouth. The reverend appears in Carolina swampland when Inman is fleeing the North Carolina Home Guard and he helps Inman get to safety. The reverend is also fleeing his townspeople, who have cut off his long hair and want to hang him for his crime. Via ferry they cross the river and then help a farmer, Junior (Giovanni Ribisi), get his dead bull out of a creek using a stolen saw. Junior takes the men home and then betrays them to the Home Guard. The reverend is shot dead when he and other chain gang members attempt to escape from the Guards. The reverend is a morally ambiguous character since he is a married man and a preacher who has an affair with a servant and then tries to kill her. His hunger for sex extends to his considering the offer from the Ferry Girl (Jena Malone) of sex for payment, and his appreciation for the women at Junior's farm. He accepts the advance of Junior's sister-in-law Mae (Kathleen Durio). The reverend cannot be blamed for the death of the Ferry Girl since she is shot by the Home Guards but then again he puts her in the position to be shot by hiring her to escort himself and Inman. Inman calls the theft of the saw un-Christian theft but the reverend steals it because he believes it will help them. He is proven wrong, since the saw is only used to help Junior. The reverend can be considered brave for yelling to the Yankee soldiers in an attempt to save the chain gang from being bayonetted by the Guards; he is then shot by one of the Guards.

Hoffman speaks with a Southern accent and wears his hair in an extra-long wavy style that fits the character's later description of having curls. Hoffman also has a moustache and goatee, and then later a beard after his hair has been cut short. His period wardrobe includes a brown coat which he wears over long johns since presumably the townspeople have stripped him in their attack upon him. The reverend might be considered a nerd being a preacher except his behavior is more loutish. He flinches at the sight and sound of the bull's head being sawn off, and yells when he quotes Scripture when his plugged bowels open and he yells, "The tribes of Israel are about to flee from the banks of Egypt." Hoffman's mannerism of heavy breathing is also used when Inman holds a gun on him. The character's humiliations continue the cinematic ones that some of the actor's other characters have endured, which here include being tied and gagged, the sudden release of his bowels (director Minghella spares us anything graphic here), his being on a chain gang, etc. Despite the grievous wrong that the reverend has done, Hoffman makes him likable. He is fortunate that the screenplay gives him some funny lines, which also include telling Inman about his strict congregation and how they've "churched men for pickin' up a fiddle on the Sabbath." He comments about the bull, "That's a rank odor from that animal," and says in reaction to its neck being sawed, "Oh well…. That is unpleasant."

Hoffman's most memorable moment may be in one in the deleted scenes, entitled "Veasey Town." In it the reverend and the chain gang are brought to a town that is presumably where he hails from. The men sit on the ground and as the reverend watches a woman and a girl walk by them, he says, "I baptizes that child." Then we see a group of Negro women walk by and he calls out "Rebecca!" to one of them. A pregnant woman—the one he tried to drown—approaches. The reverend tells her, "I've been repenting for what I did. I've walked the road of atonement. God bless you." Rebecca retreats to the group after a Guard tells her to go away.

The film was released on December 25, 2003, with the taglines "If hate sends men to war, then it must be love that brings them home," "Find your way home" and "Find the strength. Find the courage. No matter what it takes ... find the way home." Todd McCarthy in *Variety* wrote that Hoffman provided larger-than-life gusto to his portrayal. The film was a hit and received Academy Award nominations for Best Actor, Best Supporting Actress for Renee Zellweger, Best Cinematography, Best Editing, Best Original Score, and Best Original Song. Zellweger was the only winner.

Hoffman said that the film was loaded up with many different people and stories, and he felt that Minghella's script was the essence of the book but not the book. The director commented that he loved working with Hoffman. The director added that Hoffman was an extremely intelligent man who wrestled his way through work and acted in a state of high anxiety. Editor Walter Murch recalled that the deleted scene where the reverend speaks with Rebecca was meant to be placed between the chain-gang escape scene and the scene where Inman is the only survivor. Murch said that the escape scene originally had the reverend and not Inman leading the escape since the prior scene had established that he now wanted to be with Rebecca. This change also changed the plot point that Inman had resisted attempting to escape with the gang.

After Hoffman's death, Jude Law said that when the actor was on the set he raised the bar by being so truthful and demanding of himself. Law described Hoffman as very modest, always interesting, and generous. Nicole Kidman, who did not share any scenes with Hoffman, said that his death was a devastating loss, and he that he was of the greatest "actor's actors" of all time. Kidman said he would take your breath away.

On August 20, 2002, Hoffman began workshop performances of Stephen Adly Guirgis' play *Our Lady of 121st Street* at Center Stage/NY. Hoffman was also the director of the piece. Set in the Ortiz Funeral home, it involved a group of childhood friends who return to the Bronx after the death of a feared but beloved alcoholic neighborhood nun. The show was to run until September 14, 2002, but then appeared to be extended until October 12, 2002. Bruce Weber of the *New York Times* wrote that Hoffman's direction was brazenly in the spirit of high dudgeon and that the actor was helping to make LAByrinth into perhaps the most exciting troupe in the city. On October 25, 2002, it was reported that a casting problem had delayed the show's move to a new venue. Its producers had been considering the Union Square but now that seemed unlikely, but it was certain that the show would have a commercial run somewhere beginning in February 2003. On December 20, 2002, it was confirmed that the show would open in March at the Union Square Theater after all. The show had a season with previews from February 18, 2003, and ran from March 6 to July 27, 2003.

Hoffman was photographed by Gregory Crewdson in a portfolio called "Dream House" for the magazine *Portfolio*, published on November 10, 2002. For his setting, the photographer chose an empty house in Rutland, Vermont; he and Hoffman went there on a Sunday in August 2002. The photograph had him sitting in the passenger seat of a parked maroon-colored car in the middle of the road, its trunk open to reveal it filled with flowers that matched the flowers strewn across the road around the left side of the car. Hoffman, leaning out of the seat with his elbows on his knees, wore shorts and a gray sweater. Crewdson had not met the actor before and as he drove to the location's rendezvous in a shopping center parking lot he wondered how he would know him. But Hoffman was in the big empty lot, in one lone car smack in the middle of it, reading the *New York Times*. The photographer said that Hoffman knew how to make an entrance. Crewdson was very precise about every detail in his pictures and upon seeing the clothes that the actor was dressed decided to ditch the planned costume because he felt it conveyed precisely the look of the character Crewdson wanted to evoke. After the car and Hoffman were in position, he was directed not to act. Hoffman, under his breath, replied: "I get it. I'm an actor but I shouldn't act. I get it." Crewdson said that he just wanted *him*. And he got him.

The *New York Times* reported on November 15, 2002, that Hoffman was being considered for the role of Jamie in a new production of Eugene O'Neill's *Long Day's Journey into Night*. The confirmed cast included Brian Dennehy, Vanessa Redgrave and Robert Sean Leonard. It was to be directed by Robert Falls with rehearsals to begin in mid–March 2003, previews on or around April 21 and an opening night proposed for May 6. Producer David Richenthal had yet to nail down a commitment for a space. On November 22, 2002, it was reported that Hoffman had agreed to do the play. The actor said he was obsessed with O'Neill's big, sad masterwork. Hoffman commented that it was one of those plays that he had to see every time it was shown, and though it was a long play and not a happy play, it was addictive. In Hoffman's December 16, 2002, *Charlie Rose* interview he was asked about doing the play and said he was petrified in all the good ways. Hoffman said it was a daunting play and a daunting part and a lot of daunting actors to work with, which is what he wanted, but it didn't make him sleep easier. He said he was very excited about it and couldn't wait to get started. Hoffman said the run for the play was planned to be five or six months.

His next film, the Universal Pictures-Jersey Films romantic comedy *Along Came Polly* (2003), was shot from November 11, 2002, to February 2003 on location in New York, Los Angeles and Hawaii and on the Paramount backlot. Written and directed by John Hamburg, it starred Ben Stiller as Reuben Feffer, a New York City risk assessment analyst for Indursky & Sons Insurance. His wife, real estate agent Lisa Kramer (Debra Messing), leaves him on their honeymoon for Claude (Hank Azaria), a St. Barts scuba instructor. Reuben finds love again two weeks later with a former school friend, waitress and children's book writer Polly Prince (Jennifer Aniston). Hoffman played Reuben's friend Sanford "Sandy" Lyle, who as a child star appeared in the 1985 film *Crocodile Tears* where he memorably played the bagpipes. Sandy has hired cameraman Dustin (Judah Friedlander) and sound man Vic (Kevin Hart) to film his life to try and sell the documentary to the *E! True Hollywood Story* TV show, although he pretends that it is E! that has initiated the project. His delusion of grandeur is shown in the sunglasses he wears. When he asks the wedding cake decorator (Mark Adair-Rios) if he wants his autograph, the decorator says he thought he had died. Sandy is also appearing in an amateur community theater production of *Jesus Christ Superstar* as Judas although at the first performance he also takes over the title role. Sandy takes Reuben to the artists' party where he meets Polly who works there as a waitress. Sandy does not support their relationship because he thinks the couple is mismatched. The climax has Sandy reverse his position by agreeing to be Reuben's proxy at his office presentation concerning whether the company should insure Australian high-risk multi-millionaire adventurer Leland Van Lew (Bryan Brown). Sandy does this so that Reuben can go after Polly, who he learns is leaving New York. Sandy is crude in the way he has the cake decorator at Reuben's wedding pipe icing into his mouth, how he laughs at an obscene joke told at the wedding by Stan Indursky (Alec Baldwin), how he says loudly and inappropriately in an elevator that he is horny, how he has "sharted" at the party, and how he takes the grease from Reuben's slice of pizza to apply to his own.

Third-billed Hoffman wears his hair long, sometimes gelled back, and he is unshaven. His wardrobe favors mismatched colors, jackets with rolled-up sleeves and sweatpants. The role is a variation on one of Hoffman's previous louts who calls people "dude," says "cool" and smokes pot. The actor gets to do some slapstick when Sandy trips twice on the waxed floor of the wedding, in his wild dance at the wedding, playing basketball badly, and when he fights with Wonsuk (Masi Oka), the musical's Jesus, and they fall onto the stage before the show. We also get to hear him sing Jesus' part in "What's the Buzz" from the show where Hoffman performs with fey gestures.

Hoffman is funny when he does his wild dance, when he says he wants a time out at basketball because his legs are burning, and when he repeatedly clears his throat at the Indursky boardroom presentation. Perhaps his best moment is when he listens to Irving Feffer (Bob Dishy) who tells him after Sandy has walked out of the show that he has to let go of the past and just enjoy the ride. This scene pays off the idea that it is the only time in the narrative where Irving speaks, so that when he asks Sandy if he ever told him how funny he was playing the bagpipes, Sandy replies that he doesn't think he has ever heard him speak before.

The film premiered on January 12, 2004, and then given a wide release on January 16, with the tagline "For the most cautious man on Earth, life is about to get interesting." It was lambasted by Roger Koehler in *Variety*, who wrote that Hoffman reveled in playing a frustrated former teen movie star experiencing hard times. Roger Ebert in the *Chicago Sun-Times* wrote that the way Hoffman responds to having a stranger tell him how amazed he is that he's still alive in one early scene was a small masterpiece of facial melodrama. The film was a hit.

The DVD featured deleted scenes in which Hoffman appeared. One of these had him in the Groom Room of Reuben's wedding where Sandy eats crackers; when his E! film crew arrives, Sandy sends them away. Another deleted scene had Sandy playing the Air Supply song "All Out of Love" on bagpipes at the wedding to begrudging applause. The elevator scene before the artists' party had an extended moment where Sandy did more sex trash-talk but it was cut, according to director John Hamburg, because it became an issue with the rating board as the film needed a PG-13 rating. In his DVD audio commentary the director also mentioned other cut moments. These include Sandy singing in the opening performance of *Jesus Christ Superstar* and then running offstage and tackling Wonsuk. It was cut after previews because, although it was considered funny, Hamburg thought that people were ready to get on with the story. He substituted Sandy's announcement of his intention to play dual roles because that paid off the earlier scene in rehearsal where Sandy sang Jesus' part in the song. Another moment cut after previews was at a show rehearsal when Sandy yelled at the cast after singing "What the Buzz"; it was perceived as being too mean-spirited. The DVD also features outtakes, two of which show Sandy and Reuben in the scene where Sandy confesses that E! charade. In both outtakes Hoffman laughs after Stiller pushes Reuben's case against his chest when he asks Sandy to be his proxy at the office presentation, with one take having the camera on Hoffman and the second with the camera on Stiller. In both, Stiller carries on with the scene despite Hoffman's laughter, though he must be aware that the take cannot be used.

Hoffman surmised that Sandy was probably 13 when he made his film and now he was in his 30s, though neither age is given in the screenplay. He commented that the film was truly funny, not only with verbal comedy but with physical comedy making it an action-oriented film. In his 2005 interview with Alex Pappademas, Hoffman admitted that when he went to shoot the film he was probably the biggest he had ever been. He had just had his first child and the actor admitted that as his girlfriend got bigger so did he because they were just at home eating all the time.

John Hamburg said he always imagined Hoffman in the role, since while the character was a sort of slob he wanted someone who could also bring a humanity to the role. Hamburg reported that Hoffman wore a fat suit in the reshot opening wedding scene since between the time of the film's shooting and the editing he had lost a significant amount of weight. He advised that the actor was a better basketball player than Sandy was and it was in this scene, shot early in the schedule, where the director saw how Hoffman brilliantly became the character, unafraid to do pratfalls and to keep them in a tone of reality. An example of this was Sandy's wheezing which was truthful because the scene took two days to shoot and exhausted the actor. Hamburg felt that the actor was touching and vulnerable in Sandy's admission scene to Reuben, and believed that the "sharted" moment worked because the actor played it seriously rather than comically. Hamburg also reported that for the boardroom scene he changed Sandy's dialogue on the day of shooting. He had learned that Hoffman was very conscientious about learning his lines before the shooting so that he knew them well but the actor worked through the new ones and totally delivered. Hamburg said the throat-clearing was something that they came up with on the day to make the scene as awkward as possible, and that Hoffman ad-libbed some lines and played the scene beautifully as a heroic monologue though Sandy got all the facts wrong. The director reported that Hoffman and Stiller did not know each other before they made the film but they really liked each other and he felt played off each other really well.

The actor made his first appearance on the Comedy Central comedy-news-talk show *The Daily Show with Jon Stewart* on January 9, 2003, and reportedly talked about working at LAByrinth. On February 21 he made the first of three appearances on the NBC comedy-music-talk show *Late Night with Conan O'Brien*.

The February 23, 2003, *New York Times* reported that *Long Day's Journey Into Night* was to begin previews on April 26 at the Plymouth Theater. An article appeared on the same date about the production and quoted from a conference call discussion with the cast moderated by Jesse McKinley. Asked if he was haunted by the memory of Jason Robards who played Jamie in the original 1956 production, Hoffman said that his experience of working with the actor on *Magnolia* was a blessing for the job that was ahead because he only felt loved by him. Director Robert Falls said that he desperately wanted Hoffman to play the part because he thought he was absolutely nothing like Robards, and yet he thought he would bring a completely original view. Falls also knew what a "tortured bastard" Hoffman was. The actor advised that he had thought about the play a lot, long before Falls ever came to him. McKinley reminded Hoffman that he had previously said that earlier in his career he could have imagined himself as an Edmund but now he felt he was more of a Jamie. The actor confided that his older brother had introduced him to the play when he was 12, telling him it was really good and that he had to read it. When he read it, he felt at the time he was Edmund. But as he grew older, other things in his life worked on him, and now that was he was 35 he thought he could understand more about regret. He said when you're 20 you didn't understand those kinds of things as much.

Hoffman appeared in a 30-minute BBC documentary, *Once Upon a Time in Utah, Sundance* (2003), broadcast on the BBC on February 25, 2003. It was written and directed by Nick Copus. *Owning Mahowny* had screened in January at Sundance so this was presumably what enabled the actor to be included.

5

A Son, *Capote*

In March 2003, Mimi O'Donnell gave birth to Hoffman's son, Cooper Alexander. His date of birth is unknown but a March 13 *New York Times* article said that he was expected March 14. The article reported that both Hoffman and O'Donnell attended a party in the lobby of the New York Film Academy which celebrated the LAByrinth Theater Company's restaging of *Our Lady of 121st Street*.

On March 31, 2003, the *Long Day's Journey Into Night* cast had a field trip to Monte Cristo Cottage in New London, Connecticut. This was the crepuscular seaside home where the young Eugene O'Neill spent his summers and which was the setting of the play. Brian Dennehy was the only one of them who had seen the place before. They did some acting research, taking in the house's creaking floors, claustrophobic upstairs rooms and general heartbreak. After ten previews from April 26, the show did open as scheduled on May 6, 2003.

Ben Brantley in the *New York Times* praised it and wrote that Hoffman was a brilliant actor but was oddly tentative. Brantley reported that he had promisingly astute moments but there was often a blankness to him that suggested that he was treading water in the early scenes. The writer also said that Hoffman played the climactic, whiskey-fueled confrontation with Edmund with a flamboyant drunkenness that pandered to the audience while blunting the pain of the scene. On July 6, 2003, the *Times'* Margo Jefferson also reviewed the show. She said that Hoffman had clearly thought out his portrayal but what was missing was an emotional through-line. Jefferson wrote that the actor ran hot (bitter and defiant) and cold (cynically detached) and the effect was that he overacted or underplayed.

The show would run until August 31, 2003, with Hoffman reportedly not missing any performances. He would later comment that doing it nearly killed him. The show received Tony Award nominations for Best Revival of a Play, Best Actor in a Play, Best Actress in a Play, Best Featured Actor in a Play for Hoffman and Robert Sean Leonard, Best Scenic Design and Best Direction of a Play. It was believed that neither Hoffman nor Leonard would win since Denis O'Hare in *Take Me Out* was considered the hometown favorite.

The June 8, 2003, award ceremony took place at Radio City Music Hall and was televised live by CBS. It was reported that Hoffman on the red carpet patiently lumbered through an interviewer's questions, and then amazement fell over his face when it became apparent that the woman didn't appear to have a clue who he was. He then roared, "I'm Philip Seymour Hoffman!" and moved up the carpet laughing.

On September 5, 2003, *The Hollywood Reporter* said that Hoffman was to star in a new film version of *Macbeth* to be produced by Antidote Films and to be directed by Todd Louiso. This film was never made.

The actor was billed as the artistic director for the LAByrinth Theater Company's next production, Bob Glaudini's *Dutch Heart of Man.* Directed by Charles Goforth, it ran at the Joseph Papp Public Theater/Susan Stein Shiva Theater from September 25 to October 19, 2003. It was about a construction company employee named Dutch (Salvatore Inzerillo) in love with a mother-smothered waitress (Maggie Bofill); he has a series of bewildered encounters with rude, aggressive strangers.

Hoffman reportedly attended the October 2, 2003, New York opening of the comedy film *The Station Agent* (2003) at Lincoln Center and also perhaps the after-party that was held at Time. The actor was said to be there to support the film's star Peter Dinklage. On October 7, 2003, he attended a benefit for the LAByrinth Theater Company at the Daryl Roth Theater where a game of charades was held in a boxing ring set up for the occasion. The actor also presented Madonna with an award, presumably for helping the company bring one of their productions to the West End. The actor was described as looking less schlubby than usual, in a blue shirt and a tie. The actor also said he thought he found his libido at 15 years old, watching her. On October 10, 2003, Hoffman made his second appearance on *Late Night with Conan O'Brien.*

In November 2003 he attended the opening-night party for the Joseph Papp Public Theater/New York Shakespeare Festival production of the musical *Caroline, or Change.* On November 10, 2003, WENN said that Hoffman had attended a birthday bash for his friend Sam Rockwell at the plush New York venue Tai. He supposedly helped actress Famke Janssen find her lost luxury Marc Jacobs purse, scrambling on the floor with the other 500 guests.

On December 6, 2003, Hoffman attended the 26th Annual Kennedy Center Honors held at the Kennedy Centre Opera House in Washington, D.C. CBS broadcast the gala event on December 26. Honored that year for their unique and extremely valuable contributions to the cultural life of the nation were James Brown, Carol Burnett, Loretta Lynn, Mike Nichols and Itzhak Perlman. Hoffman was there to support Nichols, his *Seagull* director. The actor was seen twice, once singing a version of "That's Entertainment" transposed as "That's Pure Mike Nichols" with Meryl Streep, Candice Bergen, Christine Baranski and Patrick Wilson. Hoffman wore his hair combed back with glasses, and black suit and dark-blue tie. At the end of the number he blew a kiss at Nichols and applauded with the audience. Hoffman returned for the show's finale where Wayne Brady led the cast in "Living in America" as a tribute to James Brown; Hoffman clapped his hands to the song.

In 2003 Hoffman had a film in development, writer Anthony DiPietro's *Sweet Spot.* The plot focused on Victor Spinilli who was to be played by F. X. Vitolli. Victor, 39 years old, desperately holds onto the glorious days of his youth as a promising baseball player. Deeply moved by the death of a close friend, he realizes that the world is passing him by so he seeks a new purpose in life. Peter Gallagher was said to be scheduled to direct. The film was never made.

On January 15, 2004, Hoffman appeared on the PBS talk show *Tavis Smiley* to talk about *The Last Party* and the effect it had on his political activism. Smiley, a Negro, asked Hoffman as a white man what he thought needed to be done in Hollywood to give people of color more opportunities. The actor replied that it was up to the writers and that in LAByrinth they had writers who wrote for the actors in the company and for all different types of people. Asked if a solution was to have people of color write the parts, Hoffman said it didn't have to be that way because white people could also write those parts. Tavis reported that the actor had told him the character in *Along Came Polly* was a bit of a stretch for him because it was something he had not done before. He asked him what kinds of roles were out there that would actually stretch him as an actor. Hoffman said he wanted to do new things but it was hard.

The actor was back on *The Daily Show* on January 19, 2004. He reportedly recalled making *The Last Party*, and he also mentioned his son taking his first steps. On February 16, 2004, the *New York Times* reported that Hoffman, as actor and director and also co-artistic director of LAByrinth, was mentioned as a possible replacement producer for the Public Theater after the fall 2004 departure of George C. Wolfe. Wolfe commented that his replacement should be someone who could cultivate underground theatrical talent as well as established artists; he thought the smashing-together of those impulses made the Public Theater exciting. On October 29, 2004, it was reported that after an eight-month search, a process that included nearly 100 candidates and eventually involved interviews with about a dozen finalists, the leading candidate was said to be Oskar Eustis, the artistic director of the Trinity Repertory Company in Providence, Rhode Island. On November 17, 2004, Eustis was offered the job and accepted it. An October 3, 2004, article by Jesse Green suggested that Hoffman was never a serious candidate for the job because the committee members felt they had to stay clear of someone like him who was considered unreasonably interesting.

On February 27, 2004, it was reported that Hoffman was to join the star-studded cast of Neil LaBute's *Autobahn*, a collection of five new one-act plays for the MCC Theater for a one-time-only event on March 8, 2004, at the Little Shubert Theater. On March 9, 2004, he hosted a party and performance of LaBute's play *The Shape of Things* at the Stella Adler Acting Studio to raise money for scholarships to the school and its outreach program aimed at getting teenagers involved with theater. On March 12, 2004, the *New York Times* reported that Hoffman would direct Stephen Adly Guirgis' comedy *Last Days of Judas Iscariot* for LAByrinth Theater at the Public Theater, which was scheduled to open early in 2004. The play was said to be about the appeals case God and the Kingdom of Heaven v. Judas Iscariot.

Hoffman was credited as co-artistic director for the Joseph Papp Public Theater/New York Shakespeare Festival/LAByrinth Theater Company production of Brett C. Leonard's play *Guinea Pig Solo*. Directed by Ian Belton, it ran at the Joseph Papp Public Theater/Susan Stein Shiva Theater from May 9 to June 6, 2004. John Ortiz starred as an Iraq War veteran trying to stay sane in the jungles of New York City and pursuing a dazed, predetermined course to a grisly homicidal conclusion.

Hoffman reportedly attended the July 13, 2004, opening night performance of the Public Theater's Shakespeare in the Park production *Much Ado About Nothing* at the Delacorte Theater. When Jimmy Smits (who played Benedick) was performing a scene in the audience, he slipped and was held up by Hoffman. The actor participated in the 24-minute Cornukopia Entertainment documentary *Film Trix 2004*, which premiered at the Comic-Con International Independent Film Festival on July 22, 2004. Depicting the trials and tribulations of the film industry, the short included interviews and frolics with celebrated directors and top celebrities.

On July 27, 2004, *Playbill* reported that Hoffman had joined the cast of the upcoming film *Strangers with Candy* (2005), based on the Comedy Central TV series, then filming in New Jersey. It was written by the TV show's original cast, co-creators Amy Sedaris, Paul Dinello and Stephen Colbert, who also starred in the movie, with Dinello directing. The series, a satire of afterschool specials, centered on Sedaris, a 46-year-old ex-addict who returns to high school after 30 years and tries to be hip with kids one-third her age. Hoffman had a cameo in the comedy, filmed in New Jersey and New York.

A prequel to the TV series, it featured Sedaris as Jerri Blank, who returns to Flatpoint High School as a student after 32 years in prison in a bid to start her life over. Hoffman played Henry, a State Board of Education official who visits the school to question whether they should receive bonus funding for above-average students. He is also one of the judges of the State Science Fair where two teams from Flatpoint submit entries; he disqualifies the entry from Jerri's team and he takes back the trophy. Henry secretly loves Alice (Allison Janney), his fellow Board of Education official and judge, and is jealous of her apparent past relationship with Flatpoint's Principal Onyx Blackman (Gregory Holliman). This leads Henry to behave unprofessionally: writing a love heart to Alice on his Fair score sheet, calling her a "whore," being unable to provide the tally, and then spitefully taking back the trophy from Blackman. The role of Alice was originally intended for Natasha Richardson.

Hoffman appears in two scenes, the second being an extended one of the Fair's judging. He wears his hair short and combed down and a moustache identical to the one he wore in *Owning Mahowny*. The actor doesn't have many lines but he gestures unnecessarily in one scene, which recalls one of his mannerisms. His strongest line is when he yells "You whore!" to Alice. Director Dinello uses slow motion to show Hoffman running after the explosion, slipping on the floor and grabbing the trophy from Blackman.

The film premiered at the Sundance Film Festival in January 2005 and was then screened on June 17, 2006, at the Seattle International Film Festival. It received a limited release in New York on June 28, 2006, and then was given a wide release on July 21 with the taglines "Going to high school for the first time is always scary.... Especially the second time around" and "High school is difficult ... for a 47-year-old ex-con junkie crack whore." Dennis Harvey in *Variety* wrote that Hoffman juiced his few scenes. It was not a box office success.

On August 2, 2004, Hoffman attended a benefit performance night at the American Airlines Theatre of a playlet written by Tony Kushner from a planned longer work to be called *Only We Who Guard the Mystery Shall Be Unhappy*. The show starred John Cameron Mitchell and Patricia Clarkson and was organized by the liberal activist online group MoveOn.org. Attendees paid $25 a head and the event raised $18,000 for the group. The playlet was described as an unapologetic screed against George W. Bush and his foreign policy, using Dostoyevsky as a vehicle to examine the vagaries of political morality. Mitchell as Laura Bush talked passionately about Dostoyevsky and moral relativity to the ghosts of Iraqi children; Clarkson was an angel presiding over the ghost reading. Then the actors switched chairs, with Mitchell portraying Kushner himself as he spoke with a character who was supposed to be the "real" Laura Bush (Clarkson), who was angry at her portrayal in the preceding skit by the playwright. The show had its premiere in April 2009 at the Guthrie Theater in Minneapolis and was also staged in October 2009 at the Berkeley Repertory Theater in California. It did not make it to New York.

An August 23, 2004, *New York Times* article about writer Jerry Stahl mentioned his book, *I, Fatty*, a fictional memoir of silent film actor Roscoe "Fatty" Arbuckle. It reportedly had been optioned for a possible film project by Johnny Depp's Hollywood-based production company, Infinitum Nihil. Depp said he would not play Fatty but he would be a hands-on producer, and he could see a padded Hoffman playing Arbuckle. The film was never made.

On August 25, 2004, *The Hollywood Reporter* wrote that Hoffman was set to play Truman Capote in a new film based on the book *Capote: A Biography* by Gerald Clarke. The untitled United Artists story concentrated on the period when Capote was writing *In Cold Blood*, his so-called "nonfiction novel" about the murder of a Kansas family, published in 1965. Warner Independent Pictures had a rival Capote project about the same period entitled *Every Word Is True* set up. On October 1, 2004, it was reported that the Hoffman Capote film would be helmed by Bennett Miller from a script by Dan Futterman. The actor would also executive-produce.

An October 5, 2004, article announced that Sam Rockwell had been cast in *Last Days of Judas Iscariot* in the title role. It also quoted publicity material which stated that the play told the story of the New Testament's most infamous and unexplained ultimate sinner in

French movie card for *Capote* (2005).

a time-bending, serio-comically imagined world between Heaven and Hell. On October 24, 2004, it was reported that Hoffman had recently attended a performance of *The Democracy Project* with the Naked Angels theater troupe.

The actor next played the title role in the United Artists-Sony Pictures Classics-A-Line Pictures-Cooper's Town Productions-Infinity Media Production crime drama *Capote* (2005). It was shot from October 25 to December 1, 2004, on location in Manitoba and Winnipeg, Canada, in Harlem, New York, and in Malibu, California. The film told the story of how the writer Truman Capote went to West Kansas to write an article about the November 14, 1959, murder of a farm family by Dick Hickock (Mark Pellegrino) and Perry Smith (Clifton Collins, Jr.) for *The New Yorker*; it became the book *In Cold Blood*.

Capote's connection to the killings when he reads about them in the *New York Times* is meant to be intuitive, although his intuition cannot predict that doing the book will also end his career. He manipulates and lies to get what he needs, though he claims to feel a brotherly kinship with Perry because of their similar childhoods. Capote's boyfriend Jack Dunphy (Bruce Greenwood) accuses him of having fallen in love with Perry but he denies it, perhaps since he is aware of how he is using him, as he tells Nelle Harper Lee (Catherine Keener) that Perry is "a gold mine." Capote shows both audacity and inappropriate behavior in several scenes. These include his opening the coffin of one of the murdered Clutters in the funeral home, when he pays the prison warden (Marshell Bell) so that he can have unlimited access to Perry, and when he won't leave the room where the killers are being held before their execution when he is asked. This behavior also extends to self-centered indulgence when he claims the time taken to work through appeals for the killers is a torture of himself. Capote has to wait for the killers to be executed before he has an end to his book, but surely their suffering in prison is worse than his. Capote also treats Perry badly by effectively cutting him off after he has confessed what happened on the night of the murders, although the writer does eventually see the killers before they are executed.

The screenplay explores Capote's homosexuality with the idea of gay-acting and straight-acting behavior. Capote is shown to be an obvious homosexual because he acts and speaks like the stereotype who is aware of how he sounds and appears but does not change to be accepted by the non-gay world. By contrast his live-in boyfriend is a "masculine" homosexual who can presumably pass for straight, although the narrative never sees this tested. Capote as gay-acting attracts the attention of a Kansas cruiser but also the disdain of others. He learns he must alter his wardrobe in order to become more acceptable in his new work environment, replacing a full-length camel-hair coat and Bergdorf scarf with a more conservative blue suit and tie and overcoat. Capote also has Nelle go with him to West Kansas to help him get what he needs from the locales, with her "manly" manner likened to Jack. That Capote even has a boyfriend, let alone one like Jack, shows that he has perhaps compensated for physical attractiveness with an entertaining personality. We never see the men exchange physical intimacy and it is assumed that Jack is lost when Capote returns to New York after the executions a broken man. Part of what makes Capote socially acceptable both in Kansas and especially in New York is that he is a professional success. The screenplay shows that his alcoholism, a condition heightened by his depression, makes him hostile and it will eventually cost him the approval of his superficial society world. Capote's grief over the loss of the killers has him shutting down physically. He won't speak and he retreats into bed, with this regression underlined by Capote eating baby food spiked with Scotch. The baby food is featured earlier as what the writer feeds Perry when he goes on a hunger strike in prison so it is ironic that Capote later turns to it. A postscript to the film also gives the epitaph he wrote for his last, unfinished work which reflects the notion that doing the book led to his downfall: "More tears are shed over answered prayers than unanswered ones."

Hoffman is billed above the film's title. The actor wears his hair in a short combed-back style and sometimes wears glasses. Hoffman's casting as the 5'4" Capote may seem wrong since the actor was 5'10." But it is apparent that an effort was made to make him appear to be smaller than he actually is, including how he reportedly lost 40 pounds for the role. The actor also has a facial similarity to the real man, but it is the character's combination of nerd and lout that actually fits elements of what the actor has done before. Additionally, Capote being gay recalls some of the other gay men that Hoffman has played. Hoffman makes his character likable despite the despicable things he does, but then we also feel satisfied that Capote suffers for his evil. The actor imitates the writer's distinctive voice; his cackle while sounding funny also recalls Hoffman's own big laugh. He also uses an effeminate body language. Hoffman makes Capote's outrageous moments funny, and slows down his speech when Capote is drunk, but the actor fails to provide tears when he cries.

The screenwriter's penchant for short scenes perhaps prevents Hoffman from having one defining great scene in the narrative. The scene of the New York public reading might have been that scene except that director Bennett Miller works against it by using cutaways, long shots and shots behind Capote, and has the microphone blocking our view of his face. Miller also uses some extreme closeups of Hoffman but again they are not as off-putting as those by David Mamet in *State and Main*. The actor is memorable when Capote demonstrates excitement about meeting Perry in the sheriff's office women's prison, pleasure at the New York audience reaction to his reading from the unpublished book, and vanity when he poses for the cameras on the red carpet for the premiere of the film *To Kill a Mockingbird*.

Capote premiered on September 2, 2005, at the Telluride Film Festival, which Hoffman attended. It then screened on September 10 at the Toronto International Film Festival and on September 27 at the New York Film Festival. It was given a limited release on September 30 and then a wide release on February 3, 2006. David Rooney in *Variety* wrote that Hoffman's performance was mesmerizing and said that he impressively presented Capote with dignity and soul and depth and sensitivity. A.O. Scott in the *New York Times* wrote that Hoffman achieved an impressive physical and vocal transformation but he also conveyed, with clarity and subtlety, the complexities of Capote's temperament. Roger Ebert in the *Chicago Sun-Times* wrote that Hoffman's performance was precise and uncanny. The film, a hit, earned Academy Award nominations for Best Film, Best Director, Best Adapted Screenplay, Best Actor and Best Supporting Actress for Keener. The only winner was Hoffman.

Some scenes were written but not filmed including one where Capote and Nelle, in a diner, get information by overhearing the townspeople talking about the killings;

this was replaced by the funeral home scene. Another had Capote going inside the Kansas club the cruising man had entered, which ended up in an explicit moment in the bathroom. The scene of the *To Kill a Mockingbird* premiere was also written to feature five or six shots including a huge marquee and moving cars and a big set but it was decided that Capote's moment on the red carpet was all that was needed. Another scene, filmed but cut after Gerald Clarke objected to it, was set in Spain, where we see Capote and Jack dancing and having a make-out session. Clarke advised that the men never had such a public show of affection. Hoffman said he had Capote give the finger to Nelle in one take of the scene where she departed the Spain house in a taxi.

Hoffman reported that some scenes featured improvisation. He said that he had been friends with Richard Avedon for four or five years and Avedon had known Capote for almost all of his professional life. The actor had seen footage from the 1950s and '60s of Capote doing public readings at the 92nd Street Y and they helped him play the New York reading scene. In this scene, Hoffman used an artificial sophistication in his voice which was different from his normal speaking voice since he had heard Capote use it in the filmed readings. Hoffman felt Capote was so nervous about the night because he knew it was going to define his future. He probably wondered whether his book was as great as he thought it could be and learned that the answer was yes. Hoffman also reported that his performance as Capote on the red carpet at the *To Kill a Mockingbird* premiere was influenced by footage had seen of the real event.

Bennett Miller talked about his working relationship with Hoffman. The actor had told him early on that if something was working he wanted to be told how and why, and if something wasn't working he wanted to be told the same thing. Miller also spoke about the scenes of Capote's depression where Hoffman exuded a "Stay away from me" energy. He said the actor was a raw and open and pained anguished nerve so it was very difficult for Miller to ask for 18 or 20 takes.

The actor was interviewed about the film in the DVD short "Answered Prayers" and in the Making of *Capote* documentary. Hoffman said that when he was approached by Miller and Futterman to do the film, he knew who Capote was from the later part of his life where he did the talk show circuit. The actor said he saw these appearances when he was a kid and didn't really know what to make of them. Hoffman then read the script and some of the biography that it was based on, and he knew it was something he needed to do. The actor said what was great about the screenplay was that it wasn't a biopic (he didn't think he would have been interested in playing it if it was). It was more a fictional world and that's what was so fantastic about it. He was not interested in mimicking Capote because he said that was not interesting. Hoffman commented on the ensemble that was put together for the film and said he couldn't have thought of anyone else to have played all those parts than the people who did. Miller reported that Hoffman spent six months before shooting in preparation: losing weight, studying the voice and the physicality. The director said the role was a huge risk for the actor to take and the possibility of profound humiliation was always there, and he believed it was certainly the most challenging film role that Hoffman had ever done.

Hoffman was interviewed by Charlie Rose on September 29, 2005, about the film. Hoffman said the role was difficult because Capote was such an icon and there were a lot of people who were still alive who knew him or had seen him on television through the 1970s and early '80s. The actor read whatever he could and listened to and watched whatever he could—a great documentary by the Maysles Brothers, *With Love from Truman* (1966), helped him a lot because it was from that period and captured him in his private moments and settings.

Asked about Capote's voice, Hoffman said he wasn't very good at accents and mimicking people, so it meant that he had to work on it a lot. It wasn't as simple as affecting a feminine or a high-pitched voice; there was something else to it. Capote did something with his tongue and something with his jaw and his whole face was formed in a way to make this sound come out. It was maddening for the actor for a couple of months before he started mastering it, and even then it was difficult.

Hoffman said Capote was a great writer but agreed that while you couldn't show that, you could show his intelligence, wit and insight. He was a colorful raconteur who became almost embarrassing at times to a lot of people. Rose recalled a famous TV talk show where Capote said he thought all actors were stupid. Hoffman laughed when he heard Capote say that Brando was a dumb as a post, but he also admired the moxie he had to say it.

Hoffman said he could see how crazy Capote could make people, which was also ultimately how he got a lot of attention. The actor saw how the man was flawed beyond belief and he could be judged and criticized but he was so open that he had empathy for him. Hoffman also found Capote too bold and cocksure which was apparent from the way he walked into a room with his head tilted up with that energy. When Capote was on *Johnny Carson* he literally bounced on stage like a little bunny. The actor also felt he had an incredible strength to be able to win over a man who shot a family of four, to be able to deal with him and humiliate him to get what he wanted. Hoffman figured that what was underneath that was an incredible desire to be loved, and his confidence and courage gave Capote the ability to lie to people when he could justify it in the moment. However the grief he felt over the execution of the two killers was crushing and those incompatible feelings were the personal tragedy of the story. Apart from his drinking, there was also his pill-taking which made him lose a lot of his friends and made society reject him, which was the worst thing that could have happened to him.

Asked about Miller, the actor said he and Danny Futterman, the screenwriter, had all known each other since they were 16 years old. Hoffman advised that although it was Miller's first feature film as director, he had previously made commercials and a wonderful documentary called *The Cruise* (1998). The actor said they were all in summer school and college together and Miller was always probably the most intelligent man and wittiest men in the room. When he went to Hoffman's house with Futterman and said he had a script Futterman wrote that he wanted to direct, Hoffman was very excited. He knew that Miller would push him and challenge him and do whatever he needed to do with him to get the job done and that was what Hoffman needed and liked. The actor thought that Miller made the film taut, concise and compelling.

In the February 27, 2014, *Rolling Stone*, it was reported that the actor developed his own fitness regime to lose weight for the role. This involved going to the local basketball court and taking a one left-handed shot, which was followed by push-ups and sit-ups. Hoffman then sprinted to the other end of the court and took a right-handed shot, falling to the hardwood for more push-ups and crunches. He repeated the routine again and again.

On March 3, 2006, *Charlie Rose* reran part of the interview with Hoffman. This new episode also included part of Rose's January 17, 2006, interview with Miller. He said that Hoffman needed to go to a dark place and feel profound vulnerability and experience a level of despair that maybe people who didn't know Hoffman that well would have been uncomfortable with. Miller said that on set, the process on the outside looking in might have looked fierce and rough but they didn't have to apologize to each other about being very forward and knowing whether they had what they needed or not.

Hoffman was credited as executive director of LAByrinth for its production of Joseph Patrick Shanley's play *Sailor's Song*. Directed by Chris McGarry, it ran at the Joseph Papp Public Theater/Susan Stein Shiva Theater from November 7 to 21, 2004. It was about a man whose wife was dying, the nephew who kept him company during her coma and the two women he meets in a bar, one of whom channels the dead.

On November 2, 2004, it was reported that Eric Bogosian had been cast as Satan in *Last Days of Judas Iscariot* and that performances were to start on February 8, 2005. Hoffman would later comment that he was really intimidated about meeting Bogosian because he was an iconic figure. On February 5, 2005, it was reported that the run of *Last Days of Judas Iscariot* was to be extended from March 20 to April 3, 2005. The show opened on March 2, 2005, with Hoffman credited as co-artistic director of LAByrinth, at the Joseph Papp Public Theater/Martinson Hall.

Cast member Craig "mUMs" Grant was encouraged by Hoffman and LAByrinth to develop his one-man show *A Sucker Emcee*. Interviewed in the *New York Times* (September 14, 2014), Grant said that after an early performance of the show he wrote, he felt the performance went over everybody's head and said that Hoffman had notes for him. The actor (who was also the company's co-artistic director) commented that he felt the writing was incredible but very dense. Hoffman said it was not a play as it stood and Grant needed to scan it down like it was Shakespeare when he went to perform it—line for line. The writer said that helped him edit and the show would eventually be produced by LAByrinth at the Bank Street Theater from September 10 to October 5, 2014. It was directed by Jennie Koons.

The actor attended the 20th IFP Independent Spirit Awards on February 26, 2005, in Santa Monica, California. The show was held at a beachside tent and broadcast on television on Bravo Cable. Hoffman and Patricia Clarkson presented the award for Best Screenplay to Alexander Payne and Jim Taylor for their romantic comedy *Sideways* (2004). Hoffman looks as if he is still thin from his *Capote* shoot.

On March 9, 2005, Hoffman participated in the Knicks Cheering for Children Foundation bowling event at Chelsea Lanes. On April 4, 2005, he was among those performing at a dinner and variety show at the Angel Orensanz Foundation for the Arts to aid DreamYard, an arts education group that worked in 40 public schools in the Bronx. Hoffman reportedly attended the Partial Comfort production of Chad Beckim's play *... a matter of choice* at Chashama. Beckim's autobiographical tale told of the effect of the Second Avenue subway line's construction on three twenty-something friends—Diggs, who is white; Chastity, Latina; and Webb, gay and black—who share a Harlem apartment that is to be demolished for the project.

From April 28 to 30, 2005, Hoffman performed in live readings of two so-called sound plays, intended for radio, at St. Ann's Warehouse in Brooklyn. Set to the music of Carter Burwell and presented under the collective title "Theater of the New Ear," the plays were *Sawbones* by Joel and Ethan Coen and *Hope Leaves the Theater* by Charlie Kaufman. The Coens' play centered on the star of a television series about a frontier veterinarian (Hoffman). The program was also to be performed at the Royal Festival Hall in London on May 13, 2005, and broadcast in America in the summer on Sirius Satellite Radio. On April 28, 2005, *The Hollywood Reporter* said that Hoffman was one of the creative advisers for the annual June Filmmakers and Screenwriters Labs, scheduled for May 31 to June 30, 2005, at the Sundance Institute.

On May 9, 2005, he attended a screening of the HBO miniseries *Empire Falls* (2005) at the Temple of Dendur room in the Metropolitan Museum of Art. The series, based on a novel by Richard Russo about life in a fictional small town in Maine, was directed by Fred Schepisi. It was made by HBO Films-Marc Platt Productions-Aspetuck Productions-Stone Village Pictures Productions and shot on location in Maine. Russo also wrote the teleplay which focused on the Empire Grill restaurant manager Miles Roby (Ed Harris) and his hopes to get away from the impoverished town and own a book store in Martha's Vineyard. Hoffman played the supporting part of Charlie Mayne a.k.a. Charles Beaumont Whiting, the long-dead owner of the Whiting Textile Company and husband of Francine (Joanne Woodward as an older Francine and Carey Lowell as Francine at 40) who came to own the Grill and the town.

While married to Francine, Charlie has an affair with Miles' mother Grace (Robin Wright Penn) and wants to run away with her, although Grace is married to Max Roby (Paul Newman as the older Max and Josh Lucas as the young Max). The couple decide not to leave because of the boy, Miles (Miles Chandler). While said to be reluctant to marry anybody, Francine is presented as a cold, unloving woman and Grace is the love of Charlie's life. Francine manipulates her husband, whom she knows accidentally ran his car over their daughter Cindy (Kate Burton and Claire Winters as Young Cindy) and lies that the culprit was a hit-and-run driver in order to hold the secret over Charlie. When he buys the Empire Shirt Factory in 1959, Grace loses her job as office manager and takes one as Francine's maid, which involves caring for Cindy. Charlie goes to run the company in Mexico and returns after ten years to shoot himself in the gazebo of the Whiting home. It is suggested that he actually intended to shoot Francine but stops after seeing Cindy and commits suicide instead. It is also suggested that Grace was pregnant by Charlie although it is not stated that her second child David (Aidan Quinn) is his son. Charlie has refused to do anything to stop the repeated flooding of the Knox River, which runs by the home. This results in the flooding of the town and the drowning of Francine but restores the town to prosperity. Charlie's tombstone reads that he was born on May 22, 1915, and appeared to die on October 10, 1969, with the last digit of the date of death obscured by a weed on the stone. If these dates are correct, this means that he was 54 when he died, and 44 when he left Maine for Mexico.

The teleplay is divided into titled chapters and an epilogue, with each chapter covering a day in the town, and the actor is seen in six of the eight. He is first represented in a painted portrait of Charlie in Francine's home wearing a white hat with his face partially obscured. He is repeatedly seen in a white hat in the narrative, and favoring a white suit. Hoffman wears his hair in a longish style for the 1950s and has a beard. He uses an appropriate New England accent and, surprisingly, uses none of his usual acting mannerisms. The character is an elusive one, often seen as a vision of memory by Miles. Charlie is shown from the back when he walks to the gazebo and shoots himself so it is possible that this is a double. Russo's use of literary conceits also extends to Hoffman's last scene, where director Fred Schepisi has the ghost of Charlie talk alternatively to the adult and child Miles.

The series debuted on May 28, 2005, with the tagline "Every small town has a big story." It was nominated for Emmy Awards for Outstanding Miniseries, Outstanding Writing, Outstanding Directing, Outstanding Editing, Outstanding Art Direction, Outstanding Casting, Lead Actor, Supporting Actor for Paul Newman and Hoffman, and Supporting Actress. Only Newman won.

Hoffman said Charlie was a kind of a mysterious character but he probably influenced the storyline more than any other character. Schepisi said that Hoffman brought a wonderful upper-class attitude to it. The director added that it was because Hoffman's casting was so unexpected that made it work. Schepisi also said that it was wonderful to watch him working with Robin Wright Penn and the both of them working with Miles Chandler, because the two actors were wonderful with the boy.

On June 20, 2005, the actor appeared in the five-episode television series *Celebrity Charades* which ran on AMC on consecutive nights from June 20 to 24. It was shot at a rented downtown loft. The series, executive-produced by Bob Balaban, Chad Lowe and his wife Hilary Swank, replicated the real-life charades dinner parties they held with friends. These had ten guests eating a catered buffet dinner in between rounds of the game of running movie-themed charades, with banter and storytelling also occurring between games. This was designed to allow viewers to get to know the celebrities on a personal level. The players were divided into two teams that raced against each other, with a member of each team running to the moderator in another room to receive the next clue. After guessing five movie titles, the teams had to figure out the common link among them. The games were played to raise money for the chosen charity of each star.

Filming took place from July 12 to November 29, 2005, on the Paramount–Cruise–Wagner action-adventure *Mission: Impossible III* (2006). This was a sequel to *Mission: Impossible* (1996) which was based on the 1966–73 TV series of the same name. It was shot in China, Italy, California and Virginia from a screenplay by Alex Kurtzman, Robert Orci and J.J. Abrams and was directed by Abrams. Tom Cruise stars as Impossible Mission Force (IMF) rogue government agent Ethan Hunt, who goes after a black market trafficker, Owen Davian (Hoffman), with connections to the destructive "rabbit foot" device. Kenneth Branagh was reportedly first cast as Davian but dropped out. Albert Brooks reported that he wanted the part but Abrams told him that he was a big fan but just didn't see the actor in it.

After Ethan kidnaps Davian and takes his suitcase which contains the location of the device, Davian is rescued and kidnaps Ethan's wife, Virginia Regional Hospital nurse Julia (Michele Monaghan). He then offers to exchange her for the device. The trafficker is described as a means to an end by IMF senior operative John Musgrave (Billy Crudup) since the government would rather allow Davian to sell the device to a Middle Eastern

In lobby card for *Mission: Impossible III* (2006).

buyer which would result in a military strike and justify the American government making a return attack. Musgrave says Davian is like a weed and if he is stopped, then another like him will emerge. However Davian appears to take what Ethan does to him personally and his plan to murder Julia is payback. The narrative tells us of the bad that Davian does but the only bad things we see him do are shooting his translator (Bahar Soomekh) and attacking Ethan in the climax. He does not get to murder Julia because he is stopped by Ethan. Davian meets his demise when the two men are fighting in the street and Davian is hit by a car. Davian's line to Ethan, "You can always tell someone's character by the way they treat those they don't need to treat well," is a judgment of Ethan after he has hanged Davian outside the plane and seems to make Davian's attempt at revenge personal.

Hoffman wears his hair short and combed back, is clean-shaven and without glasses. Davian only gets two outfits: a black suit with dark green shirt and a tuxedo with black bow tie and sunglasses; he wears the latter at the Vatican event. The Vatican scene features the elaborate ruse of having Ethan disguised as Davian with the help of a facial mask generated after photographs are taken of Davian. A double is used to accommodate Hoffman playing both Davian and Ethan as Davian in these scenes, but the disparity between the height and weight of the actor compared to that of Tom Cruise is not allowed for. This is noteworthy since Cruise is only 5'7" compared to Hoffman's 5'10" and Hoffman is also heavier. The role allows Hoffman the new actions of firing a gun and kicking and punching and wrestling with Ethan. The actor manages to make Davian sympathetic for being kidnapped by Ethan, particularly in the plane sequence where director Abrams photographs Hoffman in extreme closeups and unflatteringly when he is face down hanging from the plane's opened area. It is interesting that despite his hands being tied, Hoffman still over-acts in the scene with the use of head-shaking as if to compensate for his over-gesturing mannerism that he uses in the Vatican scene. Ultimately the role is unworthy of the actor but one can assume that he accepted for it for the challenge of playing something different, and for the film's commercial appeal.

The film premiered in Rome on April 24, 2006, with Hoffman attending. It opened in the U.S. on May 5. Todd McCarthy in *Variety* wrote that Hoffman played his villain with unsparing meanness and that while he invested his scenes with a special weight and interest, his involvement hadn't been fully exploited. Peter Travers in *Rolling Stone* wrote that Hoffman played with dry wit and hardcore menace. the *New York Times'* Manohla Dargis wrote that Hoffman enlivened the film and, though he wasn't given that much to do, what he did was choice. With a sneer in his voice and a lazy slouch that telegraphed world-weariness of the most misanthropic kind, she said that the actor created an ice-blooded creature. The film did not recoup its budget costs but it would be followed by two *Mission: Impossible—Ghost Protocol* (2011) and *Mission: Impossible—Rogue Nation* (2015).

Hoffman commented that these were the best possible circumstances to be doing a film like that and that he wasn't going to be doing a lot of movies like it in his life. So when the opportunity came along and it was actually a good situation, he jumped on it. Hoffman knew that the character study wasn't going to be three-dimensional but it had visceral energy and imagination and needed to be played well. Hoffman loved the physical training and hanging out with stunt people, reporting that he did his own stunts. The actor said he was excited to work with Cruise again because on *Magnolia* "he never half-assed it, ever."

J.J. Abrams said it felt unusual to have Hoffman in the movie but he thought the actor would raise the bar. The director advised that the opening scene was originally envisaged to have Eddie Marsan threatening Ethan rather than Davian. He also reported that originally the Vatican party scene had a moment where you saw Davian arrive and get out of his car, but it was cut. For the mask scenes, Hoffman watched Cruise play the scene first and studied his physicality so he could copy it when he was playing Ethan playing Davian. This was said to be most apparent when Ethan wearing the Davian mask holds the forearms of fellow IMF agent Luther Stickell (Ving Rhames), which was a Cruise gesture.

Hoffman appeared on the television series *Henry's Film Corner* on September 3 or 4, 2005 (sources vary). On September 7, 2005, it was reported that Hoffman had attended the opening-night party for the Shakespeare in the Park production *Two Gentlemen of Verona* on August 16. The reporters wrote that they had tried to make eye contact with the actor but he waved them off, like he would a pesky fly.

On September 25, Hoffman was interviewed by Christian Moerk for a *New York Times* article about *Capote* on the telephone from the set of *Mission: Impossible III* in Los Angeles. He reported that he had sat in on the pitch to United Artists with the director and producer around two years ago. It was thought to be clutch time because other companies had shown interest but eventually passed; then six more months had been wasted by a near-investor who fell out. Hoffman said he remembered being in the room and the hopefuls were leaning forward and he said if they could have reached forward and grabbed the men they were pitching to, they would have. They knew that if what was needed hadn't come soon then it never would. Hoffman said he vouched for the writer and the director with a very strong conviction, saying, "If you believe in me, believe in them" because he felt they had all went out on a limb together. A key executive finally leaned forward and said the yes they were waiting for. Danny Rosett of United Artists said the decision to trust Hoffman and his gang had more to do with the specifics of what they proposed than the actor's currency or their close bond. Rosett said the premise of the actor in that kind of role was an obvious thing and they viewed it like Ed Harris in the biographical drama *Pollock* (2000), as his career role.

The article also reported how Miller learned soon after getting Futterman's screenplay about the competing project. As unlikely as it seemed, Warner Independent Pictures was gearing up to let Douglas McGrath direct its *Have You Heard?*, a film whose title was later changed to *Infamous* and had also been known as *Every Word Is True*. This was set to open in 2006 and used the same violent flashpoint to illuminate Capote's life.

Based on the book *Truman Capote* by George Plimpton, it presents a more sexualized view of the relationship between Capote and Perry Smith. Another difference is the performance of Toby Jones as Capote and his presentation in the narrative. Jones is 5'4", smaller than Hoffman, and the same height as the real Capote. It is possible that the impact of Jones' Capote is lessened because it was viewed after Hoffman's (*Infamous* opened on October 13, 2006). However it seems that Jones' performance is both more natural and also has an androgyny that Hoffman lacks, apparent since this Capote is repeatedly perceived to be a woman. Jones plays Capote as an obvious homosexual but mostly without the extreme feyness that Hoffman provides. This Capote is more charismatic and funny than Hoffman's but he is also shown to be less grief-stricken that Hoffman's character becomes over the loss of Perry. Jones wears the same cream-colored coat the Hoffman does in the latter part of *Capote*.

On September 26, 2005, the actor appeared at the Women's Image Network awards, broadcast on PAX Television. On the September 30 *New York Times* Hoffman was quoted after attending a *Capote* screening. He said that as a person who had been interviewed a lot, he got interested in the technique. The screening was hosted by Dominick Dunne, who had been a friend of Capote's. Also at the screening were Catherine Kenner, and Neil Simon and John Patrick Shanley, who lavished praise on Hoffman. The actor returned to *The Daily Show* on October 6 and appeared on the AMC talk show *Sunday Morning Shootout* on October 16.

Hoffman was interviewed by Gavin Edwards for the October, 20, 2005, *Rolling Stone*. Edwards had lunch with Hoffman at an Italian restaurant on New York's Upper East Side; he says Hoffman's strawberry-blond hair looks like it was styled with an eggbeater and describes how he shoved fried food into his mouth as he slouched on his seat. The writer calls him a slob but also one of the best actors in the world, though no one at the restaurant recognizes him. He said the actor didn't want to lose the ability to take the subway. Edwards suggested that the role of Capote had made the actor a favorite for the Best Actor Oscar and he quoted Paul Thomas Anderson and Hoffman's brother Gordy. Gordy wanted to thank producer Christine Vachon who made *Infamous* since he claims the competition of the rival Capote film challenged the athlete in his brother. Hoffman commented on his relationship with Mimi O'Donnell, saying he was never a Casanova and it was good to know he was waking up with someone.

The actor was interviewed by Michael Musto in the October 2005 edition of *Out Magazine*. Hoffman said he knew about *Infamous* coming out because in the business it was always something: either you couldn't get the money together or it rained and there was another movie about the same subject! Hoffman didn't wish them ill and he didn't think the films would be that similar. He said that when he told some people how he was playing Capote, they didn't know who he was and the actor's jaw dropped. These were people in their thirties and in the film business so he hoped the film would introduce the man to a lot of people. Asked if he was ever frustrated that he was usually cast as fringe characters, Hoffman replied no. He didn't see them as so fringy but he guessed Musto was right in that he had played a lot of people who lived on the outside of things. The actor said the great thing about playing Capote was that he was on the outside of things but on the inside of everything.

Hoffman was also interviewed by Alex Pappademas for *GQ.Com Magazine*'s October 2005 edition. The journalist, who met the actor at a West Village café for dinner in late July, described him as looking a little crumpled, a little slouchy and couch-creased, freckled and pale, and at least for a minute before they met he seemed befuddled in a way that was familiar. But in person, Pappademas wrote, he had a genial, surprisingly dude-like quality to him. He looked like a man you'd trust to help you move a dorm fridge or co-captain your Ultimate Frisbee team. In a crinkly, ungainly way, the writer said he is actually kind of handsome. The actor reported that the café was around the corner from the apartment he shared with Mimi O'Donnell and their two-year-old son. Hoffman commented on the issue of his being a leading man in film after playing so many supporting roles. He said there was no truth to the notion that he sat at home yearning to be a leading man, biting the knuckles of one hand in mock frustration at the notion. Hoffman advised he had had conversations where someone had wanted him to play a role that was actually bigger than the role he was interested in. But he felt that to play one leading role after another would ultimately narrow his options. People would stop seeing him as being capable of doing both kinds of roles and he wanted to make sure that doors didn't close for him. Hoffman also spoke about *Capote*.

Hoffman appeared on the ABC talk show *Live! With Kelly and Michael* on November 2, 2005, to talk about *Capote*. That same day he was on *Late Night with Conan O'Brien* for the third and last time. The actor appeared on the *2005 MTVU Woodie Awards* which was broadcast on MTV on November 9 (these awards were given to new music college students). The event was held at the Roseland Ballroom in New York. Hoffman was photographed there looking physically heavier as if he had gained back weight he had lost for *Capote*.

On December 1, Hoffman appeared on the CBS-TV talk show *The Early Show*. On the same date he was honored as one of the *GQ Magazine* Men of the Year with a dinner and after-party at Mr. Chow in Beverly Hills. On December 12, he attended the New York Film Critic's Circle Awards at the Algonquin Hotel where he gave the award to Bennett Miller for Best First Film. On December 13, he was a guest on the NBC news and talk show *Today* in New York.

6

Oscar

Hoffman was a guest on *The Tonight Show with Jay Leno* on January 3, 2006. This was shot in California. On January 9 he attended the Broadcast Film Critic's Choice Awards ceremony (aka the 11th Annual Critics' Choice Awards) at the Santa Monica Civic Auditorium where he accepted the Best Actor award. On January 10 the actor attended the National Board of Review awards ceremony held at the Tavern on the Green in Central Park. His award for Best Actor was given him by his friend Eric Bogosian; in his acceptance speech, Hoffman talked about his mom. He suggested that she, along with his girlfriend and Bogosian, were the people he thought of when he tried to ready himself for a scene. Hoffman also announced that the Best Foreign Film was the crime drama-thriller *Paradise Now* (2005).

In a January 15, 2006, *New York Times* article on Dan Futterman, he commented about the actor being the perfect choice as Capote. He said Hoffman was in touch with what would be fun to play about the man. Futterman felt there was something inherently dramatic when someone was manipulative and self-serving and he knew that the actor could bring a clarity to Capote. Hoffman was interviewed by David Edelstein for an article that appeared on the same day. The journalist lunched with the actor at a restaurant in Lower Manhattan, near Hoffman's apartment. Edelstein said he had heard two things from people who had worked with him: that he was one of the nicest and most humble performers in the business, and that on sets he could be unapproachable. Hoffman said he agreed. The actor also spoke about his role as an executive producer on *Capote*. He said in the editing room he fought with the director to make his character less attractive. Hoffman felt he could have easily cut that film and not shown him in as harsh a light but the actor believed that the way toward empathy was actually to be as hard as possible on this character, since the harder you were, the more empathy you would gain. The actor also said the training for the role was like going to the gym for hours every day, pushing his body and his voice to places he wasn't sure were within reach. Going by the awards Hoffman would receive for his performance, it appeared that a lot of people felt he had succeeded at what he was trying to achieve, although he told Edelstein that he was trying not to think too much about the upcoming Academy Awards race.

On January 15, 2006, Hoffman attended the *Vanity Fair* pre–Golden Globes party at Los Angeles' Sunset Towers. On January 16 he was awarded the Best Actor in a Film Drama Golden Globe at the ceremony held at the Beverly Hilton Hotel in Los Angeles which was televised live by NBC. Accepting the award, he joked that he wished the stage had a podium (there was only a microphone on a stand) so that the audience wouldn't see his knees shaking. Hoffman thanked, among others, Danny Futterman and Bennett Miller whom he knew had given him the best part of his life. At the backstage press room Q&A, Hoffman was asked what advice he had for his son; the actor said, "Well, he's not three yet, so I am mostly going to throw a ball back and forth with him and love him."

The actor was interviewed by John Darnton for the *New York Times* TimesTalk video program on January 27, 2006. Darnton commented on the actor looking so disheveled in *Love Liza* and asked how he came to be so comfortable in front of the camera. Hoffman said, at the end of the day, that was the profession of acting.

On January 29, 2006, he participated in the 12th Annual Screen Actors Guild Awards ceremony, held at the Shrine Auditorium in Los Angeles and broadcast live on TNT. Hoffman was shown on the red carpet before the show, arriving with Catherine Keener. He sat at the *Capote* table with Keener and other cast and crew members, and also with her introduced the film as one of the nominees for Ensemble Cast. While doing the latter, Hoffman laughed in reaction to the applause the couple received. Hoffman was nominated for the Best Male Actor in a Leading Role in a film and won. He accepted it from Hilary Swank. Hoffman thanked fellow acting nominee David Straithairn, an actor he said he had admired since he was young, and the cast of *Capote*. *The Hollywood Reporter* of January 30, 2006, quoted Hoffman on the night of the awards. He said he had experienced professional high points this awards season but nothing compared to the feeling he experienced when, as a 24-year-old novice, he landed a part in *Scent of a Woman*. Hoffman commented that he didn't think he had been more joyful since that moment, because he never thought he would be an actor.

The consensus was that Hoffman could not lose the Oscar since, as opined in the February 1, 2006, *New York Times,* he had played both a gay and famous person. His closest competition was said to be Heath Ledger for *Brokeback Mountain* but he had only played gay. Best Actor nominees David Strathairn and Joaquin Phoenix played famous persons, Edward R. Murrow and Johnny Cash respectively, but not *gay* famous persons. It was proposed that Hoffman's Capote required that he carry off an incredibly mannered character and not just sell it to the people of Kansas but to the moviegoers as well. Ledger's performance lacked the kind of audible and visible virtuosity that make people first notice the acting and then notice the story. By February 23, the odds had changed. In light of the greater box office success of *Brokeback Mountain* over *Capote*, Ledger seemed to have the edge. By February 28, Hoffman was said to be odds-on favorite to win with a 94.8 percent probability as predicted by the University of Oregon's Iain Pardoe.

On February 11, 2006, Hoffman attended the 21st annual Santa Barbara International Film Festival, which ran from February 2 to 12. He was honored with the Riviera Award, established to recognize an actor who had influenced American cinema. On February 19 he attended the British Film Awards (BAFTA) ceremony where he won the Best Actor Award for *Capote*.

The actor was interviewed by Steve Croft on the February 19, 2006, episode of the CBS documentary series *60 Minutes*. Hoffman insisted on meeting Croft and the crew in New York's Greenwich Village because he said he thought it would be easier to talk and there wouldn't be as many people around. The actor was described by the *New York Times* as being dressed like a "schlub" and by Kroft as looking as though he may have slept in the park or wandered out of a homeless shelter. A female fan recognized him and told him that he deserved the Oscar. Kroft questioned him about his "scruffy" wardrobe and wondered if that was the real Phil Hoffman or whether he was preparing for some other role. He laughed and replied "No, this is me." Hoffman used his actor mannerisms of self-conscious touching, over-gesturing and enthusiastic laughter, the latter disturbing when he laughed about his past use of drugs and alcohol.

He thought part of being an actor was staying private, because an important part of doing his job was to believe that he was someone else, and if the audience watched him and thought about how he got a divorce or something in his real life he wasn't doing it. Hoffman said that doing *Capote* had changed his life because it had altered his point of view about almost everything. He spoke about his perfectionism and how, when he didn't think he was doing well, he became unpleasant. Asked what made him so good at his job, the actor advised that he had a need to create a personal crisis for himself, to take risks, as a means to "get to the good stuff." Kroft teased Hoffman with the request for him to do Capote one more time and the actor advised that would only happen if he was drunk at a party. However Hoffman had now stopped drinking and told Kroft of his stint in rehab at the age of 22. Kroft invited Miller, Dan Futterman and Gordy Hoffman to join them for a few hands of poker. The actor thought this was a bad idea and despite the good-natured kibitzing and saying it didn't matter if they won or not, Kroft felt it was hard to tell if they were bluffing. Hoffman seemed to be concentrating on the poker game more than the others and he sandbagged Kroft and took all his money.

The actor was photographed by Inez van Lamsweerde and Vinoodh Matadin for the *New York Times'* annual "Great Performers" portfolio. Van Lamsweerde said they decided to make a double exposure to show the two sides of Hoffman: the introverted, stern, quiet side, and the actor side of him when he was more outgoing. The black and white photograph has the actor in a checked shirt with a beard. The double exposure has Hoffman seen in one image looking directly into the camera and in the second looking in profile, and he is unsmiling in both.

On February 20, 2006, Hoffman appeared on the BBC talk show *Film '72*. On February 22 he was a guest on *Late Night with David Letterman* in New York. On it Hoffman told how he and Bennett Miller made a pact with a third friend when they were all teenagers: The first one to win an Oscar would have to bark his acceptance speech like a dog and continue until he was hauled off the stage. So the actor threatened to bark on the Academy Awards show if he won the Best Actor Oscar. On February 23 Hoffman was a guest on the BBC documentary talk show *The Culture Show* and spoke about *Capote*. He was on the Spanish documentary television series *Miradas 2* on February 24.

On March 3, Hoffman attended an honorary dinner at the Ritz-Carlton for Horton Foote to celebrate his 90th birthday the next day. The event was hosted by The Signature Theater Company. On March 4 he attended the 2005 Independent Spirit Awards in Santa Monica and broadcast on the Independent Film Channel. At the show he won the Best Male Lead award for *Capote*.

On March 5, 2006, Hoffman attended the *78th Annual Academy Awards* ceremony which were held at the Kodak Theatre and televised by ABC. He wore a black suit with black shirt and silver tie. Director Louis J. Horvitz cut to him nine times during the show, sometimes so that we could see him applauding various people. The actor laughed when host Jon Stewart made the comment that *Capote* was a groundbreaking film that broke taboos "by showing America not all gay people are virile cowboys; some are actually effete New York intellectuals."

In his Best Actor acceptance speech, Hoffman thanked his mother, Marilyn O'Connor, who took him to see his first play and stayed up with him to watch the NCA finals. He said her passions became his passions and added, "Be proud, Ma, 'cause I'm proud of you and we're here tonight and it's good."

On March 6, 2006, *People Magazine* reported that Hoffman was next to appear in a short film by Tim Farmer called *Simply Leon*. Farmer was an 18-year-old senior at Fairport High School, Hoffman's alma mater, and in 2005 he had pitched a seven-second role to the actor when he visited the school. Farmer was making the short for his media class and reported that Hoffman gave him his all, even saying the f-word which wasn't scripted. The director hoped to debut the short in Los Angeles in the summer. When Farmer asked Hoffman if he had to pay him, the actor replied that he didn't require payment for saying the f-word. On March 21, 2006, Hoffman and Tom Cruise appeared on the Canadian documentary series *HypaSpace,* broadcast on Chum Television. They spoke about *Mission: Impossible III*.

In April 2006 Hoffman began the Fox Searchlight Pictures–Lone Star Film Group–This Is That Production–Ad Hominem Enterprises–Cooper's Town Productions–Savage Productions dramedy *The Savages* (2007). Scripted and directed by Tamara Jenkins, it was shot in 30 days in Arizona, Buffalo and New York City's East Village.

The story told of 42-year-old Jon (Hoffman) and his 39-year-old sister Wendy Savage (Laura Linney). He is a professor of philosophy and a college drama teacher and she's a Master of Fine Arts, a playwright and an office temp. They are called upon to move their father Leonard "Lenny" Michael Joseph Savage (Philip Bosco), who is suffering from dementia, from his home in Sun City, Arizona, to the Valley View Rehabilitation Center in Buffalo. Jon lives with the Comp Lit Critical Theory Polish teacher Kasia

Holding his Oscar for Best Actor for *Capote* (2005).

(Cara Seymour), his girlfriend of three years; her visa has expired and she is returning to Poland. He refuses to marry her (even though this would allow her to stay in the United States) because he claims that even if they married she might have to travel away from him to get a job. Jon is also writing a book on Bertolt Brecht and the narrative ends has him going to a conference in Poland to present the paper "No Laughing Matter: The Dark Comedy in the Plays of Bertolt Brecht." We are not told whether Jon finishes his book but his disorganized application to it is suggested by the piles of books shown on his couch and on the floor when Wendy comes to stay with him. This mess also suggests that Jon is a bit of a slob, since among the books are food plates. He also has an artistic rivalry with Wendy, who is awarded a grant from the Federal Emergency Management Authority to fund the artistic creation of her new play *Wake Me When It's Over*. She tells Jon that the grant is from the Guggenheim Foundation; he discovers her lie when he contacts the Foundation after failing to find her name on a published list of fellows, an action which he sees as looking out for her but she sees him as policing her. However Jon will give his approval of Wendy's play when he sees a rehearsal at the Theater for the New City. He is also critical of Wendy's sexual relationship with the married 52-year-old Larry Mendelson (Peter Friedman). Additionally Jon investigates nursing homes for his father while leaving Wendy to move Lenny's belongings out of the house and to move him from the hospital where he is staying to the airport and then on the plane from Arizona to Buffalo. He also attempts to have time away from Lenny when he tells Wendy that he wants to spend Thanksgiving doing research but then changes his mind and agrees that they both can spend the time writing. Hoffman has another good scene where he yells in anger at Wendy's idea of moving Lenny to the Greenhill Manor in Vermont, which she thinks is nicer than the Buffalo nursing home.

Hoffman is second-billed to Laura Linney. He wears his hair in a medium length, is unshaven, and wears reading glasses. Jon sometimes wears color-*un*coordinated outfits; however he also has an elegant fur-collared black long coat. Hoffman uses a feminine way of sitting cross-legged. We see him humming and singing to Lotte Lenya's "Salomon-Song" from *The Threepenny Opera*. He's is funny in expressing annoyance at his sister and he has some funny lines, like "This is not the time to regress." At the Buffalo airport he gives Lenny a look that changes from disgust to empathy. The role gives Hoffman the opportunity for farce when Jon injures his neck when playing indoor tennis with Wendy and then uses a neck brace attached to a door to relieve pressure. This scene is perhaps the actor's best in the film since it allows us to see a more likable side to the character and also gives him comedy to play. Looking a little like a rabbit in the grotesque contraption, Jon tells Wendy, "It's not funny!" when she laughs at him but Hoffman says the line in a way that tells us that he *does* think it is funny. It also helps that being in the contraption makes the actor both look and sound different to how we have previously seen Jon.

The film premiered at the Sundance Film Festival on January 19, 2007, with Hoffman attending. Interviewing the actor at a dinner at the Festival was Anthony Breznican and his wife. The writer reported on February 6, 2014, how a bit of advice given by Hoffman changed his life. Breznican told the actor how he and his wife of five years were thinking of having children and Hoffman asked him what he was waiting for.

Hoffman said that you didn't make time to be a mom and dad; that when you have a kid, you figured out how to make time for work and all the other stuff. All the priorities you had now totally shifted, whether you wanted them to or not. Hoffman told Breznican not to worry about it and just do it and said, "Trust me."

The film was screened at the Toronto International Film Festival on September 10, 2007; at the Vancouver International Film Festival on September 29; at the Chicago International Film Festival in October; at the Mill Valley Film Festival on October 4; at the Austin Film Festival on October 17; at the Hamptons International Film Festival on October 19; at the Zagreb Film Festival on October 24; at the London Film Festival on October 29; at the Savannah Film and Video Festival on November 2; and at the Thessaloniki International Film Festival on November 24. It opened in the U.S. on February 1, 2008. It was praised by Todd McCarthy in *Variety*, Manohla Dargis in the *New York Times*, Roger Ebert in the *Chicago Sun-Times*, and Peter Travers in *Rolling Stone*. Ebert wrote that Hoffman and Linney were so specific in creating their characters that we saw them as people, not elements in a plot, and that Hoffman showed how many disguises he had within his seemingly immutable presence. Travers said that Hoffman left you in awe. The film recovered its budget costs without being a box office smash and won Academy Award nominations for Best Original Screenplay and Best Actress for Linney, but won neither.

Hoffman reported that the script had been given to him a few years prior and then it kind of went away. Then it was to be made by another company and came back to him with Linney attached. Hoffman loved the script and had wanted to do. He said that what attracted him was the story of people being estranged from their parents. Hoffman said to get into the character he used his process of what was similar to himself and what was not. Jon was interested in the theater so that was something he had in common; and Hoffman also had siblings and a relationship with his father which he could call upon. Jon was also a very intellectual guy, which the actor thought he was too, to a point, though not like him. Hoffman advised that although he had not had the experience of putting his parents in a nursing home, he did speak to nursing home residents (some of the film's scenes were shot in nursing homes).

The actor found that Tamara Jenkins had a unique and honest way to tell her story. Hoffman found her to be very passionate, and because she had worked on the material for a long time she was connected to it in a deep way. This made Hoffman know that he was with somebody who was going to do everything she could to make sure that it was the best film she could make. He commented on Jenkins in a November 4, 2007, *New York Times* article, saying that the longer the shooting days got, the surer he became that she was making a good movie because Jenkins was not a compromiser. In his 2008 *Filmink* interview Hoffman added that she was very specific with the actors and very supportive. He said Jenkins knew what she wanted and that always helped. Hoffman said that he thought the writing was terrific and it was one of the best scripts he had ever read.

Jenkins advised that she didn't write the parts for any particular actors. She first cast Linney and then met with Hoffman. Jenkins said that she thought Hoffman and Linney would be really exciting together. The director held a few days of rehearsals in her apartment and she said when she preparing coffee she could hear Linney and Hoffman chatting and could tell that there was going to something good between them. Jenkins described Hoffman as an astonishing artist who had a special and unique gift, maybe because he also directed theater, which was a peripheral vision about the big picture. The actor commented that he and Linney hit it off, saying she was a real sweetheart and they had a chemistry as actors. Linney said that she and Hoffman had a lot of the same philosophies about work, which they fought for 100 percent, and she felt most people were not that brave. The actress reported that the two knew each other as acquaintances before being in the film and she had always loved his work. They would run into each other backstage and Linney would see Hoffman in New York once in a while. She said his work so good and so generous, and you could see what kinds of decisions the actor had made and how his priorities were right where they should be.

French movie card for *The Savages* (2007).

Hoffman advised that at this time in his career he was more particular about what roles he would accept, and there were a lot of things that went into the decision. He felt that there wasn't much difference between Hollywood movies and independent films, since they were both a big machine, which he found depressing. Ultimately, you were under the same gun.

On April 10, 2006, Hoffman attended a tribute to Christopher Reeve's wife Dana Reeve at a special memorial service in New York City (the actress-singer had lost her battle with lung cancer on March 6, 2006). Hoffman was said to be one of her famous pals. The private memorial was held at the New Amsterdam Theatre on 42nd Street. In mid–April *Variety* reported that Hoffman was in talks to play the ship's doctor in a new *Star Trek* film to be directed by *Mission: Impossible III* director J.J. Abrams. Abrams commented that this news was unauthorized and not entirely accurate. The director would make the science fiction action adventure *Star Trek* (2009) but Hoffman was not in the cast.

WENN reported on April 26, 2006, that the actor was heading to Australia to direct a play written by Cate Blanchett's husband, Andrew Upton. He would set up home in Sydney during his collaboration with the Sydney Theatre Company in 2007. Hoffman had been recently spotted in the audience of Upton and Blanchett's production of *Hedda Gabler* at the Brooklyn Academy of Music in New York City. The show, staged at the school's Harvey Theatre, was a revival of the Sydney Theatre Company's 2004 production, which was directed by Robyn Nevin. It ran from March 1 to March 26, 2006. Hoffman advised that he was in talks with Upton and the STC and the actor hoped it was going to happen. He decided to withhold giving any more details out of respect for his collaborators and preferred that they make all announcements. Hoffman returned to the Canadian television series *HypaSpace* on May 4, 2006. This time he attended with J.J. Abrams to talk more about *Mission: Impossible III*.

From June 19 to August 2006 Hoffman appeared in the Capitol Films¬–Funky Buddha Group–Unity Productions–Linse Film Ltd. Production crime thriller *Before the Devil Knows You're Dead* (2007). Scripted by Kelly Masterson and directed by Sidney Lumet, it was shot in New York. Lumet photographed the film on hi-definition video, which allowed him to use multiple cameras simultaneously.

The plot centers on the Hanson family who own the Hanson Jewelers store in the Westchester shopping mall. It is robbed by the Hanson sons, real estate accountant Andrew "Andy" (Hoffman) and Henry, a.k.a. Hank (Ethan Hawke) with his friend Bobby Lasorda (Brian F. O'Byrne). Andy decides to steal from his parent's business because he needs the money. Andy is a drug addict who snorts cocaine in his office and visits dealer Justin (Blaine Horton) to receive in-house intravenous treatment. He has also stolen money from his company which is discovered when an audit exposes the fraud, and he will steal from Justin to pay off Chris's brother Dex (Michael Shannon) who blackmails Hank. The robbery is bungled since the Hanson mother Nanette (Rosemary Harris) is in the store when she is not meant to be and is fatally shot. The killing will lead to Andy's father Charles (Albert Finney) seeking revenge and eventually smothering his son with a pillow when he is hospital after being shot by Bobby's wife Chris (Aleksa Palladino). Andy's decision to rob his parent's store is perhaps influenced by a feeling of a lack of love from Charles. He considers that his father prefers Hank over him and even questions whether he really is the son of Charles. The confrontation has Charles slap him at Nanette's wake, which makes Andy cry. However Andy is immediately unreactive when Gina tells him about her affair with Hank and that she is leaving him.

Hoffman gets top billing above the title although the piece is more an ensemble than a starring role for the actor. Hoffman is clean-shaven and has his hair in a combed-back style, which gives it a darker look, and he wears a variety of business suits with colored shirts and ties. We see the actor naked for the first time in a sex scene with Gina (Marisa Tomei), and also punching and shooting Justin, another user in his apartment and Dex. We see him doing drugs, prefiguring the actor's real-life struggle with drugs. Hoffman has some convincing expressions of anger. The actor's best scene is perhaps the silent one where he calmly messes up Gina's remaining belongings in the apartment after she leaves.

The film was screened at the Deauville Festival of American Cinema on September 6, 2007, and then at the Cinémathèque Française on September 9; the Toronto International Film Festival on September 13; at the Rio de Janeiro International Film Festival on September 30; at the Chicago International Film Festival in October 2007; at the Morelia Film Festival and the New York Film Festival on October 12; at the Austin Film Festival on October 18; at the Rome Film Festival on October 20; at the São Paulo International Film Festival on October 30; at the St. Louis International Film Festival on November 11; and at the San Luis Cine International Festival on November 16. It was released in the U.S. on December 7, 2007, with the taglines "No one was supposed to get hurt," "Loyalty. It's all relative" and "Greed. Betrayal. Revenge. Families can be murder." A.O. Scott in the *New York Times* wrote that Hoffman made us care about his character, the scale of whose ethical failures giving him a kind of negative grandeur. Roger Ebert in the *Chicago Sun-Times* said that Hoffman and Hawke were such intelligent actors that they pulled off that miracle that made us stop thinking of anything we knew about them. *Rolling Stone*'s Peter Travers wrote that Hoffman continued to astonish. It was a box office success.

Hoffman said that Lumet was a true master who loved directing and working with actors like no other, and despite Lumet's age (82) the film didn't smack of the work of an older man. The actor advised that the film's opening sex scene was made easier because he had known Marisa Tomei since he was 22. The actor enjoyed working with Albert Finney because he was a lot of fun; Hoffman said that every time he saw him, he wanted to have a joke to make Finney laugh. The last scene in the hospital, where Charles smothered Andy, was a concern because

French movie card for *Before the Devil Knows You're Dead* (2007).

Hoffman got frightened and panicked when he couldn't breathe and feared that Finney thought this reaction was only him acting. The scene was shot in the same hospital room where Hoffman had shot a scene for *The Savages* a few months earlier. The producers advised that the original script had Andy and Hank as friends and not brothers and Lumet made the change to increase the material's intensity. He also cut the plot point of Andy and Gina having a child, and a moment where Andy snorted a bag of cocaine after Gina leaves him. Lumet commented that the car scene where Andy cries was one of the most extraordinary scenes of acting he had been involved with, and he had been involved with some pretty good ones.

Hoffman, Lumet and Ethan Hawke appeared on the *Charlie Rose* TV show on November 30, 2007, to talk about the film. Asked why he chose the script, Hoffman advised that it was unromantic and, like other Lumet films, there was an identification with the characters that made you really look inward. He thought the film showed violence that didn't allow you distance or comfort and that's also what he loved about it. Hoffman said he also responded to the story, which was striking. The actor said he read the script a couple of years prior when someone else was directing, and then Lumet brought it back to him and that made him very interested. Lumet had reportedly asked Hoffman which part he wanted to play, believing he could have played either Andy or Hank. The actor took Andy after Hawke came along and preferred to play Hank. Hoffman reported that it really bothered him in rehearsals that Andy would call Hank "faggot," although previously the actor would never question the dark side of a character. As a person Hoffman would be disgusted to call someone that word but Andy was not. The actor said that he trusted Lumet so much because he allowed him to say or do whatever he needed to say or do and he never got in his way at all, which meant a great deal to him. Hoffman reported that another important thing that Lumet did was to allow him to be anxious and scared.

Ethan Hawke commented in the February 27, 2014, *Rolling Stone* about working with Hoffman on the film. He said had known the actor for years but this was the first and only time they worked together. Hawke advised that he found the experience more intense than he had imagined. He said it was the first time he had worked with an actor of his generation who made him nervous. If you were just being charming, he would get the wash of Hoffman's disapproval. Maria Tomei recalled that, during rehearsals, Hoffman walked around with a pad of paper with scribbles all over it. He said it was a diagram of what his character was doing but to her it looked like Egyptian hieroglyphics. Hoffman advised he had to keep "the plates spinning."

On June 23, 2006, WENN picked up the story from *U.S. Weekly* that Mimi O'Donnell was expecting her second child. She was reportedly four months along and the baby was due in November.

Hoffman was credited as co-artistic director for LAByrinth's next production with Joseph Papp's Public Theater, the Jose Rivera play *School of the Americas*. Directed by Mark Wing-Davey, it ran at the LuEsther Hall from July 6 to 26, 2006. The play was historical speculation about the final day in the life of Che Guevara in October 1967 and starred John Ortiz. On August 27, 2006, it was reported that Eric Bogosian had been persuaded by Hoffman and Ortiz of LAByrinth to reprise a recent semi-solo piece in the spring. Bogosian said he thought he was done with the solo performance thing, but after Hoffman directed him in *The Last Days of Judas Iscariot* he found that Bogosian embodied the idea of the company, to be a worker among workers, and "he couldn't be more self-effacing." It is not known whether this reprised show was produced. After Hoffman's death Bogosian said that courage was Hoffman's forte, always, and that he set his bar on the highest rung, on a rung above the highest rung. Bogosian added that the actor pushed himself relentlessly until finally his efforts virtually redefined the very endeavor called acting. He said that's what Hoffman wanted: He wanted to rock the world.

Ioncinema.com reported on July 28, 2006, that the actor was to appear in Mike Nichols' exposé on American Intelligence, *Charlie Wilson's War* with Tom Hanks and Julia Roberts. Nichols and crew were to head out to Morocco in September to begin shooting the film, based on the book by *60 Minutes* producer George Crile and written by Aaron Sorkin. On August 11, 2006, it was reported that Hoffman would also star in *Synecdoche*, the directorial debut of screenwriter Charlie Kaufman. He was to play an anguished playwright with several women in his life. On August 16, 2006, it was reported by WENN that the actor was in talks to play the Penguin in the upcoming *The Dark Knight* (2008). When the movie was made, the Penguin was not in its cast of characters.

The announcement came in October 3, 2006, that Hoffman would direct Andrew Upton's drama *Riflemind* for the Sydney Theatre Company in 2007. It was to star Hugo Weaving as the front man of a once world-famous rock and roll band that attempts to make a comeback. Hoffman had befriended Upton on the film *The Talented Mr. Ripley*. The actor advised that he had known the playwright for eight years and had always felt that he was an extraordinarily bright and talented man. Hoffman commented that the play was an original and he hoped this opportunity to collaborate with Upton and the STC would be the first of many. Weaving reported that he had not seen any of Hoffman's work as a director but he admired his screen presence. He said the actor had always been fearless, he was hugely bright and burrowed his way through to the psychological truth of a character and let it all hang out, warts and all.

Hoffman was credited as one of LAByrinth's artistic directors on Stephen Belber's play *A Small, Melodramatic Story*, which ran at the Shiva Theater of the Public Theater from October 10 to November 5, 2006. Directed by Lucie Tiberghien, it told the story of Washington, D.C., widow O (Quincy Tyler Bernstine) and her complicated relationships with two men. It was lambasted by Mark Blankenship in *Variety* and Charles Isherwood in the *New York Times*.

In October 2006, Hoffman appeared in a supporting role in Universal Pictures-Relativity Media-Participant Productions-Play Tone's *Charlie Wilson's War* (2007), a comic biography reportedly based on a true story. The film was shot on location in Morocco and at the Downey Studios in Hollywood. The title character (Tom Hanks) was a Washington Congressman who in the 1980s was on the Defense Appropriations Subcommittee and helped to convince the government to fund the covert war on the Soviets who had invaded Afghanistan. For his efforts in defeating the Soviets, Wilson was awarded the title of Honored Colleague of the CIA. Hoffman, reuniting with director Mike Nichols (after *The Seagull*), played CIA case officer Gust Avrakotos, whose position on the Afghan desk led him to consult with Wilson. Gust is said to have been with the CIA for 24 years with the bulk of that time in Greece but he has been passed over for a position in Helsinki because he is considered "coarse" and lacking in diplomatic skills. He describes himself as a "street guy" and Wilson comments that Gust is not a James Bond type of spy. He swears, chews gum at the ceremony for Wilson, smokes heavily, and makes a clumsy sexual advance to Texan heiress Joanne Herring (Julia Roberts) who helps Wilson. Gust is savvy enough to bug the bottle of Scotch he brings to Wilson so that he can hear about the indictment that the Congressman may face for attending a drug party in Vegas. Gust is also shown to have a sense of humor, albeit one that Wilson says is an acquired taste. He challenges Wilson to identify the CIA strategic weapons expert among a group of young men playing chess and then points out that the expert is Mike Vickers (Christopher Denham) as the one who obviously stands out because of his clothes. Gust tells Wilson that there is no reason why CIA business can't also be fun. When the Mossad agent Zri (Ken Stott) tells how Arabs have been trained to assassinate him and his family, Gust tells him that Americans were also trained for the same purpose. He tells a Pakistani joke that ridicules Pashtun men and advises that it loses its impact in translation. Gust also tells Wilson the Greek tale of the Zen Master and the little boy as a warning that the Soviets retreating from Afghanistan will not end strife in the country. This advice will prove to be prophetic since we see how, as opposed to the interest Congress had in Afghanistan when the Soviets were there, they now have little when Wilson requests money for the country's reconstruction.

The actor wears his hair combed back and darkened, graying at the temples and on top, with Jerry DeCarlo credited as Hoffman's hair stylist. He also wears a dark moustache, tinted glasses and a series of uncoordinated suits and ties. Gust is a variation of one of Hoffman's louts but also with a sense of humor, even if deemed inappropriate, and a sense of self-awareness. Hoffman's best scene is perhaps Gust's confrontation with Henry Cravely (John Slattery) at the CIA headquarters in Langley, Virginia, over his being passed over for the Helsinki job. The actor easily expresses Gust's rage which results in a vindictive re-smashing of Cravely's office window with an instrument he takes from the glazer, who has just replaced the glass pane after Gust having reportedly having smashed it before. After Gust walks away from Cravely's office, he asks a female secretary, "How was I?"

The film premiered on December 10, 2007, in Hollywood and was given a wide release on December 21, with the taglines "A stiff drink. A little mascara. A lot of nerve. Who said they couldn't bring down the Soviet empire," "Based on a true story. You think we could make all this up?" "When the world wasn't watching, they changed it forever," and "Based on the Outrageous True Story." Todd McCarthy in *Variety* wrote that Hoffman gave another indelible performance and vibrated with conspiratorial electricity. Roger Ebert in the *Chicago Sun-Times* said that Hoffman was a smoldering volcano of frustration and unspent knowledge. The film received a mixed reaction from *Rolling Stone*'s Peter Travers wrote that Hoffman was the film's sparking live wire. It was not a box office success but Hoffman was nominated for the Best Supporting Actor Academy Award.

The actor said he enjoyed working on the film and had been very good friends with Mike Nichols for seven years after doing *The Seagull*. Hoffman felt that Nichols was one of the industry's great artists and that getting a chance to work with him is a gift. The actor said he knew the book and when he was doing *Long Day's Journey Into Night* someone had told him that if it was ever made into a film, there was a part in it that was perfect for him. So Hoffman was amused that this was the part that Nichols offered, and he thought that was a bit serendipitous. The actor said that Nichols was like Sidney Lumet in that they were both very intelligent, highly skilled and wonderful people. They had been around a long time in theater and film, and they had a lot of resources. Hoffman also admired screenwriter Aaron Sorkin. As part of his research, the actor spent some time with Hollywood's CIA advisor Milt Bearden, who was in Afghanistan and knew Gust intimately. The real Gust passed away before they started work on the film and the actor really missed meeting up with him. Hoffman commented on the responsibility of playing another real-life person by saying that the film was not a documentary and he felt his job was to interpret the character's story and there were certain truths and facts of history that helped you inform the story and which you tried to stay true to. But the actual interactions were something to be interpreted.

Hoffman said that he and Tom Hanks hit off it and described Hanks as a "mensch" and a wonderful actor. Hoffman added that Hanks as one of the producers created a wonderful work environment. Hanks commented that had had been an admirer of Hoffman, whom he considered to be one of the finest actors that had come down the pike. Julia Roberts reported that she loved doing scenes with Hoffman because she loved him and he was such fun. Hanks commented that the day Hoffman died was a horrible day for those who worked with him, and that he was a giant talent. Sorkin would later write about the discussion he and Hoffman had on the subject of drug-taking, which occurred during a break in rehearsals for the film outside the soundstage on the Paramount lot. Both men were recovering addicts and swapped stories about their experiences. Hoffman said if one of them died of an overdose, probably ten people who were about to wouldn't, meaning that the death of a famous addict might scare a few other people on the edge into getting clean. After Hoffman was found dead, Sorkin wanted to make clear that the actor didn't die from an overdose of heroin—he died from heroin. The writer felt that people should stop implying that if Hoffman had just taken the proper amount, then everything would have been fine. Sorkin said the actor didn't die because he was partying too hard or because he was depressed. Hoffman died because he was an addict.

On October 30, 2006, the actor was scheduled to be included in the ceremony in the Frederick P. Rose Hall at Jazz at Lincoln Center for the annual Mayor's Awards for Arts and Culture. Hoffman's second child with Mimi O'Donnell, a girl named Tallulah, was born in November 2006.

On January 11, 2007, *The Hollywood Reporter* wrote more about the *Synecdoche* film that the actor was set to star in. It said that it was now called *Synecdoche, New York* and Hoffman was in negotiations for it. Indie production companies Sidney Kimmel Entertainment and Anthony Bregman's Likely Story were to produce the project based on Charlie Kaufman's original screenplay, with Kaufman and Spike Jonze also serving as producers. A spring shoot in New York was anticipated. Hoffman was to play a theater director who ambitiously attempts to put on a play by creating a life-size replica of New York inside a warehouse.

At the January 15, 2007, Golden Globes ceremony, Hoffman presented the Best Actress on a Film Drama to Helen Mirren for *The Queen*. It was reported that to get him to do the presentation the Hollywood Foreign Press Association had to enlist the help of Tom Hanks, who was then shooting *Charlie Wilson's War* with the actor. Even then, Hoffman only showed up to read the nominations and make the presentation, and after that he left. This was because the actor reportedly did not enjoy making public appearances, although award ceremonies were not as bad for him as inquisitive journalists and press junkets.

Hoffman attended the 79th Annual Academy Awards ceremony held on February 25, 2007, at the Kodak Theatre. He was introduced by host Ellen DeGeneres as "last year's Academy Award winner for Best Actor and *People* magazine's sexiest man to portray Truman Capote." The actor presented the award for Best Actress to Helen Mirren for *The Queen*. He wore his hair pushed off his forehead in a messy long style (this dread-like cornrow hairstyle was for the play he was then rehearsing, *Jack Goes Boating*). Anthony Breznican, reporting on the show for *USA Today*, met up with the actor backstage. When he saw Breznican he told him that he knew him and the writer reminded Hoffman of their 2007 Sundance dinner. The actor then said "So...?" and opened his arms expectantly. He was asking whether Breznican and his wife had made a decision about the kid. They had not and Hoffman again advised to just do it. "You'll adapt, because you have to and your priorities will clarify." This encounter helped nudge the writer into the decision to have two children.

The actor next played the title role in the LAByrinth–Joseph Papp Public Theater co-production of the Bob Glaudini comedy *Jack Goes Boating*. Directed by Peter DuBois, it ran at Martinson Hall from March 18 to April 29, 2007. The play was about a married couple (John Ortiz and Daphne Rubin-Vega) who set up two oddball friends (Hoffman and Beth Cole) on a date. Hoffman played the limousine driver Jack. He smokes a lot of marijuana, listens repeatedly to the rasta anthem "Rivers of Babylon" and wears pale-blonde dreadlocks. Cole was Connie, a compulsively chatty embalmer's assistant. The production was praised by Ben Brantley in the *New York Times* who wrote that Hoffman was unrecognizable in the part and that the actor, without ever over-sentimentalizing or patronizing his character, uncovered a light-giving touch of the poet in this seemingly prosaic creature.

The actor was interviewed by Melena Ryzik for a March 5, 2007, *New York Times* article on LAByrinth. Ryzik reported that the company's operation had improved since its inception 15 years prior and one catalyst for change had been the addition of Sam Rockwell to the ensemble. The group's creative process included retreats each summer at which everyone was encouraged to write so that new plays could be found as a framework for the group's future. Known as the Summer Intensives, these get-togethers had grown from a dozen people to a hundred who gathered for more than two weeks at Bennington College in Vermont. Readings and workshops were held although at the same time people played volleyball and swam in the lake. Hoffman commented on getting into the ensemble, which was said to require more than just acting chops. Hoffman said the company was not geared toward trying to find material that would ultimately be successful since the process kind of worked against that. Sharing the duties as co-artistic directors, it was the job of Hoffman and John Ortiz to keep the egos and the establishment in check. Ortiz was described as gregarious and talkative and Hoffman not. Beth Cole said they almost worked like good cop-bad cop. She didn't mean that Ortiz was soft and Hoffman hard, but they did complement each other. Ortiz advised that it took such a long time for he and Hoffman to act together again because Hoffman preferred to direct. Glaudini said that although the two were friends, Hoffman and Ortiz also had the competitiveness of professional athletes. He said as they were considered two of the best stage actors in the country, they were continuously in training, with a spirited repartee and a playfulness that was very good.

An article was published on March 18, 2007, in the *New York Times* about Susan Feldman, founder and artistic director of St. Ann's Warehouse, the Brooklyn performance space converted from a spice-milling factory. It was reported that the space was to be soon used by screenwriter Charlie Kaufman to direct *Synecdoche, New York* which was to star Hoffman as a theater director.

On April 20, 2007, *The Hollywood Reporter* announced that the actor would co-star in writer-director John Patrick Shanley's feature adaptation of his Broadway hit *Doubt*. The project was to be produced by Scott Rudin. In the big-screen adaptation of Shanley's Pulitzer Prize- and Tony-winning play set in 1964, Meryl Streep would play Sister Aloysius, a nun and principal of a New York Catholic school who accuses a priest (Hoffman) of sexually abusing one of his students, leading to an escalating debate over his guilt or innocence.

7

Synecdoche, New York and *Doubt*

The Sidney Kimmel Entertainment-A Likely Story- Projective Testing Service-Russia-In Production comic drama *Synecdoche, New York* went into production from May 21 to August 2007 on location in various parts of New York. The film was originally to be directed by Spike Jonze.

Charlie Kaufman's story concerned Caden Cotard (Hoffman) of Schenectady, New York. He spends decades creating an uncompromising autobiographical theater piece in a New York warehouse with recreations of New York streets and buildings and thousands of actors after receiving a hefty MacArthur "Genius" grant but it never opens. Caden is presented as a self-indulgent artist where even his production of *Death of a Salesman* is pretentious in its casting of young actors in mature roles and its upstaging use of music over dialogue, a device he repeats in the funeral scene with the speech of the pastor (Christopher Evan Welch) we see in the warehouse rehearsal. Crossing his arms in front of the *Death of a Salesman* actors at rehearsal also suggests that he is an amateur. Additionally the narrative explores Caden's relationships with women, namely his first wife, artist Adele Lack (Catherine Keener); theater assistant Hazel (Samantha Morton); his second wife, actress Claire Elizabeth Keen (Michelle Williams); and Hazel's acting double Sammy (Emily Watson). Caden's relationship with women is also demonstrated by his female therapist, Dr. Madeline Gravis (Hope Davis), who behaves unprofessionally by talking over him and being seductive. Adele's unhappiness in the marriage obviously has an impact on him as she leaves him to go to Berlin with her friend Maria (Jennifer Jason Leigh) and explore lesbian relationships. She is also unsupportive of his work since she prefers to do her own painting rather than go to his opening night. When she does go, she criticizes what he has done. In a magazine interview, Adele says that she wants to be around joyous, healthy people which Caden is not. This provides her with a rationale for abandoning him. Her comment that *Death of a Salesman* reveals nothing personal will lead to his new autobiographical show, where he even casts an actor to play himself, Sammy Barnathan (Tom Noonan), and then another (Stanley Krajewski) after Sammy commits suicide.

The marriage to Adele produces a daughter, Olive, played as a four-year-old by Sadie Goldstein and as an adult by Robin Weigert. Adele moves the four-year-old to Berlin and she later becomes a full-body floral-tattooed adult peep-show entertainer named Olive Wittgart. Claire also gives Caden a daughter named Ariel but it is Olive whose absence is more felt. Caden is shown to be obsessive about his work on the new theater piece to such an extent that he never finishes it, and also obsessive about cleaning as when he cleans his house after Adele leaves and then cleans her apartment and then lives in a closet there.

His obsessions cost him intimacy in his relationships and he is presented as a duplicitous character when he has an affair with Hazel when still married to Adele, and then sees her again and lies about it when he is married to Claire. The duplicity that Olive understands he has perpetrated to abandon her for a gay lover is a lie and not even his falsely admitting to it to her on her deathbed allows her to give forgiveness. The emotional distance their physical separation has caused is amplified by them both needing to wear translating headphones to understand each other. Caden has a moment of self-awareness and self-consciousness about his juggling of women when he talks with Hazel in a bar where he has planned to meet Claire, and asks why he is bowing when he moves away from Hazel. But ultimately he will die without a romantic partner and do so in the artifice of acting as Ellen. This illusion is the opposite of the honesty and truth which he strives for in his failed theater project.

Here Hoffman was reunited with Catherine Kenner after *Capote* and Hope Davis after *Next Stop, Wonderland*. The plot's use of *Death of a Salesman* recalls the young actor's appearance in the play and prefigures the adult actor later doing it again. Hoffman, top-billed, is clean-shaven and wears glasses, and his hair is a medium-length brown that becomes lighter and recedes and gets a bald spot and then a bald scalp as Caden ages. The aging of the character also has Hoffman wearing aging makeup, though when Millicent Weems (Dianne Wiest) acts him in the play, he dyes his hair dark, before it falls out as he ages further.

The character is one of Hoffman's introverted types although he uses the same mannerisms of over-gesturing and self-conscious touching and crossed legs. The self-conscious touching extends to Caden having crossed arms and hands on his hips when he is rehearsing with actors. Writer-director Kaufman presents the actor in unflattering moments as when Caden's forehead is cut from a bathroom accident and he bleeds profusely and requires stitches. He is a sickly man whose rotted teeth are bloodied from gum surgery, who we are told has bad body odor, pustules on his face and leg, a shaking leg, takes pills, walks with a limp and uses a cane. Kaufman also supplies two extreme and unflattering closeups of the actor as he puts drops in his eyes. Caden's proclamation to Claire that he must have sex with her because she is so beautiful reads as an unusual statement for a Hoffman character, since he rarely plays this kind of sexual aggressor. The actor has many scenes where he cries although we don't see tears. Despite Caden being presented as a depressive character, Hoffman's best scenes are perhaps when he is unintentionally funny. These include when he flirts with Hazel, when he has a seizure, and most amusingly when he salivates before eating soup. However the narrative's last scene with the actor as an old man have a poignancy with hindsight in the knowledge that Hoffman would never become an old man in real life. The film credits Sara Murphy as Hoffman's assistant and Scott Glascock as his stand-in.

The film premiered at the Cannes Film Festival on May 23, 2008. It continued to be screened at festivals including the Sarajevo Film Festival on August 22; the Toronto

International Film Festival on September 9; the Athens Film Festival on September 19; the Rio de Janeiro International Film Festival on September 27; the Sitges International Fantastic Film Festival in October 2008; the Gent International Film Festival on October 16; the Chicago International Film Festival on October 19; the Zagreb Film Festival on October 21, and the London Film Festival on October 28. The film received a limited release in the U.S. starting on October 24, and then a wide release on November 21. It was praised by Manohla Dargis in the *New York Times* who wrote that Hoffman exhaled despair with every breath, and Roger Ebert in the *Chicago Sun-Times*. Todd McCarthy in *Variety* wrote that Hoffman embodied his character completely, forcing the audience to share his every physical and emotional wound. Peter Travers in *Rolling Stone* said that Hoffman was mesmerizing. It was not a box office success.

The narrative does not specify the age of Caden or the length of his life. Hoffman advised that Caden was 40 at the beginning and that he aged to 80. One of the film's producers, Anthony Bregman, reported that the character aged up to 90 years old and the makeup team was required to age Caden over 50 years. Bregman told how when Hoffman was playing Caden at 90, during a 30-minute break he would shuffle as a 90-year-old back and forth to the craft service table to get M&M's. The producer reported that the actor took 40 minutes to go forth and back so that the company observing this action were concerned for him, though it was done because Hoffman wanted to stay in character. The actor advised that he had seven different looks for Caden and that the makeup application was exhausting, and also that the skin on his face went through a real tough period because of it.

Hoffman said he met Kaufman while doing a play (presumably *Jack Goes Boating*). Hoffman found him a charming guy. He recognized that the project was a "bear" and its nine-week shooting schedule could have easily taken 15 weeks. The actor

Japanese poster for *Synecdoche, New York* (2008).

felt Kaufman as a first-time director was wonderful and similar to the specific types of auteurs he knew: an innovator, stimulating to be around. He also observed that the director had a way with women which led to what Hoffman called the all-star team of actors. Hoffman advised he had a connection with all of the female co-stars and cited his past relationship with Keener as particularly helpful.

Kaufman said the film's idea was to take dream logic and the visceral interaction that people had with their dreams and apply it to the external world. He advised that Hoffman and Keener spent a lot of time establishing a history for the couple because they were playing a long-term relationship, one that was at its end, and Kaufman wanted to feel there was substance to it. He had the actors use improvisation in rehearsal although not all of it survived in the final screenplay. Keener shot her scenes in the first two weeks of shooting so her absence after that paralleled Caden's loss of her in the narrative.

Hoffman was interviewed about the film by Edward Douglas for the *Comingsoon* website (October 20, 2008). The actor and Kaufman appeared on the October 22, 2008, *Charlie Rose* show to talk about the film. Hoffman recalled how he went out to dinner with Kaufman and the writer pitching his screenplay, and they spent time talking about what the subject brought up for the both of them in their lives. These shared anecdotes made the actor more excited about the project, because although the subject resonated with his life, it also resonated outside himself and applied to everyone's life. Hoffman reported that he would like to direct a film but he didn't want to make it his day job because it was a "bear" to manage. He advised that even directing plays, which took a shorter time, required you to put your demons on the shelf and to allow others to be crazy. Hoffman said the tricky part that Kaufman did achieve was how to manage and still be honest because he had had other directors who were not honest. Some would not tell the actors that what they were doing wasn't working or they really hadn't gotten it.

On the same date, Hoffman was interviewed by Aaron Hills for the IFC website and commented about the film. He advised that at times he was as neurotic as Caden although the actor was not as obsessed about his physical health as Caden was. Hoffman had the same real existential questions that people started to struggle with when they were about halfway through their life. The actor thought it was a film to be seen a few times because it gave you a lot to think about and the more you took in, the more accessible it became.

Robert Downey, interviewed for the 2007 book *Film Talk: Director's at Work* by Wheeler Winston Dixon, said he was working on a new script which Jonathan Demme was going to produce, *Forest Hills Bob*, and that Hoffman and Blythe Danner had agreed to be in it. It was never made.

On July 31, 2007, it was reported that Hoffman would direct the new Stephen Adly Guirgis play *Little Flower of East Orange*. This was to be a co-production between LAByrinth and the Public Theater for its 2007–2008 season. On September 25, 2007, it was reported that Waterbury, Connecticut, officials were threatening to deny a Miramax film crew access to Naugatuck's Salem School because they didn't like the theme of the film, *Doubt*, that they had hoped to shoot there. *Doubt* was based on the Pulitzer Prize-winning play that concerned a high-voltage issue—allegations of molestation against a Roman Catholic priest—but it was ambiguous on the truth of the charges. The school principal and board members didn't want the school to be used in the film but Mayor Mike Bronko said he intended to approve it. It was stated that unless a film crew performed stunts that endangered people or property or depicted sex acts or violent incidents in full public view, the state and municipalities should have no problem.

The Andrew Upton play *Riflemind* that Hoffman directed for the Sydney Theatre Company ran from October 10 to December 8, 2007, at the Wharf 1 Theatre. Hoffman commented on the play's theme of the impact that sudden fame could have on young lives by saying that he didn't think he could have been able to handle what he was now doing if he was in his 20s. He said he got to meet a lot of people and travelled to a lot of great places, which he was grateful for but there was also a lot of pressure and weirdness. While he stayed in Sydney, it was said that Hoffman had no entourage to speak of and was his characteristic low-key self, moving about quietly on his own. Hugo Weaving said that he was a lovely man, very generous and calm, and he had an inquiring mind. Susan Prior, who was also in the cast, reported that Hoffman's process had him consistently brushing away affectation and tricks.

On October 25, 2007, Hoffman participated in a tribute to Sidney Lumet at the TheTimesCenter. The event was sponsored by the Museum of the Moving Image. The actor was credited as co-artistic director for the next co-production between LAByrinth and Joseph Papp Public Theater, the Bob Glaudini play *A View from 151st Street*. The show, directed by Peter DuBois, ran at the LuEsther Hall from October 18 to November 4, 2007. Set in Harlem, it starred Craig (muMs) Grant as street drug dealer and amateur rapper Delroy. A buy goes wrong, and this results in the shooting of police detective Daniel (Juan Carlos Hernandez).

Hoffman attended the Gotham Independent Film Awards held at the Steiner Studios in Brooklyn on November 27, 2007. He was quoted about how *Before the Devil Knows You're Dead* and the historical biography *Talk to Me* (2007) tied for the ensemble award, saying, "It's cool to share, that's what I tell my kids." The show was broadcast on the Documentary Channel on December 4, 2007.

The actor was interviewed by Steve "Frosty" Weintraub for an article published on November 28, 2007, in *Collider*. In it he spoke about *The Savages, Before the Devil Knows You're Dead* and *Charlie Wilson's War*. Hoffman was asked how difficult it was to shift from characters and whether he could leave them behind right away. He replied that he was able to do so immediately. Once he was done with something, he was done, and then getting the motor started again was actually tough when he was working a lot. Hoffman said it was like his body and mind were saying "Don't work, take a break," but he had to get it because that was life.

He was asked how the Writers Guild of America strike affected his future projects. Questioned about the *Capote* awards circuit, he said it was fun at times but was also a very stressful thing. Hoffman said he was obviously grateful and that ultimately the circuit experience was not a bad thing. When Weintraub asked the actor where he kept his Oscar, Hoffman pretended to pull it out of his jacket.

Asked what he liked to do when he wasn't working, Hoffman said he hung out with his kids. When asked if he would teach his kids about theater or acting, he advised that they were around it because of himself and his girlfriend. Their son went with them to the theater when they went and that was their introduction since it was the life they were in. He didn't think they were going to need any kind of classes or to be taught by them because they were seeing right in front of their eyes.

The Miramax Films-Scott Rudin Productions mystery *Doubt*, shot in New York, had a screenplay by its director John Patrick Shanley. He reported on the DVD audio commentary that it was filmed from December 2007 to January 2008. According to other sources, the shooting period was from September 2007 to July 2008 or from December 10, 2007, to February 2, 2008. The story was set in 1964 at the St. Nicholas Catholic school in the Bronx church parish where the Sister of Charity principal Sister Aloysius Beauvier (Streep) questions the relationship between a troubled 12-year-old Negro student, Donald Miller (Joseph Foster II), and the priest Father Brendan Flynn (Hoffman). The play had run on Broadway at the Walter Kerr Theatre from March 31, 2005, to July 2, 2006, and had starred Cherry Jones as Beavier and Brian F. O'Byrne as Flynn. It had been directed by Doug Hughes and had won Tony Awards for Best Play, Best Actress in a Play, Best Featured Actress in a Play, and Best Director of a Play. It also won for Shanley the 2005 Pulitzer Prize for Drama. Tom Hanks, John Cusack and David Hyde Pierce were considered for the role of play Father Flynn and Hoffman reportedly threatened to leave the project if Amy Adams was not cast as Sister James.

Father Flynn is presented as a sign of the new times for the church in his approach to the children: He wants to be friendlier, as opposed to the more formal approach by Sister Aloysius who is proud that the children are terrified of her. He is more approachable than her as when the student Noreen Horan (Bridget Clark) tells him how she is in love with a boy student and Flynn advises her to tell the boy. Flynn says that his caring for Donald comes out of compassion and is similar to the kindness demonstrated by the history teacher Sister James (Amy Adams), as opposed to the strictness and cruelty of Aloysius. These differing philosophies extend to how we see Flynn and Aloysius interact with their fellows where he laughs at dinner with the other priests but she has silent meals with the other nuns. Flynn is also a bit of a dandy in having and being proud of long fingernails, and keeps dried flower petals in his Bible. He also has a sweet tooth where he asks for three lumps of sugar in his tea when Aloysius has no sugar, using a ballpoint pen which she disapproves of, and suggesting "Frosty the Snowman" for the Christmas pageant which she rejects. We also see that Flynn smokes cigarettes, which we assume she would also not approve of. The fact that Flynn is Aloysius' superior perhaps allows him to take her chair in her office when he attends a meeting about the pageant, but he also closes the window blind she has opened because the sun bothers him, takes a second cup of tea that is offered to him, insults her by interpreting her opinion of the rejected song as the inspiration for a sermon on intolerance, stands as the nuns sit, and initially refuses to discuss his relationship with Donald with her.

These differences between Flynn and Aloysius make them antagonists, and her dislike for him allows for her belief that he has acted inappropriately with Donald. Flynn has a ballerina toy that he gives to Donald; we later see other students break it when he is bullied and this confirms what Flynn claims, that the boy is troubled and therefore needs special attention. This trouble will extend to what his mother (Viola Davis) tells Aloysius about Donald, that his father beats him because of his nature, which seems to be code for him being gay. We never hear from Donald as to what happened when he was alone with Flynn in the rectory. We also don't hear from Donald as to whether he did actually drink altar wine that James smells on his breath or whether Flynn gave it to him. This leads to Donald being removed from the altar boys. James sees Flynn putting Donald's undershirt in the boy's locker; Flynn explains that the boy had left it in the sacristy. The most damning incident is when James sees Flynn hug Donald after holding out his hand to help the boy stand after we see him bullied and the toy broken. Touching the children in an affectionate way is perceived as inappropriate, although the touching by Aloysius as punishment is apparently acceptable. This touching is what confirms to Aloysius that Flynn has made advances to the boy. She succeeds in removing him from the school, after Flynn resigns, though ironically we learn that he is then promoted to pastor at the St. Jerome church and school. But the narrative ends with Aloysius' belief of Flynn's abuse after she tells James that she now has doubts.

Top-billed Streep is given a star entrance by Shanley: She is first seen from behind and the reveal of her face is delayed. Second-billed Hoffman is not given the equivalent kind of coverage. As Father Flynn he is clean-shaven and he wears his hair short, sometimes combed back. As a priest Hoffman wears white-collared black robes and white-collared black pants and shirts, as well as a green and a purple vestment for church services. We also see Flynn in sweats when he plays basketball with the schoolboys. The actor uses shifty eyes to suggest an ambiguity in Flynn and his comfort level with the schoolboys also allows for the suspicion over him. Hoffman tries to make Flynn likable so that we can believe him rather than Aloysius, but doesn't quite succeed. Perhaps what he provides is the emotional separation that comes from being a priest and not a natural man, and an authoritative figure. Shanley seems to have stacked the odds against Flynn since his characterizations give her more individuality than he so that when he is removed from the narrative his absence is felt less than hers might have been. Hoffman's best scene is perhaps the 11-minute confrontation with Aloysius, where Hoffman's directness is compared to Streep's theatrical and fussy performance. The film credits Sara Murphy and Eliza Czander as his assistants and Tim Wilson as his stand-in.

The film was premiered at the AFI Film Festival on October 30, 2008, and had its Hollywood premiere on November 19, with Hoffman attending. Its New York premiere was on December 8, again with Hoffman in attendance. Its limited release began on December 12. The film was then given a wide release on December 25 with the tagline "There is no evidence. There are no witnesses. But for one, there is no doubt." Peter Travers in *Rolling Stone* wrote that Hoffman nailed every nuance in a complex role. Todd McCarthy in *Variety* wrote that Hoffman's performance was ambiguous enough to make the viewer continue to wonder about Flynn and, crucially, to fear that Aloysius might actually be right. He said the actor was particularly effective in his sermons, delivering his thoughtful remarks with a clarity and intellectual pertinence that many pastors might envy. A box office success, the film received Academy Award nominations for Best Actress for Streep, Best Supporting Actor for Hoffman, Best Supporting Actress for Adams and Davis, and Best Adapted Screenplay for Shanley. It won none of them.

Hoffman advised that he was a fan of the play but he never thought about playing Flynn until Shanley asked him to, which took the actor by surprise. Hoffman felt the play was a great piece for actors. He had seen it a couple of times but said he tried to think about it as if he hadn't seen it. The actor thought that he probably could have done the part without doing any research, but he did, talking to Father Jim, who was a friend, because Hoffman wanted to know what certain things meant. He had seen some sermons done before but he went and saw a couple while he was rehearsing.

The actor was skeptical of plays transferred to film since he said they were not always done well and they lost their power. He felt that playwrights sometimes had a hard time directing their plays but he thought Shanley knew exactly what he wanted to do. Hoffman said Shanley also had a really great way about him on the set so he had no doubt that he was the man for the job the whole time. Hoffman felt very blessed to be in that company. He had met Viola Davis in his mid–20s, had known Streep for nine years, and had done two films with Amy Adams. Hoffman said this time it was beneficial to be working with friends, and loved working with Streep.

In *Doubt* (2008).

Shanley believed that Hoffman was one of *the* most surprising, mercurial and powerful actors. He advised that he had known Hoffman for about ten years before they made the film though they had never worked together. He said he and the actor sort of circled each other, amiable and wary in equal measure. LAByrinth had produced his plays *Where's My Money?* in 2001, *Dirty Story* in 2003 and *Sailor's Song* in 2004. Streep commented that Hoffman was one of her favorite people that she had worked with in her life. Streep said that Hoffman brought so many layers to the humanity of the parts he played. Shanley advised that on the days they shot the meeting scene, Hoffman was sick with a cold that made him miserable. The actor would lie around semi-comatose until the moment he had to shoot, and then stand up and pull it all together and play it with unbelievable authority. Shanley reported that between takes, Streep would mutter to Hoffman that she knew Flynn had interfered with the boy, as a mind game to try to just get inside the actor's head and undermine him. In response, Hoffman would just chuckle and say, "Stop talking. Leave me alone," and go on with his work.

Hoffman, Shanley, Streep and Adams appeared on the December 12, 2008, *Charlie Rose* show. Shanley said he cast Hoffman against Streep to make her sweat. In the December 19, 2008, *New York Times,* Hoffman commented that, as usual for him, he struggled with the character. He said on every film he would have nights where he woke up at two in the morning and think, "I'm awful in this." In the article, Shanley reported that during the shooting, the actor seemed to be in a lot of pain. He would smoke cigarette after cigarette and stare out the window and the director was afraid to say anything to him. But after the film was finished, Hoffman would say how much fun he had.

Shanley would respond by telling him that he looked like he was in hell and the actor would just shrug and joked: "Hell? That's where I live."

In January 2008 it was reported that Hoffman was interested in appearing in Steven Spielberg's new film *The Trial of the Chicago 7*. Due to go into production later in the year, it would tell the story of the conspiracy trial which grew out of protests at the 1968 Democratic Convention. To date the film has not been made.

A Writers Guild of America strike affected the Golden Globes ceremony: The usual gaggle of stars at a rollicking, banquet-style event was replaced by a stripped-down affair modeled on a news conference. It was broadcast live on NBC on January 14, 2008, with no actors in attendance. Hoffman lost the award for Best Supporting Actor in a Film Drama for *Charlie Wilson's War* to Javier Bardem for his role the thriller *No Country for Old Men* (2007).

Hoffman was credited as co-artistic director for LAByrinth's co-production with Joseph Papp Public Theater of the Brett C. Leonard play *Unconditional*. Directed by Mark Wing-Davey, the show ran at the LuEsther Hall from February 18 to March 9, 2008. It featured nine New York stories that converged in an explosive tale of love, justice, race, rage and betrayal. It received mixed reactions from Sam Thielman in *Variety* and Charles Isherwood in the *New York Times*.

Hoffman attended the Independent Spirits Awards on February 23, 2008, in Santa Monica, California, where he won Best Male Lead for *The Savages*. Accepting the award, he said he felt as if he had gained two sisters in making the film, "the sublime" Laura Linney and director Tamara Jenkins. The show's host Rainn Wilson (from the TV comedy *The Office*) and Hoffman reportedly mock-taunted each other from the podium all day, with Wilson describing the actor's physical effect in less-than-flattering terms. Hoffman ended his speech by reporting that he was going to kick Wilson's backside. At the end of the show, Wilson got up to thank the crowd and then said he was going down to settle things with Hoffman, threatening to kill him. The throwdown between the two revealed that Hoffman's past experience as a wrestler had left him with some moves and he ended up on top, spanking Wilson. The incident wasn't pretty, since both men "sold a little crack," but it was said to be pretty damn funny.

The actor attended the 80th Annual Academy Awards ceremony on February 24, 2008, at the Kodak Theatre which was televised by ABC. He got a closeup when his name was announced as one of the Best Supporting Actors nominees. He again lost to *No Country for Old Men*'s Javier Bardem. Hoffman was reportedly not too upset by not winning, since he was said to be known as somebody with very little taste for the pomp and silliness of the awards campaign. The actor commented, "What do I really have to complain about after the past few years?" which had seen him win the Best Actor Oscar in 2005 for *Capote* and (just the day before) the best actor at the Independent Spirits for *The Savages*. Hoffman said it had been a lovely time, working on *Charlie Wilson's War* and working with Sidney Lumet. He called it a nice run for a working actor.

On the *Before the Devil Knows You're Dead* DVD audio commentary, the actor commented that he was scheduled to work with Michael Shannon on a play in February. This play was presumably Stephen Adly Guirgis' *The Little Flower of East Orange* which was produced by the Joseph Papp Public Theater and LAByrinth Theater Company.

7. Synecdoche, New York *and* Doubt

The show was described as a modern ghost story. Directed by Hoffman, it ran at Martinson Hall from April 6 to May 4, 2008. It was reported in the *New York Times* on February 24, 2008, that it was to star Ellen Burstyn as a patient in a Manhattan charity hospital. Shannon played the role of Danny, Burstyn's character's son and the play's narrator, a writer with a history of substance abuse. David Rooney in *Variety* wrote that Hoffman plowed through, pushing his cast to abrasive extremes, and the play's awkward timeshifts were negotiated with messy flourishes that lacked fluidity. Ben Brantley in the *New York Times* wrote that the production needed a more disciplined staging than Hoffman had imposed upon it.

He next appeared in the Universal Pictures-StudioCanal-A Working Title Production musical comedy *The Boat That Rocked* a.k.a. *Pirate Radio* (2009). Written and directed by Richard Curtis, it was shot from March 3 to June 18, 2008, on location in England including on the former Dutch hospital ship *Timor Challenger* moored in Portland Harbor, Dorset and at the Shepperton and Pinewood Studios in London. A British boat anchored in the north seas of England in 1966 houses the Radio Rock radio station which broadcasts rock and pop music 24 hours a day. Hoffman played the part of the Count, the only American amongst the disc jockeys. The Count has been brought in to replace British disc jockey Gavin Cavanagh (Rhys Ifans) and he holds a resentment towards him, which is intensified when he learns that Gavin slept with Elenore (January Jones), the new bride of Simon Swafford (Chris O'Dowd). The Count declares war against Gavin and he instigates the chicken game where both men compete to climb up the boat's mast before jumping into the sea. The action results in the Count having a broken arm and hand. While Gavin clearly wins the game, the Count tells him that he was wrong in his bad feeling over Gavin. The Count as an American citizen is the first to say he will not abide by the government decision that further broadcasting is illegal, and this leads the others to join him. When the boat begins to sink, he decides to stay, and we fear that he has drowned when the boat goes under. Then the Count appears in the sea.

Hoffman is top-billed but in terms of screen time he has less than Clark (Tom Sturridge), the godson of the group's leader Quentin (Bill Nighy) and who lives on board. Hoffman wears a full beard and his hair in a messy medium-length style. The Count is another variation on one of Hoffman's louts. He is also a bit of a hippie and uses "man" as an address, smokes, drinks and swears. The Count is perhaps more obnoxious than other Hoffman louts in his arrogance about his music preference. We get to see Hoffman dancing and singing a little, playing basketball and wearing a Santa suit at Christmas. The actor comically shakes his head when the Count says "stag" to suggest that the disc jockeys have a pub-crawl before the wedding of Simon. The chicken game sees Hoffman making the Count's fearful climb comic, and he asks himself why he is so fat since this inhibits his climbing ability. The actor's best scene is perhaps the quiet one he has with Clark where he claims that these are the best days of his life.

The film was released in the United Kingdom on April 1, 2009, and in the United States on November 13, 2009, with the taglines "1 Boat. 8 DJs. No Morals," "They rocked. They rolled. Then they sank," and "On air. Off shore. Out of control." It was praised by Manohla Dargis in the *New York Times* and Roger Ebert in the *Chicago Sun-Times.* Derek Elley in *Variety* wrote that Hoffman melded well with the Brit cast and Peter

Travers in *Rolling Stone* said that Hoffman had a rowdy good time of it. It was not a box office success.

Hoffman appears in several deleted scenes that are featured on the DVD of the film. These include him giving a note to Simon before the Count takes two girls to his cabin for sex; the Count leading his fellows to sabotage the station of the Radio Sunshine boat anchored near the Radio Rock boat and then the men listening to the next broadcast and hearing the result of their sabotage; the Count being introduced with his fellows by Quentin to the visiting boatload of girls who refuse to applaud Angus (Rhys Darby); the Count leaving Harold to broadcast while the fellows go on their pub crawl (Hoffman does anther funny dance); the Count taking them to see the exterior of the Abbey Road studio where the Count does a salute to The Beatles; the Count leading the fellows in exercise, and more. Another deleted scene has Gavin explain to Carl why he left the station to allow for him to be replaced by the Count. Gavin says that he was in search of the meaning of life and has returned after he discovered that the meaning was rock and roll.

Japanese poster for *The Boat That Rocked* (2009).

The actor had gotten hold of the script, read it, and was drawn to the Count because he considered himself the best DJ who had ever existed. Hoffman thought the script was funny and also oddly moving, with a serious undercurrent of how much music meant to people and how much it informed lives. He took the role because he was playing a foreigner in the almost completely British cast of characters and there was something to be said for not belonging to that tribe. Hoffman said when he showed up to film his scenes, he felt a little bit like a fish out of water but soon he was having a great time hanging out and felt like he belonged. He considered the film a real ensemble piece with no real lead in it, although if there was any protagonist it would be the Clark character, and he was just one of the DJs on the boat sharing that burden with all. Hoffman reported that the cast all took seasickness pills for the scenes shot at sea because the conditions were quite rough at times. They also had to remember to put on sunblock to avoid sunburn. The actor commented that day in and day out, being out on the boat in the middle of the water created quite an atmosphere. It would take 45 minutes to get six miles out to sea and even longer to return to the dock so the days were long. The current and the wind would constantly move the boat, and they had to have tugboats keeping the boat in position. Hoffman also said that the music selections brought him back to his own early childhood. He believed that rock and roll was one of the more important essences in his life. The actor advised that Curtis actively encouraged all the actors to improvise lines, partly because a lot of them were comedians. Hoffman considered Curtis to be a pretty sharp writer so he tried to follow what he had since that was usually funnier.

Curtis said that the character of the Count was based on the real-life American DJ Emperor Rosko. He advised that Hoffman was known to the other cast members as the Big Badger. He arrived to the film a few weeks after the other actors because of scheduling conflicts. He missed the boot camp and boat camp experiences that the other actors went through together, which was four days and three nights of living and rehearsing on the boat. Hoffman said he never slept on the boat which he was glad for because it was very tiny. From when he arrived on the set, he filmed all day every single day and he had one hour in which to learn how to be a DJ. Curtis said that Hoffman soon looked like he had been doing it all his life. The director said the actor was initially nervous but gave a brilliant performance and praised what he called Hoffman's extraordinarily naturalistic work.

Co-star Rhys Ifans commented that it was crucial that Hoffman fit in since the film was an ensemble piece and he felt the actor did with flying colors. Tom Sturridge advised that playing the Count made Hoffman's competitive edge take over. The loose way in which the movie was filmed, with cameras on shoulders, bred an environment of all these kind of massive comic egos trying to compete to seduce the camera operator and it generated an amazing energy.

Curtis advised that the mast-climbing scene was shot with stunt men, the actors perched on the side of a cliff, and green screen technology. Hoffman and Ifans only climbed five feet and then the stunt men continued, and the actor would not leave the location on the day the climbs were shot until his stuntman was safely out of the sea. Curtis also advised that the deck scene where the Count talks about the best days of his life was an idea that Hoffman came up with, since he felt that the man had a fundamental depressing streak and fought hard against it by being celebratory and determined about things. To the actor, this was more than just the Count believing that it was bad luck how the good times were over. Curtis said the idea also came from something autobiographical: He knew a man who was a pilot in World War II and, even though his life during the conflict had been at risk every day, when the war was over he could never get any joy out of life because he had lived so large. Curtis also advised that originally the Count emerged on a mast of the boat after it had capsized and then resurfaced before sinking.

The April edition of *Interview* magazine reported that Hoffman was one of many friends of the late Heath Ledger to talk about their relationship with him. Hoffman advised that he met Ledger when they were both nominated for the Best Actor Oscar in 2006. Hoffman also commented on the actor in *People* magazine on March 13, 2008.

In a March 23, 2008, *New York Times* article about British actor Simon Pegg and the sports romantic comedy film *Run, Fat Boy, Run* (2007), it was revealed that Hoffman had been under consideration for the part that Pegg eventually played: Dennis, a schlubby loser who decides to get in shape and run a marathon to get his former fiancée back. Director David Schwimmer lost the American financing for the project and when the script was eventually picked up by a British company, this made Pegg the director's "natural first choice," with the fact that he had previously worked with the actor also a consideration.

Interviewed by Lawrie Masterson in the April 6, 2008, *SMH Entertainment* magazine, Hoffman spoke about *Before the Devil Knows You're Dead*, *The Savages* and *Riflemind*. In the April 2008 *Filmink Magazine* Hoffman talked about those three films plus *Charlie Wilson's War* and winning the Oscar. He commented that at this time he felt that he was the kind of actor who made a little bit of a difference, which is something that was important to him. On winning awards for *Capote* Hoffman said it was surreal and he went through a lot of different feelings. Up until that point he had never really won any acting awards though he had been nominated for a lot of things. Then he got to have a year where he experienced going to every award show and winning every time. Hoffman said it was a good thing for him because, now that he had experienced it, it was a good reference for the rest of his life. He reported that having children had changed his priorities of working and time and scheduling things, since now it was all about spending as much time with them as he could. Hoffman said he had been working a lot lately and was looking forward to a break. Asked what a day with his four-year-old son Cooper and his two-year-old daughter Tallulah was like, the actor advised that when you played with a child the day could be anything. It was up to what struck their fancy and all his children wanted from him was to be there for them and to be focused. The article mentioned that Hoffman was scheduled to play lawyer and agitator William Kunstler in Steven Spielberg's *The Trial of the Chicago 7*, a film which still has not been made.

Hoffman next played a cameo role in the Focus Features International-Radar Pictures-Media Rights Capital comic fantasy *The Invention of Lying* (2009). Written and directed by Ricky Gervais and Matthew Robinson, it was shot in London and in Lowell, Massachusetts from April 14 to June 2008. British Lecture Films screenwriter Mark Bellison (Gervais) is in his 40s and lives in an American town at an unspecified time where people only speak the brutal truth. Fired from his job and threatened with eviction from his home, he discovers that lying makes him rich and successful and helps him to romance office executive Anna McDoogles (Jennifer Garner). Hoffman played Jim the bartender, one of the people whom Mark initially tries out his lies on and who believes whatever Mark says. Jim agrees with Mark's best friend Greg (Louis C.K.) that the thing they would do, if they could do anything in the world, would be to "touch girls' boobs" and have sex with them. Hoffman plays this character not as one of his louts, but rather with understatement as if Jim is not too bright. The actor only appears in one scene and wears the same full beard he wore in *The Boat That Rocked*.

The film premiered at the Toronto International Film Festival on September 14, 2009, and then opened in the United States on October 2 with the taglines "In a world where everyone can only tell the truth ... this guy can lie," and "In a world where everyone can only tell the truth, he's just invented the lie!" Justin Chang of *Variety* wrote that Hoffman had a brief memorable turn, and Manohla Dargis in the *New York Times* said that Hoffman was an appealing guest star. It was a box office success.

When the moviemakers tried to secure Hoffman for a cameo, his agent claimed he was too busy. Gervais emailed Hoffman that there was very little money involved as he had spent the budget on testicular implants but added, "Don't look upon them as my testicles, look at them as our testicles." Hoffman loved it and signed on. After the actor died, Gervais said it was such shocking and sad news, that he was one of the greatest actors of a generation, and a sweet, funny and humble man.

On June 22, 2008, there was a benefit reading of Stephen Adly Guirgis' play *Jesus Hopped the A Train* at New York's Town Hall, directed by Hoffman. The reading also attracted the 2000 production's entire original cast. *The Hollywood Reporter* wrote on June 26, 2008, that Hoffman and his New York-based Cooper's Town Prods. had inked a two-year, first-look deal with Overture Films. The companies set as their first project *Unconditional*, which had been produced as a play at the LAByrinth Theater Company earlier in the year. Brett C. Leonard was to adapt his own work for the screen. The film was never made.

On July 30, 2008, WENN wrote about the next installment of the *Batman* movie series and quoted *The National Enquirer* that studio bosses wanted Hoffman to play the Penguin. The rumor continued when Michael Caine, who played Alfred in the series, told MTV on September 8, 2008, at the Toronto Film Festival that Warner Bros. executives told him of their desire to secure Hoffman. On September 9 Hoffman responded to the rumor, saying no one had ever talked to him about it. He said the rumor had begun five years prior in the press and the actor found it funny. Hoffman advised that he had never met director Christopher Nolan, his interest in comic book movies was purely on a fan level, and he intended to keep it that way. The actor said that as a kid he was a big comic book collector and admitted that he didn't know if he would be a good Penguin, so he would rather see someone else do it.

WENN reported on August 8, 2008, that the actor was to make his West End debut as a director with *Riflemind*. The show was to star John Hannah and was set to open in September at London's Trafalgar Studios. On August 14, 2008, *The Hollywood Reporter* wrote that Hoffman's Cooper's Town Productions was joining with Big Beach Films to develop a film of *Jack Goes Boating*. Hoffman was said to be eyeing the project as a potential directing vehicle. The Off-Broadway play was written by Bob Glaudini and had been produced by the LAByrinth Theater Company in 2007.

When *Synecdoche, New York* was screened at the Toronto Film Festival in September 2008, Hoffman was interviewed by Paul Fischer for the Female.com.au website. The actor said he felt lucky, like he had been given more than most people should be given as actors. Hoffman advised that he wasn't trying to be selective, he just wanted to do things he wanted to do. He also said that he had to keep his gratitude in check because he knew offers of the same magnitude weren't going to come to him forever. He still thought he would get offers as he aged but there wouldn't be as much available so he wanted to take advantage of them now. Hoffman tried not to make choices based on career and admitted that there were other things that came into play, like the schedule in his life and money issues. He felt that ultimately he stayed close to his gut, following the path he had been following since he was a teenager, just moving where his heart took him. Asked if he wanted to do more comedy, Hoffman replied that he thought he did a lot of it. He was always baffled by that question, since he felt that a lot of the dramatic pieces he had done had a lot of humor in them and this is why he was drawn to them.

He said there was no film role that he wished to come back to and no sequels because he was *so* not that guy. Hoffman advised that he turned down Todd Solondz's offer to reprise the character from the film *Happiness*, suggesting that the director cast someone else because he thought it would be interesting to see them anew. Solondz did not agree at first but since Hoffman flatly refused to repeat the role, he had no choice. The actor said he also refused to replay the same parts on stage since once you had said goodbye to something, it was hard to invite that thing back. Hoffman felt that reprising a role after many years was possible if he had grown as a person and his perception of the character had changed. However, he felt that after many years there were roles that he couldn't play any more and you weren't supposed to play any more. Hoffman said you had to kind of give it up and admit that you had lost that chance, like playing Biff and Happy in *Death of a Salesman*.

The actor reported that there was no classic part that he yearned to play but that he did an episode of the children's cartoon *Arthur* for his children because he felt that was a great reason to do so. He was thought it would be fun to do a great kids' movie so that he could take his kids to the premieres, but one had not been offered to him. Hoffman also spoke about his production company Cooper's Town and the films they were trying to get off the ground. Hoffman said Emily Ziff handled the business side and he did the creative end like developing projects and working hands-on with directors or directing himself. The actor was presently directing the play *Riflemind* in London.

On September 15, 2008, Hoffman joined Cate Blanchett and Andrew Upton, co-artistic directors of the Sydney Theatre Company, and Howard Panter, the creative director and joint chief executive of the Ambassador Theater Group in London, to announce the formation of a new alliance. This was between LAByrinth, the Sydney Theatre Company and the Ambassador Theater Group which owned Trafalgar Studios of London. Panter said that the plan was to build on the new creative bridge between these international companies and to regularly produce and exchange work which might not otherwise be seen in their different cities. The first joint production was *Riflemind* with Hoffman directing, set to open that week in London's West End at the Trafalgar Studios. The play opened on September 18, 2008, with John Hannah in the lead role but the rest of the original Australian cast restored. It was to have run until January 2009 but closed early (on September 23) after brutal reviews and desultory box office sales.

The Hollywood News reported on September 29, 2008 that a sequel to *The Big Lebowski* was in the works and that Hoffman might rejoin the cast. However this film was never made.

8

Mary and Max, Jack Goes Boating

On October 1, 2008, *Variety* wrote that Hoffman had signed on to voice the leading role of Max in Icon's Aussie stop motion claymation feature *Mary and Max*. The film would look at the unlikely pen pal friendship between Mary, a chubby, lonely Melbourne, Australia, eight-year-old, and Max, a 44-year-old, severely obese Jewish man with Asperger's Syndrome living in New York. It was the first feature from writer-director Adam Elliot, whose animated comedic short *Harvie Krumpet* (2003) won the 2004 Oscar for Best Animated Short Film. Mark Gooder of Icon said that the fact that one of the world's most "in demand" actors had agreed to voice an independent Australian animation spoke volumes for the creative integrity of the project. Elliot said Max was based on a pen pal he had been corresponding with for 20 years who lived in New York and had Asperger's.

A Screen Australia/Australian Melodrama Pictures/Film Victoria-SBS Television Australia-Adorondack Pictures production, *Mary and Max* (2009) was shot in Melbourne. The film was said to be have been based on a true story. Mary Daisy Dinkle as a girl was voiced by Bethany Whitmore as a girl and by Toni Collette as a woman. She lived in the Melbourne suburb of Mount Waverley. Her friendship with Max Jerry Horovitz (Hoffman) spanned from 1976 to approximately 1990.

The two have a lot in common and in addition to their letters they also send photographs and gifts. Mary's gift of a pom-pom will have a special impact on Max as he wears it on top of his yarmulke, and she also sends him a bottle of her tears since he claims he cannot produce his own. The two are lonely despite the fact that they have human contact and pets (Max even has an invisible imaginary friend) and they love chocolate. Mary is in love with her neighbor Damian Popodopolous (voiced by Eric Bana) while Max has no romantic love. When Mary asks him about love, he has a major anxiety attack that lands him in a mental ward for eight months.

Max's neurosis also extends to his collecting flies, his cut toenails and cigarette butts from the street; he also irons and laminates and files Mary's letters. He is described as "retarded" and later is diagnosed with Asperger's Syndrome. Max's influence on Mary initially has her saving money to come and visit him, something she stops once he stops writing to her. Max never attempts to visit her in Australia, even when he wins the lottery and has the financial means to do so. Max's influence on Mary is also demonstrated when she becomes a psychology student at the university and her thesis is on Asperger's as a disorder of the mind and she uses him as a case study. It is the fact that her thesis is published as a book, *Dissecting the Asperger's Mind* with Max's photograph on the cover, which makes him break from her a second time, even though she offers to share the royalties.

Max's break causes Mary to become depressed and alcoholic and to neglect Damian whom she had married and who leaves her. Max's break is symbolized by his sending her the M typewriter hammer, which Mary will return to him when she finally goes to New York to visit him. Her friendship with Max and the hurt she has apparently caused him with the book has her sacrifice it and her career when she pulps all the books. Max's forgiveness and his gift of his collection of Noblet figurines brings her out of her depression. This also motivates her to finally visit him in New York, although Max dies the very morning of her arrival.

Max resembles Alfred Hitchcock but also Hoffman in that he has a stocky build with a protruding stomach and he is described as six feet and 353 pounds. The character is also *un*like the actor as he is bald and has a long nose and protruding ears. Hoffman uses a New York accent for Max and he also speaks Yiddish. His performance amounts to reciting four letters to Mary and also one to the New York mayor as he types. We also hear the actor breathe, gasp, moan, sigh, eat and slurp, fart, burp, snore, make robot noises and yell in anxiety and anger. An interesting plot point is that Max is unable to produce tears when he cries, since this is also lacking in Hoffman's acting range.

The film premiered at the Sundance Film Festival on January 15, 2009. It was then screened at the Berlin International Film Festival on February 9; the Edinburgh International Film Festival in June; the Paris Cinema on July 14; the Film and Art Festival Two Riversides on August 3; the Festival Internacional de Cine de Monterrey on August 21; the L'Étrange Festival on September 13; and the Buster Copenhagen International Film Festival for Children and Youth and the Athens Film Festival on September 21. It opened in the U.S. on September 25, 2009, with the taglines "Two unlikely people. Two different worlds come together in a story about a most unusual friendship" and "Sometimes perfect strangers make the best friends." Justin Chang of *Variety* wrote that Hoffman was superbly schlubby and hard to recognize. The film was not a box office success.

Hoffman's voice was recorded in a studio in New York via a remote hook-up, with another source reporting that he was piped in for two sessions in New York and London. Adam Elliot advised that the film's budget could not bring the actor to Australia; the director therefore never met Hoffman in the flesh, and only saw him on Skype when he was recording his part. Hoffman understood that the usual process was to record the voice first and then the animation was done with the help of seeing the actor's face; this was a different situation. Hoffman felt this was a better way because it wasn't about them making a character of him but him helping to inform what Elliot had created. Hoffman commented that the film was very graphic about certain things, like suicide, which made it a little more geared toward young teens and adults. He said children could see the film but there were things in it that he didn't know that he wanted *his* six-year-old to watch. (Hoffman admitted that his son *had* watched a lot of things that he probably shouldn't have, because he (Hoffman) as a parent wasn't too strict about that.) Hoffman said that Elliot made a great film, and he was really glad he did it.

On October 8, 2008, the website dreadcentral.com reported rumors that Hoffman was in talks to join Vanikoro. Xavier Gens' film told the story of Jean-Francois de Galaup, a French explorer who in 1788 mysteriously disappeared with his entire crew. The movie draws the conclusion that the ship and its crew ran afoul of cannibals on the titular island.

Hoffman's episode of the Cookie Jar Entertainment–WGBH Kids family animated comedy *Arthur* aired on October 12, 2009. The series, based on the Arthur adventure books by Marc Brown, centered on Arthur Read (Dallas Jokic), an eight-year-old aardvark, and his family and friends. The 12-minute "No Acting Please" was the first half of the 30-minute episode, written by Cusi Cram with a storyboard by Elie Klimos, Nadja Cozic and Elise Benoit. The show was directed by Greg Bailey. Hoffman voiced the part of William Fillmore Toffman, the most famous theater director in Elwood City, who has come back to stage a revival of his first play *It Began with a Whistle*. Francine (Jodie Resther), Muffy (Melissa Altro) and Fern (Holly G. Frankel) audition for the part of Little Lucie, the only kid in the play, and Fern is cast. Toffman is temporarily swayed by Muffy's attempt to be cast when she also offers him chocolate, presumably to compensate for her bad acting. However he is professional enough to give Fern a chance too, though we don't see her audition. Toffman stops a rehearsal where Fern upstages the other actors performing as she verbalizes preparation exercises, and tells her that acting is reacting and listening. When Fern delivers her line in a melodramatic way, Toffman has the actors take a break so that he can stroll with her and instruct her how to play it. After the show, where Fern messes up her line by improvising, Toffman calls it genius. Most importantly, he felt she was really listening. When he suggests for the next performance that they

Japanese poster for *Mary and Max* (2009).

restage the blocking of her scene, she asks whether they can give her another line. To this, Toffman replies that he is not the playwright, just the director, which is presumably a no.

The writer has fun with Hoffman's name as well as parodying the actor's stage credits by having Toffman credited with *True East* and *Jenny Hopped the C Train*. Hoffman is drawn as a bear with pink ears on the top of his head, light-yellow skin, blonde hair, rectangular-framed glasses, a chubby body and face and a double chin. Hoffman speaks in an amusing theatrically loud and affected voice and, interestingly, is animated to use the actor's mannerisms of self-conscious touching and over-gesturing.

On October 17, 2008, Mimi O'Donnell gave birth to her third child with Hoffman, a girl they named Willa.

Interviewed by Edward Douglas for the *Comingsoon* website (October 20, 2008), Hoffman said that he was very busy because there were a lot of things he had committed himself to that he was trying to see through. Hoffman said he was trying not to take on too many new things and he hadn't been for a while because there was theater work he needed to do. Asked whose work had influenced him, the actor advised there were a lot. He gave as examples Paul Scofield, Sean Penn, Meryl Streep, Mike Nichols, Martin Davies, Paul Thomas Anderson and other actors, directors and novelists. He said it was art. Hoffman remembered reading Arthur Miller's *All My Sons* and *Death of a Salesman* which both influenced him, seeing Al Pacino live on stage, and Dustin Hoffman in *Death of a Salesman*. He said they were all so different and they all meant so many different things but it was influential and they made up how he ultimately tried to be an actor and an artist. Hoffman said he had tried to talk to some of these people about how to avoid burnout, and quipped that they didn't want to be bothered.

His October 22, 2008, IFC interview with Aaron Hills also included questions about the theater and acting. He didn't agree that theater had become a niche medium. He acknowledged that it had changed a lot since the '50s and '60s, but Broadway was the same way since he went to New York in the '80s—still thriving and still as important as it was 20 years ago. Asked if he still worried about anything when he took on a new project, Hoffman said yes, all the time. He said it was creative anxiety—doubt, anxiety about doing it, and fears, and Hoffman felt it would never go away because of all his successes in the past. The actor agreed that he tried to raise the proverbial bar of his work after he had been praised and won an Oscar, although he knew he couldn't wipe the slate clean and be the person that no one had seen before. Hoffman also found that certain things weren't interesting to him any more, and age was a factor since being 20 was no longer interesting to him. Hills reminded the actor of some things he had said about the craft when he was younger. These included "Acting is so difficult for me that, unless the work is of a certain stature in my mind, unless I reach the expectations I have of myself, I'm unhappy." And "Sometimes I'm working on a film and someone will ask me if I'm having fun. And I'm tempted to tell them the truth: No, absolutely not."

The actor appeared in the FullDawa Films-UNESCO 20-minute documentary short *A World for Inclusion* (2008), written by David Atrakchi and Jill Van Den Brule and directed by Atrakchi. It presented the 2006 UN Convention on the Rights of Persons with Disabilities, and used footage from schools in Kenya, Finland and Turkey to addresses the situation of children with disabilities worldwide and the importance of

8. Mary and Max, Jack Goes Boating

getting them into school. The short also contained interviews and commentary from key stakeholders and experts. It was screened in Turkey on November 14, 2008.

Hoffman was back on *The Daily Show* on December 11, 2008, and then on *Entertainment Tonight* on December 12, 2008. A *New York Times* article on Hoffman (December 19, 2008) was written by Lynn Hirschberg, who had interviewed him early in the fall in London at the Trafalgar Studios where he was directing *Riflemind*. His blond hair was said to be still damp from showering and was standing in soft peaks on his head; Hirschberg wrote that it gave him the look of a very intense, newly hatched chick. Hoffman spoke about the film of *Doubt* as well as his earlier films, and acting. He told how when he was in his mid–20s, another actor had told him that acting "ain't no puzzle." Hoffman thought: 'You must be really bad, because it is a puzzle.'

It was said that due in large part to the actor's commitment to LAByrinth that the company had mounted five productions in the last year and that he was involved with every aspect of the process, from fundraising to directing to acting. Company member John Patrick Shanley also saw Hoffman tearing tickets and seating people at performances. Shanley believed that the actor was not a carefree person and refused to live lightly. He said he was hard to know and told of a party at Shanley's house that Hoffman and Mimi O'Donnell attended. The actor had on three coats and a hat and Shanley told him to take off one of them as it was hot inside. O'Donnell advised that he would maybe take one off in a half hour. Shanley felt that was a metaphor for Hoffman, who he said had a protective cocoon that he shed very slowly.

Hirschberg also saw him carrying a worn paperback copy of *Othello*. He was to portray Iago in a new production of the play in 2009 to be directed by Peter Sellars who had worked with Hoffman on *The Merchant of Venice* in 1994. Othello was to be played by John Ortiz, Hoffman's friend and fellow member of LAByrinth, which was affiliated with the production. Hoffman advised that he had never been all that interested in playing Hamlet although it was a role most actors were supposed to want to play. That, he said, was probably why the reason it had never intrigued him. The demons of Iago interested him more.

On January 15, 2009, it was confirmed that Hoffman would direct the film of *Jack Goes Boating* with filming to begin in New York on February 9. He and John Ortiz were also credited as executive producers. The Overture Films-Big Beach-Cooper's Town Productions-LAByrinth Theater Company-Olfactory Productions romantic comedy had Hoffman playing the title character, a driver for the New York Classic Limousine company run by his Uncle Frank (Richard Petrocelli). Jack begins a romance with a funeral director grief seminar telephone saleswoman, Connie (Amy Ryan). The narrative covers winter and the following summer in New York City, after Jack has learned how to swim so that he can go boating with Connie as the title suggests and also cook to make her a dinner. He has other ambitions and takes a test for the MTA, presumably to help him earn more money and to get away from his uncle (he lives in the uncle's basement). Jack is said to have never had a long-term romantic relationship and there is the suggestion that the reason is that there is something psychologically wrong with him. He comes across as a bit of a hippie with a love of reggae, specifically the song "Rivers of Babylon" which is repeatedly heard in the narrative for its "good vibes." Jack's love of reggae extends to his hair being partially dreadlocked; his hippie status is also apparent in his use of the words "mellow" and "cool." The idea that he is psychologically wounded is suggested by his closeness to his best friend Clyde (Ortiz) and the impact that the news of the infidelity of Clyde's wife Lucy (Daphne Rubin-Vega) has on Jack. (Connie works with Lucy at the office of Dr. Bob Thomas [Tom McCarthy].)

What makes his romantic relationship with Connie seem to work is that she appears to be as psychologically wounded as he is. She is an attractive woman, as opposed to Jack who is overweight with his dreadlocked hair adding to his perceived undesirability, so we wonder why she is still single. The narrative doesn't provide a backstory for her but it is telling that she is starting a new job and her reactions to Jack also show some strangeness. An example is that she won't have penetrable sex with him but she allows him to masturbate her. Connie is the victim of a subway attacker, who presses against her in a crowded carriage and pursues her when she moves. Naturally this is not her fault, but she regrets telling Jack about it when he visits her in the hospital because she feels he will not be able to forget the image. This does not prove to be the case, and Jack's letting her listen to the version of the song "Rivers of Babylon" by the Melodians is done as an act of attempted healing. Connie is also strange in wanting her first intercourse with Jack to be done where he overpowers her but does not hurt her, and he obliges.

Jack agrees to take cooking lessons from the chef Cannoli (Salvatore Inzerillo) to prepare the dinner he makes for Connie, in the same way that he takes swimming lessons from Clyde in preparation of going boating with her. The fact that he takes these lessons shows his commitment to an interest in her but also further suggests that there is something intellectually slow about him. He is also shown to be kind in a shy way when he asks permission to kiss Connie for the first time. Jack's swimming is paralleled with that of the Swimming Student (Byron West) we see at the pool who appears to be older than he and in better shape but is an amputee.

Hoffman cast 3 of the 4 actors of the original stage production in the film, including himself, and his partner, Mimi O'Donnell, who also did the original stage costumes. Amy Ryan replaces Beth Cole as Connie and the actress also reunites with him after her appearance in *Capote*. Hoffman had first met Ryan doing 2 one-act plays at the Barrow Street Theater when he was in his 20s, which was *The Author's Voice & Imagining Brad* at Greenwich House in 1999 where she was in the same cast.

The film adaptation often recalls its theatrical origins, with the long centerpiece of the dinner cooked by Jack for Connie at the apartment of Clyde and Lucy, who also attend. The scene features melodramatic acting, contextualized by the characters being high on drugs, which heightens the intensity of their emotions. However Clyde and Lucy and Connie all singing "Rivers of Babylon" to Jack, to get him to come out of the bathroom after he has become upset over the meal being ruined, reads as an embarrassing idea. Thankfully, the notion of the song having good vibes gets a nice payoff when it doesn't work to get Lucy out of the room where she has fled to get away from Clyde, and Clyde gets to step on the tape player as a final rebuff to the song.

Hoffman perhaps tries to compensate for theatricality but also giving the film short scenes, montages, subjective camera angles and slow motion effects. One notable camera angle is a goggle-cam as Jack's point of view when Clyde adjusts Jack's leaking swimming goggles. Hoffman presents Jack's visualizations of himself swimming and cooking

8. Mary and Max, Jack Goes Boating 123

without point of view so that he sees himself in a non-logical way. When Jack stands on a bridge practicing his swimming stroke, he visualizes himself swimming in the pool, and the bridge shot is superimposed over the pool shot. Slow motion is used repeatedly, but the scene where Clyde watches a row of chefs carrying plates of desserts walking in the Waldorf Hotel has context since one of the chefs is Cannoli who he knows Lucy had an affair with. Hoffman uses fast-cutting for a montage of Jack's visualization of his cooking and inter-cutting to parallel Jack boating with Connie and him swimming with Clyde, although it is a surprise that so little is made of the actual boating when we finally see it. One swimming lesson scene features a funny action that was not presumably in the play, where the Ungainly Swimmer (Ralph Osorio) swims underwater by Clyde and Jack and touches each man as he passes them.

A shock moment occurs when snow falls from a passing train onto the parked car's windshield that Jack and Clyde sit in outside a diner, with the action punctuating Clyde's comment that you take some shots from hooking up with someone long term. Hoffman reveals the result of Connie's attack in the subway by using suggestion and delay. However the scene where Lucy sees Connie's bloodied face is undercut by the theatrical contrivance of Lucy using her cell phone to ring for an ambulance in close proximity to Connie speaking on her office phone to a customer.

Hoffman spares us the scene of Connie being attacked since the aftermath is enough for us to imagine it. He also uses restraint in the scene where Jack masturbates Connie, with bed sheets covering the action and having both actors shown to be clothed. This is different from the scene where Lucy is in her underwear when Clyde attempts to re-enact the scene where Connie had been groped by Dr. Bob. We can forgive Hoffman having Rubin-Vega undressed like this because the scene plays out to show how Clyde desires her and Lucy is unable to respond to his advance. However what we can't forgive is Hoffman's general overuse of music by Grizzly Bear and additional score by Evan Lurie in the film.

Top-billed Hoffman is clean-shaven for the role and wears dreadlocks in his shoulder-length long hair. Jack has the mannerism of a clearing throat which is commented on by Lucy as something he does when he is nervous. Jack is another of Hoffman's sensitive characters who here is practically inarticulate with some loutish touches, such as how he swears when angry and smokes hashish with his friends. Hoffman as director gives himself a lot of long-held takes of Jack in silence, presumably to show his slow reactions but also to emphasize the character's isolation. He has a funny moment of slow reaction when Connie tells him that Clyde has told her that she has "nice cha-chas," and we see Jack angry and attacking Clyde when the character's smoking hashish makes them neglect the dinner. Hoffman is perhaps best in the dinner scene.

The film premiered at the Sundance Film Festival on January 23, 2010, and was then screened at the Toronto International Film Festival on September 12, 2010. It was released in the U.S. on September 17 with the tagline "In love you either sink or swim." Hoffman was photographed at the film's Los Angeles premiere at the Landmark Theater on September 13, 2010, wearing a black baseball cap, open-collar light green sport shirt, gray jacket, scuffed brown shoes and torn khaki jeans. When Cindy Adams, who said she had known the actor for centuries, commented in his clothes, Hoffman told her, "These pants fall down because I have no ass so I don't round them out enough. That's why the cuffs rip." He then scowled and added, "And is this what you'd really like to talk about tonight?"

Todd McCarthy wrote in *Variety* that Hoffman made an engagingly modest directorial debut and brought a sympathetic touch to a small dramatic piece that recalled the warm-hearted "little people" dramas of the '50s. He also said that the actor as Jack displayed a girth that would give hope to overweight romantics everywhere. Roger Ebert in the *Chicago Sun-Times* noted that director Hoffman was merciless in using himself as an actor without vanity, with his face often seen in closeup—sweaty, splotchy, and red as if he suffered from rosacea. Ebert wrote that Hoffman's gift for playing men who fear rejection, and convey such vulnerability that we are on his side, was on display here.

Hoffman reported that when he was doing the play, people would comment about how cinematic it was, since it took place in a lot of locations and there were a lot of things that happened in it that you didn't see that you could very easily see on film. Another aspect was the weather component that was important in the play, and could also help open up the piece. Bob Glaudini did a screenplay draft and gave it to Hoffman during the play's run but the actor didn't want to read it because he was doing the play; he let it sit in his dressing room. Big Beach didn't like Glaudini's screenplay draft so the play was put through one of LAByrinth's summer retreat workshops. Hoffman said it was John Ortiz who suggested Hoffman direct the film because he had directed a lot of plays with LAByrinth. The actor replied that maybe that was right but he said it took him a while to think about it. Hoffman thought that perhaps the idea of directing a film was in the back of his mind because he had been directing theater for a while and he acted in film often. The actor advised that he had tried to get someone else to play the part of Jack because he really didn't want to do both jobs, acting and directing, and he didn't want the film to be perceived as a star vehicle. However Hoffman couldn't get the person he wanted for the role, and also he had a deadline to cast. It also developed that the film was not going to be made without the actor's name as a box office guarantee.

The director reported that his learning in London that Mimi O'Donnell couldn't swim flavored his take on the character of Jack. He commented that he was concerned that the characters couldn't just be odd for the sake of being odd and although he didn't necessarily need to have the oddness explained, he found that he stopped believing in odd characters in other films after a while. However Hoffman was aware that oddness of character captured people's interest (which he never understood) and found the efforts to be comically unbelievable. Rather he wanted to tell a real story about middle-aged working class people in Manhattan, the kind of characters who were rarely if ever seen.

Hoffman loved directing the film but he didn't like also acting in it because it required too much attention and too much time. He advised that the surprises of the job were what he discovered about digital imagery, the post-production duties which he was ignorant about, and the director's relationship with the cinematographer. He was very used to having relationships with the actors because he had directed plays a lot, and with designers in the theater. Hoffman learned he sometimes had to defer in a way that theatre directors don't; when a movie is made, a group of artists bring their own sensibilities and everyone creates it together, and it's as much their film as the director's.

Amy Ryan reported the cast rehearsed the film like a play for two and a half weeks. Ryan said Hoffman as a director was specific and very generous and shared much of his own life with his actors. Hoffman spoke a lot about how personal this story was to him and she marveled at how, when they were in a scene together, he kept the balance of staying in the place where he needed to be for his character and yet (as director) he also had an eye out to everything else. Hoffman showed her that he wasn't about to take her to a place where he wasn't going to go himself, and this created an incredible trust. Ryan advised that, like other actors who directed, he had real compassion and knew what it was like to go to darker places and vulnerability, and the feeling that you might fail miserably.

John Ortiz said that Hoffman as a director was tough but he thought that was an extension of Hoffman as an actor. Ortiz thought Hoffman was really smart and extremely specific and unafraid to try many different things. The actor remarked that the director knew what the cast was capable of doing and it was always important for them to go there and find that extreme, and he was there to demand that from them. Sometimes the producers told the actors it was time to move on and the director insisted that they get things right, which was great. Ortiz reported that the dinner scene in the play only had the living room and not the bathroom where Jack retreats, or the bedroom of Clyde and Lucy. Ortiz said that he was extremely grateful for his friendship with Hoffman and how it helped them play friends in the play, since he found that sometimes playing someone's

French movie card for *Jack Goes Boating* (2010).

friend could seem forced. This was particularly good for them in the swimming scenes. Daphne Rubin-Vega said Hoffman was an intense person and he was wonderful and generous to the actors.

The actor appeared in the HBO Documentary Films—Brent Ratner documentary *I Knew It Was You: Rediscovering John Cazale* (2010), which premiered at the Sundance Film Festival on January 16, 2009. Richard Shepard directed a portrait of the life and work of the late actor Cazale, who died in 1978. Hoffman comments that Cazale was terrifically brilliant in every one of the five films he made. He said he felt that what the actor created was not necessarily what the director or the writer had envisioned. He said he would almost bet money that all the actors who worked with Cazale were inspired by him to be better, and that his seeming to be uncomfortably vulnerable must have made them rethink what they had planned to be do because he was going for it. Shepard said he wanted Hoffman in the film to get a younger actor generation's perspective. He assumed that Hoffman would be interested in participating, and it turned out he was because the actor was a fan of Cazale. The film received a News & Documentary Emmy Award nomination for Outstanding Individual Achievement in Graphic Design and Art Direction.

Hoffman apparently did not attend the Golden Globes ceremony held at the Beverly Hilton hotel on January 11, 2009. He was nominated for Best Supporting Actor in a Film but was not shown in the audience like the other nominees when they were announced by Demi Moore. The winner of the award was Heath Ledger for *The Dark Knight* (2008). Hoffman was a guest on the Spanish television series *Cinema 3* on January 31, 2009, with Amy Adams, Viola Davis, John Patrick Shanley and Meryl Streep, presumably to promote *Doubt*.

On February 7, 2009, Hoffman attended the 61st Annual Writers Guild Awards ceremony at New York City's Hudson Theatre for the Ian McLellan Hunter Award for Lifetime Achievement in Writing given to John Patrick Shanley. Wearing a ski hat to the event, Hoffman said in his speech that he was going to be a little more serious than those who had come before him. That didn't stop him having a little fun critiquing the writers' sartorial habits, as well as quoting Eugene O'Neill. He also described the event as unruly.

Hoffman was nominated for the Best Supporting Actor Academy Award for *Doubt* but the consensus was that he'd again be beaten by the deceased Heath Ledger. On February 19, 2009, the *New York Times*' David Carr predicted that Ledger would win because an indelible performance and an untimely death made it no contest, no debate. Hoffman attended the Independent Spirit Awards on February 21, 2009, in Santa Monica where *Synecdoche, New York* won the Best First Feature Award. He was reported to have worn a black skullcap to cover the blonde dreadlocked hair he was sporting for *Jack Goes Boating* which he was then filming. Hoffman commented that he would rather deal with hat jokes than crazy hair jokes.

On March 12, 2009, the *New York Times* reported that Hoffman would direct the world premiere of the Brett C. Leonard play *The Long Red Road* for the Chicago Goodman Theater's 2009–10 season. It would be the first play the actor directed for the company. On May 26, 2009, it was reported that *Othello* with John Ortiz and Hoffman as Iago was to run at the Public Theater from September 12, 2009, for 23 performances.

However it was said the season could be extended given the potential audience interest and be moved into a larger space, which would be the 860-seat Skirball Center at New York University. The Monsters and Critics website on March 20, 2009, reported that Hoffman had lost the role of Bill Clinton in *The Special Relationship* to Dennis Quaid. The film was to tell the story of Clinton's "inappropriate relationship" with White House intern Monica Lewinsky. The historical drama would eventually be made for television by director Richard Loncraine and broadcast on HBO on May 29, 2010.

WENN on April 13, 2009, published a Hoffman interview where he talked about being a reluctant Hollywood leading man. The actor said he just wanted to be a thespian who could cycle to work. Hoffman admitted to struggling to come to terms with life as a famous actor and he said he still couldn't handle awkward moments when he was recognized. He advised that when somebody stared at him in a restaurant, he thought they didn't like him or they wanted to fight him or he knew them and he had forgotten their name.

More news about his proposed film *Vanikoro* was released on May 13, 2009, by the Bloody Disgusting website. Xavier Gens advised that it was to begin shooting in New Zealand and Australia in 2010. He also described more of the plot, which mixed the story of the *USS Indianapolis* with an island of hungry cannibals. The French explorer La Perouse was wrecked on Vanikoro in 1788. The ship *Boussole* was destroyed on a reef along with most of the crew. The second ship *Astrolabe* was also wrecked, but survivors salvaged enough to build a small ship and sailed away. Two survivors remained on the island into the early 1800s.

Hoffman, interviewed by Simon Reynolds on May 14, 2009, for the website Digital Spy, voiced his frustration with his profession, saying he found acting torturous. On May 31 it was announced that Hoffman was leaving his position as co-artistic director of LAByrinth; John Gould Rubin, Stephen Adly Guirgis, Yul Vazquez and Mimi O'Donnell were taking over. In a joint statement Hoffman and John Ortiz (who was also leaving his co-artistic director position) cited family and professional responsibilities as the reason. But they said they would remain involved in the company as board members and be continually available to the new leadership as advisers. The pair added that most of all, they were excited to get to be members again, as the members were the real heart and motor of the company.

Othello opened on June 14, 2009, at Vienna's Theater Azkent as a co-production between the German Schauspielhaus Bochum company, LAByrinth and the Public Theater. It reportedly moved to Bochum, Germany, later in June. A diary was provided as a program written by Avery T. Willis who said that the production had had a nine-month rehearsal period. Larry L. Lash of *Variety* lambasted the show, writing that Hoffman spent the majority of the evening with his chin on his chest and his hands in the pockets of his ill-fitting trousers; Lash claimed that the actor simply did not know his part. On opening night, Hoffman fumbled and restarted lines, made false entrances and spent uncomfortably long periods with his palms tight against his temples as if trying to squeeze out the next line. On several occasions, the actor was said to resort to yelling "Line!" to the offstage prompter, once missing her reply and having to repeat the call.

The *New York Times* reported on September 10, 2009, that *Othello* would begin previews on September 12 and open on September 27 at the Skirball Center for the Performing Arts in Greenwich Village. The show was said to be nearly sold out before it opened. Set to run until October 4, it had been modernized and set in present-day Washington. Patrick Healy, covering the show in a September 16, 2009, article, wrote that Hoffman and John Ortiz had been close friends for 15 years both on and off the stage and as well as being co-artistic directors of LAByrinth. During that time they also celebrated the births of each other's children and commiserated over the highs and lows of their beloved New York sports teams. Ortiz commented that there was something powerful and provocative about Hoffman and himself playing these parts, given their history as friends, and he wanted to take that into the relationship between Iago and Othello. Director Peter Sellars reported that although neither actor had previously done the play he had them both in mind for the roles from the start. Hoffman advised he had never seen a production of the play and after rereading it when he was offered the part of Iago, he was genuinely surprised by all the things he got out of it that contradicted the accepted thoughts and images. Rather than draw on the occasional bumps in the road in the friendship, the actor said his performance instead tapped into his affection for Ortiz. Sellars advised that he planned to continue performances of the production in other cities with as many of the current cast members as possible over the next five years and ultimately to film the production with Hoffman and Ortiz.

Marilyn Stasio in *Variety* commented that Hoffman's offbeat casting as Iago was the most provocative thing about the eccentric production, and said he made canny use of his unprepossessing presence, wearing it like a costume to dupe the rubes. She reported that when the actor was called upon to bellow his lines at the top of his voice, which she felt was one of the show's more bizarre directorial choices, he used his goofy grin and soft insinuating voice to chilling effect. She also stated that Hoffman grasped the essence of Iago's evil power: how the man was smarter than everyone else and how his keen understanding of human psychology made him dangerous. Ben Brantley in the *New York Times* described Hoffman as one of the best stage and screen actors of his generation and said he had created a provocative portrait of a man burned to an ashen, angry nihilism by years of unrewarded service. He pointed out that Hoffman had played this part more satisfyingly in the movie *Before the Devil Knows You're Dead*. The *New York Post* reported on October 2, 2009, that the show's audiences were unenthusiastic; on one recent night most of them left at intermission. Someone who stayed reported that Sellars came onstage to urge those in the back to move to the now empty seats in the front of the theater.

WENN reported on November 30, 2009, that Moviefone.com placed Hoffman at number 5 in their list of the unsexiest men in Hollywood. On December 2, *Variety* announced that the actor would reunite with Paul Thomas Anderson on a dark take on the role of faith and religion on the American landscape. The drama, tentatively set up at Universal, had Hoffman playing the Master, a charismatic intellectual who launches his own faith-based organization in 1952. The movie would revolve around the conflict between the Master and Freddie, his young lieutenant who begins to have doubts about the movement. The film was to have a $35 million budget, with Universal having first rights to the project when Anderson turns in a completed script. The director hoped to shoot in 2010.

Hoffman attended the Kennedy Center Honors at the John F. Kennedy Center for the Performing Arts in Washington on December 5, 2009. Hoffman was seen several times during its December 29 CBS broadcast, at one point applauding Robert De Niro and Bruce Springsteen, two of that year's award recipients.

On December 17, 2009, the actor attended a lunch celebrating the new Coen Brothers comedy *A Serious Man* (2009), and reportedly dissected the mural on the walls of the Monkey Bar. On December 19 he was reported to have attended a party at the Thompson Smyth Tribeca hotel to celebrate the 29th birthday of Jake Gyllenhaal. The holiday party benefited God's Love We Deliver.

WENN reported on January 19, 2010, that Hoffman had been invited to reprise his *Big Lebowski* role in an X-rated version of the Coen Brothers film, *The Big Lebowski—A XXX Parody*. Perhaps aware that the actor would not accept his offer, director Lee Roy Myers also put a call-out to lookalikes and fans to fill the non-sex and sex roles. As expected, the actor did not do the film.

At the Sundance Film Festival where Hoffman was in attendance for *Jack Goes Boating*, it was announced on January 28, 2010, that the actor was to produce the psychological drama *The Well*, to be written and directed by Tim Guinee. The story centered on a well-to-do New York couple (to be played by Guy Pearce and Mary-Louise Parker) whose obsessive pursuit of salvation ultimately leads to destruction. The film was never made. Hoffman also announced plans to make *Mr. Crumpaker and the Man from the Letter*, a comedy from writer-director Kazuo Ohno. It was the story of an overbearing boss who starts a quest to discover the meaning of life, despite having absolutely no capacity for introspection or self-examination. Hoffman had already appeared in a few scenes from the film, shot as part of the Sundance Filmmakers Lab, and was now trying to get financial backing to make the whole thing on the strength of those snippets. The actor was to produce the result as part of his Cooper's Town Productions company. To date the film remains in development. *Variety* announced that there were two other projects the company were to produce: One was a sports drama based on the Dean Colvard novel *Mixed Emotions*, about the civil rights movement within the Mississippi State University basketball program in the 1960s. The novel followed Colvard, then president of MSU, and his conflicted stance when he abolished the rule prohibiting him from playing racially integrated teams. Tim Guinee and writer-director Ali Selim were set to adapt. The second was *The Farm*, a tale about a father (Manny Howard) who reinvigorates his life and marriage when he creates a functioning farm in his Brooklyn backyard. The yarn was based on Howard's *New York Magazine* cover story, which he was developing into a novel. Writer-director Donal Lardner Ward was set to adapt.

On January 29, 2010, the website Collider.com reported that Hoffman appeared in Shane Salerno's already finished two-hour documentary on the life of author J.D. Salinger, as a person influenced by work of the fiction writer who died on January 27, 2010. *Salinger* (2013) was 5 years in the making. The Weinstein Company–A Story Factory production was based on the book by Paul Alexander. Hoffman, who appears twice, is one of many actors interviewed in the film; he comments about the impact of *The Catcher in the Rye*. Hoffman says the book was magical and made you wonder how Salinger put it together the way he did. He added that you were so grateful to him and you wanted to go find him, just like Salerno was doing. In commenting on Salinger's becoming a recluse, Hoffman presumably brought his experience of being a public figure to the writer's dilemma. The actor says he understood why anyone who was becoming famous would stop it. He felt you were born with a right of anonymity where you could walk the streets and have private thoughts while you were among other people. Hoffman said that people who had never had that change in their life didn't think about it and didn't question it. To them, it just *was*.

The film premiered at the Toronto International Film Festival on September 5, 2013, and was then given a limited American release on September 6, with the tagline "Uncover the mystery but don't spoil the secrets!" The film received a mixed review by Andrew Barker in *Variety* but was lambasted by A.O. Scott in the *New York Times* and Peter Travers in *Rolling Stone*. It was not a box office hit.

Director Salerno commented that he'd had trouble getting big names to participate in the film, but after Hoffman agreed to do it, other people began getting on board. Salerno said it was like the filmmakers now had a seal of authenticity. The director felt the interviews Hoffman gave were as good as those of the Yale professors Salerno spoke with. He said that Hoffman was as smart as they come.

Hoffman directed *The Long Red Road* for the Chicago Goodman Theater. Running from February 22 to March 21, 2010, the play centered on Sam (Tom Hardy), a far-gone drunk living on a South Dakota Indian reservation, trying to forget his role in a tragic accident involving his family. Visited by someone from his past, he is forced to face his guilt and the man he has become. Steven Oxman in *Variety* wrote that Hoffman let the action develop very slowly and the playing had a hyper-realistic feel even as the director layered the action in the two locations on top of each other. Oxman said that Hoffman was careful to allow no humor, perhaps for justified fear of making light of the subject, which was a noble choice, but it also had its consequences.

The March 3, 2010, *People* magazine proposed that Hoffman be cast as Capt. Jonas Grumby, a.k.a. the Skipper, in the announced Warner Bros. film of the 1960s TV sitcom *Gilligan's Island*. It wrote that the actor could bring the right balance of comedy and heft to the role. To date the film remains in development. Hoffman was a presenter at the March 5, 2010, Independent Spirit Awards, held at La Live's event deck in Los Angeles. On March 19, *The Guardian* reported that Hoffman was in the running to play Daniel Johnston in an upcoming biopic. The film's writer-producer David Miller advised that he had begun work on an epic superhero story about the troubled singer. Miller said Hoffman had reached out to him because he was a huge Johnston fan. Gabriel Sunday was to direct and star as the young Daniel. The film was never made.

Hoffman appeared in the TV documentary series *Made Here,* shot in New York and broadcast on May 2, 2010. The show explored the lives of New York performance artists.

It was reported on May 14, 2010, that Hoffman was in talks to join Bennett Miller's new film *Moneyball*. It had been set to begin filming the previous year before Sony abruptly pulled the plug on director Steven Soderbergh's vision. The script and Brad Pitt's co-star Demetri Martin were scrapped but the studio was able to keep Pitt aboard with a polished script by Aaron Sorkin based on Michael Lewis' book *Moneyball: The Art of Winning an Unfair Game*. Pitt was to star as Oakland A's manager Billy Beane who, with the help of a number-crunching assistant (Jonah Hill), builds a successful team with the lowest payroll in the league. Hoffman would play the team's manager, Art Howe, and filming was expected to begin in July in Los Angeles.

In June, Hoffman appeared on the talk show *Motion Pictures Live!*, shot in Hollywood. The episode was titled "Strong Women." It was reported on June 23, 2010, that the actor had been interested in appearing in Great Hope Springs for Escape Artists. The film, written by Vanessa Taylor Writer, was about a married couple (to be played by Meryl Streep and Jeff Bridges), who after 30 years together attend an intense counseling weekend to decide the fate of their marriage. Hoffman wanted to play the role of the counselor, but his participation was in question because of schedule conflicts with *The Master*. Jessie Neilson, then Mike Nichols was to direct this romantic comedy.

Hoffman reportedly attended the *American Film Institute Salute to Mike Nichols* on June 26, 2010, at the Sony Pictures Studios in Los Angeles; he cannot be seen in the televised version. On June 27, *The Hollywood Reporter* wrote that Kevin Spacey had been cast in the New Line crime comedy *Horrible Bosses* (2011) in a part that he had beaten out Hoffman for. This was Dave Harken, the boss of Jason Bateman, who was to play one of three best friends who decide to kill each other's bosses. The film, released in 2011, was a hit. Spacey reprised his role in the sequel *Horribe Bosses 2* (2014), another hit.

On the July 12, 2010, episode of the comedy TV series *Very Mary-Kate*, Josh Ruben did an impersonation of Hoffman in two sketches. In one, he is the acting coach of Mary-Kate (Elaine Carroll). Ruben wears an obvious blonde wig and large-framed glasses to be Hoffman, with a brown cardigan buttoned to his neck over a shirt. He sits in a slouched manner where he uses the actor's mannerisms of excessive hand-gesturing and enthusiastic laughing. Ruben's Hoffman gives her a note to say "Mountain Dew" and not "Mountain Dude," and he hits on her for sex. Mary-Kate's room features a painted portrait of Hoffman, with long hair, glasses and a moustache. The episode also had Ruben as Hoffman repeatedly coming to Mary-Kate's apartment door for Halloween dressed consecutively in costumes as a fireman, a monster, a cat, a ghost—and undressed. Now Ruben has a beard and also uses Hoffman's heavy breathing mannerism. The second skit references the actor's Oscar and *Love, Liza*.

In *Moneyball* (2011).

Shooting for the Columbia sports

biography *Moneyball* reportedly took place from the week of July 17 to October 6, 2010. The film had a screenplay by Steven Zallian and Aaron Sorkin based on a story by Stan Chervin and the book by Michael Lewis. It was directed by Bennett Miller and shot on location in Boston and in California. Brad Pitt stars as 44-year-old Billy Beane, general manager of the Oakland Athletics baseball team. He assembles a team on a lean budget by employing computer-generated analysis to acquire new players for the 2002 season. He does this with the help of an economics graduate, 20-year-old Peter Brandt (Jonah Hill), and leads the team into an unprecedented winning streak. Art Howe (Hoffman), the team's manager, disagrees with Billy's tactics of replacing players mid-season but his coaching still leads the team to the ALDS elimination game and close to the World Series last game. It is Art's decision to bring on Scott Hatterberg (Chris Pratt) in the September 4, 2002, game against Kansas City. Scott's home run hit leads to the team's winning streak.

The film reunites Hoffman with his *Capote* director. The actor, third-billed after Pitt and Hill, is clean-shaven and has a shaven head. The actor doesn't have any great scenes and he has few lines but he underplays Art's anger and disapproval of Billy's tactics, particularly in the manager's strategic movement of players.

The film premiered at the Toronto International Film Festival on September 9, 2011, where Hoffman appeared with Pitt, Hill and Miller. At a press conference, Hoffman talked about the character of Billy, saying that he found it inspiring that there was a man in the middle of his life who turned back into his life and became obsessed with having to deal with what came before. He said it was also inspiring because he, Pitt and Miller were at that point in their lives, so Billy's struggle spoke to them. At the Festival, Miller advised that one of his next projects was a book Hoffman had found for them to adapt, although he did name it.

Moneyball opened in Oakland, California, on September 19, 2011, with Hoffman attending. It received a wide release on September 23, with the tagline "What are you really worth?" Peter DeBruge in *Variety* wrote that Hoffman was surly and skeptical. The film was a box office success and earned Academy Award nominations for Best Film, Best Adapted Screenplay, Best Actor for Pitt, Best Supporting Actor for Hill, Best Editing and Best Sound Mixing. It won none of the awards. The DVD has two deleted scenes that feature Hoffman, entitled "Billy tells Art to play Bradford." The first scene has Art dressing into his Athletics uniform when Billy comes into his office. Billy suggests that Art bring out Chad Bradford (Casey Bond) instead of Mike Magnante (Derrin Ebert) as the first batsman out of the pen for the next game after the team has won seven games. Art does not follow Billy's suggestion, which leads to the second scene where Billy goes to the dugout to confront Art about it since Magnante has been unsuccessful. We see Art leaving the field and walking to the dugout. Billy points out that they are both on camera and that the boos they heard are for Art. The first scene also has Art comment on Billy's days as a baseball player when he tells him that he could have coached him up.

The actor said that accepting the film was a no-brainer (he loved baseball) and that he had a great time. The real Art Howe commented that Hoffman physically didn't resemble him in any way because he was a little on the heavy side, and the way he portrayed him was very disappointing and probably 180 degrees from what he really was.

The actor advised that he hoped to meet him one day and tell him that he did not actively play the man as he really was. He wondered if the writers should have taken Howe's real name off as they did with Jonah Hill's character, who was based on Paul DePodesta. Hoffman knew there was no way he could fill out who Howe was with what was written, and so he agreed that Howe had every right to be unhappy. The actor acknowledged that it was not a fair representation of him as a person whatsoever but the story was about something else.

9

A Late Quartet, The Master

On July 15, 2010, it was reported that *The Master* was set to begin filming in August. Hoffman was to play a man who creates a faith-based organization that blossoms into an empire in the 1950s; this led to talk of the film being a rather thinly disguised swipe at Scientology.

On August 18, 2010, news that a film about Google founders Sergey Brin and Larry Page was in the works based on the Ken Auletta book *Googled*. One of the casting ideas reportedly pitched was Hoffman as Google chief executive Eric Schmidt, a man described as composed, articulate and just a little edgy. To date this film has not been made. On August 31, 2010, it was reported that the actor was to appear in George Clooney's film version of the Off-Broadway play *Farragut North,* with shooting to start in February 2011. The play, written by former Democratic political operative Beau Willimon, was a political drama about campaign dirty tricks. Willimon also wrote the screenplay. Hoffman replaced Brad Pitt in the part of the hard-bitten veteran boss of a 20-something presidential campaign spinmeister-wunderkind, Stephen Myers, to be played by Chris Pine.

Hoffman was in Seattle in September 2010 promoting *Jack Goes Boating.* He then took it to the Toronto International Film Festival for a September 12, 2010, screening. The actor was a guest on CBS's comedy and music talk show *The Late Late Show with Craig Ferguson*, shot in Los Angeles and broadcast on September 13, 2010. Hoffman promoted *Jack Goes Boating* and spoke about his commitment to acting, LAByrinth, the theater, directing and *Doubt*. Hoffman was in good humor and self-deprecating. He commented that because he is poor at doing accents and he speaks sloppily anyway, he has to stay in character if it requires an accent when filming, even on a break. This is because he finds it really hard to get back to it if he stops. Hoffman also spoke about his kids who were now seven, almost four and almost two. Asked if he took drugs, the actor said that he would like to but he didn't any more.

He was interviewed by Tasha Robinson for the A.V. Club website for *Jack Goes Boating* for an article that was published on September 15, 2010. Hoffman spoke about being famous and the empathy process. He advised that he was at the point where he was so famous that he pulled away from other people, and that it was definitely trickier for him, in certain circumstances, to enter into the crowd. Asked if he was worried about being typecast as the sad, troubled, awkward character he played in various movies, Hoffman said he felt he had played more parts that weren't the sad type—but Hoffman found they were the ones that sat with people.

9. A Late Quartet, The Master

WENN reported that on September 16, 2010, at the New York premiere of *Jack Goes Boating* at the New York Yacht Club, Hoffman assisted a man (one of his friends from LAByrinth) who fainted on the red carpet. The actor rushed over to help and waited with his friend until medics arrived and then helped the man out of the venue. On September 19, he attended the LAByrinth Poker benefit sponsored by the Borgata Hotel Casino & Spa at the Soho House in New York. There he was quoted on his philosophy of child-raising, saying it was fundamental that children develop a sense of security with help from their families at an early age. Hoffman said the most important tip that you could ever get as a parent was that you had to tell your kids that you loved them, and not assumed they knew. He thought it was important to be physically affectionate with them so that they got used to being hugged and having their hands held. Those things were the most important so that the children knew that you weren't going anywhere.

On September 22, Hoffman was back as a guest on the *Tavis Smiley* talk show. It was reported on September 20, 2010, that production on *The Master* had been postponed indefinitely. Hoffman commented to Playlist that he didn't have any new information, and that he wasn't being obtuse. He didn't quite know what the problem was but hoped he would be part of something soon, saying that it would be great to work with Paul Thomas Anderson again. On September 23, reports about the actor's participation in the film *Great Hope Springs* resurfaced with Mike Nichols on board as director and James Gandolfini now set to co-star with Meryl Streep. It was said that no deal had been signed but all parties were highly interested, and recently even did a table read. Jeff Bridges had been set to play the husband in June, but the deal never came together. Hoffman was available for the part of the marriage counselor now that *The Master* had halted production. Filming was to begin in March 2011. The film would be shot as *Hope Springs* in August 2011 with David Frankel as director, Tommy Lee Jones replacing Bridges, and Steve Carell cast as the counselor, Dr. Feld. It was a box office hit.

Hoffman went to Australia to direct the Sydney Theatre Company production of *True West* which ran from November 2 to December 18, 2010, at Wharf 1. The cast included Brendan Cowell as Austin and Wayne Blair as Lee. Jason Blake in *The Sydney Morning Herald* wrote that Hoffman's production was well governed, very secure and looked as you might imagine it should, save for its deliberately jarring scene changes. Blake said what was unique was the casting of an Aboriginal man (Blair) and an Australian Anglo-Saxon (Cowell) as brothers. Brendan Cowell reported that Hoffman was an incredibly intense man who approached acting with vigor and intensity. Cowell said he had never known anyone who took acting so seriously and that he pushed him to a new level.

In Sydney, Hoffman and his family rented a house in Bondi for several months. It was reported on September 25, 2010, that his seven-year-old son Cooper was saved by Bondi Rescue Lifeguard Troy "Gonzo" Quinlan after the boy was swimming in the shallows near a riptide in the water. Hoffman was reportedly watching his son, unaware that the tide could have dragged the boy away, when the lifeguard rolled up in his buggy and told him of the danger. Quinlan said he had no idea who Hoffman was until he went back to the lifeguard tower and was told. The family were said to have stayed in Australia for four months, and also spent time at Palm Beach and at the lavish home of the Packers. Brendan Cowell reported that Hoffman would go for morning jogs and loved the beach.

Hoffman was interviewed about *Jack Goes Boating* for the Fall 2010 issue of *Under the Radar* magazine by Chris Tinkham. He reported that he would shoot the film *Moneyball* the next summer. WENN reported on September 29, 2010, that Hoffman was plotting his return to Broadway in a revival of Arthur Miller's play *Death of a Salesman*. The actor was said to have teamed with Mike Nichols to resurrect the play in New York in 2011. Hoffman would play Willy Loman. Brian Dennehy, who last played the part on Broadway in 1999, commented that he knew the play fascinated Hoffman. Dennehy said Hoffman saw him do it in London and they spent a lot of time talking about it afterward. On September 30 it was reported that the start date for *Farragut North* had been pushed back to March 2011 and that Ryan Gosling had replaced Chris Pine.

Also on September 29, Hoffman was a guest on the Canadian comedy music and news television show *The Hour* a.k.a. *George Stroumboulopoulos Tonight*, which was shot in Ontario. The actor spoke about directing *Jack Goes Boating*, *Mary and Max* (which he calls *Max and Mary*), the stage show *Othello*, acting, friendship, fatherhood and his mother. Asked to name the silliest thing he has done for love, Hoffman tells a story about Mimi O'Donnell being silly. He reported how she bent over when she was leaving a voice message telling him she would go out with him, because she had been told this was the way to avoid sounding nervous.

On October 1, 2010, it was reported that the actor would possibly take on the role of Venom in the reboot of the *Spider-Man* film franchise. The character had been played by Topher Grace in *Spider-Man 3* (2007) and seemingly killed in that film. It was described as a sentient alien in a gooey, almost liquid-like form, which required a host to bond around for its survival and in return gave its host enhanced powers. The action adventure fantasy *The Amazing Spider-Man* (2012) was released on schedule, but the character of Venom was not in the narrative.

On October 20, 2010, the *New York Times* confirmed that Hoffman would appear as Willy Loman in a new Broadway production of *Death of a Salesman* for director Mike Nichols in the fall. Nichols advised that the actor had been eager to play the part for a while and the two of them had been planning this production for months. Nichols and Hoffman both wanted Linda Emond to play Linda Loman. At the age of 43, Hoffman was considered too young for the part that was written as a man in his 60s although he was seen as his younger self in flashbacks and memories. Lee J. Cobb, who originated the part on Broadway in 1949, was only 38 when he played it. George C. Scott was 48 in 1975, Dustin Hoffman 47 in 1984, and Brian Dennehy 61 in 1999. Nichols remarked that the character was different ages over the course of the play—young, middle-aged, old—but what mattered was finding the right man to play the part. The director said he was thrilled to be doing the play with Hoffman.

Hoffman attended the Marrakech International Film Festival in Morocco where *Jack Goes Boating* was screened on December 10, 2010. He commented that he was eager to direct another film and was just waiting for the right script. Hoffman said he didn't know what it would be but he did like small stories that crept up on you and become bigger than they were, where there was something very tragic happening before your eyes but you couldn't put your finger on it. On December 18, 2010, the actor was back as a guest on the Spanish television series *Cinema 3*. In December the actor held two public readings of the new Stephen Adly Guirgis play *The Motherf**ker with the Hat* he directed for LAByrinth at the Cherry Pit Theatre. The play was scheduled to open on Broadway in the spring.

On January 11, 2011, Hoffman was reported to have signed to appear in Yaron Zilberman's feature debut, *A Late Quartet*. Scripted by Zilberman and Seth Grossman, the film involved a quartet whose members have performed together for 25 years and who have to adjust to one of them retiring due to Parkinson's disease. Hoffman was to replace Ethan Hawke, whose casting in the film had been announced in August 2010. Hoffman was to play the part of the second violinist whose desire for more solos leads him to have an affair with his jogging partner, leaving him remorseful and saddened by the state of his marriage.

On January 17, 2011, Hoffman participated in a special benefit production of *Being Harold Pinter* at the Public Theater. He was one of a group of guest actors that raised $25,000 for the Belarus Free Theatre troupe. During a section of the play in which letters from political prisoners were read, Hoffman was one of ten performers who stepped onto the stage to deliver the often wrenching testimonies. On January 20, Hoffman attended Joe's Pub for an evening devoted to the release of Lapham's Quarterly's Winter 2011 issue *Celebrity*. Lewis Lapham, the editor and founder of the publication, presided over a discussion of celebrity, a performance and readings from the journal.

It was reported on January 27, 2011, that a massive in New York City snowstorm had temporarily halted production on *A Late Quartet*. Fifteen inches of snow blanketed the city, closing airports and shutting down production on TV and film projects. The RKO Pictures-Opening Night Production-Concept Entertainment-Spring Pictures-Unison Films musical drama was also known as *Performance* (2012). The story concerned the Fugue String Quartet which featured cello Peter Mitchell (Christopher Walken), viola Juliette "Jules" Gerbert (Catherine Keener), first violin Daniel Lerner (Mark Ivanir) and second violin Robert Gelbart (Hoffman).

The group has played internationally for 25 years but now Peter has contracted Parkinson's disease and he announces that their first concert in the new season will be his last. This news makes Robert want to alternate chairs with Daniel so that he can have a chance to play first violin, an idea that is discouraged by Jules and Daniel. Robert feels that their disapproval is saying that he is not good enough to so do, and this rejection from his wife in particular leads to him have sex with the dancer Pilar (Liraz Charhi) with whom he jogs. When Jules learns of the affair she asks Robert to move out of their home. Robert resents Daniel being first violin since he believes he has led the group into a direction Robert does not like and he misses the challenge he faced when he first began playing. He also feels that Daniel's application is rigid and monotonous and self-loving and safe. Robert asks him to unleash his passion which Robert seems to do when he has the affair with Pilar, and which Daniel also does when he has his own affair with the daughter of Robert and Jules, violin student Alexandra "Alex" Gelbart (Imogene Poots). Robert perhaps is uncomfortable with the fact that Daniel had a relationship with Jules before she met him, and wonders if she only married him because Robert got her pregnant. He is angry when he learns of Daniel's affair with Alex and Robert punches him. Robert has threatened to leave the group if the alternating chair idea is not used and he walks out on a rehearsal after punching Daniel. The concert sees Peter stop playing since he claims he cannot keep up with the others and he has cellist Nina Lee (playing herself) replace him. Before the group resumes playing, Daniel closes his notebook and the others do the same, this action suggesting that Daniel is unleashing his passion in another way since Robert has criticized him for only playing with notes. However Daniel plays first violin and Robert plays second violin so this anticipated compromise is not made.

The film sees Hoffman reunited with Keener (who had appeared in *Capote* and *Synecdoche, New York*) and Christopher Walken (from the stage production of *The Seagull*). The actor appears with short hair and a beard that he shaves during the narrative so that he is seen clean-shaven in the opening concert scene that is repeated at the film's end. He is also seen clean-shaven in the film on the group. Hoffman does an imitation of Walken when he describes how he was approached to be in the quarter (Robert's imitation is poor). Robert is a mix of one of Hoffman's introvert and extrovert characters, since his being a musician suggests he is an introvert but his swearing and drinking demonstrates extrovert qualities. We see Hoffman semi-naked in the shower. The actor is good in the scene at Sotheby's where he talks to Jules backstage about the compromises of their marriage and asks if she really loves him, and he expresses resentful anger at Daniel who visits him to discourage the idea of wanting to alternate chairs. Hoffman's best scene is perhaps when he is confronted by Jules, who finds Robert and Pilar together when they couple meet so Pilar can return his violin case. He ranges from being embarrassed at seeing Jules (who is aware that Robert has cheated on her with Pilar) to being vulnerable in asking her to forgive him. The confrontation scene also features the film's funniest line, where Jules says, "You took this whole alternating chairs a little too far, don't you think?" The film credits Nanae Iwata and Keiko Tokunaga as his violin coaches.

The film premiered at the Toronto International Film Festival on September 10, 2012, and was then screened at the Edmonton International Film Festival on October 4; the Hamptons International Film Festival on October 5; the Austin Film Festival on October 21; the Starz Denver Film Festival on November 1; and was then given a limited U.S. release on November 2 with the tagline "No arrangement is more beautiful ... or more complicated." Justin Chang in *Variety* wrote that the emotional precision of Hoffman's performance was matched by how convincing he looked at his instrument. Stephen Holden in the *New York Times* said that the actor gave an exceptional performance. Roger Ebert pointed out that Hoffman was frequently seen in roles that don't really test him so it was a pleasure to see him sounding his depths. Peter Travers of *Rolling Stone* said that Hoffman and Keener played off each other with artful intensity and pure feeling.

Hoffman said the film's drama was life, where people make mistakes and everything becomes unraveled and feelings started to come out. Hoffman said he had as a teacher a young Asian woman who was incredible and talented. He remembered that she wouldn't lie and she came to see him in a play he was in and she told Hoffman she didn't like it. The actor reported that he worked so they could get as much footage of him faking playing the instrument as well as possible. Hoffman advised that he got into the violin thing because it wasn't acting so he got to go someplace and work on something that wasn't his day job. He said he didn't play after finishing the film because ultimately he felt he wasn't very good.

Catherine Keener said that she remembered every moment of working with Hoffman, saying he gave so much. She recalled the scene where Robert poured out his heart to Jules at the auction and she just stood listening to him. Keener said to prepare for the scene, Hoffman had told her "Don't come near me right now" and because a lot of what she did was informed by what her acting partner did, she did it that way.

The Exclusive Media Group-Cross Creek Pictures-Crystal City Entertainment-Smokehouse and Appian Way Production drama *The Ides of March* was filmed from February 7 to April 2, 2011, on location in Michigan, Cincinnati and Kentucky. It was directed and co-written by George Clooney, based on Beau Willimon's Off-Broadway play *Farragut North*, which had run at the Linda Gross Theatre from November 12 to 25, 2008, under the direction of Doug Hughes. In the movie, Ryan Gosling starred as 30-year-old Stephen Meyers, media consultant for the campaign of Pennsylvania Governor Mike Morris (Clooney). Morris is running for the Democratic primary election seat in Ohio against Arkansas Senator Pullman (Michael Mantell). Hoffman plays campaign manager Paul Zara, Stephen's boss. Brad Pitt was originally cast in the role. Paul is said to value loyalty in his workers so when he learns that Stephen has met with Pullman campaign manager Tom Duffy (Paul Giamatti) who offers him a job, he has Stephen fired. Paul claims that Stephen has been disloyal in not immediately telling him about the meeting although Stephen does so later. Paul justifies his action of firing Stephen since he tells how he had been offered a job for an opposing candidate 20 years prior and told his candidate about it; the candidate advised him to take the job if he wanted it, but then he declined the offer out of loyalty. However Paul's ideas about loyalty may have changed since he also implies that he is jealous that the offer from Tom did not go to him instead of Stephen. Paul leaks the information about the job offer to *New York Times* reporter Ida Horowitz (Marisa Tomei) to enable him to fire Stephen. Stephen outmaneuvers Paul when he blackmails Morris into firing Paul and replacing him with Stephen, since Stephen has knowledge of the affair Morris had with 20-year-old intern Molly Stearns (Evan Rachel Wood).

In *The Ides of March* (2011).

This film reunited third-billed Hoffman with Marisa Tomei from *Before the Devil Knows You're Dead*. He is clean-shaven and his medium-length hair looks more white-gray than blonde. Paul is a variation on one of Hoffman's louts in that while he is intelligent and politically savvy, he also smokes, speaks coarsely and swears. His clothes also present his occasional lack of finesse when he repeatedly wears an uncoordinated red tie with a blue suit. His best scene is perhaps the one where Paul tells Stephen that he plans to fire him. Hoffman uses subdued anger to express Paul's disapproval of Stephen.

The film premiered on August 31, 2011, at the Venice Film Festival, with Hoffman attending. It was then screened at the Toronto International Film Festival on September 9, the Athens Film Festival on September 23 and the Zurich Film Festival on September 24. It opened in the U.S. on October 5 with the taglines "Ambition seduces. Power corrupts" and "Is This Man Our Next President?" Hoffman also attended this opening. Justin Chang of *Variety* commented that Hoffman and Giamatti were so well cast that they warranted more scenes together. Roger Ebert in the *Chicago Sun-Times* wrote that both actors made some front-of-the-stage monologues plausible under the closer scrutiny of a camera. The film was a box office success and earned an Academy Award nomination for Best Adapted Screenplay. It lost to Alexander Payne, Nat Faxon and Jim Rash for the comedy *The Descendants* (2011).

Hoffman advised that he was interested in politics but had no desire to be a politician. He said it was hard not to be disenchanted because every day he read about how nothing could get done and there was a lot of stonewalling going on, and it was maddening how in the country a minority of people were controlling the argument. Hoffman observed that every minute detail of a politician's life was scrutinized by the media. He commented that Clooney was involved in so many aspects of the business (producing, directing, writing and obviously acting) and all of those things fed into the tools he had on the movie set. Hoffman didn't think all actors should direct because to do so, one had to think a certain way or deal with things a certain way which was the opposite way of an actor. However he thought Clooney definitely knew how to lead a film.

The actor was present at the film's screening at the BFI London Film Festival on October 22, 2011. At the press conference he was seen with Clooney and Evan Rachel Wood. The actor was also quoted in an October 20, 2011, article on the Virgin Media website about the film. He responded to the question of whether a similar movie about backstabbing and behind-the-scenes wrangling could be made about Hollywood. Hoffman believed the backgrounds were quite different as movies but he guessed a story could be told.

Clooney reported that for the scene where Paul reveals to Stephen that he had leaked the information about him to Ida, there was an end moment also shot where the two men yelled at each other, although Clooney knew he wasn't going to use it. Additionally the director advised that he deliberately didn't write dialogue for the scene where Paul gets into Morris' car after his affair with Molly has been discovered, because he wanted the audience to imagine instead what was said. Clooney advised that all the actors he cast were his first choices, and that Hoffman joined the company after they had been shooting for three weeks. He reported that he played basketball with Hoffman and that he was a good athlete.

After Hoffman's death, Clooney said his loss was heartbreaking and something he couldn't comprehend. He later said that Hoffman was loved and a friend to all actors in the community, an incredible talent who died way too young. The director said it was difficult for him to do the New York premiere for a war drama he directed, *The Monuments Men* (2014), two days after the death since he always thought of Hoffman in the city. Clooney said Hoffman was such a great actor because he was so instinctive that directing him was picking and choosing as he didn't need to tell him what to do. All he had to do was turn him loose and Hoffman would give him three choices and the director would do three takes with him. The first take would be very quiet and calm, the second just raging with screaming and spitting and yelling, and then one in between. Clooney said it was so much fun because it gave him options which didn't always happen with actors, since they had usually decided on something and that's what they did. Hoffman was always experimenting and wanting to push it a little bit. Clooney also reported that Hoffman wasn't a manically intense actor because when he called cut, it was easy for him to go home or to join him for dinner. Clooney thought the actor seemed to be very happy at that point in his life, and he saw him many times after the making of the film. They had dinner in Berlin a few months before Hoffman died and he seemed to be having a tougher time, though Clooney had no understanding of what was going on his mind and in his life that got him to that place. Clooney said he would like to think that Hoffman's death was an accident but what got him to a point where he did what he did was hard to understand. He felt that the problem with the situation was that there wasn't a great lesson to be learned and nothing good to come out of it. Talking about the dangers of drug use was not new and not the lesson. Therefore Clooney believed that Hoffman's death was as pure a tragedy as he had ever known.

Ryan Gosling reported that Hoffman yelled at him during the shooting but he needed it because, although he hadn't realized it, he had gotten lazy. Gosling learned a lot from watching Hoffman work. He advised that Hoffman put it all on the line for every single take and that was hard to do but somehow he managed to do it. Gosling reported that the older actor didn't suffer fools gladly and on a base level it was terrifying to work with him.

On March 16, 2011, *Deadline Hollywood* reported that Hoffman's Cooper's Town Productions and eOne Television were developing a project entitled *Upstate* for HBO. It was being written by Brett C. Leonard and Bob Glaudini and centered on recently laid-off Roy Perkins, who relocates his family to rural America to become a correctional officer in a new private prison run for profit. As the town and his family prosper, Roy encounters conflict and danger inside and outside the prison walls. Hoffman was also acting as co-executive producer on the show, which was to be broadcast later in the year. The project never got past the script stage. WENN reported that Hoffman attended a preview of Chris Rock's Broadway show *The Motherf**ker with the Hat* on March 17, 2011. The LAByrinth company was one of the producers of the show, which was written by Stephen Adly Guirgis and directed by Anna D. Shapiro. It ran at the Gerald Schoenfeld Theatre from April 11 to July 17, 2011.

WENN reported on March 23, 2011, that Neil Strauss, the writer of the script for the movie adaptation of Motley Crüe memoir *The Dirt*, saw Hoffman as Ozzy Osbourne.

Drummer Tommy Lee recently stated that Rob Zombie was on board to direct the film, but Zombie has since denied that. The film remains in development.

The actor participated in the HBO & Poetry Foundation made-for-television special *A Child's Garden of Poetry* (2011). Directed by Amy Schatz, the show (broadcast on April 28, 2011) won the 2011 Outstanding Children's Program Emmy Award. In it, Hoffman read "The Road Not Taken" by Robert Frost, with animation created and designed by Maciek Albrecht, sound effects and original music by Lesley Barber, Andrew Hollander and Joby Talbot. Hindsight makes one consider that the actor, like the character of the poem, perhaps took the wrong road in the choice he made in his personal life that led to his death.

Hoffman took *Jack Goes Boating* to the Edinburgh International Film Festival where it was screened at the George Square Theatre in June 2011. He was interviewed by Kaleem Aftab for the website The List in an article which was published on May 27, 2011, and updated on June 17, 2011. Hoffman commented that when he was directing the film, during takes he would walk back to the monitor and drive everyone crazy by saying, "I look awful." Hoffman advised that he relied upon everyone with him and their input to get through.

In a May 6, 2011, *New York Times* article about film director Dan Rush and his new comedy *Everything Must Go,* Rush said that he considered Hoffman for the leading role of an alcoholic sales representative who loses his job and his wife. He got the idea from a big wall portrait of the actor done by his photographer friend Peter Falk, with whom Rush shared a Los Angeles workspace. The director said he wanted an actor with a proven track record of bringing sad-sack characters to life, but eventually chose Will Ferrell.

It was reported on May 13, 2011, that Hoffman had appeared in a PSA video that featured a special group of celebrities who had come together to support fundraising in a relief effort for the March 11, 2011, earthquake and tsunami that had struck Japan. The videos were organized by actor Ken Watanabe and produced by Cross Media International and the Center for Asian American Media and the organization Unite for Japan. Under the latter title they had been screened at the Los Angeles Asian Pacific Film Festival on April 28, 2011. Hoffman appeared once on the PSA, with an underscore of the song "Amazing Grace." Hoffman stood in an office; windblown trees were seen outside the window. He held a white sign with black lettering: "Hope Heal Love." There were Japanese letters under the words, presumably the Japanese translation of the words.

On June 2, 2011, Hoffman plugged *Jack Goes Boating* on the BBC talk show *The Culture Show.* It was reported in *Variety* on June 8 that the actor had been offered a role in Summit Entertainment's *Now You See Me* (2013), a heist thriller to be directed by Louis Leterrier. The film had a script by Boaz Yakin and Edward Ricourt and followed a crack FBI squad caught in a game of cat-and-mouse with a super-team of the world's greatest illusionists, who pull off a series of bank heists during their performances and shower the audiences with the loot. Hoffman was reportedly offered one of the leads but then it was decided to age them down and he did not appear.

Shooting began for the Joanne Sellar-Ghoulardi Film Company-Annapurna Pictures Production drama *The Master* (2012) from June 9 to September 4, 2011, in Hawaii, Nevada and various locations in California. Writer-director Paul Thomas Anderson's film centered on mentally unstable ex-Marine and photographer Freddie Quell (Joaquin Phoenix) who in March 1950 meets the philosopher-author Lancaster Dodd (Hoffman), a.k.a. The Master, when he stows away on the yacht *Alethia* on which Dodd and his followers are sailing to New York. Freddie stays with the group (they describe their faith as The Cause), which involves using a processing method of recalling a person's past life. Dodd processes Freddie but he proves to be a destructive force to the group with his alcoholism where Dodd is tempted and chided for doing so by his wife Peggy (Amy Adams). The new recruit also acts as muscle, beating up John More (Christopher Evan Welch), a man who questions Dodd at a party hosted by Mildred Drummond (Patty McCormack), attacking the police that serve a civil warrant against Dodd, and attacking another man who criticizes Dodd's second published book. Dodd likes Freddie because he says he inspires him to write even though Freddie goes back on his promise to Peggy to stop drinking. Freddie also amuses Dodd, which is apparent when they roll around on the ground together after hugging, and Dodd thinks he can "cure the insane" of Freddie with his teachings, though it is clear that Freddie is not smart enough to understand what he is being taught. There is also the suggestion that Freddie's loyalty is questionable since it is feared that he may steal Dodd's unpublished work—something which expressed in a deleted scene between Freddie and Mark (Rami Maler). Dodd perhaps likes Freddie because he acts out the violence Dodd wants to, although Dodd disapproves of the behavior, and Dodd rewards him with a position of trust in the group. Dodd's expressed anger at anyone who questions his philosophy, his taste for liquor and smoking, and the civil warrant Mildred orders against him for wrongful withdrawal of funds also suggest that Dodd is morally flawed. However Freddie uses the game of motorbike riding to leave the group and he leaves again when he is invited to stay after visiting the school set up in England. Dodd's impact on Freddie is shown after he leaves where he processes Winn Manchester (Jennifer Neala Page) when he makes love to her.

The Master was Hoffman's fifth appearance for Anderson after *Hard Eight, Boogie Nights, Magnolia* and *Punch-Drunk Love.* The film also saw the actor reunited with Amy Adams from *Doubt.* The actor wears his hair short and combed back with a moustache and is clean-shaven, and he appears physically lighter than in *Moneyball.* His costumes are colorful period items as well as a cowboy outfit and a biker's outfit of leather jacket and jeans. Hoffman uses a formal speech pattern except for when he expresses anger. The character is a combination of extrovert and introvert, since Dodd is an intellectual who writes, philosophizes and makes speeches but also smokes and drinks and yells and swears. Hoffman is funny in his comic pleasure at the wedding of Elizabeth (Ambyr Childers) and Mark and also in the beginning of his speech at The Cause's Phoenix congress. We also see him being masturbated by Peggy though it is not graphically shown, riding a motorbike, singing and dancing to the song "I'll Go No More a Roving" and singing "On a Slow Boat to China." The first song is delivered in a fey manner by Hoffman, although Anderson has the performance break the melody and the actor is upstaged by the sight of naked women and also cutaways to the observing Freddie. The performance of the second song is also upstaged by Anderson's camera coverage of Phoenix and Freddie's reaction. Hoffman gets a funny line in the prison scene where Dodd and Freddie share adjacent cells: Freddie smashes the cell's toilet and Dodd comments, "Your fear of capture and imprisonment is an implant from millions of years ago." The scene also features a funny moment where both men swear simultaneously at each other. In Hoffman's best scene, Dodd is confronted by John More at Mildred's party. Dodd repeatedly ignores the question from More as he is processing Margaret O'Brien (Barbara Brownell), and then defends his philosophy with growing anger until he erupts with yelling "Pig fuck!" since he believes that More is grilling him rather than wanting a conversation and asks questions that he already knows the answers to.

The film premiered on September 1, 2012, at the Venice Film Festival, which Hoffman attended. The film was then screened at the Toronto International Film Festival on September 7. It was given a limited release on September 14 and then a wide release on September 21. Justin Chang in *Variety* wrote that Hoffman simply mesmerized. A.O. Scott in the *New York Times* said that the actor brought his character to life with the flair and precision of a great concert pianist and presented an integrated, highly nuanced, supremely Methodical self to the camera. Peter Travers in *Rolling Stone* wrote that Hoffman was never finer, with a monumental *tour de force* here as a do-gooder-turned-silky-charlatan, which topped all his previous portrayals in Anderson films. Roger Ebert in the *Chicago Sun-Times* said that Hoffman suggested the charisma that a character like L. Ron Hubbard must have had. The film did not recoup its production costs but it received Academy Award nominations for Best Actor for Phoenix, Best Supporting Actor for Hoffman and Best Supporting Actress for Adams. All three lost, Hoffman defeated by Christoph Waltz for the Western *Django Unchained* (2012).

The DVD features deleted scenes in a collection called "Back Beyond." Hoffman appears in 12 of them. Additionally there are scenes that explain some plot points regarding Dodd, and a scene that has three goofs. The deleted scenes include: Dodd and Freddie on the yacht where Dodd tell him that he thinks they have known each other before and asking him if he would like to do away with harm from his past life; Dodd at Mildred's party suggesting to the unseen Mildred that he demonstrate his processing on Margaret and then preparing her for it by making her comfortable lying in the sofa, with a flash suggesting that that the session is being photographed; Dodd carrying Freddie in the scene where they roll on the ground outside the Philadelphia house; Dodd watching and applauding Elizabeth firing a rifle in the desert and walking with Freddie; Dodd and Freddie walking in the desert and finding the buried box of Dodd's second book; Dodd eating a meal and Mark asking him if it is possible for books to kill people (Dodd says it is); Dodd and Freddie bringing the second book manuscript to Dodd's office and Dodd asking Freddie to guard it overnight after he leaves; Dodd dancing in reaction to Melora Walters singing "A-Tisket A-Tasket" with two musicians with new words for The Master at the Phoenix congress, then joining her to sit at the piano to be kissed by and hug her; Dodd in the Phoenix crowd applauding when Freddie is presented with a jacket for being first lieutenant for The Cause; Dodd preparing to be photographed in his office and dressed as a cowboy in the desert and laughing as he is photographed by Freddie; and Dodd dancing with and applauding Freddie after the concentration exercise.

The scenes that don't feature Hoffman but still have a narrative impact include Mark telling Freddie how in 1945 Dodd had died for seven minutes during an operation in an army hospital and he came back with a storm of vision and creative output that led him to write his second book, which supposedly led 12 people that read it to go insane or commit suicide; Freddie asking Mark how much Dodd's unpublished manuscript would be worth; and Freddie leaving a note on a noticeboard at the England school that says "Gone to China," which pays off the scene where Dodd sings "On a Slow Boat to China." The goof scene also has a narrative impact since in it Dodd smokes a Kool cigarette Freddie lights for him after Freddie's processing; this later pays off Dodd asking Freddie to bring him Kools to England because they don't have them there. The goof scene has Hoffman initially laughing after Dodd's line of "I like Kools. Minty flavor." We hear a voice (presumably Anderson's) say to do it one more time; after Phoenix lights Hoffman's cigarette, Hoffman repeats the lines, but laughs again. The third time it is Phoenix who laughs at Hoffman's lines, which makes Hoffman laugh.

The character of Dodd was reported to be inspired by—though not entirely modeled on—Scientology's L. Ron Hubbard. But Hoffman said the film was not about Scientology and that when you saw the film you would see that he was not even trying to play Hubbard. He said he never thought of Hubbard but rather many other people, like Orson Welles, who had that gravitas and personality and aura. Hoffman admitted that the film was influenced and inspired by some of the events around Scientology but ultimately it wasn't a film about it. To the actor's mind, Dodd led a very successful movement, and the film got the point where the movement was starting to go bad where it might be turning into a cult.

Hoffman said it was very nerve-wracking to sing in the film, though it was perfect for that scene. He said he could hold a note, but he had admiration and respect for the people who could actually do that in front of 2000 people. Asked about

Japanese poster for *The Master* (2012).

working with Anderson, Hoffman reported that he had never worked with a filmmaker so willing to reinvent himself. Anderson said that Phoenix was the first choice for the part of Freddie but the actor was then doing his *I'm Still Here* shtick. The director would have conversations with Hoffman where they would wonder how much longer Phoenix would be doing that, since it was reported that the actor had been living that fat, crazy bearded life for six to eight months. This is why Anderson turned to Jeremy Renner to play the part before it ended up working out with Phoenix.

In a *New York Times* article on Phoenix (September 4, 2012), Hoffman talked about his co-star's casting in the film. When he was proposed by Anderson (who said Hoffman needed a formidable opponent), Hoffman said Phoenix scared him, in a good way. Hoffman advised that he had already met him a couple times but they didn't know each other. They had been at the same 2006 Oscar ceremony when Hoffman won Best Actor for *Capote* and Phoenix was nominated as Best Actor for the musical biography *Walk the Line*. Hoffman advised that when they met for the first rehearsal they never brought up their prior acquaintance or what they had talked about which Hoffman thought was kind of great. The actor said about the scene where Freddie and Dodd hugged and rolled around on the ground that it came out of something he and Anderson had always done together. Hoffman and the director had known each other since their 20s and he recalled one time when Anderson was falling in love and came to see him. They were in a bar in the middle of the day although they weren't drunk and Anderson was very happy and he started grabbing Hoffman and they ended up wrestling. The actor said it got so rambunctious that the bar owner almost kicked them out. It was playful but disturbing because it was two grown men, and the behavior came out of excitement and camaraderie and friendship. Hoffman said that for the film, he and Anderson had maybe talked about this kind of action a few days prior to shooting the scene but the actor didn't want to tell Phoenix. He kept it in the back of his mind and when they came to do the scene, Hoffman told Anderson that he was going to try something that Phoenix was unaware of. However, the actor felt that he knew his co-star well enough that he knew he would react and that it would lead to something. Hoffman thought that this scene encapsulated physically what the film was about.

It was reported that making the film led to Hoffman having a relapse of his alcoholism, and that he had his first drink in 23 years at the wrap party. Perhaps this was influenced by the fact of Dodd being tempted to drink by Freddie in the narrative.

Hoffman was a guest speaker at the Film Society of Lincoln Center's retrospective for director Sidney Lumet, who had died on April 9, 2011. Entitled "Prince of the City: Remembering Sidney Lumet," the festival ran from July 19 until July 25, 2011, with screenings at the Walter Reade Theatre. On June 27, Hoffman had spoken lovingly at a tribute to Lumet by the Film Society at Alice Tulley Hall. He discussed starring in Lumet's final feature, *Before the Devil Knows You're Dead*.

The *New York Times* reported on August 12, 2011, that Mike Nichols' production of *Death of a Salesman* was to open in March 2012 at the Barrymore Theater. The Independent Filmmaker Project and the Film Society of Lincoln Center announced on September 13, 2011, that Hoffman was one of the mentors for Emerging Visions, a collaborative program to take place during that year's New York Film Festival. The program was to take place on October 3 at Lincoln Center's Elinor Bunin Munroe Film

Center with 25 emerging filmmaking talents attending with a documentary or narrative feature that had been selected from IFP and the Film Society of Lincoln Center's talent pool. They would be paired with an established director or producer who would mentor them, offering guidance and connections to filmmakers on both their current projects and careers. Each filmmaker would receive mentorship and year-round support from both organizations through annual memberships and participation in panels and events. It was not announced who was to be mentored by Hoffman.

Hoffman attended the 55th BFI London Film Festival and a television special was screened on the British Sky Arts channel on October 12, 2011. On October 18, he attended the Paris opening on *The Ides of March*. The actor also attended the afterparty at L'Arc, a 19th-century townhouse mansion at the top of the Champs-Élysées that had been converted into a nightclub-restaurant. Hoffman reportedly sat a table with George Clooney and renowned French actresses Catherine Deneuve and Juliette Binoche. He was also in London on October 19, 2011, for the film.

The actor was interviewed by Simon Hattenstone for an interview that was published in *The Guardian* on October 29, 2011. The reporter mentioned film writer David Thomson's comment that the actor was no longer stretching himself; Thomson wondered why he didn't do a reverse De Niro, lose weight for jobs, and surprise us with his svelteness. The actor said that he had lost weight for roles before but he considered the idea of the romantic leading man now to be myth. He felt they didn't exist any more and, if they did, he actually found those characters uninteresting. Hoffman advised that now his family came first and he said that he had to remember to not kill himself. He said he was so different when he started out, more moody, more mercurial. As a young man, Hoffman felt it was all or nothing, but now as an older man he was confident that there would be another film and another relationship, or he would die. But if he was alive, he knew that life was going to keep throwing things at him.

On the December 10, 2011, episode of *Saturday Night Live,* Jason Sudeikis impersonated Hoffman in a New Year's Eve spoof. *The* February 7, 2012, *Hollywood Reporter* revealed that the actor was in final negotiations to star in the thriller *A Most Wanted Man* for Anton Corbijn. The Andrew Bovell script was based on John le Carré's bestselling spy novel. The story followed a British banker who tries to aid a young Muslim immigrant targeted by the U.S., German and British secret services after he is taken in by a Turkish family in Hamburg. Hoffman was to play the head of the German secret spy organization, and shooting was said to begin in Hamburg in September 2012.

The actor was interviewed for the 2012 book *The Muses Go to School,* published by the New Press. Edited by Herbert Kohl and Tom Oppenheimer, it was a collection of inspiring stories about the importance of arts in education. Hoffman said what he wanted for his children was for the arts to be taught with other disciplines like math and science and sports so that they could be all integrated because that was what life was like. He felt education had to be structured to understand that that was the way creative minds could be developed. Hoffman knew that his son was lucky because he was his kid and travelled with him and walked into many theaters. The actor said his son understood acting and they talked about plays and performances but Hoffman also loved sports and he liked to utilize creative energy and creative talk through sports with him. He reported that for ten years he had been working with a public school in the Bronx which had kids of the lower-income areas from sixth grade up, helping them to raise money. Hoffman joined with them through his theater company and the school had taken part in LAByrinth shows.

The actor was interviewed at WNYC's The Greene Space in February 2012 when he was in rehearsal for *Death of a Salesman* where he talked about the play and his acting past. Hoffman reported that the play was emotionally draining and demanded a lot of him but the experience was also thrilling. He said he would now never think of looking at how other actors had done the role because he thought what they did would get stuck in his head in a weird way, even though he had seen Dustin Hoffman play it on stage and televised clips of the Lee J. Cobb version. Hoffman talked about the idea of being too young to play Willy Loman and said that the literalness of the character's age was not the issue. Hoffman said Mike Nichols *was* the production to him. The actor advised that the director had mentioned the part to him a while back and it just kind of stuck in his head, and he thought he fought it for a long time, but Nichols kept on him about it. Hoffman said their work together was very fruitful and challenging and incredibly entertaining and a loving experience.

Death of a Salesman began its preview performances on February 14, 2012. The previews were to begin on February 13, but this date had to be cancelled because Hoffman was ill with the flu. Photographs published in the *New York Times* showed that Hoffman was clean-shaven for the part and that his hair was cut in a short period style. In a *Times* article, Mike Nichols said he wanted Hoffman because of his endlessly curious nature and his determination to figure things out. The director advised that those qualities initially unnerved him during rehearsals in 2001 for *The Seagull* where Hoffman played Konstantin. Nichols recalled how one day Hoffman was very loud, one day he couldn't hear him, one day he wasn't doing the right blocking and when he asked what was going on, Hoffman said he had to do all the things he wasn't going to ultimately do. And Nichols said indeed he didn't do them. He advised that the actor searched for his performances, and how he did it was completely mysterious to Nichols. Co-star Andrew Garfield advised he had grown close to the older actor out of admiration and he particularly respected his choice of emotionally intense and vanity-free roles. Hoffman had told him to chase whatever he respected and if it happened to make him a bunch of money, that was fine, and if it didn't that was also fine.

After 30 previews the show opened on March 15, 2012, and would run till June 2, 2012. Despite the show's success, there was no extension due to scheduling commitments for members of its cast.

Some of Hoffman's past co-workers attending on opening night were Julianne Moore and Meryl Streep. Marilyn Stasio in *Variety* said that Hoffman was a superb actor going for the gold. Ben Brantley in the *New York Times* wrote that the actor was deeply thoughtful and uncomfortably cast. He said there were instances of piercing emotional conviction throughout, but Hoffman didn't give the illusion of the younger Willy's certainty of the belief in false gods. Unlike the titan Willy of Brian Dennehy of 1999, whose tragedy was how the hope-inflated man has all the air go out of him, this Willy was pre-shrunk. Charles Isherwood wrote about the production in an article that was published on April 20, 2012. In it he said that Hoffman's performance felt constricted, and a little monotonous, lacking in the full range of emotional dynamics that the role demanded. When Isherwood returned to the show almost a month after it had opened, he found that the actor had burrowed more deeply into his characters' troubled psyche and connected to the material on a more visceral level.

Hoffman reported in his later interview for *Esquire* that it was a very hard job physically and spiritually. Following the actor's death, it was said that he was never the same after doing it. David Bar Katz reported that the play tortured him and that Hoffman confided to him that he didn't want to act in theater again after its run for a while. The playwright also commented in the February 27, 2014, *Rolling Stone* that the actor was miserable during the entire run of the play, and that putting himself through the experience on a continual basis rewired his brain. Ethan Hawke said he never saw Hoffman drink until *Death of a Salesman*, and reportedly Hoffman told a friend that after 23 years sober, he felt he could risk drinking in moderation. Hoffman later reflected on the balance artists may or may not strike between creating art and living their lives. He said when he was in a play he didn't function very well and when he was doing *Death of a Salesman* it was petrifying.

The show was nominated for the Tony Awards for Best Revival of a Play, Best Actor in a Play for Hoffman, Best Featured Actor in a Play for Andrew Garfield, Best Featured Actress in a Play for Linda Emond, Best Lighting Design of a Play, Best Sound Design of a Play, and Best Direction of a Play for Mike Nichols. In the May 12, 2012, *New York Times*, Ben Brantley predicted that Hoffman would win Best Actor though James Corden should win for *One Man, Two Guvnors*. On June 7, 2012, Patrick Healy wrote in an article that Corden and Hoffman were believed to be tied in voting but Hoffman seemed to have the edge in the era of the struggling everyman. The only Tony Awards that *Death of a Salesman* won were for Best Play Revival and Nichols.

On March 30, 2012, it was reported that FX had put in development *Inside*, a drama from playwright-screenwriter Kyle Jarrow and Philip Seymour Hoffman's Cooper's Town Productions. The semi-serialized cop drama followed a San Francisco homicide detective who discovers his real father is a convicted serial killer who claims to be innocent of murdering the cop's mother. Hoffman was to executive produce. The television series was never made.

The actor attended a special luncheon held at the Four Seasons Restaurant to honor Mike Nichols on April 23, 2012. When the director introduced the cast of *Death of a Salesman*, he called Hoffman one of the greatest actors of our time. After Nichols was done, the actor reportedly stood and blew him a kiss. Hoffman said he was going to be directing Mark Ruffalo on a project by Kenneth Lonergan, and had plans to direct both film and theater. Hoffman commented that after finishing the play's run, he needed to give his emotional psyche a rest.

It was reported on May 17, 2012, that the actor had confirmed his commitment to star in *A Most Wanted Man*. On May 18, Hoffman presented the 78th annual Drama League Awards for Distinguished Play to John Robin Baitz's *Other Desert Cities* at a luncheon ceremony at the Marriott Marquis Times Square. It was announced on May 20 that the actor was to star in *Hate Mail* with Robert Pattison and Scarlett Johansson. It was never made.

Hoffman attended the Theatre World Awards held at the Belasco Theatre. The awards were to honor actors who had made an outstanding achievement in a Broadway or Off-Broadway debut. Hoffman presented an award to his *Death of a Salesman* co-star Finn Wittrock. The older actor said Finn had set the bar for a part that was set back in the '40s, and he thought he would set the bar for every part.

On June 10, 2012, a white-bearded Hoffman attended the 2012 Tony Awards, held at the Beacon Theatre and televised live by CBS. There was a cut to Hoffman when his nomination for Best Actor in a Play was announced by Candice Bergen. Hoffman lost the award to James Corden for *One Man, Two Guvnors*.

10

The Hunger Games: Catching Fire, A Most Wanted Man

It was reported on June 11, 2012, that the actor had decided to leave his agency, Paradigm, where he had been for years. Hoffman reportedly informed them of this in the previous few days, and for now he planned on going it alone. On the same day it was also reported by *Variety* that the actor had been offered the role of the new Plutarch Heavensbee in the *Hunger Games* sequel *Catching Fire*. Heavensbee took over as the new Gamemaker following the demise of Seneca Crane (Wes Bentley) in the original film. One source said that the series' producer Lionsgate had made the actor the offer, but another said they refused to comment. But with shooting set to begin later in the summer or in the fall, more news was expected very soon.

Reports from June 22, 2012, seemed to confirm the actor's casting in *The Hunger Games: Catching Fire*, and Lionsgate announced it on July 9. The deal was reportedly made right before the Fourth of July holiday. The film was due to start filming in the autumn.

On August 1, 2012, it was announced in the *New York Times* that the actor would direct again for LAByrinth for their 2012–2013 season. The play was a new comedy by Bob Glaudini, *A Family for All Occasions*; it was to be produced in the spring of 2013 at the Bank Street Theater. It was reported on September 8, 2012, that Hoffman was present at the Venice Film Festival to accept the Best Actor prize that he shared with Joaquin Phoenix for *The Master*. He accepted for Phoenix and also Paul Thomas Anderson, who won the Best Director prize (both of them had left for Toronto, the next stop on the festival circuit).

The Color Force-Lionsgate Production sci-fi thriller *The Hunger Games: Catching Fire* (2013) had a screenplay by Simon Beaufoy and Michael deBruyn based on the novel of the same name by Suzanne Collins. Directed by Francis Lawrence, it was filmed in Atlanta, Georgia, Oahu, Hawaii, and New Jersey from September 10, 2012, to March 2013. The story was a sequel to *The Hunger Games* (2012) which introduced the televised games held in the dystopian future in the totalitarian nation of Panem. Now victors Katniss Everdeen (Jennifer Lawrence) and Peeta Mellark (Josh Hutcherson) tour the districts on a train before being made to participate in the seventh anniversary games.

Hoffman's Plutarch Heavensbee apparently plots with the Capitol's President Snow

(Donald Sutherland) to stop Katniss being considered to be a heroine of the Mockingjay rebels, by having the peace-keeping forces persecute the villagers of her home District 12. He also invents a wrinkle for the 75th anniversary games, a Third Quarter Quell, which sees Katniss having to fight with Peeta and other male and female tribute teams. Plutarch's game has the tributes battling to survive in a jungle arena under a dome, and he provides hourly threats like poison fog, monkeys, sea waves, lightning and blood. He expects that Katniss will be discredited when she turns against her allies Peeta, Finnick Odair (Sam Claflin), Mags (Lynn Cohen), Johanna Mason (Jena Malone), Beetee (Jeffrey Wright) and Wiress (Amanda Plummer) to win the game, which will also help to discredit the revolution. She disrupts the game when she uses an electronic wire to fire into the dome's force field which cuts off the power to the Capitol's control room surveillance. When Katniss is brought back to a hovercraft, it's revealed that Plutarch is loyal to the revolutionaries and his mission is said to be to get her out of the games because she is Mockingjay.

The film sees Hoffman reunited with Jeffrey Wright, who appeared with him in *The Ides of March,* and Jena Malone from *Cold Mountain.* Hoffman, seventh-billed, has the belly that he lost for *The Master* (he retained it for his subsequent films). Plutarch has one main costume, a dark blue shirt with knee-length black coat and black pants, though he also has a purple vest during the games and at the film's end. Hoffman's character doesn't provide him with much of an acting challenge, though he adds some smiles and humor to his apparent baddie to suggest the revealed duplicity. He is appropriately earnest when we learn he is working in the revolution.

The film premiered in London on November 11, 2013, and then opened in the U.S. on November 18 with the taglines "Every revolution begins with a spark," "Remember who the enemy is," "The sun persists in rising, so I make myself stand" and "Remember, girl on fire, I'm still betting on you." Hoffman attended the Los Angeles premiere and later said that it was crazy like the Oscars, weird and exciting. He said when he was offered the part he really didn't know what it was about so he started to read the books, and by the end of the third book he was just blown away by what the writer did. He also predicted that the franchise would be a real exciting series for many years. Peter DeBruge of *Variety* wrote that Hoffman's appearance was a casting coup, and Peter Travers in *Rolling Stone* said that Hoffman gave a witty, wily performance that added to the film's class-act casting choices. Manohla Dargis in the *New York Times* wrote that Hoffman looked uncomfortable. A box office success, it was followed by the sequels *The Hunger Games: Mockingjay—Part 1* (2014) and *The Hunger Games: Mockingjay—Part 2* (2015), both of which also featured Hoffman.

The DVD features deleted scenes and three have Hoffman in them. "A Wrinkle" shows the conversation between Snow and Plutarch where he suggests the wrinkle to have Katniss and the other tributes eliminated. In this scene Snow speaks of the jabberjays which prefigures their appearance in the game. We see drawings of them and he advises that they were organic spy mutts who were outmoded but some escaping birds had mated with mockingbirds to become mockingjays. In "Switching Envelopes" Plutarch is seen walking in a corridor and then down a staircase to unlock a compartment which holds a sealed envelope. He replaces the envelope with one he produces from his pocket and burns the original.

10. The Hunger Games: Catching Fire, A Most Wanted Man   153

Top: Hoffman at left with Woody Harrelson and unidentified extras in *The Hunger Games: Catching Fire* (2013). *Bottom:* Hoffman in *The Hunger Games: Mockingjay—Part 1* (2014).

Hoffman said that when he was offered the part, he also went and saw the first film which he thought was pretty good. The actor said he had bought his son the books and he was going to read them with him. The actor took the role because he liked the people involved, thinking it was a great group of actors and a great environment. He was attracted to the character because it was an interesting role. The actor felt that, although his role in the film wasn't big, that would change with the Mockingjay sequels, which he was looking forward to.

Francis Lawrence reported that locking Hoffman down for the role took more patience than persuasion: The actor was in the middle of *Death of a Salesman* when he was approached and said he wasn't really interested in entertaining anything until he was done with that. Lawrence beefed up Hoffman's role since most of Plutarch's action came in the last installment of the series, *Mockingjay*. The director thought the actor was amazing in the film and considered himself lucky to have him. Lawrence advised that a moment was cut from the party scene where Plutarch flashes Katniss a pocket watch with a hologram of the mockingjay on its face because it was believed this ruined the film's surprise of Plutarch's true allegiance. It was thought that the moment might work if Katniss thought he was only messing with her but ultimately it was decided that the symbolism was too ambiguous. Lionsgate co-president Erik Feig commented that they wanted Plutarch to be scheming, brilliant and masterful, and they knew Hoffman could deliver on all fronts. Co-producer Bryan Unkeless said that Hoffman brought substance to the role: He had experience, intelligence and depth. It was reported that many of the actors were in awe of him when he arrived on the set. Josh Hutcherson said that watching him was like going to an acting class.

On September 13, 2012, Hoffman, interviewed by Peter Travers for the ABC celebrity interview show *Popcorn*, spoke about *The Master* and Paul Thomas Anderson. Asked why he wasn't in Anderson's *There Will Be Blood* (2007), Hoffman said there was no part for him in it. The actor said he had helped the director with reading the script and that Anderson was always looking for a part for Hoffman but couldn't find one in it. Hoffman realized that their friendship had the priority so if he was never in another Anderson film, he felt that would be fine and the actor would be grateful for the Anderson films he *had* been in.

He laughed about the perception of him as a serious actor with photographs of him in the *New York Times* with his hand to his forehead, with Hoffman admitting to being kind of a nut. He said he didn't strategize his role choices so that he would do a comic role after a serious one, or a bad guy role like the one in *Mission: Impossible III* as a change of pace. Rather the actor chose unexpected roles like that because he thought they would be fun and he said there was a lot more of himself in those roles that people realized. Hoffman wanted to have a good time. Travers ended his interview with a request for Hoffman to sing. The actor claimed he could not sing but Travers gave the example of his singing in *The Master* as proof that he could. Hoffman refused to sing "On a Slow Boat to China" even after Travers began singing it to try to get him to join in.

On September 17, 2012, *Variety* reported that Hoffman was to direct the Depression Era ghost story *Ezekiel Moss* for Mandalay Pictures. The script by Keith Bunin followed an imaginative small-town boy who befriends a mysterious drifter who may have the ability to communicate with the dead. The film was to be co-produced by Emily Ziff of Hoffman's Cooper's Town Productions. Co-producer Anthony Bregman stated that Hoffman was an unsurpassed artist as an actor and director, on stage and in film. Fellow co-producer Amy Schulman commented that Hoffman was one of the great talents of our generation and they were thrilled to be in his capable hands.

The Film4 crime thriller *A Most Wanted Man* was shot from September 23 to November 23, 2012, on location in Berlin and Hamburg, Germany. It had a screenplay by Andrew Bovell with additional writing by Stephen Cornwell, based on the novel by John le Carré, and was directed by Anton Corbijn. Grigory Dobrygin starred as 26-year-old Issa Karpov, a Russian-Chechen escaped militant Muslim jihadist who illegally immigrates to Hamburg seeking asylum. Hoffman played the part of Gunther Bachmann. The head of an unlawful anti-terrorist intelligence unit in Hamburg, he spies on Issa and his contacts, Sanctuary North human rights lawyer Annabel Richter (Rachel McAdams) and Brue Freres private banker Thomas "Tommy" Brue (Willem Dafoe). Gunther also liaises with the U.S. Embassy representative in Berlin, Martha Sullivan (Robin Wright), and has a desire to capture Dr. Faisal Abdullah (Homayoun Ershadi), who may have links to militant Islamist groups like Al-Qaeda. Gunther believes that Issa will give the ten million Euro money his drug lord father Colonel Grigori Borisovich Karpov has left in Brue's bank to Abdullah. Learning that Issa does not want the money, Gunther has Annabel kidnapped so that he can persuade her to make Issa agree to give the money to Abdullah. When Abdullah makes the deal, it's decided that he will be taken by Gunther's unit, with Gunther acting as a fake taxi driver to pick up Abdullah. Their plan is sabotaged by other government agents who take him and Issa instead—and betray Gunther's promise of asylum for Issa. These betrayals are apparently not new for Gunther since his backstory includes an assignment in Beirut where he lost some of his network men when American agents made a mistake. Gunther is presented as an honorable man who says he wants to make the world a better place. He is willing to compromise and give Issa asylum in order to use him to get Abdullah as a bigger target and to neutralize a potential terrorist action.

The film was dedicated in loving memory of Hoffman, who is top-billed. He is clean-shaven though also has some stubble, and wears no glasses and his hair is medium-length. Hoffman uses a German accent and also speaks in German. The role lets us see him perform the actions of driving cars, smoking, drinking, running in the street, pushing through a crowd at a disco, pushing Annabel and playing the piano. We see Gunther embrace his colleague Irna Frey (Nina Hoss) in the street though it is to cover their surveillance of Annabel so it is an action devoid of romantic attachment. Gunther is another combination for Hoffman of playing a character who is both an introvert and an extrovert. His extrovert behavior includes swearing and compulsive smoking and drinking, but when he punches a man in a bar who has slapped a woman, it is presented as an act of chivalry.

The actor supplies some humor to Gunther, as well as a deadly stare to show his contempt for other officials to whom he has to answer, and unemotional sadness. The latter quality is presumably a hangover from the Beirut experience but also perhaps due to the dark worlds that his job requires him to enter. Hoffman has his late-period actor gravitas and a new stillness. He uses a manipulative tenderness when he hugs and touches the face of his agent Jamal (Mehdi Dehbi), and later touches him again when he arranges for Jamal to abandon his father who is Abdullah. Hoffman's best scene is perhaps in the climax when Gunther yells in rage at the betrayal when Abdullah is taken from him. Director Corbijn holds the camera on a long closeup of the actor's face in reaction and then films him from behind as he walks away. Although Corbijn cuts to Irna's reaction, he returns to a long closeup of Hoffman in his car before he drives away and then has a long shot of Hoffman's back with his face seen in the driver's rear mirror. If this film was the last screened of Hoffman's, his last moment where Gunther gets out of the taxi and leaves the frame would have been a resonant cinematic exit for the actor.

The film premiered on January 14, 2014, at the Sundance Film Festival, which Hoffman attended. He can be seen in YouTube footage being photographed standing with Corbijn, Willem Dafoe, Rachel McAdams and Grigory Dobrygin. In a *National Enquirer* article (February 17, 2014), friends of Hoffman said that he appeared pasty and disheveled at Sundance. Anton Corbijn felt that the actor did not look well, and it was only when the director looked back later that he saw that Hoffman was actually more disheveled than he had realized. Corbijn thought it was just the way he operated.

In an Associated Press interview Hoffman said that he had never read a John Le Carré novel which now he felt was a sin because he was such a wonderful writer. He said that when he read it, there was something about that story that spoke to him about where he was in his life. The actor said that making the film was very satisfying, far more than most he had been on. Asked about the awards circuit, Hoffman said when he was nominated for *Capote* he and Bennett Miller made a pact to do everything and go to everything so then they would never have to do it again. And so he had never done it again and only went to what he had to go to and he was very grateful for that, since it avoided cynicism which could set in after the repeated experiences began to wear on one.

A Most Wanted Man was given a limited release on July 22, 2014, before being given a wide release on August 1. Justin Chang in *Variety* wrote that Hoffman brought a superb world-weary quality to the role. Manohla Dargis in the *New York Times* said that the actor invested his role with gravity and his performance was so finely etched that the film became, almost inescapably, something of a last testament. Peter Travers in *Rolling Stone* wrote that Hoffman's performance was a master class in acting, and that we would not see the actor's like again. The film was a box office success.

Twenty years before *A Most Wanted Man* was shot, Hoffman had been to Hamburg to do a play, presumably *The Merchant of Venice*. He said when he came back he stayed at the same hotel, the Atlantic. Hoffman said he didn't immediately remember it as the same hotel but when he did he had the weird feeling of being home again. He felt he was lucky to be asked to do the film and that Corbijn felt he was good enough to play the part. Hoffman said that Corbijn was a gorgeous man with a terrific artistic sensibility who looked at everything in a unique way.

Corbijn had previously met Hoffman on a 2011 photo shoot for *Vogue* (Corbijn was the photographer). When Corbijn drove him to the location, Hoffman didn't say much so he thought that he really disliked him. The director said it was an odd situation because it had been arranged for him to meet the actor to talk about the film, and then *Vogue* had also asked him to photograph Hoffman, totally unrelated. The photography session was scheduled on the same day as the meeting and Corbijn was told that Hoffman was only able to have the meeting in the afternoon because he had this photo shoot in the morning. So when the actor arrived for the shoot, he was confused. Corbijn said that while they we were waiting for some pants to be tailored for Hoffman, they talked about the film. The director advised that the film was originally to be shot in the summer and the reason it was switched to autumn was that Hoffman was not available in the summer. Corbijn said he considered no one else for the part and what made him think of the actor was his amazing body of work, and how he looked for that role. You could see him as a German who ate too much food though the director believed that the actor's incredible talent was that he could play any character and make him believable. Corbijn thought that Hoffman was tremendous in the film and got the impression that he was a tortured soul, though he never thought the actor was doing drugs during filming. He felt that the actor was an artist and artists were sensitive people who needed other people to help them and make them feel good. Corbijn advised that he and Hoffman had one disagreement about shooting a scene Hoffman didn't feel he was ready to film, but after they argued, the two figured out how to work together.

Corbijn reported that the actor watched a rough cut of the film with him. The two spent some time together only two weeks prior to Hoffman's death, and Corbijn said that the actor seemed in a good place despite some issues he had to deal with. The director said Hoffman was the most gifted actor he had ever worked with. Corbijn agreed that the poignancy related to his death was that he appeared to be on the verge of a breakthrough, as he was starting to be considered a bona fide leading man. The director felt it was hard for Hoffman to get leading

Chinese poster for *A Most Wanted Man* (2014).

roles, but if you looked at the ones that he did, they were so good you could not believe he wasn't always the leading actor.

Willem Dafoe commented that he liked working with Hoffman very much. Dafoe saw the film at Sundance when Hoffman was also present; according to Dafoe, he seemed gregarious enough and then a couple of weeks later he heard the news of his death. The actor said it stayed with him and added a layer to watching the character in the film who obviously had real conflict and real pain, and it made it natural to think of Hoffman and the circumstances of his death. Nina Hoss said she was a huge fan of Hoffman's and she was really excited to meet him and to watch him work. She advised that he such a great colleague and it was really lovely to work with him.

John le Carré, interviewed in the *New York Times* (April 18, 2013), commented that the actor's performance as Truman Capote was the best single performance he had seen on screen. The writer stated that Hoffman was his personal choice to play George Smiley, the central character in many of his other novels, should he ever be portrayed by an American. He commented that the actor had an intelligence that came at you like a pair of headlights and enveloped you from the moment he grabbed your hand. Le Carré joked that Hoffman wasn't much of a lover on screen, and initial talks of giving him a bedroom scene were scrapped. Le Carré also saw that Hoffman was troubled and said he was burning himself out before your eyes. He felt nobody could live at his pace and stay the course, and in bursts of startling intimacy the actor needed you to know it. Le Carré said whenever Hoffman left the room, you were afraid you had seen the last of him.

Le Carré said more about the actor in a July 20, 2014, *New York Times* article he wrote. The writer advised that he had spent five hours at most with the actor on the set of the film. Le Carré recalled that a novelist friend of his was asked to leave by Hoffman because the actor said something about her presence bothered him. The woman had been standing in a group 30-odd yards away from him, just watching, and even though Hoffman didn't know her Le Carré said the actor just sniffed her out. The writer said Hoffman's intuition was luminous from the instant you met him, as was his intelligence. He described him as a shining, artistic polymath. He would greet you by putting a huge arm round your neck and shoving a cheek against yours, or hug you to him like a big, pudgy schoolboy, then stand and beam at you while he took stock of the effect. Le Carré advised Hoffman greeted him as if he'd been waiting to meet the writer all his life, which he suspected was how he greeted everyone. The writer said that the actor took stock of everything, all the time, that it was painful and exhausting work, and probably in the end his undoing. The world was too bright for him to handle—he had to screw up his eyes or be dazzled to death. Le Carré ended the article by saying that we shall wait a long time for another Philip.

Hoffman was in Venice's Hotel Excelsior when he was interviewed by Robbin Collin for a *Telegraph* article published on October 23, 2012. He did not appear to have shaved in days, maybe weeks, and the whole lower half of his face and upper neck were flecked with fluffy silver hair. Hoffman was there to talk about *The Master* after the film had had its world premiere at the Venice Film Festival the previous month.

He was interviewed by James Mottram in the ballroom of the Venetian Hotel for an October 28, 2012, *Independent* article on *The Master*. Hoffman spoke about the press' interest in his private life. He attended the Classic Stage Company production of Anton Chekhov's play *Ivanov* which ran at the East 13th Street/CSC Theatre from November 11 to December 9, 2012. This was directed by Austin Pendleton and starred his friend Ethan Hawke in the title role. Hoffman was said to be beloved by friends in the theater for always seeing and supporting their work. Hawke reported that at the time the actor seemed different and more troubled. Hoffman told him how he loved the play, with its study of depression, but it affected him. Hawke said it was a little upsetting to see this and he observed that his friend was not at his happiest.

The November 2012 *Esquire* featured a Hoffman interview by Scott Raab in which he talked about *Moneyball*, *The Master* and *Death of a Salesman*. He advised that he didn't write at all because he just wasn't a screenwriter but hoped that maybe someday he would. Hoffman said he had quit smoking a year ago but found he was also addicted to food. He had gained weight while doing *Death of a Salesman* and he was now trying to lose it, since he couldn't carry the extra weight because his knees and hips were "fucked." Hoffman said he wasn't working out as much as he wanted to, but it was more about the eating and that the weight would come off if he stopped with the bread and the pie. The actor reported that when he was getting ready to do *The Master* he lost weight and it was the best he had felt in a long time—he was around 200 pounds, which was thin for him. Hoffman said his family had thick builds and his ideal weight was 205, and when he did *Capote* he was rail-thin at 195 and it was the only time he had a six-pack. One of Raab's favorite quotes of the actor's was, "It isn't easy to love something as much as you love a child."

The December 15, 2012, episode of *Saturday Night Live* spoofed the animated television holiday classic *A Charlie Brown Christmas* and featured Beck Bennett again impersonating the actor, now playing Pigpen. The three-minute skit was entitled "You're a Rat Bastard, Charlie Brown" and was said to be a performance from the New York Actor's Studio.

When the actor and his nine-year-old son Cooper were photographed at a Knicks gam, *E! News* made much of the two Hoffmans' replicate poses with power fist poised mid-air and open-mouth yells. On January 10, 2013, Hoffman attended the 18th Annual Critics' Choice Movie Awards, held in Santa Monica and broadcast by the CW television network. He also attended the 19th Annual Screen Actors Guild Award on January 27, broadcast by the Turner Television Network. The event was held at the Shrine Exposition Center in Los Angeles and Hoffman was nominated for Outstanding Performance by a Male Actor in a Supporting Role for *The Master*. He lost to Tommy Lee Jones for the biographical drama *Lincoln* (2012).

The *New York Times* predicted on February 21, 2013, that Hoffman was a long shot for the Oscar with their pick being Robert De Niro for the romantic comedy *Silver Linings Playbook* (2012). The Academy Awards ceremony was held on February 24, at the Dolby Theatre in Hollywood and was televised by ABC. Octavia Spencer presented the award for Best Supporting Actor. Hoffman was in attendance and was shown when his nomination was announced sitting with ten-year-old Cooper. When the audience applauded Hoffman he smiled and touched his son's head. Christoph Waltz won for the western *Django Unchained* (2012). Hoffman was also featured in the E! Live from the Red Carpet special that aired on E! Entertainment Television on February 25, 2013.

The actor attended the First Time Festival in early March 2013 in New York. He presented *Jack Goes Boating* and did a Q&A in the First Exposure series. *Deadline Hollywood* reported on March 20 that his next film *God's Pocket* was to be directed by John Slattery.

The Hoffman-directed LAByrinth production of *A Family for All Occasions* opened on April 25 and ran till May 26, 2013. The comedy presented a dysfunctional family that experienced upheavals when the daughter of a recent retiree (Jeffrey DeMunn) brought her new boyfriend home. It received a mixed reaction from Marilyn Stasio in *Variety* but was lambasted by Charles Isherwood in the *New York Times* who described Hoffman's direction as listless. In *Rolling Stone*'s February 27, 2014, article on the actor's death, the show's managing director Danny Feldman commented that Hoffman obsessed over every aspect of the production. Feldman recalled that from the napkin holder on the dining room table, every minute detail was debated and thought out. He said even after opening night, Hoffman was still working because he felt they were still in rehearsal.

Rolling Stone reported that two days after the show opened, the actor checked himself into rehab after prescription drugs had triggered a relapse of his heroin use. Hoffman told TMZ that he checked himself into an East Coast facility on May 14 for a ten-day heroin detox. He said he had relapsed back into addiction in 2012. Playwright and friend Bob Glaudini reported that the actor-director displayed no sign of difficulties in rehearsal, saying he was present and creative and there was no dealing with the wayward artist. Another source reported that Hoffman had fallen off the wagon while he was filming *The Hunger Games: Catching Fire* and he was away from his family, and that everyone was proud of the decision he made to get better.

In the May 15, 2013, *Variety*, more details emerged on *God's Pocket*. Park Pictures Features announced that John Slattery had adapted the screenplay with Alex Metcalf from the novel by Pete Dexter. Park Pictures Features was to produce it in partnership with Hoffman's Cooper's Town Productions and Slattery's Shoestring Pictures. The film would be set in the gritty blue-collar neighborhood of God's Pocket. Hoffman was to play Mickey, whose crazy stepson Leon is killed in a construction accident. He finds himself stuck in a life-and-death struggle between a body he can't bury, a wife he can't please and a debt he can't pay. Producer Sam Bisbee commented that he was glad Hoffman was on board to help bring John Slattery's beautiful film to life.

On May 31, 2013, press reports about the actor's rehab stay said he was now back at work filming a movie in Europe. Hoffman credited a great group of friends and family for encouraging him to seek help. On June 11 he appeared onstage at the 2013 Envision Awards in New York City and reportedly looked exuberant, at ease. Hoffman was presented on June 12 at a dinner by the Film Society of Lincoln Center and Jaeger-LeCoultre as one of the new Advisory Board members for the new Filmmaker in Residence initiative. The program was designed to support filmmakers at an early stage in the creative process. One annually nominated artist would have the opportunity to refine or develop their work through master classes, mentorships, cultural exchanges and enrichment programs with Center members and the public. The initiative was to launch in September 2013.

On June 25, 2013, it was reported that Hoffman had joined the cast of the serial killer thriller *Child 44* which was filming and being directed by Daniel Espinosa in Prague. In the Soviet Union of the Stalin-era, security guard and former war hero Leo Demidov (Tom Hardy) investigates a series of child murders. There was no word on Hoffman's role.

Interviewed by Katie Calautti for a *Huffington Post* article (July 2, 2013), Hoffman commented about the process of choosing roles. He said that if something didn't feel right he just didn't do it and that his days of acting just for acting's sake were gone. The actor had to know why he was going to do something and he was grateful to be in a position where he could think that way since most actors could not. They had to take the job they were offered because they needed the money but Hoffman would only take the jobs that he knew he cared about. He said that he had done readings for Paul Thomas Anderson's comic crime drama *Inherent Vice* (2014) and he presumed that he hadn't been offered a part because he wasn't right for it.

The actor's next film, shot in New York and New Jersey, was Park Pictures-Cooper's Town Productions-Shoestring Pictures' *God's Pocket* (2014), shot in 24 days, with the filming ending in mid–July 2013. The film had a screenplay by John Slattery and Alex Metcalf based on the novel by Pete Dexter, and it was directed by Slattery. It was set in the summer in the Philadelphia neighborhood of God's Pocket and told the story of Mickey "Mick" Scarpato (Hoffman), an alcoholic gambler in the employ of Arthur "Bird" Capezio (John Turturro) and a driver for Scarpato Meat. Mick is married to Jeanie (Christina Hendricks); her 23-year-old son from a previous marriage, Leon Hubbard (Caleb Landry Jones), is a day laborer on a construction site and is killed by Lucien "Old Lucy" Edwards (Arthur French). The narrative centers on the three days prior to Leon's funeral where Mick scrambles to cover the funeral expenses, and then shows how he leaves God's Pocket and joins Bird in Florida.

The film was a reunion for Hoffman with Slattery, who had appeared with him in *Charlie Wilson's War* as an actor, and with Molly Price, who had appeared with Hoffman in the play *Death of a Salesman.* The film gives the actor an end credit "in memory of" Hoffman. He was one of its producers and the actor is top-billed over the title. He is seen enacting the actions of having sex, driving a car and a truck, carrying meat and the corpse of Leon, tripping over Leon's body and falling in the street, vomiting, running in the street and lying on the road. We also see Hoffman semi-naked in Mick's sex scene with Jeanie and when he is in a bath. Mick has a sense of being downtrodden which makes him not react as violently as expected though he is violent in speech in swearing which with his drinking presents him as loutish. He does slap funeral director Smilin' Jack Moran (Eddie Marsan) but it is in self-defense. His street fighting at the film's climax is an attempt to defend alcoholic newspaper columnist Richard Shellborn (Richard Jenkins), who is attacked by patrons of the Hollywood Bar. Mick would seem to have a reason to join in the attack since he hears how Richard has had sex with Jeanie, but he does not do so. Despite his mannerisms, Hoffman's performance has a pleasing stillness. He is funny when tolerating the drunken advice of Eleanor (Prudence Wright Holmes) in the bar and when arguing with Nick (Carmine Kamigiletti) when he is trying to offload meat. Hoffman's finest moment may be his watching a horse race on a television screen at the racetrack turf club where the horse he has bet on loses. The film credits Chris Barnes as Mick's stunt double with his work including the scenes where

Mick falls in the back of the funeral home and in the street when running after his truck.

The film premiered on January 17, 2014, at the Sundance Film Festival, which Hoffman attended. He was interviewed by Krista Smith for *Vanity Fair* on January 20, 2014; it was shot on video. Hoffman pulled a few faces as he listened to questions and his mood seemed jovial. The film was next screened at the Sarasota Film Festival on April 11, 2014, and then given a limited release on May 9 with the tagline "The only thing they can't forgive is not being from God's Pocket." Justin Chang in *Variety* wrote that every character was so sketchily written that even reliably great actors like Hoffman came off as non-entities. Stephen Holden in the *New York Times* said that the actor gave a solid performance. The film was not a box office success.

The DVD features deleted scenes and Hoffman is seen in two of them. In one, Mick is seen walking to the Hollywood Bar, and in the second he gives the barman McKenna (Peter Gerety) a package of meat and drinks beer.

Hoffman reported that he and John Slattery had lived in the same neighborhood and they would see each other at shows and every time they did they would stop and talk. Then this script came along and Hoffman read it and he couldn't get it out of his head—he read it about five times. The simple humanity of Mick, who was doing what he was doing for someone else, appealed to him. Hoffman said it was tragic that there was somebody who was trying so desperately to make something work while everyone else knew it was never going to work. But this man didn't know it and that killed Hoffman and that's what he couldn't shake.

The actor said that Slattery knew what he was doing, and knowing that he had long wanted to make the film, Hoffman was just lucky enough to jump on Slattery's passion bandwagon and ride it. Another appealing element for him about the film was that every week in shooting he got to work with a great actor, and he said that it was the other actors who kept him coming back to work. Hoffman said he had to drag Caleb Landry Jones (6'1"), who played Leon, around in the rain, which was not easy. Hoffman also commented on the fall he took when Mick runs after the meat truck. He said he wore butt-pads to protect himself, and the day the scene was shot it was seriously hot.

Hoffman reported that he watched the film when he attended the Sundance Film Festival and had a rare enjoyable experience. He really hadn't watched a film he was in with an audience in over a decade—when he did so, he got self-conscious.

Slattery confirmed that he had known Hoffman for years, through LAByrinth and having done *Charlie Wilson's War* together. Slattery first offered Hoffman the part of Richard Shelburn and he sent back word that he wanted to play Mick, an idea that the director quickly realized was a great one. Hoffman's participation got the film made, and also motivated the other actors to come on board. Slattery kept scheduling meetings but because the actor was working they kept missing each other. Once they sat down, the director thought that Hoffman was going to say he wished he could do the film but he was too busy. However the surprise was that the actor told Slattery that he couldn't shake the script because he found it extraordinarily moving. The director reported that above and beyond all the skill Hoffman had emotionally, technically and physically, he just brought who he was to the part and he wasn't afraid to do that and that's what made him as special as he was. Slattery also reported that for the scenes where Mick drove the truck, Hoffman was unable to drive a stick shift. The problem was overcome with truck doubling and the actor given an automatic shift, which he drove in shots of Hoffman inside the truck. To help the illusion, sound effects were added for the shifting. Slattery said that Hoffman used his influence as one of the film's producers to have the director use a different, more effective take in the scene where Mick argues with Nick, because the actor felt one was funnier. Slattery said that this was evidence that the actor had the technical gift of remembering every single take filmed, which was even more surprising given how deeply he was into character when acting when shooting.

The director advised that his last contact with Hoffman occurred three days before the actor died. Hoffman apparently sent Slattery a photograph of them together at Sundance, with a note saying "This made my day." The director commented that he found the message bittersweet and his friendship with Hoffman was meaningful because at that point in Slattery's life he didn't discover many people he could connect with like that. Co-star Christina Hendricks commented that she found herself bringing her A-game for Hoffman and called the opportunity to work with him a dream come true. In a May 2014 interview she added that the company had obviously been grieving, but it didn't take away from how special it was, at the time, and how special it was now. Hendricks said that the fact that Hoffman was in it and they got to work with him was extraordinary, and now they had this beautiful finished product that they hoped people will still want to see. The actress was surprised by the actor's death and said that they were together at Sundance the week before, where he seemed fantastic. Hendricks said she knew he had had problems in the past but she really did think it was in the past.

On July 26, 2013, *The Hollywood Reporter* wrote that Hoffman was to star in the Showtime comedy pilot *Trending Down* as Thom Payne, a man who becomes obsolete when his advertising agency is taken over. The pilot was described as a blistering attack on our youth-obsessed culture, and a darkly comic examination of what it means to matter. Or matter not. Shalom Auslander created the comedy and was to write and executive produce alongside Hoffman under the Cooper's Town Productions banner. On July 30 it was reported that production would begin on the East Coast in the fall. Cast member Kathryn Hahn, interviewed by Christina Radish for *Collider* on August 28, 2013, said that they were to start rehearsals in the next week and that John Cameron Mitchell was directing the pilot.

On August 29, 2013, it was reported that Hoffman had been replaced in the part of Major Kuzmin in *Child 44* by Vincent Cassell. The film was not a box office success.

Hoffman next returned to the *Hunger Games* film series: The film adaptation of Suzanne Collins' novel *Mockingjay* was going to be split into in two films which were shot back to back. Filming of the Lionsgate presentation of *The Hunger Games: Mockingjay—Part 1* (2014) took place from September 23 to October 2013 at the Eue/Screen Gems Studios and on locations in Atlanta, Georgia, and Paris, France. The screenplay was by Peter Craig and Danny Strong, and the director again was Francis Lawrence. The story has Katniss Everdeen (Jennifer Lawrence) recruited by the underground rebels based on District 13 who are led by President Alma Coin (Julianne Moore) to be the Mockingjay to unite the districts against the Capitol and to be the lightning rod and the face of the revolution. Plutarch Heavensbee (Hoffman) sends Katniss to District 12 to see the devastation that has occurred there as a way to overcome her reluctance to be what he wants her to be. The rebels have saved Katniss' sister Primrose (Willow Shields) and her mother (Paula Malcomson), who are on the hovercraft, and Plutarch recues Effie Trinket (Elizabeth Banks) from imprisonment to be Katniss' advisor and to give her a new Mockingjay outfit. He also wants Katniss to appear in a "propo" (propaganda video) for the rebels and sends her to District 8 to film it where she can perform unscripted since her attempts to do it scripted are unsatisfactory. Plutarch employs Cressida (Natalie Dormer) to direct the commercial; Cressida also films Finnick Odair (Sam Claflin) to speak in lieu of Katniss as a decoy to the covert rescue operation undertaken to liberate tributes from inside the Capitol. Plutarch is merely a witness to this action, as is Katniss, since the operation is led by Gale Hawthorne (Liam Hemsworth) and Colonel Boggs (Mahershala Ali). We do see Plutarch mouthing the speech that Alma makes to the rebels at the film's end, which implies that he wrote it.

The film is dedicated "in loving memory" to Hoffman. He is billed seventh in the film, which reunited him with Julianne Moore (*Boogie Nights* and *Magnolia*). Hoffman again is unshaven and wears a new costume of brown-gray military jumpsuit with a shoulder bag and a matching jacket. Hoffman delivers an extended look at Alma after their meeting with Katniss, which falsely suggests perhaps he has a duplicitous agenda. He is amusing in his frustration when directing Katniss in the commercial in the hovercraft setting. As with *The Hunger Games: Catching Fire*, there were no great acting challenges for him.

The film was released on November 10, 2014, in London and on November 21 in the U.S. with the taglines "Fire burns brighter in the darkness" and "The courage of one will change the world." Peter Travers (*Rolling Stone*) wrote that Hoffman went beyond the call of franchise duty to find the bruised soul in a master manipulator, and that seeing him go out with such playful panache was one of the film's unalloyed joys. Justin Chang in *Variety* wrote that Hoffman was among those who again brought a crucial measure of grown-up authority to the Youth Audience proceedings, and Manohla Dargis in the *New York Times* said he was loose, funny and stingingly real.

The DVD features deleted scenes, one of which has Hoffman in a scene where Plutarch takes Katniss and Gale through a plant nursery to a garden where Beetee (Jeffrey Wright) shows them hummingbirds.

Francis Lawrence said that Hoffman died while the film was in post-production. He added that the actor liked to keep talking about things and unlike a lot of other actors who liked to talk about it and then nothing changes, he could actually change his performance. Lawrence said it was amazing to see the layers of nuance and subtext that were added. The director advised that in the scene where Plutarch directs Katniss in making the propo, Hoffman and Jennifer Lawrence had fun improvising off each other so that Lawrence had a choice of different versions. He also said that in the scene where the Capitol bombers attack the rebel base, Hoffman changed the expected performance for Julianne Moore's benefit. The script had Plutarch being scared but Hoffman played him tough and strong for Moore's shots so that her reaction to him would be just as strong. For Hoffman's shots, he jumped from being strong to being scared and also added some levity in Plutarch's fear. Lawrence advised that this created an interesting dynamic between the two actors that really worked for the scene.

Julianne Moore commented that Hoffman was a wonderful actor and she felt really one of the best of his generation and said that his death was a tragic loss. When she was interviewed by ABC News she agreed that the film was a celebration of his work. Later she added that Hoffman was imaginative and fully developed and engaged and always got the most out of every scene.

The actor attended the New York Film Festival gala tribute to Cate Blanchett at Lincoln Center and a Sony Pictures Classics luncheon at Le Cirque on October 3, 2013. On the October 5 episode of *Saturday Night Live*, Taran Killam and Beck Bennett impersonated the actor; in a skit, Bennett's Hoffman auditions for the film *50 Shades of Gray* (2015). Footage of the comic being made up as Hoffman was viewed on YouTube; two photographs of the actor are displayed on the makeup table. The brunette Bennett is given a blonde beard, a blonde wig and glasses.

On November 6, 2013, Hoffman attended the opening night of the LAByrinth production of Dominique Morisseau's drama *Sunset Baby* at the Bank Street Theater. The play centered on Nina (DeWanda Wise) a Brooklyn drug dealer, and her reunion with her estranged father, Kenyatta (John Earl Jelks), a former black revolutionary. Directed by Kamilah Forbes, it ran until December 15. The *New York Times* reported that Hoffman sat in the back for the performance and posed for paparazzi at the cast party. The show was praised by the *Times*' Ben Brantley.

Filming for the Color Force-Lionsgate science fiction adventure *The Hunger Games: Mockingjay Part 2* (2015) began on December 2, 2013, and was completed on June 20, 2014. It was shot at the Studio Babelsberg in Germany, and on locations in Atlanta, Paris and Berlin. The screenplay was by Peter Craig and Danny Strong, based on Suzanne Collins' novel *Mockingjay*, and it was again directed by Francis Lawrence. Katniss Everdeen (Jennifer Lawrence), now symbolized as the rebels' mockingjay, participates in a District 13 star squad advance on the Capitol City in District 2 so that she can kill President Snow (Donald Sutherland). Hoffman reprised his role as Plutarch Heavensbee, the right-hand man of President Alma Coin (Julianne Moore). They ask Katniss to be in the frontline of the rebels' advance but spin her rogue action into their own plan, which is televised. When the rebels defeat Snow's peace-maker forces, Plutarch supports Coin's desire to Panem's interim president but he also supports Commander Paylor (Pettina Miller) who is made president after Coin is assassinated by Katniss. Plutarch also advises Katniss in a letter that she is pardoned of the killing of Coin.

Hoffman is billed 7th below the film's title and appears in 8 scenes. Some of the actor's appearances, such as the shots of him at the planned execution of Snow and his attendance at Paylor's inauguration, look to be compromised. The scene where Plutarch's letter to Katniss is read to her by Haymitch Abernathy (Woody Harrelson) was presumably the one that Hoffman had yet to film before his premature death on February 2, 2014, since it seems to be an obvious opportunity for a monologue. Francis Lawrence advised that the scene was originally filmed as a more direct eulogy to Hoffman. He said they actually had extra dialogue and they wanted it to feel like a tribute to him. However this was taken out because Lawrence said it changed the thematic meaning of what that scene was. However he still felt partially because both Jennifer Lawrence and Woody Harrelson knew that there was an element to it that was a tribute to Hoffman, maybe some of that still came through. Plutarch's absence at the victor's meeting Coin holds would seem to be another one that the actor should have been in.

In his scenes, Hoffman uses his actor mannerisms of over-gesturing and self-conscious touching. In what is the actor's final screen appearance it is regrettable that it should be in this franchise, and despite the scenes not shot, in this particular film. Again Hoffman delivers a likeable, bemused performance, but it is one that provides no challenge for him. Finally, Plutarch has little screen time because his involvement in the plot is minor and this is a sad swansong to an actor that deserves better. *The Hollywood Reporter* wrote in its review of the film that "this great actor goes out with a whimper rather than a bang." Hoffman's best moment is perhaps his scene with Coin where they are talking about their spin on Katniss going rogue. The fact that it is with Moore alone is redemptive of Hoffman's legacy since she is an actor of comparable gravitas, and his exit from the frame can be viewed as a sad farewell to the actor.

The film was first released in Berlin on November 5 2015 and then on November 16, 2015 in the United States with the taglines "The revolution is about all of us," "The fire will burn forever," "A creature as unquenchable as the sun," and "Nothing can prepare you for the end." It was praised by Peter DeBruge in *Variety* and Manohla Dargis in the *New York Times*. DeBruge wrote that Hoffman added welcome resonance to his scenes. Dargis said that he was one of the many familiar faces who flashed by so quickly that they feel like guests who have popped in only to say goodbye. However she wrote that Hoffman's popping in was moving. The film was a box office success.

11

The End

It was reported around Christmastime 2014 that Hoffman moved out of the $4.4 million apartment on Jane Street in Greenwich Village that he co-owned and shared with Mimi O'Donnell and their children. The couple had supposedly purchased the 3-bedroom apartment in 2008. Hoffman rented another apartment a few blocks away in a 4-story red brick building in a fashionable neighborhood of the West Village, where many other actors keep homes. The property was in the building called Pickwick House and the address was thought to be 35 Bethune Street. The building's superintendent said that the actor only lived in the new apartment about 2 months.

Friends of Hoffman confirmed that O'Donnell had asked him to leave their apartment for the sake of his children as he was battling a huge drug habit. A source reported that it was known that he was struggling to stay sober, and O'Donnell had given him some tough love and told him he needed some time away from the kids and to get straight again. Another source reported that Hoffman had actually taken the new place to begin with because he couldn't memorize lines with 3 kids running around. The couple were living separate lives but Hoffman still saw his children every day, because he was a devoted father and was especially close to his son Cooper. The actor was reported to regularly play weekend basketball with him and was often photographed with Cooper at Knicks games in Madison Square Garden. Stephen Adly Guirgis advised that Hoffman and O'Donnell were constantly in touch and that the actor would have moved back into their shared apartment the moment he was clean. O'Donnell was said to be committed to the actor and he was committed to her.

The suggestion that Hoffman and O'Donnell had separated because he had had an affair was refuted. The idea that his relationship with his assistant, Isabella Wing-Davey, was also a romantic one was denied. Hoffman was simply mentoring her into the business and had met her since she was the daughter of his close friend, Mark Wing-Davey, who chaired the graduate acting department at Tisch School of the Arts. The actor and Mark had worked together at the Public Theater and Hoffman had known Isabelle since she was a child. He had brought her into his company to be his development person when she was finishing her graduate work at Tisch. She was known to be highly skilled and highly talented, and didn't just get the job with Hoffman because of her family connections. The actor was also credited as one of the associate producers on *Candlesticks* (2012) an 11-minute comedy short that Wing-Davey had directed.

Hoffman had reportedly been attending 12-step meetings in the West Village over several years and was also the sponsor for other actors. Playwright David Bar Katz said that the actor's struggle with addiction was one he took seriously. He said Hoffman was sober for over 25 years and conquered it to the greatest degree one can, given the nature of it. Katz advised that the actor was against every aspect of drug use. Katz would later say in a February 17, 2014 *National Enquirer* article how he regularly saw Hoffman use drugs and that he had partied with him a number of times and had seen him do heroin.

On January 16, 2014 it *The Hollywood Reporter* announced that Showtime had picked up Hoffman's comedy television series for its schedule. It had been formerly known as *Trending Down* and was now entitled *Happyish*. Hoffman commented on it when asked by an Associated Press interview at the Sundance Film Festival on January 19, 2014. He said that he had been corralled in by writer and producer Shalom Auslander and David Nevins, the president of entertainment for Showtime. Hoffman said he shot the pilot in New York where he lived which was nice. He loved working with Auslander because the actor thought what the show's creator wanted to do was pretty unique. Hoffman said he would have to find out what the result was and that it was another journey and another experience. He advised that he was really looking forward to working more with Auslander because he was quite a guy.

Hoffman was interviewed for *The Hollywood Reporter* at Sundance on January 18, 2014 with John Slattery and Christina Hendricks. He had medium-length hair, his glasses and was unshaven and wore a pea-green colored cardigan with the sleeves pulled up to the elbows over a similar colored t-shirt and pants. Hoffman was seen laughing with the others before the interview and he held a bottle of water in his right hand which he drank from. The actor's face blushed red when he joked in the interview and when he spoke he used his actor mannerisms of self-conscious touching and over-gesturing. One comment Hoffman made was that he had first come to Sundance when he was 25, not to support a film he had there but to support a friend of his who was in a short that Paul Thomas Anderson had directed. The actor remembered sleeping on a floor somewhere in a hotel room where a bunch of people were staying.

He was photographed by Victoria Will on January 19, 2014 at the Sundance Film Festival while promoting *A Most Wanted Man*. Three of these photographs show the actor in different moods, and in both he has stubble, his medium-length hair is ruffled, and he wears a dark-colored jacket over a light blue-gray sweater. In 1 photo Hoffman wears glasses and smiles and his arms are crossed. The second photo has him still with his arms crossed and with his glasses but looking down, as if he is not aware that the shot is being taken. The third photo sees Hoffman unsmiling and without his glasses. This shot had Hoffman being described as looking chillingly vacant and somber and, after the actor's death, was used to present him in a prefiguring fatal mood. However the photographer suggested that this latter pose was a performance, since she stated that during the shoot Hoffman appeared to be having a great time. Will added that she found him to be just a regular guy and very approachable.

Anthony Breznecan had his last encounter with Hoffman at Sundance where he found the actor sitting alone in the Entertainment Weekly studio, waiting to have his portrait taken with the cast of *God's Pocket*. The writer reminded Hoffman how he once gave him the advice to have children rather than wait to do so. The actor at first looked uncertain and then smiled as he remembered, and then opened his arms in an expectant gesture, waiting to see what had happened. Breznecan showed Hoffman pictures of his two children on his iPhone and the actor grabbed the writer by the shoulders and shook him. Still studying the phone Hoffman said "I was right, right? I've got three of my own now." Breznecan felt that the actor did not look well, saying he looked disheveled and he was quiet, morose, and more than a bit lost. However the writer advised that when Hoffman spoke about his children he radiated pride. Breznecan would report that the actor was a common sight around his Greenwich Village neighborhood, often pushing a stroller, and he was devoted to those kids he talked about with such adoration. Despite his demons, it was apparent that Hoffman's role of fatherhood was one he loved so much that he wanted everyone he met to play it too.

Hoffman at the Sundance Film Festival on January 19, 2014 (photograph by Victoria Will).

At Sundance it was reported that Hoffman had confessed to a stranger that he was a heroin addict. Speaking to the *New York Post*, Washington Life magazine co-publisher John Arundel said he had a chance encounter with Hoffman and he recalled that he didn't immediately recognize him and asked what he did for a living. After the actor told him that he was a heroin addict he then took off his "sloppy hat" and Arundel recognized him. When the publisher said his name, Hoffman replied, "Bingo!" and then added, "I just got out of rehab." Arundel commented that the exchange made it obvious that Hoffman wanted people to know that he was in recovery mode.

The idea that Hoffman seemed disheveled, reticent and rumpled at Sundance was later rationalized by friends as a supposed sign of his pending demise. They pointed out that the actor would often appear that way, as if he had been out partying all night, when in fact he had just awakened from a night's sleep. Howard Cohen, a president of Roadside Attractions, the distributor that brought *A Most Wanted Man* to the festival had his own story. He reported that when he saw Hoffman he said hello to the actor and described him as very gracious and friendly. Hoffman told the executive that he was happy to be there and Cohen said they had a very normal interaction. Elsewhere at the festival, the actor spoke of having little time to see movies lately, but said he had enjoyed the animated adventure comedy *Frozen* (2013) with his children. In January 2014 Hoffman had been spotted in the audience at the Broadway revival of *Waiting for Godot* which had opened at the Cort Theatre on November 24, 2013, and would run until March 30, 2014. Samuel Beckett's tragicomedy ran in repertory with Harold

Pinter's drama *No Man's Land*, with the same cast, and both shows were directed by Sean Mathias. In the week prior to Hoffman's death he reportedly spoke with theatre artists who said that he was preoccupied with some future film possibilities and his coming Showtime series. He was to return to Atlanta the next week. David Bar Katz had texted him about getting together for one of their frequent steak and coffee dinners before he left.

On January 25, 2014, the writer Tatiana Pahlen had run into Hoffman at the elevator of the 92nd Street Y where she had gone for a swim. She said he was there to pick up one of his children. The two had met a couple of years earlier, when he performed a reading at Joe's Pub for a party for the magazine Lapham's Quarterly. A similar event was planned for the Monday of February 3, 2014, but Hoffman had told Pahlen he would not be involved this time since he planned to be back in Atlanta, shooting *The Hunger Games*. It was said that the actor had 1 week left of shooting on the film. Pahlen commented that he seemed happy, if "a little hyper," and noted that his skin was in very bad shape. It was reported that the actor had dined at La Bonbonniere restaurant on the Monday of January 27, 2014, eating a cheeseburger and drinking water. This was said to be one of Hoffman's favorite eateries and the manager, Marina Cortez, said that he seemed happy. She said before he left he was singing. Less than a week before Hoffman died it was claimed that he had called a reporter from the set of *The Hunger Games* and supposedly sounded incoherent, slurry and barely awake in the middle of the afternoon. He was said to keep forgetting the names of people he had worked with.

Hoffman was photographed on January 30, 2014, in an Atlanta airport bar smoking and drinking, and then unconscious in his seat on a flight bound for New York. The actor was also photographed being driven away from the flight by an airport cart in New York. The bar photographs taken by a diner in a restaurant next door to the Hyatt hotel show Hoffman talking with an unknown woman as he sits at the bar. He appears to be clean-shaven and wears his glasses and his hair in a long-style, wearing a dark green-dark brown coat with a high collar and a similarly-colored baseball cap. The diner who took the photographs, which were published by TMZ.com, reported that Hoffman appeared sketchy and intoxicated and he made multiple trips to the bathroom, which alerted the fellow patron's attention. However the photograph makes it unclear what was in the actor's glass. At the airport Hoffman's condition was such that Theresa Fehr, a home warranties executive based in Houston, mistook him for a street person. Fehr said she noticed a man—not immediately recognizing him—being escorted to the security checkpoint by a female Transportation Security Administration agent. She just thought it was really odd that this street person was at the airport. Hoffman had put his shoes on the belt and then tossed his belt there, and Fehr could tell he was very intoxicated. She turned to the agent and commented how the man looked like that actor that had three names. The agent confirmed that's who it was. The agent said she saw Hoffman trying to put his belt on and his pants were about to fall off and his belly was hanging out. She said to him, "Dude, I hope you don't lose your pants," and he reportedly looked at her with a dazed expression.

The photograph of Hoffman in his plane seat has him supposedly unconscious with his head resting on his chest and his hands clasped together. At the airport he was described as drunk and disheveled, although he does not look disheveled in the photograph. The plane photograph was said to have been taken just after his drinking session in the downtown Atlanta bar. According to the passenger who took the picture, Hoffman was out like a light almost as soon as he took his seat. He was said to have later awakened and was described as groggy and again "disheveled," and it was reported that as soon as the flight touched down Hoffman was put on an airport cart and driven away. Hoffman was seen driven away after the flight to La Guardia Airport from the gate in a motorized cart by Andrew Kirell, an editor of Mediaite, a blog that covers the media. Kirell said he recognized the actor right away because he was a huge fan and he said it was remarkable how awful he looked.

On January 31, 2014, it was announced in *The Hollywood Reporter* that Jake Gyllenhaal and Amy Adams were set to star in Ezekiel Moss which Hoffman planned to direct. Gyllenhaal was to play the title character and Adams was to play Iris, the emotionally fragile widowed mother of the boy Joel whom Ezekiel befriends. She runs a boarding house in a small town overrun by religious fervor and falls in love with Ezekiel. To date the film has not been made. Producer Anthony Bregman commented that it was a project that Hoffman had put a lot into over a long period of time because he loved it. The actor had also been asked by Anton Corbijn to appear in a small role in his next film, a biopic about James Dean and Dennis Stock, a photographer for *Life* magazine, who changed each other's lives. Corbijn said Hoffman was trying to find a way to make it work. This film was entitled *Life* (2015) and was planned to shoot in February, 2014 in Canada. Hoffman was to play the part of John Morris, a photo editor for *Life*, and the actor was replaced by Joel Edgerton. The film was released in the United States in December 4, 2015. Another film project that Hoffman was involved with through his production company, Cooper's Town, was based on an untitled 2010 script about the racial dynamics of college basketball in the 1960s.

The actor was last seen alive on Saturday February 1, 2014. Early in the day he was seen at The Chocolate Bar on 8th Avenue, which was said to be one of Hoffman's favorite places to take his kids. Reportedly he was there for his standing order of a four-shot espresso. The assistant manager, Kate St. Cyr, had seen him then and reported that the actor looked really happy. She said he seemed fine and he had been in a great mood lately. St. Cyr described Hoffman as a really sweet man and dad who would often take his children to the store for ice cream in the summer. A neighbor of his reported that he had also seen the star early in the day buying tissues and soda at a nearby grocery store. He added that Hoffman looked gray and not well.

Mimi O'Donnell told police she saw him at 2 p.m. on the street near his apartment, though another source said that he met O'Donnell and their children at a playground. Around 5 p.m., the actor was sighted by Paul Pabst, executive producer of the sport program *The Dan Patrick Show*. Pabst was walking with his members of his family in the Village. His sister called out to Hoffman, who turned and gave her a high-five. Pabst's sister commented to him that the actor didn't look good and Pabst felt he looked "out of it." Sources differ as to the time of the next sighting at the West Village restaurant Automatic Slims where he was said to be a regular. One said it was around 7 p.m., another at 7:30, and another around 8. Hoffman was seen with two men and he reportedly ate a cheeseburger and drank cranberry and soda for dinner and appeared to a witness to be totally fine. The witness commented that the men the actor was with seemed liked industry people, and the actor behaved a in a low-key and friendly manner. The witness said that none of the three presented like they were looking to party. The person also reported that Hoffman had visited the restaurant occasionally, always kept a low profile, and appeared to be a nice guy. It was not noted when he departed but the bar closed for a private party at 9:30 p.m., and by then the actor was long gone.

At 8 p.m. Mimi O'Donnell said she telephoned Hoffman and that he seemed to be under the influence of drugs and sounded high. He sent David Bar Katz a text at 8:44 that read, "you wanna watch the second half of the knicks heat game at Bethune." Katz later claimed that the fact that Hoffman wanted him to come over meant that he did not want to be doing drugs, because he never did them in his presence. This was in opposition to the claim in the *National Enquirer* article that Katz said he had seen the actor freebasing cocaine the night before he died. The playwright told the *New York Times* on February 25, 2014, how Hoffman had once told him that addiction was when you do the thing you most don't want to be doing. The actor sent a second text 14 minutes later, at 8:58 that read "like 10:15." Another friend reportedly spoke to Hoffman by phone around 9 p.m. although it is not known who the person was and what transpired.

Fox News reported a man had come forward claiming he saw the actor buying drugs that evening. The passerby claimed he saw a very sweaty Hoffman withdrawing a large sum of money from an ATM by his home before handing it over to two men wearing messenger bags. The man reportedly added the actor looked "like shit." Police investigators later determined from surveillance videos from the bank that Hoffman made 6 ATM transactions for a total of $1,200 inside D'Agostino, a supermarket near his home. He is said to have repeatedly withdrawn $200 during an hour, with gaps of several minutes between withdrawals. He was described by the passerby as looking disheveled. It was reported that Hoffman was seen giving the money to two men, whom police suspected to be the ones who supplied him with heroin.

Katz said he did not see the invitation to watch the game until more than an hour after it was sent. At 11:30 p.m., after seeing the texts, he texted Hoffman: "just got out of dinner. Where r u?" There was no reply. The playwright said that they were planning to go to the Super Bowl together that Sunday. He said that he had seen the actor the previous week and he was clean and sober, his old self. Katz really thought this chapter of Hoffman's life was over and described what happened to his friend as an awful relapse.

Hoffman died on Sunday, February 2, 2014, at the age of 46. In an eerie coincidence, a few days before several news outlets erroneously reported he had passed away, prompting his reps to issue a denial of the death hoax. One source almost believed that the actor had a death wish, saying he was too deep, too private, too sensitive, and it was like all the craziness of celebrity was just too much for him. Hoffman was discovered unresponsive on the bathroom floor of his Greenwich Village apartment in what a New York police source described as an apparent drug overdose. He had been expected to pick up his children on Sunday at 9 a.m. at a nearby playground but failed to show up, which led Katz and Isabella Wing-Davey to go to his apartment. The *National Enquirer* reported that Katz had received a frantic phone call from Mimi O'Donnell after Hoffman had failed to pick up his children, which led Katz to go to the apartment. Katz had contacted Wing-Davey to get the apartment keys since the front door was double-locked.

11. The End

The pair found Hoffman at 11:30 a.m. on the bathroom floor wearing boxer shorts and a t-shirt and his glasses, with a needle still in his arm. The needle in the arm was in ironic counterpoint to the actor reportedly having told his friend Stephen Adly Guirgis that you didn't have to die with one to be a great artist. 911 was called and the police attended with Emergency Medical Service workers declaring the actor dead on the scene.

In Hoffman's apartment there were said to be scores of plastic heroin packets recovered, though the number of packets varied according to sources. Authorities were working to determine whether the drugs were mixed or tainted with anything else. There were also reportedly 5 empty packets in the trash. In addition there were reported to be found unused syringes, a charred spoon and various prescription medications. These included: the blood-pressure drug clonidine hydrochloride, known to be used for treating opiate withdrawal; the addiction-treatment drug buprenorphine; vyvanse, a drug used to treat attention-deficit hyperactivity disorder; hydroxyzine, which can be used to treat anxiety; and methocarbamol, a muscle relaxer. Some of the medications were said to be anti-depressants that Hoffman appeared to not have a script for. A police spokesperson said that the direction of the investigation was going to depend, in large part, on the findings of the medical examiner and the findings of the lab tests. An autopsy was to begin on Monday but the results were not expected until at least Tuesday.

Also found by police in the actor's apartment were two small diaries. In them Hoffman reportedly described being troubled by demons and wrote about drug deals, and his struggle to overcome his addiction with Narcotics Anonymous meetings. Some of the entries appeared to have been written while he was in rehab for heroin abuse. Others were scrambled and illegible, with sentences running into each other as though the actor was high when he put pen to paper. Some of the entries were described as stream of consciousness and difficult to follow. One line referred to "Frank who always owes money" and on the same page Hoffman wrote about a 15-year-old girl from Texas. While the entries were said to definitely contain some soul-searching there was also a fair amount of rambling that didn't make sense. However on February 12, 2014, it was reported that police had also found in the diaries entries that suggested that Hoffman was in a love triangle with O'Donnell and an unnamed woman he had recently gotten involved with.

On Sunday afternoon onlookers gathered near the building and the entire block was cordoned off by police. Just before 7 p.m., after investigators spent the entire afternoon and much of the evening going in and out of Mr. Hoffman's apartment, the crime scene van moved to make way for the medical examiners wagon to pull up to the building. After remaining in the apartment all day, the actor's body was finally taken from his home just before 7 p.m. Police flanked both sides of the van all the way to the buildings entrance. After ten somber minutes, a stretcher was wheeled out carrying a figure covered in black plastic and was loaded into the wagon before being quickly whisked away with blaring horns and blinding blue and red lights.

Hoffman was survived by his longtime partner, Mimi O'Donnell and their three children—son Cooper, 10, and daughters Tallulah, 7, and Willa, 5. Others included his mother Marilyn O'Connor, his brother Gordon, and two sisters Jill Hoffman DelVecchio and Emily Hoffman Barr. In a statement issued through Hoffman's publicist, his family said that they were devastated by the loss of their beloved Phil and appreciated the outpouring of love and support they had received from everyone.

Members of the LAByrinth Theatre Company were said to be in a state of shock. The actor Felix Solis commented in an interview that Hoffman was their hero and their leader. An article in the *New York Times* on February 3, 2014, wrote about the actor's work in the theatre. It stated that his devotion to LAByrinth was so great that, six years prior, he had made a personal loan of $350,000 to the company, which typically had a six-figure annual budget, to help it through a tough patch. The managing director, Danny Feldman, reported that the company was only able to pay back some of the amount and they still owed him $125,000, though Hoffman never asked for any of it back. The actor was planning to act in a staged reading of the play *Doubt* in the spring for LAByrinth and he was also to direct a play in the near future.

In the *New York Times* obituary of February 2, 2014, Bruce Weber wrote that Hoffman was perhaps the most ambitious and widely admired American actor of his generation, who gave three-dimensional nuance to a wide range of sidekicks, villains and leading men on screen and embraced some of the theatre's most burdensome roles on Broadway. Weber said Hoffman did not cut the traditional figure of a leading man, though he was more than capable of leading roles, citing the supporting roles that earned the actor Academy Award nominations and also his Best Actor Academy Award for *Capote*. He commented that Hoffman was prolific and versatile and willing to explore the depths of not just creepy or villainous characters, but especially unattractive ones.

In *Variety* on February 2, 2014, Justin Chang wrote that Hoffman, over the course of an astonishing career cut devastatingly short, made an art of playing aggressively, defiantly unlovable characters. He added that the actor's formidable range and classically honed technique went beyond twisted, lumpen sad sacks, rich and strange though they were. He emerged from obscurity and evolved from a well-regarded character actor into a lead player of tremendous intelligence, stature and emotional force.

Appraising the actor in the *New York Times* on February 3, 2014, A.O. Scott wrote that he was an unusually fine one, who had a special combination of talent, discipline and fearlessness. Scott said that whatever Hoffman did he nearly always did something memorable, and his death revealed, too soon and too late, the astonishing scale of his greatness and the solidity of his achievement. He wrote that we did not lose just a very good actor. We may have lost the best one we had. It was said that in a medium that prized glamor and flash he offered the opposite in film: untidy, imperfect, shy, awkward and eminently real people. And despite his outsized talent, he was relentlessly humble.

Tributes for Hoffman came from co-workers like Mark Wahlberg, Julianne Moore, Anton Corbijn, Jude Law, Todd Louiso, Patrick Fugit, June Squibb, Amos Poe, George Clooney, Brett Ratner, and Nicole Kidman. Julianne Moore, who had co-starred with the actor in *The Hunger Games: Mockingjay Part 2*, commented that she felt so fortunate to have known and worked with the extraordinary actor, she was deeply saddened by his passing, and her thoughts and condolences were with his family. When interviewed for the November 2014 issue of *More Magazine*, Moore was asked about Hoffman. In response her face reportedly became flushed with emotion, and she commented "What is there to say? It was a terrible, ridiculous, untimely loss." Moore added that Hoffman was an extraordinary talent and a lovely human being.

John Ortiz commented that he was in shock. He said that in their 20s and 30s, there was so much partying going on, but he never once saw Hoffman take a drop of alcohol or any illegal drugs in his life. Ortiz added that he saw a great future ahead for the actor and they had told each other they would be in their 90s doing Broadway together. It was something the pair would joke about all the time.

Hunger Games director Francis Lawrence issued a joint statement with producers Jon Kilik and Nina Jacobson, Suzanne Collins and Jennifer Lawrence to say that words could not convey the devastating loss they were all feeling. They added that the actor was a wonderful person and an exceptional talent, their hearts are breaking, and their deepest thoughts and condolences went to his family. Francis Lawrence himself commented that it was about as horrible a thing that could happen and was just completely tragic. Lionsgate described Hoffman as a singular talent and one of the most gifted actors of our generation. They said they very fortunate that he graced their *Hunger Games* family, that losing him in his prime was a tragedy, and they sent their deepest condolences to Hoffman's family.

The actor had been due to return to the film on February 3, 2014, and Francis Lawrence said after a brief shutdown, the production half-heartedly resumed. He reported that you could have heard a pin drop that first day back, and they all gathered and said something about Hoffman and for him. Lawrence confirmed that it was tough getting back into work and trying to find a groove again because it had created a deep sense of sadness for everyone and had thrown them all. Lionsgate released a statement affirming that the majority of the actor's scenes had been completed but then it was announced that Hoffman would be digitally recreated for a major scene involving his character that had yet to be shot. However Francis Lawrence advised that there was no intention to fake a performance, and that he had rewritten Hoffman's two remaining scenes to compensate for the actor's absence giving his dialogue to other actors. He also dropped the actor's appearance in other scenes where he had no dialogue, and said that there would be no digital manipulation or CG fabrication of any kind. Lawrence thought that Hoffman was one of the greatest actors of all time and to try to fake a Philip Seymour Hoffman performance would have been catastrophic and he would never want to do that. The director just thought the solution he provided was the best way to be able to get around such a horrible thing. A Lionsgate representative commented that Hoffman's performances in both remaining movies would be up to the best of his craft and they felt it was a good tribute to him.

Variety wrote on February 2, 2014, that Hoffman's death had impacted Showtime's new series roster for 2014, since he had been scheduled to take on the lead in *Happyish*. Showtime had given the project a ten-episode order in January month for a planned premiere later in the year. It was reported that the 30 minute single-camera pilot had been shot in September but production had yet to start on the series, with creator and executive producer Shalom Auslander and his writing staff working on scripts. Showtime executives were said to be reeling from the news of Hoffman's death and would not comment on the fate of *Happyish*. But they released a statement regarding his death, saying that he was one of our generation's finest and most brilliant actors, and also a gifted comedic talent. Showtime said it was a great privilege and pleasure to work with him and they were all absolutely devastated by this sudden loss, and their thoughts went out to his family at this very difficult time.

The website *Indiewire* reported that a clip from the pilot had been previewed at the Television Critics Association press tour in January to much positive response. The site also published a photograph of Hoffman in the pilot, and he appeared without glasses and clean-shaven with short-length hair and also looking surprisingly thin. On February 3, 2014, it was reported that the series was unlikely to continue, since the late actor drove every scene of the pilot. The source added that it was hard to imagine a way in which it could go on. The role would have to be recast and there weren't any other actors in serious consideration. If it did move forward, the premiere would be delayed as the pilot would be needed to be reshot.

Shalom Auslander also issued a statement on Hoffman's passing, saying that the world was no damned place to have a heart, and Phil had the biggest, brokenest heart of anyone he had ever met. He added that the actor was a beautiful person in a hideous world, and a great actor, too.

On February 4, 2014, sources revealed that Hoffman predicted his own death. The actor reportedly was on a heroin binge 6 weeks before he died, and told friends he feared he was destined to fatally overdose. A source advised that in December Hoffman told them he had started injecting himself with heroin and couldn't kick it. He said he would kick it for a few days and then fall off the wagon. The actor had gone back to Narcotics Anonymous in a desperate attempt to clean up but much to his great frustration it didn't work. Hoffman was described as often looking disheveled and dirty in the last 6 weeks of his life, and at one point someone asked him how bad his problem was. He supposedly replied that if he didn't stop he knew he was going to die. Hoffman was also said to be drinking excessively which opened the door to many bad decisions when it came to heroin use. Ironically the actor was considered a guru by those at AA because he had been sober for so long, and he would give inspirational talks to people who attended.

In *The Hollywood Reporter* on February 5, 2014, Todd McCarthy wrote about Hoffman. He said was a consummate character actor whose talent was so genuine and deep that nothing could prevent him from becoming a complete performer, which sometimes included being a leading man and star as well. McCarthy wrote that Hoffman played a startlingly wide range of characters and he caught the eyes of talented younger directors. McCarthy also commented that he had seen the actor at his last Sundance and he didn't look good. He said Hoffman's demeanor was pasty, drained, and a bit distracted but he charitably attributed this to what his part had required in *A Most Wanted Man* and that he would recover and readjust for his next part. McCarthy concluded by writing that the actor went all the way with the talents he had, further and more often than many. But his vital time as an artist should have lasted at least twice as long.

Marquees of Broadway theatres in New York were dimmed on the night of Wednesday February 5, 2014, at 7:45 p.m. for one minute in memory of the actor. Charlotte St Martin, executive director of the Broadway League, described Hoffman as a true artist who loved theatre and said that they would always be grateful for his boundless and profound talent that he shared with the Broadway stage. LAByrinth held a candlelight vigil for him in the courtyard of the Bank Street Theater at 6:30 p.m. on the same night. The weather at the vigil was snowing with a winter storm and it was noted that none of the votive candles held aloft by the hundreds gathered were extinguished by the steady drizzle. It is here that Eric Bogosian read the eulogy to his friend which spoke of Hoffman's setting his bar on a rung above the highest rung and how his efforts redefined acting.

A private wake was held for the actor on February 6, 2014, at the Frank E. Campbell Funeral Home on the Upper East Side 1076 Madison Avenue from 5 to 9 p.m. Those who attended include Mimi O'Donnell, Isabelle Wing-Davey, Amy Adams, Michelle Williams, Meryl Streep, Cate Blanchett, and Joaquin Phoenix.

On February 7, 2014, a private funeral was held at New York's Church of St. Ignatius Loyola at 980 Park Avenue at noon and last for 90 minutes. Hoffman was transported in a mahogany-colored coffin. Around 400 mourners attended including Hoffman's mother Marilyn O'Connor, brother Gordy, and his partner Mimi O'Donnell and her 3 children. Also in attendance was David Bar Katz, Cate Blanchett with husband Andrew Upton, Spike Lee, Meryl Streep, Amy Adams, Joaquin Phoenix, Michelle Williams, Mary-Louise Parker, Brian Dennehy, Joel Cohen, Ellen Burstyn, Louis C.K., Justin Theroux, Paul Thomas Anderson, John C. Reilly, Ethan Hawke, Laura Linney, John Slattery, Marisa Tomei, Jake Gyllenhaal, Eric Bogosian, Billy Crudup, Julianne Moore, Anna Paquin, Vanessa Redgrave, and Mike Nichols. Blanchett did a reading during the service, and the ceremony was described by playwright Jose Rivera as beautiful and very much a ritual of healing and remembering.

On February 10, 2014, it was reported that a large mural memorializing Hoffman had popped up in the East Village. It was the work of street artist Michael DeNicola, a.k.a. Ink Lungs, and the Centre-fuge Public Art Project, painted onto a trailer. The piece, done in black and white with "P.S.H. RIP" written on it, was located on First Street between First and Second avenues.

Cate Blanchett dedicated her BAFTA Best Actress award for *Blue Jasmine* (2013) to Hoffman at the ceremony on February 16, 2014. She said the actor had a monumental talent, generosity and an unflinching quest for the truth both in life and in art, and he would be missed by many. Blanchett added that Hoffman had continually raised the bar, and concluded with "Phil, buddy, you bastard, this is for you. I hope you're proud."

People magazine of February 17, 2014, put Hoffman on the cover with an article on his death entitled "His Tragic Final Days." The article by Michelle Tauber, et al, reported that Hoffman had been seen by a neighborhood friend in the spring of 2013 at the Barrow Street Alehouse after his return from rehab. The friend said the actor ordered half of a beer. The barman teasingly asked Hoffman why he couldn't splurge for a whole beer. The friend then realized that the actor only wanted half a beer because he was trying not to drink.

Locals in the actor's West Village neighborhood reported on his troubles, where he had happy and seemingly darker private moments. They observed that Hoffman would go to Oliver's restaurant with his son, Cooper, to have lunch and would be seen talking and laughing for hours. But then at night, Hoffman would be hunched over the bar alone, looking very dark and depressed. Another source reported that the actor would stumble into his apartment after late nights out, needing to be helped into the building. The article also had a quote from Matthew Warchus who directed Hoffman in *True West* for Broadway. The tortured part of the actor came from his not settling. The audience benefited but it was a mixed blessing for the artist to have those standards. The article ended on a light note, when *Capote* producer Michael Ohoven was quoted. He said he couldn't grasp how somebody so intelligent and with enormous willpower could succumb to the terrible disease of addiction. However all Ohoven could think about was that Hoffman was sitting up there and giving one of his dark, big chuckles.

On February 19, 2014, it was reported that the bulk of Hoffman's estate was to go to Marianne aka Mimi O'Donnell, according to a will filed in New York court on February 18, 2014. She was also named the estate's executor, though the exact value of it was unknown. Hoffman's will was dated October 2004 and in it he set up a trust fund for his then only child, Cooper, and requested that the boy be raised in New York, Chicago or San Francisco. If that was not possible, the actor requested that his son visit the U.S. cities at least twice a year. The will said that the purpose of this request was so that Cooper would be exposed to the culture, arts and architecture the cities offered.

Claims made in a *National Enquirer* article that David Bar Katz and Hoffman were lovers were denied by Katz in the *New York Times* on February 25, 2014. The playwright said he had been alerted to the *Enquirer* story when it appeared online on February 5, 2014, and his first response was that the late actor would have gotten a kick out of it. The playwright claimed he had not spoken with *The Enquirer* that week, or ever, and that Hoffman had never used drugs in his presence, though he had spoken often with him about addiction and his pursuit of sobriety. Katz filed a libel suit and *The Enquirer* withdrew the article and apologized, saying they had been duped by a person claiming to be Katz.

The *New York Times* also reported on the American Playwriting Foundation Katz had formed in honor of Hoffman. This had been funded by the money Katz had received from the settlement with the *National Enquirer* and its publisher American Media Incorporated. The foundation had a prize of an annual grant of $45,000 for an unproduced play. The award was to known as the Relentless Award, honoring the late actor's dogged pursuit of artistic truth, with the settlement amount enough to allow for a grant to be given for years to come.

Katz said that the settlement he had reached with the newspaper wasn't for a personal payment but rather something meaningful to a person as demanding as Hoffman. The actor and he reportedly often talked about how it was a tragedy that playwrights couldn't survive being playwrights and how nice it would be if they could make their rent and still have an occasional steak. The article described how Katz and Hoffman met about 15 years prior through friends in the film world, but became close when their children wound up in the same Greenwich Village school. They would often stop for breakfast after the school drop-off and one of Hoffman's favorite pictures was of the two of them in the Waverly diner in December 2011. This photograph was taken by a waiter with the actor's phone and shows the couple sitting on red-colored seats that appear to be backless. Oddly neither of the men are looking at the camera in the shot, which has Katz looking away and Hoffman looking at the plate in front of him. The actor holds a cup in his right hand and his left rests on the table. Hoffman's hair is combed back and he wears his glasses and a beard, as well as black clothes.

11. The End

The February 27, 2014, edition of *Rolling Stone* magazine had Hoffman on its cover in a photograph by Martin Schoeller. The photo was taken in September 2003 in New York and had the actor looking into the camera in a shot that showed his head and shoulders and had him wearing a dark-colored shirt. Hoffman has a slight beard and moustache and his hair is combed back, with the freckles on his face exposing the sensitive quality of his skin. The look on the actor's face is strangely haunting, since his expression is so ambiguous that it is up to the viewer to define it. Since the photograph accompanies an article about Hoffman's death it seems appropriate to read the look as one of confusion and sadness, as if he himself is questioning why he has died. The article by David Browne was accompanied by photographs of the actor in *Almost Famous*, *Death of a Salesman*, *Boogie Nights*, *Capote*, *The Master*, and *Charlie Wilson's War*. There were also photos of Hoffman with Mimi O'Donnell and two of their children at the beach, his school photo and one of him applying makeup for a school show, at Sundance in January, and riding a bike in his neighborhood.

The article recalled Hoffman telling the magazine in 2005 how he was then sober and the only vices that had remained were pure mouth—cigarettes and food, but probably cigarettes more than food. The actor had said that parts of him were off-limits, and no one knew him or understood him. Playwright and friend Stephen Adly Guirgis spoke about the actor's hopes for the future, and reported that he wanted to be done with playing the sad-sack loser, the guy who was jerking off. He said Hoffman loved those characters and honored them, but when he did *A Late Quartet* he said it was his best performance, and the actor never talked that way about himself. Guirgis said that the actor was troubled and private, and he played those characters so well because he knew something about guilt and shame and suffering. Hoffman understood something dark and sad about human behavior. He didn't romanticize life on the edge and Guirgis felt Hoffman personified the gifted person who suffered from the work it took to exercise their gift. Ethan Hawke commented that Hoffman went to war for his art.

David Bar Katz dismissed the idea that Hoffman's life was on a downward spiral and said if anything he was on an upward spiral. He commented that his friend wasn't the type to care too much about having won an Oscar. Hoffman appreciated it and wasn't contemptuous of awards, but to him getting it was the equivalent of getting an easy laugh.

Hoffman's financial generosity extended to giving money to LAByrinth as well as paying for friend's rent. However he didn't spend on his own appearance. Mimi O'Donnell being a costume designer allowed her to introduce new clothes into the actor's wardrobe. But it is said that Hoffman would find a way to make them look like he had been wearing them for 20 years. His lack of vanity extended to self-deprecation about his physical appearance. 2 years prior he had showed up for a television interview in Manhattan on a bicycle, dripping with sweat, and dragging the bike into an elevator. He reportedly waved off an offer of makeup saying that it really couldn't have helped. But friends believed Hoffman had looked more frayed than usual in his last months. Katz would see him every morning as they dropped off the kids to school when the actor was doing *Death of a Salesman* on Broadway in 2012 and said Hoffman had been deeply affected by it. The playwright blamed the addiction for the actor's death, saying that it found a way back in, the way it had used Hoffman as a kid being an addict. Katz thought that the addiction saw an adult with incredible willpower who was saying that had hadn't had a drink or used drugs in his adult life and maybe the adult thought he could handle it. The playwright answered the question of how such a consummate professional with such a large degree of self-control for so long had tumbled off the wagon just long enough for a fatal fall. Katz said what happened was one tragic moment. He said Hoffman had his "shit together" and wanted to live and the clichéd narrative of a downward spiral was not the reality.

On February 28, 2014, the New York medical examiner ruled Hoffman's death as an accidental drug overdose and caused from acute mixed drug intoxication. The mix comprised of heroin, cocaine, amphetamines, and benzodiazepines, which have sedative and muscle relaxant properties that can be used to treat anxiety disorders. The other prescription drug found in Hoffman's system was an amphetamine "upper" which was often used to give an enhanced feeling of wakefulness and focus. Mixing the heroin and cocaine together in the same syringe was known as speedballing and also powerballing. This was the same deadly combination that claimed the lives of actors River Phoenix, John Belushi and Chris Farley. The use of pharmaceutical opioids benzodiazepines or barbiturates along with amphetamines was an extremely deadly cocktail of drugs that could cause a strong physical dependence and withdrawal symptoms.

After Hoffman's body was found, police were said to have launched a manhunt to identify the pusher who sold him the heroin. Robert Aaron Vineberg, a 57-year-old drug dealer, was charged with felony drug possession on February 5, 2014, in connection with the death, though he denied supplying the drugs that killed Hoffman. A young couple who lived next door to Vineberg's 302 Mott Street apartment were charged with misdemeanor cocaine possession. During the arrest the police seized packets of heroin. The couple were underground DJ Max Rosenblum, 22, and Parsons Design College School student, Juliana Luchkiw, also 22. A fourth person was also arrested in the raid but charges were later dropped. Vineberg, Rosenblum and Luchkiw were all held without bail after being arraigned on the same day. None of them appeared to have a criminal history of drug sales and Vineberg and Luchkiw had no prior arrests. Rosenblum had been previously arrested in March 2010, charged with possession of a small amount of narcotics and selling alcohol without a license at a Lower East Side club. He also had two other arrests but the records were sealed. Vineberg was said to have been an acquaintance of Hoffman's. Officials said no link had been established between the people arrested and what the police believe to be the actor's fatal overdose.

Robert Vineberg was interviewed in jail on Rikers Island and denied selling Hoffman the drugs that killed him. He insisted he hadn't seen the star since October or even heard from him since December. In an article in the *New York Times* that was published on April 11, 2014, Vineberg said that he had met the late actor sometime in 2013 through mutual friends. He said they were kindred spirits who spoke about books and art, and their addictions. They exchanged text messages to keep one another on the straight and narrow. Vineberg said Hoffman urged him to try suboxone, a controversial prescription painkiller used to treat heroin addiction. However the messages ended in the fall. Vineberg told the *New York Post* that in October the actor was at the Mott Street apartment where he got high. In December Hoffman had reportedly left him a voicemail saying that he was now clean. However after this the pair had apparently fallen out of touch. Vineberg said that he could have saved Hoffman in February if he had known he was in town, by suggesting that go to an AA meeting. He felt that if he was with the actor, his death would not have occurred.

Vineberg described him as a normal guy, someone you wouldn't know was an Oscar winner. But he also said Hoffman was a hardcore addict with a 10 bag a day heroin habit. Though he denied supplying the actor with drugs in February, when asked if he had ever sold him drugs, he refused to answer. Vineberg said he was devastated by Hoffman's death and offered his condolences to his family. He suggested that the actor's brief stint off the drugs may have made him more susceptible to overdose. When one was clean for that long of a time, he said, the body didn't have the tolerance to take as much. Vineberg commented on the actor's death by saying that people make choices in life, and they should be allowed to do whatever they want. If that was Hoffman's choice, he was really sad but he respected it. Vineberg said the actor was an adult, and since he had been doing drugs for a while he knew what he was up against. He felt that nobody killed him—Hoffman killed himself, and more horrible was the way he was being portrayed in death which nobody needed. Vineberg claimed to be a scapegoat in the Hoffman case. His attorney insisted there was no evidence to suggest he had supplied the actor with the deadly narcotics, stating the pair were true friends who had bonded over and struggled with the dangerous use of narcotic drugs.

Variety on March 1, 2014, reported that just in time for the Academy Awards, a gold statue resembling an Oscar with a syringe in its arm was erected at Hollywood Boulevard on February 28, 2014. The artist behind the sculpture, known as Plastic Jesus, advised that the work was inspired by Hoffman's recent death, although Plastic Jesus said his cousin and his cousin's wife also overdosed on heroin. The 8-foot-tall store mannequin was meant to call attention to "Hollywood's best kept secret" as noted on its pedestal and break the stigma attached to drug use. After a city official threatened to confiscate the artwork, Plastic Jesus removed the statue, though he said he planned to bring it back on Sunday for the Awards show.

On the March 2, 2014, Academy Awards ceremony held at the Dolby Theatre in Hollywood, Hoffman was included in the In Memoriam tribute. He was credited as actor for *Capote* and the screen showed an image from the film as well as a black and white photograph of Hoffman with beard and medium-length hair and wearing a checked-patterned shirt. He was looking away from the camera in the photograph and he was unsmiling. Hoffman's place in the tribute was the last, perhaps because his death was so recent or perhaps because it was decided that his loss was the year's greatest.

Kathryn Hahn had co-starred in the pilot of *Happyish* with Hoffman and commented on March 12, 2014, about his death and working with him. She said she loved and respected him because it was challenging working with him which made his loss all the devastating and as awful as one could imagine. Hahn advised that she would never forget the 3 weeks that they spent together that changed her as a human and an artist. She said it was a long process, but they did finally get to make it. The actress felt that Hoffman was the bravest and the most open with his soul on the outside of his body. Hahn said he loved actors and it didn't matter where you were in your career, he was there to make you feel comfortable, the best that you could be. She believed he was an extraordinarily talented, beautiful human.

On June 3, 2014, it was reported that Hoffman would be seen in an animated short from August 9, 2014, which PBS Digital Studios would stream and which could be viewed on YouTube.com. The short was one of the 5-minute shorts entitled *Blank on Blank*, which were created with the Rubin Museum of Art. The one with Hoffman talked about happiness and saw him in conversation with Simon Critchley, which had been recorded, live on December 17, 2012. The short had animation by Patrick Smith. Hoffman was presented as a black and white figure, with medium-length hair, glasses and a beard. The character wore a black sweater and was mostly drawn to resemble a mailbox, with one large body part and two stubby legs, though at other times it had normal long legs. The short also featured a sepia-colored photograph of Hoffman, with beard and glasses and wearing a baseball cap and a horizontal-striped shirt. In the short the actor differentiated between pleasure and happiness. Hoffman said he killed pleasure, taking too much of it, like having too much coffee which made you miserable. He said he did it often and there was no pleasure that he hadn't actually made himself sick on. Hoffman advised that he had thought about the issue a lot in his life lately and had gotten nowhere with it, and he wondered if there was a period when he was happy or just not aware. He said now that he had three children and that when he saw them enjoying each other, and then they let him enjoy them in turn, that brought him a feeling which he said was happiness.

The actor said there were moments when something else creeped in which he thought was his own childhood and a different kind of reflection—on his shortcomings and inadequacies, incapabilities and powerlessness. This was discouraging to Hoffman and made him think his happiness had ended. He said that as he got older the past kept trying to creep in and ruin what he had, but some great literary person said life was brutal which is also what made it memorable. Hoffman felt that in his acting he had to somehow allow people to identify with the worst inside themselves so that they could have that person in their art and in their minds. Otherwise these kind of characters were too easy to dismiss and he felt that his not being wildly different from other people meant that they too identified with them and their source. Hoffman also spoke about medication and how it made you come up to the lip of death, so learning how to die was learning how to live. The actor also spoke about his hesitance in public speaking, fearful that he was the stupidest man alive and that no one would take anything he had to say to be meaningful. He ended with: "So don't listen." Hoffmann's full conversation is available on the Rubin Museum website.

It was reported on June 5, 2004, that Hoffman had been lined up to direct an episode of the television comedy series *Louie*, loosely based on the life of Louis CK, a divorced comedian with two kids living in New York. The episode was to feature Jeremy Renner as the young Louie. Renner would appear in the episode entitled "In The Woods" that was broadcast on June 9, 2014, and this was directed by Louis C.K. It was reported on July 18, 2014, that Showtime's president David Nivens said that there was a chance that *Happyish* would be recast with an actor to replace Hoffman. The network was reportedly still interested in making the series because they were so impressed with the five scripts that the show' creator Shalom Auslander had written.

On July 21, 2014, it was revealed in court documents that Hoffman had strongly stipulated that he did not want his children to be considered trust fund kids. In the

Manhattan Surrogate's Court, his accountant, David Freidman, attested that he recalled conversations with him in the year before his death. Friedman said the topic of a trust was raised for the actor's kids and summarily rejected by Hoffman. Instead he declared that he wanted his money to go to his partner Mimi O'Donnell with the expressed faith that she would take care of their children. Although his existing will had been drawn up before the birth of their younger children it was declared by the court appointed attorney James Cahill, Jr., that there was nothing suspicious about it and that it should be approved by the court. However it was proposed by others that Hoffman's reasoning may not have been the most fiscally sound one.

Since he and O'Donnell were not married, taxes would devour about $15 million of the estimated $35 million estate. If the couple had been married the money could have been passed to her tax-free. Hoffman had reportedly told David Freidman that they had not married because the actor did not believe in the institution. But by placing his faith in O'Donnell the actor's intention was clear. Forgoing a trust fund was not meant to be a punishment but rather a gift. Hoffman's hope was presumably that his children would grow up to be curious, independent and contributing people. Perhaps it was felt that he didn't want to leave them mere money but what money couldn't buy—experience and opportunity—which would be a legacy they could be proud of.

On August 28, 2014, the *New York Times* reported that all the drug-selling charges against Robert Vineberg were dropped by the Manhattan district attorney because of evidentiary issues that had come to light. The two police officers who first interrogated Vineberg after his arrest had not read him his Miranda rights. Vineberg pleaded guilty on August 26, 2014, to possession of heroin, a lesser felony, and agreed to serve five years' probation, perform community service, continue drug addiction treatment and to forfeit money confiscated during his arrest. Vineberg again painted himself a scapegoat who people blamed because of his connection to Hoffman and denied ever selling the actor drugs. He said, at some level, it was like the Salem witch trials and you couldn't have a witch-hunt without a witch, and he was just unlucky enough to be the guy. The article reported how Vineberg had provided a variation on his story about whether he had sold drugs to Hoffman. Originally he had denied doing so, but then at a June 25, 2014, hearing he advised that he rarely sold to Hoffman because the actor didn't like the quality of Vineberg's heroin. He now advised that he had made this statement after his arrest because he was sick from withdrawal from the drug. Vineberg expressed visible relief after the hearing though he commented that the worst part was that he still lost his friend. But while he celebrated, still no one had ever been arrested and charged with selling drugs to Hoffman.

Variety reported on October 22, 2014, that Steve Coogan had replaced the actor in *Happyish*. On April 23, 2015, they wrote that others considered for the part had been Jim Carrey, Will Ferrell, Edward Norton and John C. Reilly. Coogan had appeared in *The Boat That Rocked* though he had no scenes with Hoffman. The role was reimagined as a British expat working in the United States and filming was to take place in New York in December.

Reminders of Hoffman's death came with the news of the death of Mike Nichols on November 19, 2014, and when the *New York Times* on December 30, 2014, recalled those deaths that shocked and had endured in the public memory in the past year.

Hoffman was mentioned where it was said that his performances were not just acclaimed but something of an event—must-see brilliance in action.

April 26, 2015, saw the screening of *Happyish*, with a reminder that Steve Coogan had replaced Hoffman in the series. It was lambasted by Brian Lowry in *Variety* and Alessandra Stanley in the *New York Times* and the series cancelled after 10 episodes of the first season. May 13, 2015, saw an article in the *New York Times* about Mimi O'Donnell seeking solace in theater as the artistic director of LAByrinth after her partner's death. There was a poem about Hoffman in the new collection of poetry by Nick Flynn called "My Feelings" which was published Graywolf Press on June 2, 2015. Flynn's poem about the actor, entitled "Philip Seymour Hoffman" was described in the *New York Times* as presenting an unvarnished look at the mind games that addicts play with themselves. November 20, 2015, saw the release of *The Hunger Games: Mockingjay Part 2*.

And 2016 promises the release of the 4 Hawk/Defendshee Productions/Neboya Collective documentary biography *Starring Austin Pendleton* (2016) directed by Gene Gallerano and David H. Holmes for which Hoffman was interviewed. The wide releases of *A Most Wanted Man, God's Pocket, The Hunger Games: Mockingjay Part 2* and the documentary allow us a posthumous reminder of Hoffman's prolificacy and mastery of his craft.

Appendix
Appearances on Film, Television and Theater

Films

Szuler a.k.a. *Cheat* (1991). Part: Martin. Excerpts are viewable on YouTube.
Triple Bogey on a Par 5 Hole (1991). Part: Klutch. DVD released by Fisher Klingenstein Films on August 9, 2013.
My New Gun (1992). Part: Chris. DVD released by Sony Pictures Home Entertainment on September 28, 2004.
Leap of Faith (1992). Part: Matt. DVD released by Paramount on September 23, 2003.
Scent of a Woman (1992). Part: George Willis, Jr. DVD released by Universal on April 29, 1998.
Joey Breaker a.k.a. *Cool Agent* and *Agent Breaker* (1993). Part: Wiley McCall. Video released by Paramount on September 15, 1993.
My Boyfriend's Back (1993). Part: Chuck Bronski. DVD released by Walt Disney Video/Mill Creek on September 3, 2002.
Money for Nothing a.k.a. *Joey Coyle* (1993). Part: Cochran. DVD released by Mill Creek Entertainment on May 10, 2011.
The Getaway (1994). Part: Frank Hansen. DVD released by Universal on May 27, 1998.
When a Man Loves a Woman (1994). Part: Gary. DVD released by Touchstone Home Entertainment on February 15, 2000.
Nobody's Fool (1994). Part: Officer Raymer. DVD released by Paramount on September 9, 2003.
Hard Eight (1996). Part: Young Craps Player. DVD released by Sony Pictures Home Entertainment on June 26, 2003.
The Fifteen Minute Hamlet (short) (1996). Parts: Bernardo, Horatio and Laertes. Excerpts are viewable on YouTube.
Twister (1996). Part: Dusty. DVD released by Warner Home Video on November 3, 2009.
Boogie Nights (1997). Part: Scotty J. DVD released by New Line Home Video on April 7, 1998.
"Try" music video (1997). Excerpts are viewable on YouTube.
Culture (1997). Part: Bill. Unavailable.
Next Stop Wonderland (1998). Part: Sean. DVD released by Miramax on May 9, 2000.
The Big Lebowski (1998). Part: Brandt. DVD released by Polygram USA Video on October 27, 1998.
Montana (1998). Part: Duncan. DVD released by Sony Pictures Home Entertainment on June 10, 2003.
Happiness (1998). Part: Allen. DVD released by Lions Gate on April 27, 1999.
Patch Adams (1998). Part: Mitch Vroman. DVD released by Universal on June 11, 2002.
Flawless (1999). Part: Russell Zimmerman. DVD released by MGM on April 25, 2000.

The Talented Mr. Ripley (1999). Part: Freddie Miles. DVD released by Warner Bros. on June 27, 2000.

Magnolia (1999). Part: Phil Parma. DVD released by New Line Home Video on August 29, 2000.

Almost Famous (2000). Part: Lester Bangs. DVD released by Warner Bros. on March 13, 2001.

The Directors: The Films of Anthony Minghella (1999). Part: Himself. DVD out of print.

State and Main (2000). Part: Joseph Turner White. DVD released by New Home Line Video on June 19, 2001.

The Last Party 2000 (2001). Part: Himself. DVD released as *The Party's Over* by Film Movement on February 9, 2004.

Love Liza (2002). Part: Wilson Joel. DVD released by Sony Pictures Home Entertainment on May 27, 2003.

Punch-Drunk Love (2002). Part: Dean Trumbell. DVD released by Sony Pictures Home Entertainment on June 24, 2003.

Red Dragon (2002). Part: Freddy Lounds. DVD released by Universal Studios on April 1, 2003.

25th Hour (2002). Part: Jacob Elinsky. DVD released by Touchstone Home Entertainment on May 20, 2003.

Owning Mahowny (2003). Part: Dan Mahowny. DVD released by Sony Pictures Home Entertainment on October 14, 2003.

Cold Mountain (2003). Part: Reverend Veasey. DVD released by Miramax Lionsgate on April 26, 2011.

Along Came Polly (2003). Part: Sanford Lyle. DVD released by Universal on June 8, 2004.

Film Trix 2004 (2004). Part: Himself.

Strangers with Candy (2005). Part: Henry. DVD released by Image/Thinkfilm on July 27, 2006.

Capote (2005). Part: Truman Capote. DVD released by Sony Pictures Home Entertainment on March 21, 2006.

Mission: Impossible III (2006). Part: Owen Davian. DVD released by Paramount on October 30, 2006.

The Savages (2007). Part: Jon Savage. DVD released by 20th Century Fox on April 22, 2008.

Before the Devil Knows You're Dead (2007). Part: Andrew Hanson. DVD released by ThinkFilm on April 15, 2008.

Charlie Wilson's War (2007). Part: Gust Avrakotos. DVD released by Universal on April 22, 2008.

Synecdoche, New York (2008). Part: Caden Cotard. DVD released by Sony Pictures Home Entertainment on March 10, 2009.

Doubt (2008). Part: Father Brendan Flynn. DVD released by Miramax on April 7, 2009.

A World for Inclusion (2008). Part: Himself.

The Boat That Rocked (2009). Part: The Count. DVD released by Focus Features on April 13, 2010.

The Invention of Lying (2009). Part: Jim the Bartender. DVD released by Warner Home Video on January 19, 2010.

Mary and Max (2009). Part: Max Jerry Horowitz. DVD released by MPI Home Video on June 15, 2010.

Jack Goes Boating (2010). Part: Jack. Hoffman also directed. DVD released by Overture Films/Anchor Bay Entertainment on January 18, 2011.

I Knew It Was You: Rediscovering John Cazale (2010). Part: Himself. DVD released by Oscilloscope on November 9, 2010.

Moneyball (2011). Part: Art Howe. DVD released by Sony Pictures Home Entertainment on January 10, 2012.

Appearances on Film, Television and in Theater 187

Unite for Japan (2011). Part: Himself. Excerpts are viewable on YouTube.
The Ides of March (2011). Part: Paul Zara. DVD released by Sony Pictures Home Entertainment on January 17, 2012.
A Late Quartet (2012). Part: Robert Gelbart. DVD released by 20th Century Fox on February 5, 2013.
The Master (2012). Part: Lancaster Dodd a.k.a. The Master. DVD released by Weinstein on February 26, 2013.
Candlesticks (2012). Hoffman was the associate producer. Excerpts are viewable on YouTube.
Salinger (2013). Part: Himself. DVD released by Anchor Bay. Only available as a Region 4 DVD.
The Hunger Games: Catching Fire (2013). Part: Plutarch Heavensbee. DVD released by Lionsgate on January 1, 2014.
A Most Wanted Man (2014). Part: Gunther Bachmann. DVD released by Lionsgate on November 4, 2014.
The Hunger Games: Mockingjay—Part 1 (2014). Part: Plutarch Heavensbee. DVD released by Lionsgate on March 6, 2015.
The Hunger Games: Mockingjay—Part 2 (2015). Part: Plutarch Heavensbee.
Blank on Blank (2014). Part: Himself. Excerpts are viewable on YouTube.
Starring Austin Pendleton (2016). Part: Himself.

Television

Law & Order (February, 5, 1991). Part: Steven B. Hanauer. DVD released by Universal on June 4, 2013.
The Yearling (April 24, 1994). Part: Buck. DVD released by Vivendi Entertainment on December 7, 2010.
It Is Now Our Time. Part: Himself/Launcelot Gobbo. Excerpts are viewable on YouTube.
Liberty! The American Revolution (November 23, 1997). Part: Joseph Plumb Martin. DVD released by PBS Direct on November 18, 2003.
Charlie Rose Show (May 30, 2000). Part: Himself. DVD released by Charlie Rose on September 18, 2006.
Inside the Actors Studio (June 4, 2000). Part: Himself. Excerpts are viewable on YouTube.
Charlie Rose Show (December 16, 2002). Part: Himself. DVD released by Charlie Rose, Inc. on August 16, 2006.
Jon Stewart (January 9, 2003). Part: Himself.
Late Night with Conan O'Brien (February 21, 2003). Part: Himself.
Once Upon a Time in Utah, Sundance (February 25, 2003). Part: Himself.
Late Night with Conan O'Brien (October 10, 2003). Part: Himself.
The 26th Annual Kennedy Center Honors (December 26, 2003). Part: Himself.
Tavis Smiley (January 15, 2004). Part: Himself.
Jon Stewart (January 19, 2004). Part: Himself.
20th IFP Independent Spirit Awards (February 26, 2005). Part: Himself. The show is viewable on YouTube.
Empire Falls (May 28, 2005). Part: Charlie Mayne a.k.a. Charles Beaumont Whiting. DVD released by HBO Studios on August 28, 2007.
Celebrity Charades (June 20, 2005). Part: Himself.
Henry's Film Corner (September 3, 2005). Part: Himself.
Women's Image Network Awards (September 26, 2005). Part: Himself.
Charlie Rose (September 29, 2005). Part: Himself. DVD released by Charlie Rose on August 10, 2006.
Jon Stewart (October 6, 2005). Part: Himself.
Sunday Morning Shootout (October 16, 2005). Part: Himself.

Live! with Kelly and Michael (November 2, 2005). Part: Himself.
Late Night with Conan O'Brien (November 2, 2005). Part: Himself.
2005 MTVU Woodie Awards (November 9, 2005). Part: Himself.
The Early Show (December 1, 2005). Part: Himself.
Today (December 13, 2005). Part: Himself.
The Tonight Show with Jay Leno (January 3, 2006). Part: Himself.
The 11th Annual Critics' Choice Awards (January 9, 2006). Part: Himself.
The 63rd Annual Golden Globe Awards (January 16, 2006). Part: Himself.
12th Annual Screen Actors Guild Awards (January 29, 2006). Part: Himself.
60 Minutes (February 19, 2006). Part: Himself. Excerpts are viewable on YouTube.
Film '72 (February 20, 2006). Part: Himself.
Late Night with David Letterman (February 22, 2006). Part: Himself.
The Culture Show (February 23, 2006). Part: Himself.
Miradas 2 (February 24, 2006). Part: Himself.
78th Annual Academy Awards (March 5, 2006). Part: Himself.
The Oprah Winfrey Show (March 6, 2006). Part: Himself.
Corazón de ... (March 6, 2006). Part: Himself.
HypaSpace (March 21, 2006). Part: Himself.
HypaSpace (May 4, 2006). Part: Himself.
64th Annual Golden Globes Awards (January 15, 2007). Part: Himself.
79th Annual Academy Awards (February 25, 2007). Part: Himself.
Charlie Rose (November 30, 2007). Part: Himself. DVD released by Charlie Rose on October 30, 2008.
Gotham Independent Film Awards (December 4, 2007). Part: Himself.
80th Annual Academy Awards (February 24, 2008). Part: Himself.
Charlie Rose Show (October 22, 2008). Part: Himself. DVD released by Charlie Rose on June 5, 2009.
Jon Stewart (December 11, 2008). Part: Himself.
Entertainment Tonight (December 12, 2008). Part: Himself.
Charlie Rose Show (December 12, 2008). Part: Himself. DVD released by Charlie Rose on December 18, 2009.
Cinema 3 (January 31, 2009). Part: Himself.
2009 Independent Spirit Awards (February 21, 2009). Part: Himself.
Cinetipp (April 18, 2009). Part: Himself.
Arthur (October 12, 2009). Part: William Fillmore Toffman. The show is viewable on YouTube.
The Kennedy Center Honors: A Celebration of the Performing Arts (December 29, 2009). Part: Guest. Excerpts are viewable on YouTube.
Made Here (May 2, 2010). Part: Himself.
Motion Pictures Live! (June 2010). Part: Himself.
The Late Late Show with Craig Ferguson (September 13, 2010). Part: Himself. Excerpts are viewable on YouTube.
Tavis Smiley (September 22, 2010). Part: Himself.
The Hour (September 29, 2010). Part: Himself. Excerpts are viewable on YouTube.
Cinema 3 (December 18, 2010). Part: Himself.
A Child's Garden of Poetry (April 28, 2011). Part: Himself (voice). DVD released by HBO Studios on November 8, 2011.
55th BFI London Film Festival (October 12, 2011). Part: Himself.
Popcorn (September 13, 2012). Part: Himself. The interview is viewable on YouTube.
18th Annual Critics' Choice Movie Awards (January 10, 2013). Part: Himself.
19th Annual Screen Actors Guild Awards (January 27, 2013) Part: Himself.
The Oscars (February 24, 2013). Part: Himself. Excerpts are viewable on YouTube.
E! Live from the Red Carpet (February 25, 2013). Part: Himself.

Theater

A Breeze in the Gulf (dates unknown). Rochester, New York. Part: unknown.
Henry IV Parts I and II (July 4 to 15, 1989). Williamstown Theatre Festival, Massachusetts. Parts: member of the funeral procession, Peter Bullcalf.
Mother Courage (August 1989) Venue: unknown. Part: Peasant Son.
King Lear (dates unknown). Hole Theatre, New Jersey. Part: Edgar.
Food and Shelter (May to June 1991). Vineyard Theatre, New York. Part: Earl.
The Merchant of Venice (October 12 to November 5, 1994). Goodman Theater, Chicago. Part: Launcelot Gobbo.
Divine Horseman (December 13 to 16, 1995). LAByrinth Theatre Company. Part: unknown.
Shmoo (Dates unknown). LAByrinth Theatre Company. Part: Producer.
Greensboro: A Requiem (February 9 to 25, 1996). McCarter Theater, Princeton, New Jersey. Parts: Klansman David Matthews and an F.B.I. agent.
The Skriker (April 23 to May 26, 1996). Joseph Papp Public Theatre, New York. Part: Raw Head and Bloody Bones.
Queen Latina and Her Power Posse Versus the Evils of Society (October 26, 1996, to March 1, 1997). LAByrinth Theatre Company. Part: unknown.
Race, Religion, Politics (April 9 to 27, 1997). LAByrinth Theatre Company. Part: unknown.
Defying Gravity (November 2, 1997, to January 4, 1998) American Place Theatre. New York. Part: C.B.
Shopping and Fucking (February 2 to March 8, 1998). New York Theatre Workshop. Part: Mark.
The Author's Voice (May 11 to 29, 1999). Greenwich House, New York. Part: Gene the Gnome.
In Arabia, We'd All Be Kings (June 23 to July 17, 1999). LAByrinth Theatre Company, Center Stage, New York. Hoffman directed.
Dreaming in Tongues (December 20, 1999) LAByrinth Theatre Company, Center Stage, New York. Hoffman co-produced.
Stopless (January 5 to 29, 2000). LAByrinth Theatre Company, Center Stage, New York. Hoffman co-produced.
True West (March 2 to July 29, 2000). Circle in the Square, New York. Parts: Lee and Austin.
Jesus Hopped the "A" Train (July 18 to August 12, 2000). LAByrinth Theatre Company, Center Stage, New York. Hoffman directed.
Jesus Hopped the "A" Train (November 29 to December 31, 2000). East 13th Street/CSC Theatre, New York. Hoffman directed.
The Seagull (August 12 to 26, 2001). New York Shakespeare Festival, Delacorte Theater, New York. Part: Konstantin.
Glory of Living (October 30 to December 1, 2001) Manhattan Class Company. Hoffman directed.
The World of Nick Adams (November 19, 2001). Avery Fisher Hall, New York. Part: unknown.
Jesus Hopped the "A" Train (March 6 to June 2002). Donmar Warehouse and Arts Theatre, London. Hoffman directed.
Miscast (April 8, 2002). Manhattan Class Company Supper Club. Part: unknown.
Our Lady of 121st Street (August 20 to October 12, 2002). LAByrinth Theatre Company, Center Stage, New York. Hoffman directed.
Our Lady of 121st Street (March 6 to July 27, 2003). LAByrinth Theatre Company, Union Square Theater, New York. Hoffman directed.
Long Day's Journey Into Night (May 6 to August 31, 2003). Plymouth Theatre, New York. Part: Jamie.
Dutch Heart of Man (September 25 to October 19, 2003). LAByrinth Theatre Company, Joseph Papp Public Theater/Susan Stein Shiva Theater, New York. Hoffman was the LAByrinth artistic director.
Autobahn (March 8, 2004). Manhattan Class Company Theater, Little Shubert Theater, New York. Part: unknown.

Guinea Pig Solo (May 9 to June 6, 2004). Joseph Papp Public Theater/New York Shakespeare Festival/LAByrinth Theater Company, Stein Shiva Theater. Hoffman was the LAByrinth co-artistic director.

Sailor's Song (November 7 to 21, 2004). LAByrinth Theatre Company, Joseph Papp Public Theater/Susan Stein Shiva Theater, New York. Hoffman was the LAByrinth executive director.

Last Days of Judas Iscariot (March 2 to April 3, 2005). LAByrinth Theatre Company, Joseph Papp Public Theater/Martinson Hall, New York. Hoffman was the LAByrinth co-artistic director.

Sawbones (April 28 to 30, 2005). Theater of the New Ear, St. Ann's Warehouse, Brooklyn. Part: the frontier veterinarian.

School of the Americas (July 6 to 26, 2006). LAByrinth Theatre Company/Joseph Papp's Public Theater, LuEsther Hall, New York. Hoffman was the LAByrinth co-artistic director.

A Small, Melodramatic Story (October 10 to November 5, 2006). LAByrinth Theatre Company, Shiva Theatre of the Public Theater, New York. Hoffman was the LAByrinth co-artistic director.

Riflemind (October 10 to December 8, 2007). Sydney Theatre Company, Wharf 1 Theatre. Hoffman directed.

A View from 151st Street (October 18 to November 4, 2007). LAByrinth Theatre Company/ Joseph Papp Public Theater, LuEsther Hall, New York. Hoffman was the LAByrinth co-artistic director.

Unconditional (February 18 to March 9, 2008). LAByrinth/Joseph Papp Public Theater, LuEsther Hall, New York. Hoffman was the LAByrinth co-artistic director.

The Little Flower of East Orange (April 6 to May 4, 2008). LAByrinth/Joseph Papp Public Theater, Martinson Hall, New York. Hoffman directed.

Jesus Hopped the A Train (June 22, 2008). Town Hall, New York. Hoffman directed.

Riflemind (September 18 to 23, 2008). LAByrinth Theatre Company/Sydney Theatre Company/Ambassador Theater Group, Trafalgar Studios, London. Hoffman directed.

Othello (June 14 to June 2009). LAByrinth Theatre Company/Joseph Papp Public Theater/ Schausplelhaus Bochum, Theater Azkent, Germany. Part: Iago.

Othello (September 27 to October 4, 2009). LAByrinth Theatre Company/Joseph Papp Public Theater/Schausplelhaus Bochum, Skirball Center for the Performing Arts, New York. Part: Iago.

The Long Red Road (February 22 to March 21, 2010) Goodman Theatre, Chicago. Hoffman directed.

True West (November 2 to December 18, 2010). Sydney Theatre Company, Wharf 1. Hoffman directed.

The ____ with the Hat (December 2010). LAByrinth Theatre Company, Cherry Pit Theatre. New York. Hoffman directed.

Being Harold Pinter (January 17, 2011). Belarus Free Theatre, Joseph Papp Public Theater, New York. Part: unknown.

Death of a Salesman (March 15 to June 2, 2012). Barrymore Theater, New York. Part: Willy Loman.

A Family for All Occasions (April 25 to May 26, 2013). LAByrinth Theatre Company, Bank Street Theater, New York. Hoffman directed.

Bibliography

Adams, Cindy. "Early Signs 'Things Weren't Right' with Philip Seymour Hoffman." *Page Six*. February 3, 2014. Retrieved August 12, 2015, from http://www.pagesix.com.
Adams, Thelma. "What Philip Seymour Hoffman Told Us About Grieving." *Yahoo Movies!* February 14, 2014. Retrieved April 22, 2015, from http://www.yahoo.com.
Affleck, Casey. *I'm Still Here*. They Are Going to Kill Us Productions, 2010.
Aftab, Kaleem. "Profile: Philip Seymour Hoffman, Director and Star of Jack Goes Boating." *The List*. June 17, 2011. Retrieved August 12, 2015, from http://www.edinburghfestival.list.co.uk.
Ahozie, Lorna. *Evolution of an American Filmmaker*. EMC West/Buena Vista Television/Disney Enterprises, 2003.
Allen, Jenny. "Weddings/Celebrations: Vows; Brooke Williams and Joshua Liberson." *New York Times*. February 16, 2003. Retrieved May 8, 2015, from http://www.nytimes.com.
Allen, Nick. "Tsr Exclusive: 'Jack Goes Boating' Interview with Actor/Director Philip Seymour Hoffman and Actor John Ortiz." *The Scorecard Review*. September 21, 2010. Retrieved August 13, 2015, from http://www.thescorecardreview.com.
Allon, Yoram, Cullen, Del, and Patterson, Hannah. *Contemporary North American Film Directors: A Wallflower Critical*. London: Wallflower Press, 2002.
Anderson, Jeffrey M. "'Liza' Wide Open." *Combustible Celluloid*. January 12, 2003. Retrieved April 22, 2015, from http://www.combustiblecelluloid.com.
Anderson, Paul. *The Dirk Diggler Story*. 1988. Viewed March 8, 2015 on YouTube.com.
_____, et al. DVD Cast Audio Commentary. *Boogie Nights*. Platinum Series. New Line Home Video, 2007.
Anderson, Paul Thomas. DVD Director's Audio Commentary. *Boogie Nights*. New Line Home Video, 2007.
Anderton, Ethan. "Philip Seymour Hoffman Joining Ethan Hawke for 'A Late Quartet.'" *Firstshowing*. January 6, 2011. Retrieved September 13, 2015, from http://www.firstshowing.net.
Andreeva, Nellie. "FX Developing Cop Drama Produced by Philip Seymour Hoffman." *Deadline Hollywood*. March 30, 2012. Retrieved November 21, 2015, from http://www.deadline.com.
_____. "HBO Developing Rural Drama Produced by Philip Seymour Hoffman." *Deadline Hollywood*. March 16, 2011. Retrieved November 15, 2015, from http://www.deadline.com.
_____. "Showtime on Philip Seymour Hoffman's Death; Future of His Series 'Happyish' Uncertain." *Deadline TV*. February 3, 2014. Retrieved September 17, 2015, from http://www.deadlinetv.com.
Aviles, Omar. "Hoffman Directs Jack." *JoBlo*. January 16, 2009. Retrieved November 9, 2015, from http://www.joblo.com.
Bagley, Christopher. "Judging Amy." *W Magazine*. June, 2006. Retrieved May 19, 2015, from http://www.wmagazine.com.
Bahr, Lindsey et al. "Shock and Awe: Hollywood Reacts." *Entertainment Weekly*. February 14, 2014: 35–36.
Barker, Andrew. "Film Review: 'Salinger.'" *Variety*. September 3, 2013. Retrieved October 5, 2015, from http://www.variety.com.
Barnes, Brooks. "For the Oscar Nominees, Fake Fog and Air Kisses." *New York Times*. February 4, 2013. Retrieved September 10, 2015, from http://www.nytimes.com.
Barron, James. "Boldface Names … a Friend in High Places." *New York Times*. August 3, 2001. Retrieved April 17, 2015, from http://www.nytimes.com.
Bartelmay, Ryan. "Philip Seymour Hoffman." *Believer*. February, 2004. Retrieved April 20, 2015, from http://www.beleivermag.com.
Bartyzel, Monica. "Paul Thomas Anderson's Next Film, 'The Master,' 'Postponed Indefinitely.'" *Moviefone*. September 20, 2010. Retrieved November 14, 2015, from http://www.moviefone.com.
Batistick, Mike. "Enter the Labyrinth." *Time Out New York*, August 3–10, 2000: 139.

Bibliography

Beauchamp, Jean Manuel. "Hoffman Is the Macguffin in Hard Eight." *Scribd*. Retrieved March 4, 2015, from http://www.scribd.com.

Bellamy, Jason. "Shadows and Light: 25th Hour." *The Cooler*. February 9, 2014. Retrieved May 13, 2015, from http://www.coolercinema.blogspot.com.au.

Benioff, David. *25th Hour* DVD Audio Commentary. Touchstone Home Entertainment, 2003.

Berk, Philip. "The Actor's Actor." *Filmink*, vol. 8.13, 2008: 52–55.

Berke, Richard L. "Sex! Drugs! (And Maybe a Little War)." *New York Times*. December 16, 2007. Retrieved July 19, 2015, from http://www.nytimes.com.

Bernstein, Jacob. "At the New York Premiere of 'Her,' a Party Makes Do Without Its Voice." *New York Times*. October 16, 2013. Retrieved September 15, 2015, from http://www.nytimes.com.

_____. "His Death, Their Lives." *New York Times*. February 7, 2014. Retrieved October 19, 2015, from http://www.nytimes.com.

Bigsby, Christopher. *The Cambridge Companion to David Mamet*. Cambridge, NY: Cambridge University Press, 2004.

Blackhall, Sue. *Billy Nighy—The Unauthorised Biography*. London, UK: John Blake Publishing, 2010.

Blake, Jason. "Casting Adds Bite to Feuding Brothers." *The Sydney Morning Herald*. November 4, 2010. Retrieved August 17, 2015, from http://www.smh.com.au.

Blake, Leslie (Hoban). "Theater News: At the Labyrinth Theatre Company, A-Mazing Things Happen." *TheaterMania*. January 25, 2000. Retrieved April 16, 2015, from http://www.theatermania.com.

Blankenship, Mark. "Review: 'A Small, Melodramatic Story.'" *Variety*. October 24, 2006. Retrieved June 20, 2015, from http://www.variety.com.

Bloom, Julie. "Arts, Briefly. Collaboration Onstage." *New York Times*. September 15, 2008. Retrieved August 3, 2015, from http://www.nytimes.com.

_____. "Artsbeat: Hoffman Gets Turn at Director's Chair on the Big Screen." *New York Times*. January 16, 2009. Retrieved August 14, 2015, from http://www.nytimes.com.

Blosser, John, and Brette Trost, and Robert Hartlein. "Inside Philip Seymour Hoffman's Tragic Final Hours." *National Enquirer*: February 17, 2014: 20 -24.

Blunt, Tom. "First Time Fest Nyc: Philip Seymour Hoffman on the Perils of Directing Oneself." *Word & Film*. March 5, 2013. Retrieved August 13, 2015, from http://www.wordandfilm.com.

Boule, Jean-Pierre, and Ursula Tidd. *Existentialism and Contemporary Cinema: A Beauvoirian Perspective*. New York: Berghahn Books, 2012

Boyle, Louise. "A Final Farewell to Philip Seymour Hoffman: Tragic Actor's Devastated Family and Friends Say Goodbye at New York Funeral." *Daily Mail*. February 8, 2014. Retrieved October 20, 2015, from http://www.dailymail.co.uk.

_____. "Philip Seymour Hoffman Cause of Death Ruled Accidental and Revealed to Be 'Acute Mixed Drug Intoxication' of Heroin, Cocaine and Prescription Pills." *Daily Mail*. March 1, 2014. Retrieved October 14, 215 from http://www.dailymail.co.uk.

Brantley, Ben. "American Dreamer, Ambushed by the Territory." *New York Times*. March 15, 2012. Retrieved September 2, 2015, from http://www.nytimes.com.

_____. "At Its Best, a Season That Made the Leap Into Life." *New York Times*. June 4, 2000. Retrieved April 10, 2015, from http://www.nytimes.com.

_____. "The General in His High-Tech Labyrinth." *New York Times*. September 28, 2009. Retrieved August 16, 2015, from http://www.nytimes.com.

_____. "Judas Gets His Day in Court, but Satan Is on the Witness List." *New York Times*. March 3, 2005. Retrieved May 16, 2015, from http://www.nytimes.com.

_____. "A Little Less Than Kind, But Very Much Kin: Ambivalence, Pain and Family Ties ." *New York Times*. April 7, 2008. Retrieved July 25, 2015, from http://www.nytimes.com.

_____. "Theater Review: A Mother's Haunting Presence in O'neill's Unraveling Family." *New York Times*. May 7, 2003. Retrieved May 13, 2015, from http://www.nytimes.com.

_____. "Theater Review: A Shocker That Aims to Preach." *New York Times*. February 3, 1998. Retrieved March 14, 2015, from http://www.nytimes.com.

_____. "Theater Review: Anachronism in a T-Shirt, Bewildered by a Fast-Moving World. " *New York Times*. September 30, 2003. Retrieved May 15, 2015, from http://www.nytimes.com.

_____. "Theater Review: Finding Out What It's Like to Really Be Your Brother." *New York Times*. March 10, 2000. Retrieved March 21, 2015, from http://www.nytimes.com.

_____. "Theater Review: In Her World, Normalcy Includes the Grotesque." *New York Times*. November 16, 2001. Retrieved April 16, 2015, from http://www.nytimes.com.

_____. "Theater Review: Locked Up in a Place Far Beyond Redemption." *New York Times*. November 30, 2000. Retrieved March 19, 2015, from http://www.nytimes.com.

_____. "Theater Review: Prolonging the Punch of a Lone Punch Line." *New York Times*. May 22, 1999. Retrieved March 17, 2015, from http://www.nytimes.com.

_____. "Theater Review: Streep Meets Chekhov, Up in Central Park." *New York Times*. August 13, 2001. Retrieved April 17, 2015, from http://www.nytimes.com.
_____. "Theater Review: You Can Take the Soldier Out of the War, But You Can't…" *New York Times*. May 10, 2004. Retrieved May 15, 2015, from http://www.nytimes.com.
_____. "Theater: The Tonys." *New York Times*. May 12, 2012. Retrieved September 5, 2015, from http://www.nytimes.com.
_____. "Those Who Traffic in Spin Can Get Caught in the Cycle." *New York Times*. November 12, 2008. Retrieved August 21, 2015, from http://www.nytimes.com.
_____. "Yes, Survival's Important. But Then What?" *New York Times*. November 27, 2013. Retrieved October 15, 2015, from http://www.nytimes.com.
_____. "The Zen Art of Life Maintenance (Pass the Bong, Please)." *New York Times*. March 19, 2007. Retrieved July 12, 2015, from http://www.nytimes.com.
Breznican, Anthony. "The Night Philip Seymour Hoffman Changed My Life…" *Entertainment Weekly*. February 6, 2014. Retrieved July 7, 2015, from http://www.ew.com.
_____. "Philip Seymour Hoffman Returns in Aching Animated Short." *Entertainment Weekly*. June 3, 2014. Retrieved November 30, 2015, from http://www.ew.com.
Browne, David. "Cameron Crowe on How Philip Seymour Hoffman Became Lester Bangs." *Rolling Stone*. February 14, 2014. Retrieved April 8, 2015, from http://www.rollingstone.com.
_____. "Philip Seymour Hoffman." *Rolling Stone*, February 27, 2014: 48–53.
Brunner, Rob. "'Hunger Games': Philip Seymour Hoffman on Playing Plutarch in 'Catching Fire.'" *Entertainment Weekly*. August 3, 2012. Retrieved September 20, 2015, from http://www.ew.com.
Brunsting, Joshua. "Film Society of Lincoln Center Holding Sidney Lumet Retrospective." *Criterioncast LLC*. June 27, 2011. Retrieved November 18, 2015, from http://www.criterioncast.com.
Buchanan, Kyle. "Catherine Keener on Making Music with Philip Seymour Hoffman (And Her Biggest Oscar Priority)." *Vulture*. November 2, 2012. Retrieved September 13, 2015, from http://www.vulture.com.
Bunbury, Stephanie. "Interview: Philip Seymour Hoffman." *The Sydney Morning Herald*. October 20, 2012. Retrieved September 12, 2015, from http://www.smh.com.au.
Busis, Hillary. "Philip Seymour Hoffman Really, Really Doesn't Want to Talk About Scientology, You Idiot!" *Entertainment Weekly*. September 7, 2012. Retrieved September 13, 2015, from http://www.ew.com.
Bustos, Kristina. "Jake Gyllenhaal, Amy Adams Join Philip Seymour Hoffman's Ezekiel Moss." *Digital Spy*. February 2, 2014. Retrieved September 22, 2015, from http://www.digitalspy.com.au.
_____. "Katy Perry, Jason Sudeikis in 'Snl's 'New Year's Eve' Spoof." *Digital Spy* December 11, 2011. Retrieved November 20, 2015, from http://www.digitalspy.com.
Callauti, Katie. "Philip Seymour Hoffman & Christopher Walken on 'A Late Quartet,' 'The Hunger Games' & P.T. Anderson." *The Huffington Post*. July 2, 2013. Retrieved September 9, 2015, from http://www.huffingtonpost.com.
Campbell, Mary Schmidt, and Randy Martin. *Artistic Citizenship: A Public Voice for the Arts*. New York: Routledge, ©2006.
Canby, Vincent. "Review/Film: The 'Cute Kids' of a Couple of Crooks." *New York Times*. March 21, 1982. Retrieved December 23, 2014, from http://www.nytimes.com.
_____. "Sunday View: 'Capeman' Doesn't Fly, Despite the Music." *New York Times*. February 8, 1998. Retrieved March 14, 2015, from http://www.nytimes.com.
_____. "Theater Review; When Communists Clashed with Nazis and the Klan." *New York Times*. February 12, 1996. Retrieve January 5, 2015, from http://www.nytimes.com.
Cardwell, Diane, with Faiza Akhtar, and Melena Z. Ryzik. "Boldface Names." *New York Times*. July 18, 2003. Retrieved May 15, 2015, from http://www.nytimes.com.
Carr, David. "The Contenders, the Show and the Spectacle." *New York Times*. February 19, 2009. Retrieved August 14, 2015, from http://www.nytimes.com.
_____. "'Doubt' and Doubts of a Workingman." *New York Times*. December 4, 2008. Retrieved August 3, 2015, from http://www.nytimes.com.
_____. "Hype-Dappled Landscape." *New York Times*. December 12, 2008. Retrieved August 3, 2015, from http://www.nytimes.com.
_____. "In Cold Print: The Genre Capote Started." *New York Times*. July 13, 2005. Retrieved June 4, 2015, from http://www.nytimes.com.
_____. "In Movies, Big Issues, for Now." *New York Times*. January 18, 2006. Retrieved June 18, 2015, from http://www.nytimes.com.
_____. "One Last Best Shot at Calling the Oscars." *New York Times*. March 3, 2006. Retrieved June 20, 2015, from http://www.nytimes.com.
_____. "Paul Giamatti, the Unlikely Leading Man." *New York Times*. May 7, 2006. Retrieved June 20, 2015, from http://www.nytimes.com.

_____. "The Universe According to Kaufman." *New York Times*. October 19, 2008. Retrieved August 3, 2015, from http://www.nytimes.com.

_____. "The Wrestler." *Medium*. February 4, 2014. Retrieved October 20, 2015, from http://www.medium.com.

_____, and Michael Cieply,. "'Atonement' Wins Best Drama at Globes." *New York Times*. January 14, 2008. Retrieved July 20, 2015, from http://www.nytimes.com.

Carter, Bill. "Showtime Finds a Replacement for Philip Seymour Hoffman." *New York Times*. October 23, 2014. Retrieved November 1, 2015, from http://www.nytimes.com.

Carvell, Nick. "John Slattery on Directing Philip Seymour Hoffman in His Last Lead Role (And Jon Hamm's Gq Cover)." *GQ*. August 11, 2014. Retrieved September 23, 2015, from http://www.gq-magazine.co.uk.

Cerasaro, Pat. "2010 Flashback—Indepth Interview: Philip Seymour Hoffman." *Broadway World*. February 3, 2014. Retrieved August 12, 2015, from http://www.broadwayworld.com.

Chai, Barbara. "'Death of a Salesman' Does Lunch." *The Wall Street Journal*. April 23, 2012. Retrieved November 21, 2015, from http://www.blogs.wsj.com.

_____. "Philip Seymour Hoffman, Christopher Walken on 'A Late Quartet.'" *The Wall Street Journal*. February 5, 2013. Retrieved September 8, 2015, from http://www.blogs.wsj.com.

_____. "Philip Seymour Hoffman Explains Why Bloody 'Hunger Games' Is Good for Kids." *The Wall Street Journal*. February 5, 2013. Retrieved September 19, 2015, from http://www.blogs.wsj.com.

Chaiklin, Rebecca, and Philip Seymour Hoffman. *The Last Party 2000* DVD Audio Commentary. Film Movement, 2005.

Chan, Sewell. "Arts, Briefly. City's Culture Arm Turns 30." *New York Times*. October 31, 2006. Retrieved July 11, 2015, from http://www.nytimes.com.

Chang, Justin. "Film Review: 'The Hunger Games: Mockingjay—Part 1.'" *Variety*. November 10, 2014. Retrieved September 21, 2015, from http://www.variety.com.

_____. "Justin Chang Remembers Philip Seymour Hoffman: A Master of His Screen Craft." *Variety*. February 2, 2014. Retrieved November 27, 2015, from http://www.variety.com.

_____. "Review: Mary and Max." *Variety*. January 15, 2009. Retrieved July 27, 2015, from http://www.variety.com.

_____. "Review: The Invention of Lying." *Variety*. September 30, 2009. Retrieved August 1, 2015, from http://www.variety.com.

_____. "Review: The Ides of March." *Variety*. August 31, 2011. Retrieved August 19, 2015, from http://www.variety.com.

_____. "Review: 'The Master.'" *Variety*. September 1, 2012. Retrieved September 1, 2015, from http://www.variety.com.

_____. "Review: 'A Late Quartet.'" *Variety*. September 11, 2012. Retrieved September 8, 2015, from http://www.variety.com.

_____. "Sundance Film Review: 'God's Pocket.'" *Variety*. January 18, 2014. Retrieved September 23, 2015, from http://www.variety.com.

_____. "Sundance Film Review: 'A Most Wanted Man.'" *Variety*. January 19, 2014. Retrieved October 2, 2015, from http://www.variety.com.

Chaw, Walter. "Love Notes: FFC Interviews Todd Louiso and Philip Seymour Hoffman." *Film Freak Central*. February 2, 2014. Retrieved April 22, 2015, from http://www.filmfreakcentral.net.

Chi, Paul. "Steve Coogan Talks Replacing Philip Seymour Hoffman in Showtime's 'Happyish.'" *Variety*. April 21, 2015. Retrieved December 1, 2015, from http://www.varietycom.

Chivers, Sally. *The Silvering Screen: Old Age and Disability in Cinema*. Toronto, Buffalo, London: University of Toronto Press, 2011.

Cieply Michael. "Artsbeat: Seeking Universal Life Lessons in Story of Baseball Nerdery." *New York Times*. September 9, 2011. Retrieved August 22, 2015, from http://www.nytimes.com.

_____. "As Studios Cut Back, Investors See Opening." *New York Times*. November 14, 2010. Retrieved August 18, 2015, from http://www.nytimes.com.

_____. "Filmmaker's Newest Work Is About ... Something." *New York Times*. April 18, 2012. Retrieved September 5, 2015, from http://www.nytimes.com.

Cipriani, Casey. "Film Society of Lincoln Center Selects Phillip Seymour Hoffman, Marisa Tomei and More for Filmmaker in Residence Advisory Board." *Indiewire*. June 13, 2013. Retrieved November 23, 2015, from http://www.indiewire.com.

_____. "'Mad Mens' John Slattery Talks to Indiewire from the Set of 'God's Pocket,' His Directorial Debut Starring Philip Seymour Hoffman and Christina Hendricks." *Indiewire*. July 24, 2013. Retrieved September 10, 2015, from http://www.indiewire.com.

Clement, Rene. *Plein Soleil*. Robert et Raymond Hakim/Paris Film, 1960.

Clooney, George, and Grant Heslov. *The Ides of March* DVD Audio Commentary. Sony Pictures Entertainment, 2012.
Cockrell, Eddie. "Review: 'State and Main.'" *Variety*. August 28, 2000. Retrieved April 6, 2015, from http://www.variety.com.
Cohen, Patricia. "Artsbeat: Live and in Print: Lapham's Celebrities." *New York Times*. January 11, 2011. Retrieved August 18, 2015, from http://www.nytimes.com.
Cohn, Lawrence. "Review: 'Joey Breaker.'" *Variety*. March 9, 1993. Retrieved December 29, 2014, from http://www.variety.com.
Collin, Robbie. "The Master: Philip Seymour Hoffman on His 'Scientology' Movie." *The Telegraph*. October 23, 2012. Retrieved September 12, 2015, from http://www.telegraph.co.uk.
Collins, Lauren. "A Night Out With: Kerry Washington: Politics and Shabu Shabu." *New York Times*. October 24, 2004. Retrieved May 16, 2015, from http://www.nytimes.com.
Comentale, Edward P., and Aaron Jaffe. *The Year's Work in Lebowski Studies*. Bloomington: Indiana University Press, 2009.
Conard, Mark T. *The Philosophy of Spike Lee*. Lexington, KY: University Press of Kentucky, 2011.
_____. *The Philosophy of the Coen Brothers*. Lexington, KY: University Press of Kentucky, 2009.
Connelly, Brendan. "Matt Reeves 'Let the Right One In' Remake Casting Rumors." *SlashFilm*. September 23, 2009. Retrieved November 10, 2015, from http://www.slashfilm.com.
Corbijn, Anton. Video interview for *A Most Wanted Man*. July 25, 2014. Viewed October 3, 2015 on YouTube.com.
Corliss, Richard. "The Ides of March: Ladies and Gentlemen, President George Clooney." *Time*. October 6, 2011. Retrieved August 20, 2015, from http://www.entertainment.time.com.
Correal, Annie and Newman, Andy. "New York Today: A Treacherous Wintry Mix." *New York Times*. February 5, 2014. Retrieved October 16, 2015, from http://www.nytimes.com.
Crowe, Cameron, et al. DVD Audio Commentary. *Almost Famous* Bootleg Edition. Dreamworks Video, 2001.
Cruise, Tom and Abrams, J.J. *Mission: Impossible III* DVD Audio Commentary. Paramount, 2006.
Curtis, Richard, et al. *The Boat That Rocked* DVD Audio Commentary. Focus Features, 2010.
Da Cunha, Chris, and Mike Jay. *Charlie Rose*. October 22, 2008. Charlie Rose Inc., 2008.
_____, and *Charlie Rose*. December 12, 2008. Charlie Rose Inc., 2008.
Daly, Steve. "Who Should Be Cast in the Gilligan's Island Movie?" *People*. March 3, 2010. Retrieved November 12, 2015, from http://www.people.com.
Dargis, Manohla. "Between Heaven and Earth, Room for Ambiguity." *New York Times*. December 11, 2008. Retrieved July 22, 2015, from http://www.nytimes.com.
_____. "Dreamer, Live in the Here and Now." *New York Times*. October 23, 2008. Retrieved July 14, 2015, from http://www.nytimescom.
_____. "Going to Extremes and Getting Personal in 'Mission: Impossible Iii." *New York Times*. May 5, 2006. Retrieved June 6, 2015, from http://www.nytimes.com.
_____. "Review: 'The Hunger Games: Mockingjay Part 2,' Katniss's Final Battle." *New York Times*. November 19, 2015. Retrieved November 20, 2015, from http://www.nytimes.com.
_____. "Rock Boys' Adventure, with BBC as the Enemy." *New York Times*. November 12, 2009. Retrieved August 1, 2015, from http://www.nytimes.com.
_____. "A Search and Destroy Thyself Mission." *New York Times*. July 24, 2014. Retrieved October 2, 2015, from http://www.nytimes.com.
_____. "Striking Where Myth Meets Moment." *New York Times*. November 21, 2013. Retrieved September 14, 2015, from http://www.nytimes.com.
_____. "Stuck on a Family Hamster Wheel, Mile After Mile, Year After Year." *New York Times*. November 28, 2007. Retrieved July 5, 2015, from http://www.nytimes.com.
_____. "Throwing a Digital-Age Curveball." *New York Times*. September 22, 2011. Retrieved August 22, 2015, from http://www.nytimes.com.
_____. "Up from Rubble to Lead a Revolution." *New York Times*. November 20, 2014. Retrieved September 21, 2015, from http://www.nytimes.com.
_____. "A World Where Truth Turns Out Not to Be Beauty." *New York Times*. October 2, 2009. Retrieved August 1, 2015, from http://www.nytimes.com.
Darnton, John. Philip Seymour Hoffman. TimesTalks video interview. *New York Times*. January 27, 2006. Viewed June 18, 2015 on http://www.nytimes.com.
David, Laura, and Jed Dannenbaum. *The Making of Almost Famous*. HBO/Laura Davis Prodictions/Dreamworks/Columbia Pictures Industries, 2000.
Dawtrey, Adam. "Curtis Sets Sail on Universal's 'Boat.'" *Variety*. March 4, 2008. Retrieved August 1, 2015, from http://www.variety.com.
Day, Elizabeth. "Christina Hendricks: 'My Agency Dropped Me When I First Agreed to Play Joan in Mad

Men.'" *The Guardian.* August 3, 2014. Retrieved October 13, 2015, from http://www.theguardian.com.

De Bont, Jan and Fangmeier, Stefen. Twister DVD audio commentary. *Twister.* Warner Home Video, 2011.

DeBruge, Peter. "Film Review: 'The Hunger Games: Mockingjay—Part 2.'" *Variety.* November 4, 2015. Retrieved November 20, 2015, from http://www.variety.com.

———. "Review: 'Moneyball.'" *Variety.* September 8, 2011. Retrieved August 23, 2015, from http://www.variety.com.

———. "Review: The Hunger Games: Catching Fire." *Variety.* November 12, 2013. Retrieved September 14, 2015, from http://www.variety.com.

Del Signore, John. "Philip Seymour Hoffman Street Art Tribute Goes Up in East Village." *Gothamist.* February 10, 2014. Retrieved October 20, 2015, from http://www.gothamist.com.

Denby, David. "*Fool*'s Gold." *New York Magazine*, January 16, 1995: 56- 57.

Dennen, Laura. "Philip Seymour Hoffman Is Digging Seattle." *SeattleMet.* September 10, 2010. Retrieved August 14, 2015, from http://www.seattlemet.com.

Desowitz, Bill." Film: Back to the 70's; The Extraordinary Adolescence of Cameron Crowe." *New York Times.* September 10, 2000. Retrieved April 10, 2015, from http://www.nytimes.com.

Ditzian, Eric. "The Stars Come Out for Tonight's Independent Spirit Awards." *MTV.* March 5, 2011. Retrieved November 12, 2015, from http://www.moviesblog.mtv.com.

Dixon, Wheeler Winston. Film Talk: *Directors at Work.* Piscataway, NJ: Rutgers University Press, 2007.

Doom, Ryan P. *The Brothers Coen: Unique Characters of Violence.* Santa Barbara, CA: ABC-CLIO, 2009.

Douglas, Edward. "Philip Seymour Hoffman Visits Synecdoche, New York." *Comingsoon.* October 20, 2008. Retrieved July 18, 2015, from http://www.comingsoon.net.

Douthat, Ross. "Philip Seymour Hoffman, R.I.P.." *New York Times.* February 3, 2014. Retrieved October 14, 2015, from http://www.nytimes.com.

Dowd, Kathy Ehrich. "Philip Seymour Hoffman Poses for Haunting Photo Weeks Before Death." *People.* February 3, 2014. Retrieved October 12, 2015, from http://www.people.com.

Dretzka, Gary. "An Interview with Richard Kwietniowski." *Movie City News.* April 23, 2003. Retreived May 18, 2015, from http://www.moviecitynews.com.

Dunn, Jamie. "Third Time's the Charm: Anton Corbijn on a Most Wanted Man." *The Skinny.* September 2, 2014. Retrieved October 3, 2015, from http://www.theskinny.co.uk.

Dunn, Jancee. "True Grit." *Time Out New York*, February 17–24, 2000: 15–18.

Durbin, Karen. "Breaking Out of the Mold." *New York Times.* September 10, 2010. Retrieved August 17, 2015, from http://www.nytimes.com.

Dwyer, Jim. "Truth and a Prize Emerge from Lies About Hoffman." *New York Times.* February 25, 2014. Retrieved October 29, 2015, from http://www.nytimes.com.

Ebert, Roger. "Review: A Late Quartet." *Roger Ebert.* October 31, 2012. Retrieved September 8, 2015, from http://www.rogerebert.com.

———. "Review: Jack Goes Boating." *Roger Ebert.* September 22, 2010. Retrieved August 8, 2015, from http://www.rogerebert.com.

———. "Review: Moneyball." *Roger Ebert.* September 21, 2011. Retrieved August 23, 2015, from http://www.rogerebert.com.

———. "Review: Pirate Radio." *Roger Ebert.* November 11, 2009. Retrieved August 1, 2015, from http://www.rogerebert.com.

———. "Review: The Ides of March." *Roger Ebert.* October 5, 2011. Retrieved August 19, 2015, from http://www.rogerebert.com.

———. "Review: The Master." *Roger Ebert.* September 19, 2012. Retrieved Septemer 1, 2015, from http://www.rogerebert.com.

———. "Reviews: Almost Famous." *Roger Ebert.* September 15, 2000. Retrieved April 7, 2015, from http://www.rogerebert.com.

———. "Reviews: Along Came Polly." *Roger Ebert.* January 16, 2004. Retrieved May 10, 2015, from http://www.rogerebert.com.

———. "Reviews: Before the Devil Knows You're Dead." *Roger Ebert.* November 1, 2007. Retrieved July 7, 2015, from http://www.rogerebert.com.

———. "Reviews: Boogie Nights." *Roger Ebert.* October 17, 1997. Retrieved March 7, 2015, from http://www.rogerebert.com.

———. "Reviews: Capote." *Roger Ebert.* October 20, 2005. Retrieved June 1, 2015, from http://www.rogerebert.com.

———. "Reviews: Charlie Wilson's War." *Roger Ebert.* December 20, 2007. Retrieved July 10, 2015, from http://www.rogerebert.com.

———. "Reviews: Cold Mountain. " *Roger Ebert.* December 24, 2003. Retrieved May 22, 2015, from http://www.rogerebert.com.

_____. "Reviews: Doubt." *Roger Ebert*. December 10, 2008. Retrieved July 22, 2015, from http://www.rogerebert.com.
_____. "Reviews: Flawless." *Roger Ebert*. November 24, 1999. Retrieved April 4, 2015, from http://www.rogerebert.com.
_____. "Reviews: Happiness." *Roger Ebert*. October 23, 1998. Retrieved March 14, 2015, from http://www.rogerebert.com.
_____. "Reviews: Hard Eight." *Roger Ebert*. February 27, 1997. Retrieved March 3, 2015, from http://www.rogerebert.com.
_____. "Reviews: Leap of Faith." *Roger Ebert*. December 18, 1992. Retrieved December 26, 2014, from http://www.rogerebert.com.
_____. "Reviews: Love Liza." *Roger Ebert*. February 7, 2003. Retrieved April 17, 2015, from http://www.rogerebert.com.
_____. "Reviews: Magnolia." *Roger Ebert*. January 7, 2000. Retrieved April 5, 2015, from http://www.rogerebert.com.
_____. "Reviews: Mission Impossible Iii." *Roger Ebert*. May 4, 2006. Retrieved June 6, 2015, from http://www.rogerebert.com.
_____. "Reviews: Nobody's Fool." *Roger Ebert*. January 13, 1995. Retrieved February 19, 2015, from http://www.rogerebert.com.
_____. "Reviews: Owning Mahowny." *Roger Ebert*. May 16, 2003. Retrieved May 18, 2015, from http://www.nytimes.com.
_____. "Reviews: Patch Adams." *Roger Ebert*. December 25, 1998. Retrieved March 27, 2015, from http://www.rogerebert.com.
_____. "Reviews: Punch-Drunk Love." *Roger Ebert*. October 18, 2002. Retrieved May 2, 2015, from http://www.rogerebert.com.
_____. "Reviews: Red Dragon." *Roger Ebert*. October 4, 2002. Retrieved May 4, 2015, from http://www.rogerebert.com.
_____. "Reviews: Scent of a Woman." *Roger Ebert*. December 23, 1992. Retrieved December 28, 2014, from http://www.rogerebert.com.
_____. "Reviews: State and Main." *Roger Ebert*. December 22, 2000. Retrieved April 6, 2015, from http://www.rogerebert.com.
_____. "Reviews: Synecdoche, New York." *Roger Ebert*. November 5, 2008. Retrieved July 14, 2015, from http://www.rogerebert.com.
_____. "Reviews: The Big Lebowski." *Roger Ebert*. March 6, 1998. Retrieved March 10, 2015, from http://www.rogerebert.com.
_____. "Reviews: The Getaway." *Roger Ebert*. February 11, 1994. Retrieved January 1, 2015, from http://www.rogerebert.com.
_____. "Reviews: The Invention of Lying." *Roger Ebert*. September 30, 2009. Retrieved August 1, 2015, from http://www.rogerebert.com.
_____. "Reviews: The Savages." *Roger Ebert*. December 20, 2007. Retrieved July 5, 2015, from http://www.rogerebert.com.
_____. "Reviews: The Talented Mr. Ripley." *Roger Ebert*. December 24, 1999. Retrieved March 29, 2015, from http://www.rogerebert.com.
_____. "Reviews: 25th Hour." *Roger Ebert*. January 10, 2003. Retrieved May 10, 2015, from http://www.rogerebert.com.
_____. "Reviews: Twister." *Roger Ebert*. May 10, 1996. Retrieved March 5, 2015, from http://www.rogerebert.com.
_____. "Reviews: When a Man Loves a Woman." *Roger Ebert*. May 6, 1994. Retrieved January 1, 2015, from http://www.rogerebert.com.
Edelman Borden, Marian. *Paul Newman: A Biography (Greenwood Biographies)*. Santa Barbara, CA: ABC-Clio, 2011.
Edelstein, David. "Back Door Blues. What Spike Lee's 25th Hour Is Really About." *Slate*. December 19, 2002. Retrieved May 13, 2015, from http://www.slate.com.
_____. "Pervert, Vampire, Lout. Perfectly Nice Guy, Though." *New York Times*. January 15, 2006. Retrieved December 26, 2014, from http://www.nytimes.com.
Edgington, K., and Thomas Erskine, and James M. Welsh. *Encyclopedia of Sports Films*. Plymouth, UK: Scarecrow Press, 2010.
Edwards, Gavin. "Truman Show." Rolling Stone, October 20, 2005: 38.
Egan, Kate. *Catching Fire: The Official Illustrated Movie Companion*. New York: Scholastic Inc., 2013.
Eggerstein, Chris. "'Mockingjay' Director on the Philip Seymour Hoffman Tribute that Didn't Make It in the Film." *Hitfix*. November 19, 2015. Retrieved December 1, 2015, from http://www.hitfix.com.

Eisenberg, Eric. "Interview: The Ides of March's Ryan Gosling." *Cinemablend*. October 6, 2011. Retrieved August 20, 2015, from http://www.cinemablend.com.

Elley, Derek. "Review: "The Boat That Rocked."" *Variety*. March 29, 2009. Retrieved August 1, 2015, from http://www.variety.com.

Elliot, Adam. *Mary and Max* DVD Audio Commentary. MPI Home Video, 2010.

Enk, Brian. "Gallery: Stars March Down the 'Ides' Red Carpet." *Next Movie*. October 6, 2011. Retrieved November 20, 2015, from http://www.nextmovie.com.

Fahraeus, Anna and Jonsson, AnnKatrin. *Textual Ethos Studies, or Locating Ethics*. Amsterdam, NY: Rodopi, 2005.

Falsani, Cathleen. *The Dude Abides: The Gospel According to the Coen Brothers*. Grand Rapids, MI: Zondervan, 2009.

Falsetto, Mario. *Anthony Minghella: Interviews*. Jackson: University Press of Mississippi, 2013.

Feinberg, Scott. "Interview: Sam Rockwell, an Actor with Character (And "Conviction")." *Scott Feinberg*. January 7, 2011. Retrieved November 16, 2015, from http://www.scottfeinberg.com.

Finn, Robin. "Public Lives: A Broadway Baby Without a Minute to Spare." *New York Times*. September 10, 2003. Retrieved May 15, 2015, from http://www.nytimes.com.

_____. "Public Lives; 'Seagull's' Wings Help Span a 30-Year Career." *New York Times*. August 8, 2001. Retrieved April 17, 2015, from http://www.nytimes.com.

Firestone. Lonnie. "Actors Celebrate Their Broadway and Off-Broadway Debuts." *Backstage*. June 6, 2012. Retrieved November 21, 2015, from http://www.backstage.com.

Fischer, Paul. "Hoffman Thrives on Taking Risks." *Female.com.au*. Retrieved July 18, 2015, from http://www.female.com.au.

_____. "Philip Seymour Hoffman, Catherine Keener, Jeremy Northam and Christopher Walken Comprise 'A Late Quartet.'" *Deadline*. January 10, 2011. Retrieved September 13, 2015, from http://www.deadline.com.

Fleming, Mike, Jr. "Google Founders Will Get Film Treatment." *Deadline Hollywood*. August 18, 2010. Retrieved August 17, 2015, from http://www.deadline.com.

_____. "ICM Partners Signs 'Mad Men's Christina Hendricks." *Deadline Hollywood*. March 20, 2013. Retrieved November 23, 2015, from http://www.deadline.com.

Florino, Rick. Philip Seymour Hoffman talks 'Jack Goes Boating,' music and more." *I Am Rogue*. September 17, 2010. Retrieved August 12, 2015, from http://www.imarogue.com.

Fonseca, Nicholas. "Philip Seymour Hoffman. Capote." Special Oscar Guide. *People*, 2006: 40.

Formo, Brian. "A Most Wanted Man: Anton Corbijn on Philip Seymour Hoffman." *Crave*. July 23, 2014. Retrieved October 3, 2015, from http://www.craveonline.com.

Fowler. Brandy. "Philip Seymour Hoffman's Showtime Series Happyish "Unlikely" to Continue Production." E. February 2, 2014. Retrieved September 17, 2015, from http://www.eonline.com.

Franklin, Garth. "Hoffman Is le Carré's 'Most Wanted Man.'" *Dark Horizons*. May 17, 2012. Retrieved November 21, 2015, from http://www.darkhorizons.com.

French, Alex, and Howie Kahn. "Livin' Thing: An Oral History of 'Boogie Nights.'" *Kottke*. December 10, 2014. Retrieved March 8, 2015, from http://www.kottke.org.

Frevele, Jamie. "Let's Compare Two Philip Seymour Hoffman Characters: Plutarch Heavensbee and Scotty from Boogie Nights." *Boing Boing*. July 11, 2012. Retrieved March 8, 2015, from http://www.boingboing.net.

Gallagher, Brian. "Ryan Gosling Heading to 'Farragut North.'" *Movieweb*. September 30, 2010. Retrieved November 14, 2015, from http://www.movieweb.com.

Gans, Andrew. "Carol Burnett and Mike Nichols to Receive 2003 Kennedy Center Honors." *Playbill*. August 6, 2003. Retrieved June 1, 2015, from http://www.playbill.com.

_____. "Philip Seymour Hoffman Will Direct New Keith Bunin Film 'Ezekiel Moss.'" *Playbill*. September 18, 2012. Retrieved September 22, 2015, from http://www.playbill.com.

Garner, Dwight. "John Le Carré Has Not Mellowed with Age." *New York Times*. April 18, 2013. Retrieved September 14, 2015, from http://www.nytimes.com.

Gates, Anita. "Television/Radio: It Shares Custody, but PBS Gets the Tonys First." *New York Times*. June 4, 2000. Retrieved April 10, 2015, from http://www.nytimes.com.

Genzlinger. Neil. "On the Cover." *New York Times*. May 22, 2005. Retrieved May 19, 2015, from http://www.nytimes.com.

_____. "Theater Review: Sparks Are Flying with Beatrice and Benedick in Central Park." *New York Times*. July 14, 2004. Retrieved May 15, 2015, from http://www.nytimes.com.

Gertel, Elliot. *Over the Top Judaism: Precedents and Trends in the Depiction of Jewish Beliefs and Observances in Film and Television*. Lanham, ML: University Press of America, 2003.

Giddins, Gary. *Warning Shadows: Home Alone with Classic Cinema*. New York, London: W. W. Norton & Company, 2010.

Bibliography

Gilman, Greg. "Matt Damon Thinks Philip Seymour Hoffman Was 'One of the Best Actors to Ever Live.'" *The Wrap*. February 6, 2014. Retrieved December 7, 2015, from http://www.the wrap.com.

Gioino, Catherina. "'Jack Goes Boating' Interview with Philip Seymour Hoffman and Amy Ryan." *The Young Folks.Com*. March 18, 2013. Retrieved August 13, 2015, from http://www.theyoungfolks.com.

Gittel, Noah. "Philip Seymour Hoffman's Final Starring Role Hints at a Brilliant Career Third Act We'll Never See." *Film School Rejects*. August 1, 2014. Retrieved November 30, 2015, from http://www.filmschoolrejects.com.

Glieberman, Owen. "The Master." *Entertainment Weekly*. February 14, 2014: 31–37.

Goldberg, Lesley. "Philip Seymour Hoffman, Kathryn Hahn to Star in Showtime Pilot 'Trending Down.'" *The Hollywood Reporter*. July 26, 2013. Retrieved November 26, 2015, from http://www.hollywoodreporter.com.

_____. "Showtime's Philip Seymour Hoffman Comedy, Joshua Jackson Drama Picked Up to Series." *The Hollywood Reporter*. January 16, 2014. Retrieved September 17, 2015, from http://www.hollywoodreporter.com.

Goldberg, Matt. "Meryl Streep, James Gandolfini, and Philip Seymour Hoffman May Star in Mike Nichols' Great Hope Springs." *Collider*. September 23, 2010. Retrieved November 14, 2015, from http://www.collider.com.

_____. "Philip Seymour Hoffman Still Had 7 Days Left to Film on the Hunger Games: Mockingjay—Part 2; Will Still Be Released on Schedule." *Collider*. February 3, 2014. Retrieved September 17, 2015, from http://www.collider.com.

_____. "Screenwriter Shane Salerno Has Already Locked a 2-Hour JD Salinger Documentary." *Collider*. January 29, 2010. Retrieved November 12, 2015, from http://www.collider.com.

Goodman, J. David. "Hoffman's Heroin Points to Surge in Grim Trade." *New York Times*. February 4, 2014. Retrieved October 15, 2015, from http://www.nytimes.com.

_____. "3 Arrested on Drug Charges as Police Pursue Hoffman Case." *New York Times*. February 5, 2014. Retrieved October 17, 2015, from http://www.nytimes.com.

Goodman, Roger, and Alan P. Haines. *The 81st Annual Academy Awards*. Academy of Motion Picture Arts and Sciences/ABC, 2009.

Goodman, Tim. "Bzzzzzzz: All the Upcoming Buzz Shows You Need to Know About." *The Hollywood Reporter*. February 5, 2014. Retrieved September 17, 2015, from http://www.hollywoodreporter.com.

Gordinier, Jeff. "Review: Looking Inward in Poetry Books from Ron Padgett and Nick Flynn." *New York Times*. July 9, 2015. Retrieved November 1, 2015, from http://www.nytimes.com.

Graham, Bill. "Phillip Seymour Hoffman's Shingle Announce Bevy of Projects, Including the Well with Guy Pearce and Mary-Louise Parker." *Collider*. January 29, 2010. Retrieved November 12, 2015, from http://www.collider.com.

Green, Bill, et al. *I'm a Lebowski, You're a Lebowski*. New York: Canongate Books, 2013.

Green, Jesse. "Where Have You Gone, Impresarios?" *New York Times*. October 3, 2004. Retrieved May 16, 2015, from http://www.nytimes.com.

Greene, Andy. "Philip Seymour Hoffman Looks Back at 'The Big Lebowski.'" *Rolling Stone*. February 2, 2014. Retrieved March 10, 2015, from http://www.rollingstone.com.

Gross, Jessica. "Christopher Walken Isn't as Weird as You Think." *New York Times*. November 9, 2012. Retrieved September 5, 2015, from http://www.nytimes.com.

Guerrasio, Jason. "IFP & Film Society of Lincoln Center Unveil Emerging Visions." *Filmmaker*. September 13, 2011. Retrieved November 18, 2015, from http://www.filmmakermagazine.com.

Gussow, Mel. "Control Freak, Finagler and Hollywood Legend." *New York Times*. April 29, 2003. Retrieved May 15, 2015, from http://www.nytimes.com.

_____. "Review/Theater; Disneyland as Antidote for Poverty." *New York Times*. June 2, 1991. Retrieved April 16, 2015, from http://www.nytimes.com.

Hallet, Bryce. "Riflemind." *The Sydney Morning Herald*. October 12, 2007. Retrieved July 20, 2015, from http://www.smh.com.au.

Hamburg, John. *Along Came Polly* DVD Audio Commentary. Universal Studios, 2004.

Hamilton, Jack. "The Moment Philip Seymour Hoffman Became a Star." *Slate*. February 2, 2014. Retrieved March 8, 2015, from http://www.slate.com.

Hamilton. Jake. "Philip Seymour Hoffman Interview: Jack Goes Boating." September 27, 2010. Viewed August 13, 2015 on YouTube.com.

Hampton, Wilborn. "Theater Review: a Lot of Degradation and a Little Bit of Humor." *New York Times*. July 21, 1999. Retrieved March 19, 2015, from http://www.nytimes.com.

Hantke, Steffen. *Horror Film: Creating and Marketing Fear*. Jackson: University Press of Mississippi, 2004.

Harvey, Dennis. "Review: 'Strangers with Candy.'" *Variety*. March 1, 2005. Retrieved May 18, 2015, from http://www.variety.com.

Hasty, Katie. "Christina Hendricks Brought Her A-Game for Philip Seymour Hoffman at Sundance." *HitFix*. January 20, 2014. Retrieved October 12, 2015, from http://www.hitfix.com.

_____. "Philip Seymour Hoffman on Director-Actor John Slattery: 'He Knows What He's Doing.'" *HitFix*. January 19, 2014. Retrieved October 12, 2015, from http://www.hitfix.com.

_____. "Philip Seymour Hoffman Talks Music, What's to Be Learned from 'Pirate Radio.'" *Hitfix*. November 13, 2009. Retrieved August 2, 2015, from http://www.hitfix.com.

Hattenstone, Simon. "Philip Seymour Hoffman: 'I Was Moody, Mercurial ... It Was All or Nothing.'" *The Guardian*. October 29, 2011. Retrieved December 21, 2014, from http://www.the guardian.com.

Haun, Harry. "In Defying Gravity, a National Tragedy Becomes a Personal One." *Playbill*. October 31, 1997. Retrieved March 17, 2015, from http://www.playbill.com.

Hawke, Ethan, and Sidney Lumet, and Philip Seymour Hoffman. *Before the Devil Knows You're Dead* DVD Audio Commentary. ThinkFilm, 2008.

Hay, Carla. "Philip Seymour Hoffman Looks Back at Directing the Movie 'Jack Goes Boating.'" *Examiner.com*. February 2, 2014. Retrieved August 13, 2015, from http://www.examiner.com.

Healy, Patrick. "Artsbeat: A Lucrative Start for 'Death of a Salesman.'" *New York Times*. February 21, 2012. Retrieved August 22, 2015, from http://www.nytimes.com.

_____. "Artsbeat: 'Death of a Salesman' Coming to Broadway with Philip Seymour Hoffman." *New York Times*. October 20, 2010. Retrieved August 18, 2015, from http://www.nytimes.com.

_____. "Artsbeat: More Than Attention Must Be Paid: 'Salesman' Sets Record Ticket Price." *New York Times*. June 12, 2012. Retrieved September 5, 2015, from http://www.nytimes.com.

_____. "Artsbeat: 'Othello' and 'Hamlet' Cast Updates." *New York Times*. July 30, 2009. Retrieved August 14, 2015, from http://www.nytimes.com.

_____. "The Friends Who Hold the Enemies Closer." *New York Times*. September 16, 2009. Retrieved August 15, 2015, from http://www.nytimes.com.

_____. "Philip Seymour Hoffman, Willem Dafoe, Suzan-Lori Parks on Public Theater's Lineup." *New York Times*. May 26, 2009. Retrieved August 14, 2015, from http://www.nytimes.com.

_____. "'Salesman' Revival on Broadway to Turn a Profit." *New York Times*. May 16, 2012. Retrieved September 5, 2015, from http://www.nytimes.com.

_____. "Searching for the Life of a Salesman." *New York Times*. March 8, 2012. Retrieved August 25, 2015, from http://www.nytimes.com.

_____. "Tapping a Rough-And-Tumble Life." *New York Times*. December 24, 2010. Retrieved August 17, 2015, from http://www.nytimes.com.

_____. "That Tony Pool: Few Sure Bets." *New York Times*. June 7, 2012. Retrieved September 5, 2015, from http://www.nytimes.com.

_____, and Michael Cieply. "Hollywood Was Just One of His Stages." *New York Times*. February 4, 2014. Retrieved October 15, 2015, from http://www.nytimes.com.

Heath, Paul. "Phillip Seymour Hoffman Playing the Villain in Spider-Man Reboot?" *The Hollywood News*. October 3, 2010. Retrieved November 15, 2015, from http://www.thehollywoodnews.com.

Heffernan, Virginia. "A Small Town Tangled in a New England Knot." *New York Times*. May 27, 2005. Retrieved May 19, 2015, from http://www.nytimes.com.

Hernandez, Ernio. "Our Lady of 121st Street Ends Off-Broadway Run at Union Square, June 29." *Playbill*. June 12, 2003. Retrieved May 3, 2015, from http://www.playbill.com.

_____. "Stage Stars Hoffman, Janney, Johnston, Theroux, More Join "Strangers with Candy" Movie." *Playbill*. July 27, 2004. Retrieved May 19, 2015, from http://www.playbill.com.

Herring, Joanne King. *Diplomacy and Diamonds: My Wars from the Ballroom to the Battlefield*. New York: Center Street, 2011.

Hewitt, Hugh. "David Mamet on Philip Seymour Hoffman." *Hugh Hewitt*. February 3, 2014. Retrieved April 6, 2015, from http://www.hughhewitt.com.

Hickey, Patrick, Jr. "Review Fix Exclusive: Philip Seymour Hoffman Interview: A Star on and Off the Camera." *Review Fix*. February 9, 2010. Retrieved August 13, 2015, from http://www.reviewfix.com.

Hill, Derek. *Charlie Kaufman and Hollywood's Merry Band of Pranksters, Fabulists and Dreamers: An Excursion into the American New Wave*. Harpenden: Kamera, 2008.

Hills, Aaron. "Interview: Philip Seymour Hoffman on "Synecdoche, New York."" *IFC*. October 22, 2008. Retrieved July 17, 2015, from http://www.ifc.com.

Hirschberg, Lynn. "Has Paul Newman Finally Grown Up?" *New York Magazine*, December 12, 1994: 36–43.

_____. "A Higher Calling." *New York Times*. December 19, 2008. Retrieved December 22, 2014, from http://www.nytimes.com.

_____. "His Way." *New York Times*. December 19, 1999. Retrieved April 5, 2015, from http://www.nytimes.com.

Hiscock, John. "Ricky Gervais Interview for 'The Invention of Lying.'" *The Telegraph*. September 25, 2009. Retrieved August 1, 2015, from http://www.telegraph.co.uk.

Hoby, Hermione. "Willem Dafoe Interview for a Most Wanted Man: 'I'm Not Mad and I'm Not Bad.'" *The Telegraph*. September 6, 2014. Retrieved October 4, 2015, from http://www.telegraph.co.uk.
Hoffman. Regan. "Standing Ovation: Philip Seymour Hoffman in 'Magnolia.'" *Backstage*. October 21, 2013. Retrieved April 5, 2015, from http://www.backstage.com.
Hogan, Michael. "Look Out, Will Ferrell: Zach Galifianakis Wants to Play Ignatius Reilly." *Moviefone*. October 2, 2011. Retrieved November 18, 2015, from http://www.news.moviefone.com.
Holden, Stephen. "Film Review; Movie Folk, It Turns Out, Are Subject to Venality." *New York Times*. December 22, 2000. Retrieved April 6, 2015, from http://www.nytimes.com.
_____. "First a Killing, Then a Code of Silence." *New York Times*. May 8, 2014. Retrieved September 23, 2015, from http://www.nytimes.com.
_____. "'Flawless': Drag Queen Rescues a Disabled Cop." *New York Times*. November 24, 1999. Retrieved April 4, 2015, from http://www.nytimes.com.
_____. "Movie Review: Suspense-Filled Puzzle Draped in a Dark Mood." *New York Times*. February 28, 1997. Retrieved March 3, 2015, from http://www.nytimes.com.
_____. "'Next Stop Wonderland': Love Lies in an Emerson Quotation." *New York Times*. April 21, 1998. Retrieved February 26, 2015, from http://www.nytimes.com.
_____. "Review/Film: In the Show-Biz Jungle, Seeking a Gentler Life." *New York Times*. May 14, 1993. Retrieved December 29, 2014, from http://www.nytimes.com.
_____. "Review/Film: Prom Night Was Never Like This." *New York Times*. August 6, 1993. Retrieved December 29, 2014, from http://www.nytimes.com.
_____. "A Romance Battles the Odds: Risk Assessor Woos Daredevil." *New York Times*. January 16, 2004. Retrieved May 10, 2015, from http://www.nytimes.com.
_____. "The Strings Play On; the Bonds Tear Apart." *New York Times*. November 1, 2012. Retrieved September 8, 2015, from http://www.nytimes.com.
Horowitz, Joshua. *The Mind of the Modern Moviemaker: Twenty Conversations with the New Generation of Filmmakers*. London: Penguin, 2006.
Horvitz, Louis J. *The American Film Institute Salute to Mike Nichols*. American Film Institute/ Land Prime Original Prodiction, 2010.
_____. *The 80th Annual Academy Awards*. Academy of Motion Pictures Arts and Sciences, 2008.
_____. *The Kennedy Center Honors*. CBS, 2003.
_____. *The 78th Annual Academy Awards*. Academy of Motion Pictures Arts and Sciences/ABC, 2006.
_____. *The 79th Annual Academy Awards*. Academy of Motion Pictures Arts and Sciences, 2007.
Horyn, Cathy. "Dressing the Part for Tony." *New York Times*. June 10, 2003. Retrieved May 15, 2015, from http://www.nytimes.com.
Hunter, Craig. "Philip Seymour Hoffman Joins All-Star Serial-Killer Thriller 'Child 44.'" *Hollywood News*. June 27, 2013. Retrieved May 18, 2015, from http://www.hollywoodnews.com.
Ingle, Zachary. *Fan Phenomena: The Big Lebowski*. Chicago, IL: Intellect Books, 2014.
Isherwood, Charles. "Artsbeat: Making 'Salesman' His Own, Despite Kazan's Shadow." *New York Times*. March 8, 2012. Retrieved August 22, 2015, from http://www.nytimes.com.
_____. "A Play That Resounds in the Heart and the Gut." *New York Times*. April 20, 2012. Retrieved September 5, 2015, from http://www.nytimes.com.
_____. "Review: 'Defying Gravity.'" *Variety*. November 15, 1997. Retrieved March 17, 2015, from http://www.variety.com.
_____. "Review: 'The Glory of Living.'" *Variety*. November 15, 2001. Retrieved April 16, 2015, from http://variety.com.
_____. "Review: 'The Seagull.'" *Variety*. August 12, 2001. Retrieved April 20, 2015, from http://www.variety.com.
_____. "A Shot in the Night and Its Aftermath." *New York Times*. October 19, 2007. Retrieved July 19, 2015, from http://www.nytimes.com.
_____. "A Stranger Bearing Gifts." *New York Times*. May 12, 2013. Retrieved September 14, 2015, from http://www.nytimes.com.
_____. "Strangers in a Very Dark New York Night." *New York Times*. February 19, 2008. Retrieved July 25, 2015, from http://www.nytimes.com.
_____. "Struggling with the Truth About the Men in Her Life." *New York Times*. October 25, 2006. Retrieved June 20, 2015, from http://www.nytimescom.
_____. "Waltzes by Strauss, Philosophies by the Sea Bag." *New York Times*. November 8, 2004. Retrieved May 16, 2015, from http://www.nytimes.com.
Itzkoff, Dave. "Successful Comic and Rodent Tries Unfamiliar Role: Sports Fan." *New York Times*. August 24, 2009. Retrieved August 14, 2015, from http://www.nytimes.com.
Jagernaut, Kevin. "Amy Adams & Jake Gyllenhaal Join Philip Seymour Hoffman-Directed 'Ezekiel Moss' & More." *Indiewire*. February 1, 2014. Retrieved September 22, 2015, from http://www.indiewire.com.

James, Caryn. "Faces from the Screen, Now Life Size." *New York Times*. February 24, 2008. Retrieved July 25, 2015, from http://www.nytimes.com.
_____. "Film Review: Paul Newman in Blue-Collar Gear." *New York Times*. December 23, 1994. Retrieved January 2, 2015, from http://www.nytimes.com.
_____. "Reviews/Film: In the Tire Tracks of Another Sultry Pair." *New York Times*. February 11, 1994. Retrieved January 1, 2015, from http://www.nytimes.com.
_____. "The Tease: For Your Consideration: Sappy Hallmark Moments." *New York Times*. March 2, 2006. Retrieved June 20, 2015, from http://www.nytimes.com.
_____. "The Winner Is ... Only Acting Gay." *New York Times*. November 20, 2005. Retrieved June 6, 2015, from http://www.nytimes.com.
Jay, Mike. *Charlie Rose*. May 30, 2000. Rose Communications/WNET Thirteen, 2000.
_____. *Charlie Rose*. December 16, 2002. Charlie Rose, Inc./WNET Thirteen, 2002.
_____. *Charlie Rose*. September 29, 2005. Charlie Rose, Inc./WNET Thirteen, 2005.
_____. *Charlie Rose*. March 3, 2006. Charlie Rose, Inc./WNET Thirteen, 2006.
_____. *Charlie Rose*. November 30, 2007. Charlie Rose, Inc./WNET Thirteen, 2007.
Jefferson, Margo. "On Writers and Writing: Alone with O'neill." *New York Times*. July 6, 2003. Retrieved May 15, 2015, from http://www.nytimes.com.
Johnson, Ross. "For Those Who've Tired of Glory and Riches." *New York Times*. January 15, 2006. Retrieved June 7, 2015, from http://www.nytimes.com.
Johnson, Zac. "Philip Seymour Hoffman Leaves Rehab After Snorting Heroin." *US Weekly*. May 31, 2013. Retrieved November 23, 2015, from http://www.usmagazine.com.
Jones, Jenny M. *The Big Lebowski: An Illustrated, Annotated History of the Greatest Cult Film of All Time*. Minneapolis, MN: Voyageur Press, 2012.
Juggernauth, Kevin. "Philip Seymour Hoffman Was Planning to Shoot a Part in 'Louie,' Jeremy Renner Appearing in Next Episode." *Indiewire*. June 16, 2014. Retrieved November 30, 2015, from http://www.blogs.indiewire.com.
Kamp, David. "Have You Seen This Man?" *GQ*, January 2001: 106–111.
Kandra, Greg. "Why Philip Seymour Hoffman Deserves a Catholic Funeral." *CNN*. February 6, 2014. Retrieved December 22, 2014, from http://www.cnn.com.
Kaufman, David. "Theater: A 'Gym' for Acting, It's a Company, Too." *New York Times*. December 10, 2000. Retrieved March 19, 2015, from http://www.nytimes.com.
Kavanaugh, Dan. *Directed by Sidney Lumet: How the Devil Was Made*. Mirage Productions/ThinkFilm, 2008.
Kay, Glenn, and Michael Rose. *Disaster Movies: A Loud, Long, Explosive, Star-Studded Guide to Avalanches, Earthquakes, Floods, Meteors, Sinking Ships, Twisters, Viruses, Killer Bees, Nuclear Fallout, and Alien Attacks in the Cinema!!!!* Chicago, IL: Chicago Review Press, 2006.
Keeton, Patricia, and Peter Scheckner. *American War Cinema and Media Since Vietnam: Politics, Ideology, and Class*. New York: Palgrave Macmillan, 2013.
Kehr, Dave. "Film: A Poet of Love And Chaos in the Valley." *New York Times*. October 6, 2002. Retrieved May 2, 2015, from http://www.nytimes.com.
Kemmerle, Karen. "The '25th Hour' Is Spike Lee's Unheralded Masterpiece." *Tribeca*. Retrieved May 13, 2015, from http://www.tribecafilm.com.
Kennedy, Randy. "The Dead and Dostoyevsky, in a War with Bush." *New York Times*. August 4, 2004. Retrieved May 16, 2015, from http://www.nytimes.com.
Kenny, J. M. *The Medical Value of Laughter*. Patch Adams Collector's Edition DVD. Universal Studios Home Video, 1999.
Kerr, Dave. "At the Movies: Brotherly Symbiosis." *New York Times*. January 10, 2003. Retrieved May 8, 2015, from http://www.nytimescom.
_____. "Film in Review: 'The Party's Over.'" *New York Times*. October 24, 2003. Retrieved April 24, 2015, from http://www.nytimes.com.
Khatchatourian, Maane. "'Hunger Games: Mockingjay' Director Didn't Use CGI for Philip Seymour Hoffman Scenes." *Variety*. November 15, 2014. Retrieved September 21, 2015, from http://www.variety.com.
_____. "Local Artist Erects Oscar Statue Shooting Heroin in Hollywood." *Variety*. March 1, 2014. Retrieved November 27, 2015, from http://www.variety.com.
Kilday. Gregg. "Film: Simply Flawless." *The Advocate*. November 23, 1999: 69–72.
King, Lynnea Chapman. *The Coen Brothers Encyclopedia*. London UK: Rowman & Littlefield, 2014.
King, Susan. "A Family Project for the Hoffmans." *Los Angeles Times*. January 3, 2003. Retrieved April 22, 2015, from http://www.articles.latimes.com.
Klady, Leonard. "Review: 'When a Man Loves a Woman.'" *Variety*. April 25, 1994. Retrieved January 1, 2015, from http://www.variety.com.
Knegt, Peter. "Tucci and Clarkson to Host Celeb-Heavy Gotham Awards." *Indiewire*. November 15, 2010. Retrieved November 15, 2015, from http://www.indiewire.com.

Koehler, Roger. "Review: 'Along Came Polly.'" *Variety*. December 28, 2003. Retrieved May 10, 2015, from http://www.variety.com

Kohl, Herbert, and Tom Oppenheim. *The Muses Go to School*. New York: The New Press, 2012.

Koppelman, Charles. *Behind the Seen: How Walter Murch Edited Cold Mountain Using Apple's Final Cut Pro and What This Means for Cinema*. Berkeley: CA: New Riders, 2004.

Kramer, Jessica. "Philip Seymour Hoffman Rocks the Boat in Pirate Radio." *Flavorwire*. November 13, 2009. Retrieved August 1, 2015, from http://www.flavorwire.com.

Krazit, Tom. "We're Feeling Lucky: CNET Casts the Google Movie." *CNET*. August 20, 2010. Retrieved August 17, 2015, from http://www.cnet.com.

Krcatovich, Dustin. "Philip Seymour Hoffman's Disturbing, Beautiful Role in Happiness." *Esquire*. February 4, 2014. Retrieved March 25, 2015, from http://www.esquire.com.

Krimmer, Elizabetth, and Susanne Kord. *Contemporary Hollywood Masculinities: Gender, Genre, and Politics*. New York: Palgrave Macmillan, 2011.

Labrecque, Jeff. "Movies: Philip Seymour Hoffman as Lester Bangs: 'Almost Famous' Star Patrick Fugit Remembers." *Entertainment Weekly*. January 18, 2015. Retrieved April 9, 2015, from http://www.ew.com.

Lane, Christina. *Magnolia*. West Sussex, UK: John Wiley & Sons, 2011.

Lange, Brent. "Philip Seymour Hoffman Leaves Paradigm (Exclusive)." *The Wrap*. June 11, 2012. Retrieved November 21, 2015, from http://www.thewrap.com.

Lash, Larry L. "Review: 'Othello.'" *Variety*. June 15, 2009. Retrieved August 16, 2015, from http://www.variety.com.

Lawrence, Francis, and Nina Jacobson. *The Hunger Games: Catching Fire*. DVD Audio Commentary. Lionsgate, 2014.

_____, and _____. *The Hunger Games: Mockingjay—Part 1*. DVD Audio Commentary. Lionsgate, 2015.

LeDuff, Charlie. "Film; Box Office He Wants, Not a Drink." *New York Times*. December 15, 2002. Retrieved May 6, 2015, from http://www.nytimes.com.

Lee, Spike. 25th Hour DVD Director's Commentary. Touchstone Home Entertainment, 2003.

Legel, Laremy. "Interview: Philip Seymour Hoffman and John Ortiz Talk Jack Goes Boating." *Film.com*. September 24, 2010. Retrieved August 12, 2015, from http://www.film.com.

Lehman, Daniel. "78th Annual Drama League Award Winners Announced." *Backstage*. May 18, 2012. Retrieved November 21, 2015, from http://www.backstage.com.

Leland, John. "'An Addict with Friends.'" *New York Times*. April 11, 2014. Retrieved October 30, 2015, from http://www.nytimes.com.

_____. "Drug-Selling Charges Dropped Against Man Arrested in Philip Seymour Hoffman Case." *New York Times*. August 28, 2014. Retrieved October 31, 2015, from http://www.nytimes.com.

Lesnick, Silas. "Dianna Agron and Dominique Mcelligott Up for Spider-Man ?" *Comingsoon*. October 1, 2010. Retrieved November 14, 2015, from http://www.comingsoon.net.

_____. "Philip Seymour Hoffman and Kathryn Hahn Board Showtime's Trending Down." *Comingsoon.Net*. July 30, 2013. Retrieved November 26, 2015, from http://www.comingsoon.net.

_____. "Philip Seymour Hoffman Boards Child 44." *Comingsoon.Net*. June 25, 2013. Retrieved November 26, 2015, from http://www.comingsoon.net.

_____. "Vincent Cassel Takes Child 44." *Comingsoon.Net*. August 29, 2013. Retrieved November 26, 2015, from http://www.comingsoon.net.

Levy, Emanuel. *Cinema of Outsiders: The Rise of American Independent Film*. New York, London: New York University Press, 2001.

_____. "Review: 'Boogie Nights.'" *Variety*. September 21, 1997. Retrieved March 7, 2015, from http://www.variety.com.

_____. "Review; 'Flawless.'" *Variety*. November 21, 1999. Retrieved April 4, 2015, from http://www.variety.com.

_____. "Review: 'Magnolia.'" *Variety*. December 9, 1999. Retrieved April 5, 2015, from http://www.variety.com.

Levy, Shawn. *Paul Newman: A Life*. New York: Three Rivers Press, 2009.

Leydon, Joe. "Review: 'Last Party 2000.'" *Variety*. April 11, 2002. Retrieved April 24, 2015, from http://www.nytimes.com.

_____. "Review: 'Patch Adams.'" *Variety*. December 13, 1998. Retrieved March 27, 2015, from http://www.variety.com.

Leyland, Richard. "The Making of The Big Lebowski." Polygram Entertainment, 1998. Collector's Edition DVD *The Big Lebowski*. Gramercy Pictures, 2005.

Lim, Dennis. "After 50 Years, Still No Time for Cheap Sentiment." *New York Times*. October 21, 2007. Retrieved July 19, 2015, from http://www.nytimes.com.

_____. "Artsbeat: Venice Film Festival: 'Pieta' and 'The Master' Come Up Winners." *New York Times*. September 8, 2012. Retrieved September 5, 2015, from http://www.nytimes.com.

_____. "A Director Continues His Quest." *New York Times*. December 27, 2012. Retrieved September 5, 2015, from http://www.nytimes.com.
_____. "A Star Swerves a Bit; He's Fine with That." *New York Times*. September 4, 2012. Retrieved September 5, 2015, from http://www.nytimes.com.
_____. "Unblinking Look at Death Without Nobility." *New York Times*. November 4, 2007. Retrieved July 19, 2015, from http://www.nytimes.com.
Lippe, Adam. "A Podcast with Amy Ryan, Star of Gone Baby Gone and Jack Goes Boating." *A Regrettable Moment of Sincerity*. September 29, 2010. Retrieved August 8, 2015, from http://www.regrettablesincerity.com.
Littleton, Cynthia. "'Happyish': Jim Carrey Among Actors Considered to Replace Philip Seymour Hoffman." *Variety*. April 23, 2015. Retrieved December 1, 2015, from http://www.variety.com.
_____. "Status of Showtime Series Unclear After Philip Seymour Hoffman's Death." *Variety*. February 2, 2014. Retrieved November 27, 2015, from http://www.variety.com.
Louiso, Tod, and Gordy Hoffman, and Philip Seymour Hoffman. *Love Liza* DVD Audio Commentary. Sony Pictures Home Entertainment, 2003.
Lowry, Brian. "TV Review: 'Happyish.'" *Variety*. April 3, 2015. Retrieved September 21, 2015, from http://www.variety.com.
Loynd, Ray. "TV Review: CBS' 'Yearling' a Worthwhile Remake." *Los Angeles Times*. April 23, 1994. Retrieved March 1, 2015, from http://www.articles.latimes.com.
Luchetti, Laura, and Timothy Bricknell. *Climbing Cold Mountain*. Ciccia Bomba Production/4 Ventures Limited, 2004.
Lumenick, Lou. "Long Distance Dialogue." *New York Post*. January 15, 2009. Retrieved November 11, 2015, from http://www.nypost.com.
Lundy, Karen Saucier, and Sharyn Janes. *Community Health Nursing: Caring for the Public's Health*. Sudbury, MA: Jones & Bartlett Learning, 2009.
Luscombe, Belinda. "Exclusive: Watch Philip Seymour Hoffman Talk About His Last Film." *Time*. July 17, 2014. Retrieved October 2, 2015, from http://www.time.com.
Lussier, Germain. "Paul Thomas Anderson Interviews Philip Seymour Hoffman About Jack Goes Boating." *Collider*. September 14, 2010. Retrieved August 12, 2015, from http://www.collider.com.
Lyman, Eric J. "Venice 2012: Michael Jackson Biopic 'Bad 25' Talk of the Town Heading into Weekend." *The Hollywood Reporter*. August 31, 2012. Retrieved November 22, 2015, from http://www.hollywoodreporter.com.
Lyman, Rick. "Arts in America: A Political Interlocutor Is Learning on the Job." *New York Times*. August 17, 2000. Retrieved April 24, 2015, from http://www.nytimes.com.
_____. "Slump Vexes Creators of 'Almost Famous.'" *New York Times*. October 19, 2000. Retrieved April 10, 2015, from http://www.nytimes.com.
McBride, Walter. "Photo Coverage: Starry Opening Night Arrivals for Death of a Salesman." *Broadwayworld*. March 16, 2012. Retrieved September 3, 2015, from http://www.broadwayworld.com.
McCarthy, Todd. "'The Hunger Games: Mockingjay, Part 2': Film Review." *The Hollywood Reporter*. November 4, 2015. Retrieved November 20, 2015, from http://www.hollywoodreporter.com.
_____. "Review: Charlie Wilson's War." *Variety*. November 28, 2007. Retrieved July 10, 2015, from http://www.variety.com.
_____. "Review: 'Cold Mountain.'" *Variety*. December 7, 2003. Retrieved May 22, 2015, from http://www.variety.com.
_____. "Review: Doubt." *Variety*. November 6, 2008. Retrieved July 22, 2015, from http://www.variety.com.
_____. "Review: 'Happiness—Dark Side of 'Happiness' Explores Sexual Taboos.'" *Variety*. May 18, 1998. Retrieved March 14, 2015, from http://www.variety.com.
_____. "Review: Jack Goes Boating." *Variety*. January 14, 2010. Retrieved August 8, 2015, from http://www.variety.com.
_____. "Review: 'Love Liza.'" *Variety*. January 22, 2002. Retrieved April 17, 2015, from http://www.variety.com.
_____. "Review: 'Mission: Impossible Iii.'" *Variety*. May 2, 2006. Retrieved June 6, 2015, from http://www.variety.com.
_____. "Review: 'Montana.'" *Variety*. January 19, 1998. Retrieved February 23, 2015, from http://www.variety.com.
_____. "Review: 'My New Gun.'" *Variety*. May 12, 1992. Retrieved December 25, 2014, from http://www.variety.com.
_____. "Review: 'Next Stop Wonderland.'" *Variety*. January 21, 1998. Retrieved February 26, 2015, from http://www.variety.com.

_____. "Review: Nobody's Fool." *Variety*. December 11, 1994. Retrieved January 2, 2015, from http://www.variety.com.

_____. "Review: 'Red Dragon.'" *Variety*. September 26, 2002. Retrieved May 3, 2015, from http://www.variety.com.

_____. "Review: 'Synecdoche, New York.'" *Variety*. May 23, 2008. Retrieved July 14, 2015, from http://www.variety.com.

_____. "Review: 'The Big Lebowski.'" *Variety*. January 19, 1998. Retrieved March 10, 2015, from http://www.variety.com.

_____. "Review: 'The Getaway.'" *Variety*. February 9, 1994. Retrieved January 1, 2015, from http://www.variety.com.

_____. "Review: 'The Savages.'" *Variety*. January 21, 2007. Retrieved July 5, 2015, from http://www.variety.com.

_____. "Review: 'The Talented Mr. Ripley.'" *Variety*. December 12, 1999. Retrieved March 29, 2015, from http://www.variety.com.

_____. "Review: 'Twister.'" *Variety*. May 10, 1996. Retrieved March 5, 2015, from http://www.variety.com.

_____. "Todd McCarthy on Philip Seymour Hoffman: 'Never a False or Self-Conscious Note.'" *The Hollywood Reporter*. February 5, 2014. Retrieved November 27, 2015, from http://www.hollywoodreporter.com.

McClintock, Pamela. "Indie Awards Show a Cowboy Spirit." *Variety*. March 4, 2006. Retrieved December 12, 2015, from http://www.variety.com.

_____. "The Long-Gestating Project Will Be Directed by Philip Seymour Hoffman." *The Hollywood Reporter*. January 31, 2014. Retrieved February 22, 2015, from http://www.hollywoodreporter.com.

McCrank, Mary E. "Chasing Philip." *Rochester Magazine*, May/June 2000: 44-47, 65–66.

McDonald, William. "Looking Back: Those We Lost in 2014." *New York Times*. December 30, 2014. Retrieved November 1, 2015, from http://www.nytimes.com.

McElroy, Steven. "Arts, Briefly: Footnotes." *New York Times*. October 3, 2006. Retrieved June 20, 2015, from http://www.nytimes.com.

_____. "Arts, Briefly: Footnotes. " *New York Times*. June 2, 2008. Retrieved August 3, 2015, from http://www.nytimes.com.

_____. "Artsbeat: Labyrinth Gets New Leaders." *New York Times*. May 31, 2009. Retrieved August 14, 2015, from http://www.nytimes.com.

_____. "Shakespeare, Singing and Solo Shows Galore." *New York Times*. September 10, 2009. Retrieved August 15, 2015, from http://www.nytimes.com.

McGee, Celia. "St. Ann's Mother Hen and Her Crowded Nest." *New York Times*. March 18, 2007. Retrieved July 12, 2015, from http://nytimes.com.

_____. "Writer and Director Will Confer at Home." *New York Times*. August 27, 2006. Retreived June 20, 2015, from http://www.nytimes.com.

McGowan, Todd. *Spike Lee*. Urbana: University of Illinois Press, 2014.

McGrath, Douglas. *Infamous*. Warners Independent Pictures/Killer Films/John Wells Production, 2006.

McGuire, Paul. "The Secret Life ... Philip Seymour Hoffman, and "Owning Mahowny.'" *Bluff Magazine*. March, 2014. Retrieved May 18, 2015, from http://www.bluff.com.

McIntyre. Gina. "'Hunger Games: Mockingjay' Director on Jennifer Lawrence and Philip Seymour Hoffman." *Hero Complex*. November 20, 2014. Retrieved September 20, 2015, from http://www.herocomplex.latimes.com.

McKinley, James C. "Lawyer Says Man Arrested in Hoffman Case Isn't Dealer." *New York Times*. February 15, 2014. Retrieved October 20, 2015, from http://www.nytimes.com.

McKinley, James, Jr. "Artsbeat: Son of a 'Salesman': Andrew Garfield Will Play Biff Loman in Broadway Revival." *New York Times*. August 12, 2011. Retrieved August 18, 2015, from http://www.nytimes.com.

McKinley, Jessie. "Arts, Briefly: A New 'Judas.'" *New York Times*. October 5, 2004. Retrieved May 16, 2015, from http://www.nytimes.com.

_____. "Arts, Briefly: Drama at the Public Theater." *New York Times*. October 23, 2004. Retrieved May 15, 2015, from http://www.nytimes.com.

_____. "Committee Approves 'Contact' for Tony Award Consideration." *New York Times*. April 14, 2000. Retrieved April 10, 2015, from http://www.nytimes.com.

_____. "For Public's New Director, Big Shoes Loom." *New York Times*. November 18, 2004. Retrieved May 15, 2015, from http://www.nytimes.com.

_____. "Forget Belmont, Tony Races Are Here ... the 'Featured' Spotlight." *New York Times*. June 6, 2003. Retrieved May 15, 2015, from http://www.nytimes.com.

_____. "A Night Out With/The Broadway Babies; That Rarity, a Sizzling Opening Night Party." *New York Times*. March 12, 2000. Retrieved March 21, 2015, from http://www.nytimes.com.

_____. "On Stage and Off ... a Cottage Small." *New York Times*. April 4, 2003. Retrieved May 8, 2015, from http://www.nytimes.com.

_____. "On Stage and Off ... Americans in London." *New York Times*. March 1, 2002. Retrieved April 24, 2015, from http://www.nytimes.com.

_____. "On Stage and Off ... Back to Directing." *New York Times*. May 25, 2001. Retrieved April 24, 2015, from http://www.nytimes.com.

_____. "On Stage and Off ... Fanning the Flames." *New York Times*. October 25, 2002. Retrieved May 6, 2015, from http://www.nytimes.com.

_____. "On Stage and Off ... Filling Shoes." *New York Times*. June 16, 2000. Retrieved April 10, 2015, from http://www.nytimes.com.

_____. "On Stage and Off ... Homeless Shows Seek Theaters." *New York Times*. November 15, 2002. Retrieved May 6, 2015, from http://www.nytimes.com.

_____. "On Stage and Off." *New York Times*. September 28, 2001. Retrieved April 16, 2015, from http://www.nytimes.com.

_____. "On Stage and Off." *New York Times*. December 20, 2002. Retrieved May 6, 2015, from http://www.nytimescom.

_____. "On Stage and Off ... O'Neill in His Future." *New York Times*. November 22, 2002. Retrieved May 6, 2015, from http://www.nytimescom.

_____. "On Stage and Off ... Profitable Anticipation Hooray for Hollywood." *New York Times*. September 15, 2000. Retrieved April 24, 2015, from http://www.nytimes.com.

_____. "On Stage and Off ... 'Sea Gull' Among the Birds." *New York Times*. February 2, 2001. Retrieved April 24, 2015, from http://www.nytimes.com.

_____. "On Stage and Off ... Seeking a Nest for 'Sea Gull.'" *New York Times*. December 22, 2000. Retrieved April 17, 2015, from http://www.nytimes.com.

_____. "On Stage and Off ... Those Characters." *New York Times*. November 12, 1999. Retrieved March 23, 2015, from http://www.nytimes.com.

_____. "Public Is Set to Appoint Providence Director." *New York Times*. November 17, 2004. Retrieved May 15, 2015, from http://www.nytimes.com.

_____. "Rhode Island Director in Talks to Take Over Public Theater." *New York Times*. October 29, 2004. Retrieved May 15, 2015, from http://www.nytimes.com.

_____. "Tony Forecast: Dramatic Races, Musical Chairs." *New York Times*. June 2, 2000. Retrieved April 10, 2015, from http://www.nytimes.com.

Macauley, Scott. "Play Ping Pong with Susan Sarandon for the Ifp." *Filmmaker*. November 23, 2010. Retrieved November 15, 2015, from http://www.filmmakermagazine.com.

Malanowski. Jamie. "A Talent for Characters You Love And/Or Hate." *New York Times*. November 21, 1999. Retrieved March 23, 2015, from http://www.nytimes.com.

Malkin, Mark. "News/ Hunger Games: Philip Seymour Hoffman Snags Major Role in Catching Fire." *E!* July 9, 2012. Retrieved November 21, 2015, from http://www.au.eonline.com.

Mandell, Jonathan. "Theater/The Tony Awards: Behind the Scene; Backstage at 'Journey,' a Diet Coke Distillery." *New York Times*. June 1, 2003. Retrieved May 15, 2015, from http://www.nytimes.com.

Mann. Michael. *Manhunter*. De Laurentiis Entertainment Group, 1986.

Mapstone, Lucy. "'Faking His Performance Would Have Been Catastrophic': Mockingjay Director Chose Not to Finish Philip Seymour Hoffman's Final Scenes in Hunger Games Movie with Cgi." *Daily Mail Australia*. November 17, 2014. Retrieved September 21, 2015, from http://www.dailymail.co.uk.

Marche, Stephen. "Philip Seymour Hoffman's Perfect Scene in Boogie Nights." *Esquire*. February 2, 2014. Retrieved March 8, 2015, from http://www.esquire.com.

Marks, Peter. "Theater Review; Finding Saints on the Space Shuttle." *New York Times*. November 5, 1997. Retrieved March 12, 2015, from http://www.nytimescom.

_____. "Theater; the Stars Favor Chekhov." *New York Times*. August 5, 2001. Retrieved April 17, 2015, from http://www.nytimes.com.

Maslin, Janet. "An Actor Whose Talents Are the Sum of His Parts." *New York Times*. October 8, 1997. Retrieved March 7, 2015, from http://www.nytimes.com.

_____. "'The Big Lebowski': Comic Oddballs Hurling Bowling Balls." *New York Times*. March 6, 1998. Retrieved March 10, 2015, from http://www.nytimes.com.

_____. "Film Festival Review: Faulty Families: Music Is Easy Listening and Dessert Is Hard to Take." *New York Times*. October 9, 1998. Retrieved March 14, 2015, from http://www.nytimes.com.

_____. "Film Review: Entangled Lives on the Cusp of the Millennium." *New York Times*. December 17, 1999. Retrieved April 5, 2015, from http://www.nytimes.com.

_____. "Film Review: Stealing a New Life, Carnal, Glamorous and Worth the Price." *New York Times*. December 24, 1999. Retrieved March 29, 2015, from http://www.nytimes.com.

_____. "Film Review: Take Two Giggles, Twice Daily: Physician, Squeal Thyself." *New York Times.* December 24, 1998. Retrieved March 14, 2015, from http://www.nytimes.com.
_____. "Film Review: Twister." *New York Times.* May 10, 1996. Retrieved March 5, 2015, from http://www.nytimes.com.
_____. "The New Season/Film; A Generation Moves Past 'Promising.'" *New York Times.* September 12, 1999. Retrieved March 23, 2015, from http://www.nytimes.com.
_____. "Review/Film: Scent of a Woman: Al Pacino, Indulging a Lust for Life." *New York Times.* December 23, 1992. Retrieved December 28, 2014, from http://www.nytimes.com.
_____. "Review/Film: Steve Martin as a Healer with Faith Only in Lies." *New York Times.* December 18, 1992. Retrieved December 26, 2014, from http://www.nytimes.com.
_____. "Review/Film: When a Man Loves a Woman: A Woman Under the Influence." *New York Times.* April 29, 1994. Retrieved January 1, 2015, from http://www.nytimes.com.
_____. "Review/Film: Wry Tale of Bored Wife and Her Gun." *New York Times.* October 30, 1992. Retrieved December 25, 2014, from http://www.nytimes.com.
Masterson, Laurie. "Devil in the Detail." *STM Entertainment.* April 6, 2008: 4–5.
Mayshark, Jesse Fox. *Post-Pop Cinema: The Search for Meaning in New American Film.* Westport, CT: Greenwood Publishing Group, 2007.
McNairy, David. "WGA Backs Strike Authorization." *Variety.* October 19, 2007. Retrieved July 7, 2015, from http://www.variety.com.
McNulty, Charles. "Review: 'The Author's Voice/Imagining Brad.'" *Variety.* May 24, 1999. Retrieved March 14, 2015, from http://www.variety.com.
McVeigh, Dave, and Scott McVeigh. "The Making of Twister." *Twister* DVD featurette. HBO/Warner Bros./Incue, 1996.
Meehan, Paul. *Horror Noir: Where Cinema's Dark Sisters Meet.* Jefferson, NC: McFarland, 2010.
Messer, Lesley. "How Philip Seymour Hoffman's Death Affected 'Hunger Games Mockingjay 1.'" *ABC News.* November 24, 2014. Retrieved September 21, 2015, from http://www.abcnews.go.com.
Michaels, Sean. "Philip Seymour Hoffman in Talks to Play Daniel Johnston?" *The Guardian.* March 19, 2010. Retrieved November 12, 2015, from http://www.theguardian.com.
Mikelbank, Peter. "George Clooney & Stacy Keibler Enjoy Dinner and a Movie in Paris." *People.* October 19, 2011. Retrieved November 20, 2015, from http://www.people.com.
Milano, Valerie. *Gwyneth Paltrow.* Winnipeg, Canada: ECW Press, 2000.
Milfull, Tim. "Cinema: An Interview with Adam Elliot." *MC Reviews.* April 5, 2009. Retrieved July 28, 2015, from http://www.reviews.media-culture.org.au.
Miller, Bennett, and Adam Kimmel, *Capote* DVD Audio Commentary. Sony Pictures Home Entertainment, 2006.
Miller, Bennett, and Philip Seymour Hoffman. *Capote* DVD Audio Commentary. Sony Pictures Home Entertainment, 2006.
Miller, Paul. *The 2000 Tony Awards.* Walter C. Miller Productions.
Minghella, Anthony. DVD Audio Commentary. *The Talented Mr. Ripley.* Warner Bros., 2000.
_____, and Walter Murch. *Cold Mountain* DVD Audio Commentary. Miramax, 2004.
Minow, Neil. "Interview: Amy Ryan of 'Jack Goes Boating.'" *Belief.Net.* Undated. Retrieved August 13, 2015, from http://www.beliefnet.com.
Mitchell, Elvis. "Film Review: Just an Average Bland, Obsessive, Embezzling Banker." *New York Times.* May 2, 2003. Retrieved May 13, 2015, from http://www.nytimes.com.
_____. "Taking a Bite Out of Crime." *New York Times.* October 4, 2002. Retrieved May 4, 2015, from http://www.nytimes.com.
Modell, Josh. "Philip Seymour Hoffman Makes Unrequited Affection Funny (And Heartbreaking)." *A.V. Club.* February 3, 2014. Retrieved March 8, 2015, from http://www.avclub.com.
Moerk, Christian. "Answered Prayers: How 'Capote' Came Together." *New York Times.* September 25, 2005. Retrieved June 4, 2015, from http://www.nytimes.com.
Molloy, Tim. "Philip Seymour Hoffman's 'Happyish' Could Still Be Recast for Showtime." *The Wrap.* July 18, 2014. Retrieved September 22, 2015, from http://www.thewrap.com.
_____. "Philip Seymour Hoffman's Showtime Series Shot Just One Episode." *The Wrap.* February 2, 2014. Retrieved September 17, 2015, from http://www.thewrap.com.
Mongelli, Lorena, and Elizabeth Hagen, and Bob Fredericks. "Hoffman's Grieving Girlfriend Steps Out as Funeral Plans Begin." *New York Post.* February 4, 2014. Retrieved October 19, 2015, from http://www.nypost.com.
Monk, Katherine. "Philip Seymour Hoffman: Tragic End to a Remarkable Career." *Vancouver Versun.* February 3, 2014: B5.
Morgan, Clare. "Blanchett's Touch Fails to Save West End Play." *The Age.* October 20, 2008. Retrieved July 20, 2015, from http://www.theage.com.au.

Morgan, Conor. "Scene Stealers: Philip Seymour Hoffman in Punch-Drunk Love." *One Room with a View*. July 8, 2014. Retrieved May 2, 2015, from http://www.oneroomwithaview.com.

Morgan, Louis. "Alternate Best Supporting Actor 2004: Philip Seymour Hoffman in *Along Came Polly*." *Actor Oscar Blog*. September 14, 2014. Retrieved May 13, 2015, from http://www.actoroscar.blogspot.com.au.

Morrison, Stephen J. "The Making of Red Dragon." *Red Dragon* DVD Collector's Edition. Universal City Studios/Herzog Productions, 2002.

Mottram, James. "Philip Seymour Hoffman: 'You're Not Going to Watch the Master and Find a Lot Out About Scientology.'" *The Independent*. October 28, 2012. Retrieved September 12, 2015, from http://www.independent.co.uk.

_____. *Sundance Kids: How the Mavericks Took Back Hollywood*. London, UK: Faber & Faber, 2011.

Mueller, Matt. "Venice: 'The Master' Press Conference; Cruise & Anderson Still Friends." *Indiewire*. September 2, 2012. Retrieved November 22, 2015, from http://www.blogsindiewire.com.

Murray, Rebecca. "Laura Linney Discusses the Savages." *About.com*. Retrieved July 5, 2015, from http://www.movies.about.com.

_____. "Philip Seymour Hoffman Talks About the Savages." *About.com*. Retrieved July 5, 2015, from http://www.movies.about.com.

_____, and Fred Topel. "Philip Seymour Hoffman Talks About '25th Hour.'" *About.com*. Retrieved May 10, 2015, from http://www.movies.about.com.

Musto, Michael. "Voices. Philip Seymour Hoffman." *Out*, October, 2005: 88, 90.

Nathan, Sara, et al. "Philip Seymour Hoffman Pictured Drinking at a Bar and Asleep on a Plane Days Before Deadly Drug Binge." *Daily Mail*. February 3, 2014. Retrieved October 5, 2015, from http://www.dailymail.co.uk.

Naylor, David. "The Making of the Mission." DVD Group, Inc. Production for Paramount Home Entertainment. Paramount Pictures, 2006.

Neale, April. "Julianne Moore on Most Memorable Roles, Missing Phillip Seymour Hoffman and More for More." *Monsters & Critics*. October 27, 2014. Retrieved November 30, 2015, from http://www.monstersandcritics.com.

Nemiroff, Perry. "Interview: Pirate Radio's Philip Seymour Hoffman." *CinemaBlend*. November 11, 2009. Retrieved August 2, 2015, from http://www.cinemablend.com.

Nesselson, Lisa. "Review: 'Before the Devil Knows You're Dead.'" *Variety*. Retrieved July 7, 2015, from http://www.variety.com.

Newman, Jason. "Philip Baker Hall Remembers 'Genius' Philip Seymour Hoffman." *Rolling Stone*. February 2, 2014. Retrieve November 27, 2015, from http://www.rollingstone.com.

Nissim, Mayer. "Hoffman 'Was Confused by Synecdoche.'" *Digital Spy*. May 15, 2009. Retrieved November 10, 2015, from http://www.digitalspy.com.

Nordyke, Kimberly. "Philip Seymour Hoffman Talks to THR, Jokes Around in One of His Final Interviews (Video)." *The Hollywood Reporter*. February 2, 2014. Retrieved November 27, 2015, from http://www.hollywoodreporter.com.

O'Connell, Sean. "Ethan Hawke Enlists in Indie 'Quartet' Drama." *Hollywoodnews*. August 6, 2010. Retrieved September 13, 2015, from http://www.hollywoodnews.com.

_____. "How Philip Seymour Hoffman's Death Changed the Hunger Games." *Cinema Blend*. Undated. Retrieved September 21, 2015, from http://www.cinemablend.com.

Onda, David. "'A Late Quartet' Director on Faking Music, Walking with Walken." *Xfinity*. November 8, 2012. Retrieved September 13, 2015, from http://www.xfinity.com.

Orloff, Brian. "Michelle Williams, Naomi Watts Pay Tribute to Heath Ledger." *People*. March 13, 2008. Retrieved November 7, 2015, from http://www.people.com.

Oxman, Steven. "Review: 'The Long Red Road.'" *Variety*. February 22, 2010. Retrieved August 16, 2015, from http://www.variety.com.

Pappademas, Alex. "Leading Man. His Aim Is Tru." *GQ.com*, October 2005: 186, 188, 190, 192.

Parker, Tyler. "Examining a Classic: Phillip Seymour Hoffman's Old School Let It Rain Dance." *Ballerball*. January 17, 2014. Retrieved May 13, 2015, from http://www.ballerball.com.

Paulson, Michael. "Mimi O'donnell Seeks Solace in Theater After Philip Seymour Hoffman's Death." *New York Times*. May 15, 2015. Retrieved November 1, 2015, from http://www.nytimes.com.

Paur, Joey. "Sundance 2010: Jack Goes Boating—Philip Seymour Hoffman's Directorial Debut." *Geektyrant*. Undated. Retrieved August 14, 2015, from http://www.geektyrant.com.

Paymer, David et al. *State and Main* DVD Cast Audio Commentary. New Home Line Video, 2001.

Payne, Greg. "Catching Fire': Philip Seymour Hoffman Explains Why He Joined the Franchise." *Screen Rant*. August 6, 2012. Retrieved September 16, 2015, from http://www.screenrant.com.

Perkins, Claire. *American Smart Cinema*. Edinburgh Edinburgh University Press, 2012.

Perse, Tobias. "The Life of Reilly." *Time Out New York*, February 17–24, 2000" 19–20.

Pfeiffer, Lee. "Cinema Retro Covers Sidney Lumet Tribute at Lincoln Center." *Cinemaretro*. June 28, 2011. Retrieved November 18, 2015, from http://www.cinemaretro.com.
Phillips, Gene D. *Out of the Shadows: Expanding the Canon of Classic Film Noir*. Plymouth, UK: Scarecrow Press, 2012.
Piepenburg, Erik. "Hey, Kids, Let's Put on a Reading!" *New York Times*. January 20, 2011. Retrieved August 18, 2015, from http://www.nytimes.com.
Pincus-Roth, Zachary. "Meryl Streep and Philip Seymour Hoffman to Star in Doubt Film." *Playbill*. April 19, 2007. Retrieved July 22, 2015, from http://www.playbill.com.
Pogrebin, Robin. "Both Tonys for Directing Go to Michael Blakemore; 'Kiss Me, Kate,' 'Contact,' 'Aida,' and 'Copenhagen' Are Among Multiple Winners." *New York Times*. June 5, 2000. Retrieved April 10, 2015, from http://www.nytimes.com.
_____. "'Hairspray' and 'Long Day's Journey' Have Grip on Tonys." *New York Times*. June 9, 2003. Retrieved May 15, 2015, from http://www.nytimes.com.
_____. "'Hairspray' Leads Field of Tony Nominees." *New York Times*. May 13, 2003. Retrieved May 14, 2015, from http://www.nytimes.com.
_____. "Special Twists This Year in the Competition Called Tony Madness." *New York Times*. May 31, 2000. Retrieved April 10, 2015, from http://www.nytimes.com.
_____. "Stage Electricity: Alternating Current." *New York Times*. March 28, 2000. Retrieved March 21, 2015, from http://www.nytimes.com.
_____. "Theater: Pitching in for Paul Newman and Other American Icons." *New York Times*. November 18, 2001. Retrieved April 24, 2015, from http://www.nytimes.com.
_____. "Theater: The Tony Awards: The Award Theater People Hate and Love." *New York Times*. May 21, 2000. Retrieved April 10, 2015, from http://www.nytimes.com.
_____. "3 Leaders Wanted: Arts Lovers/Math Skills/Charisma. Thick Skin Req'd." *New York Times*. February 19, 2004. Retrieved May 15, 2015, from http://www.nytimes.com.
_____. "Tony Nominations Mirror a Small World." *New York Times*. May 9, 2000. Retrieved April 10, 2015, from http://www.nytimes.com.
Pomerance, Murray. *Shining in Shadows: Movie Stars of the 2000s*. New Brunswick, New Jersey, London: Rutgers University Press, 2012.
Popick, John. "Mourning and Huffing." *City Newspaper*. Retrieved April 22, 2015, from http://www.rochestercitynewspaper.com.
Pow, Helen. "Philip Seymour Hoffman's Incoherent Ramblings About Drug Deals and His 'Demons' Revealed in Secret Diaries." *Daily Mail*. February 12, 2014. Retrieved October 14, 2015, from http://www.dailymail.co.uk.
Prigge, Stephen. *Movie Moguls Speak: Interviews with Top Film Producers*. Jefferson, NC: McFarland, 2004.
Prince, Stephen. *Firestorm: American Film in the Age of Terrorism*. New York: Columbia University Press, 2013.
Pulliam, June, and Anthony J. Fonseca. *Encyclopedia of the Zombie: The Walking Dead in Popular Culture and Myth: The Walking Dead in Popular Culture and Myth*. Santa Barbara, CA: ABC-Clio, 2014.
Punzi, Maddalena Pennacchia. *Literary Intermediality: The Transit of Literature Through the Media*. Bern 9, Switzerland: Peter Lang, 2007.
Purnick, Joyce. "Metro Matters: Free Theater, but the Lines? Unspeakable." *New York Times*. July 30, 2001. Retrieved April 17, 2015, from http://www.nytimes.com.
Quinn, Karl. "Philip Seymour Hoffman's Death Won't Delay the Hunger Games Sequels." *The Sydney Morning Herald*. February 3, 2014. Retrieved September 19, 2015, from http://www.smh.com.au.
Quirk, Lawrence J. *Paul Newman: A Life, Updated*. Plymouth, UK: Taylor Trade Publications, 2009.
Raab, Scott. "Philip Seymour Hoffman: The ESQ&A." *Esquire*. October 10, 2012. Retrieved August 23, 2015, from http://www.esquire.com.
Rabin, Nathan. "The Epic Uncool of Philip Seymour Hoffman." *Dissolve*. January 25, 2015. Retrieved May 3, 2015, from http://www.thedissolve.com.
Radish, Christina. "Kathryn Hahn Talks ... Trending Down..." *Collider*. August 28, 2013. Retrieved November 26, 2015, from http://www.collider.com.
Ramirez, Anthony, with Melena Ryzik. "Boldface. the Bluebird of Famousness." *New York Times*. January 10, 2006. Retrieved June 7, 2015, from http://www.nytimes.com.
Rance, Mark. *That Moment—Magnolia Diary*. Three Legged Cat Productions/New Line Home Video, 2000.
Ratner, Brett, and Ted Tally. *Red Dragon* DVD Audio Commentary. Universal Studios, 2003.
Rebello, Stephen. "Film. Taking a New Gamble." *The Advocate*, June 10, 2033: 56–57.

Reed, Ryan. "John Slattery Opens Up About His Fallen Friend, Philip Seymour Hoffman." *Rolling Stone*. March 19, 2014. Retrieved October 13, 2015, from http://www.rollingstone.com.

Reisz, Toby. "Inside the Talented Mr. Ripley." Paramount Pictures/Mirimax Film Group, 1999.

Renner, Pamela. "Review: 'Jesus Hopped the 'A' Train.' " *Variety*. December 10, 2000. Retrieved April 14, 2015, from http://www.variety.com.

Reynolds, Simon. "Hoffman: 'Acting Is Torturous.'" *Digital Spy*. May 14, 2009. Retrieved November 10, 2015, from http://www.digitalspy.com.

Rich, Frank. "American Pseudo." *New York Times*. December 12, 1999. Retrieved April 10, 2015, from http://www.nytimes.com.

Rich, Katie. "Dianna Agron Up for Spider-Man Love Interest, Plus Philip Seymour Hoffman for Venom?" *Cinemablend*. October 1, 2010. Retrieved November 14, 2015, from http://www.cinemablend.com.

Richards, David. "Theater Review; Sellars's Merchant of Venice Beach." *New York Times*. October 18, 1994. Retrieved January 4, 2015, from http://www.nytimes.com.

Rissmandel, Paul. "Remembering Philip Seymour Hoffman in "Pirate Radio."" *Radio Survivor*. February 3, 2014. Retrieved August 1, 2015, from http://www.radiosurvivor.com.

Robertson, Campbell. "Coming Attractions at the Public. " New York Times. July 31, 2007. Retrieved July 12, 2015, from http://www.nytimes.com.

_____, with Joe Bescia, and Melena Z. Ryzik. "Boldface: in Which We Avoid Puns on the Word 'Match.'" New York Times. August 26, 2005. Retrieved June 4, 2015, from http://www.nytimes.com.

_____, with Kari Haskell, and Winter Miller. "Boldface: Oh, Her Again." *New York Times*. March 16, 2006. Retrieved June 20, 2015, from http://www.nytimes.com.

_____, with Lily Koppel. "Boldface: Able Was I Ere I Saw the Bouncer." *New York Times*. April 7, 2005. Retrieved May 16, 2015, from http://www.nytimes.com.

_____, with Luke Jerod Kummer. "Boldface: Other Voices, Other Lobes." *New York Times*. September 30, 2005. Retrieved June 6, 2015, from http://www.nytimes.com.

_____, with Melena Z. Ryzik. "Boldface Names ... Does She Know the Name of the Play?" *New York Times*. July 15, 2004. Retrieved May 15, 2015, from http://www.nytimes.com.

_____, with Paula Schwartz, and Joe Brescia. "Boldface: In Which We Are Envious of the Australians." *New York Times*. May 13, 2005. Retrieved May 19, 2015, from http://www.nytimes.com.

_____, with Regis Morris, and Paula Schwartz. "Boldface: Kingsley Was Later Found in Imperioli's Trunk." *New York Times*. January 17, 2006. Retrieved June 18, 2015, from http://www.nytimes.com.

_____, with Winter Miller, and Kari Haskell. "Boldface: Drama! Show Tunes! National Security Policy!" *New York Times*. February 1, 2006. Retrieved June 19, 2015, from http://www.nytimes.com.

Robinson, Tasha. "Philip Seymour Hoffman." *A.V. Club*. September 15, 2010. Retrieved August 10, 2015, from http://www.avclub.com.

Rohter, Larry. "Artsbeat: Hoffman to Direct in Coming Labyrinth Theater Season." *New York Times*. August 1, 2012. Retrieved September 5, 2015, from http://www.nytimes.com.

_____. "Artsbeat: Support for Belarus Theater Troupe Includes Rally, Benefits and a Chicago Engagement." *New York Times*. January 19, 2011. Retrieved August 18, 2015, from http://www.nytimes.com.

Rooney, David. "Review: 'Capote.'" *Variety*. September 2, 2005. Retrieved June 1, 2015, from http://www.variety.com.

_____. "Review: 'The Little Flower of East Orange.'" *Variety*. April 6, 2008. Retrieved July 25, 2015, from http://www.variety.com.

_____. "Review: '25th Hour.'" *Variety*. December 13, 2002. Retrieved May 10, 2015, from http://www.variety.com.

Rosenfeld, Megan. "Money for Nothing." *The Washington Post*. September 15, 1993. Retrieved December 30, 2014, from http://www.washingtonpost.com.

Russell, Carolyn R. *The Films of Joel and Ethan Coen*. Jefferson, NC: McFarland, 2001.

Ryan, Kathy. "Three Views of Philip Seymour Hoffman." *New York Times*. February 3, 2014. Retrieved September 18, 2015, from http://www.nytimes.com.

Ryzik, Melena. "The Carpetbagger: A Jewish Film for the Soul." *New York Times*. December 21, 2009. Retrieved August 16, 2015, from http://www.nytimescom.

_____. "The Carpetbagger: Albert Brooks Finds a New Use for His Character's Backstory." *New York Times*. January 11, 2012. Retrieved August 22, 2015, from http://www.nytimes.com.

_____. "The Carpetbagger: The Carpetbagger's 2013 Oscar Predictions." *New York Times*. February 21, 2013. Retrieved September 14, 2015, from http://www.nytimes.com.

_____. "Rats to Riches: Buddies on a Theatrical Journey." *New York Times*. March 5, 2007. Retrieved July 11, 2015, from http://www.nytimes.com.

Schepisi, Fred, and Richard Russo. *Empire Falls* DVD Audio Commentary. HBO Films, 2007.
Schillinger, Liesl. "Celebrities Opt to Be Heard Rather Than Seen." *New York Times*. April 10, 2005. Retrieved May 16, 2015, from http://www.nytimes.com.
Schneider, Jeff, and Justin Kroll, "Philip Seymour Hoffman to Direct 'Ezekiel Moss.'" *Variety*. September 17, 2012. Retrieved September 22, 2015, from http://www.variety.com.
Schorn, Daniel, and John Hamlin. "Philip Seymour Hoffman Gets Candid." *60 Minutes*. February 16, 2006. Retrieved July 8, 2015, from http://www.cbsnews.com.
Schou, Solvej. "Catherine Keener on Playing Viola and Mining Emotions with Philip Seymour Hoffman in 'A Late Quartet.'" *Entertainment Weekly*. October 31, 2012. Retrieved November 22, 2015, from http://www.ew.com.
Schwartz, Paula, with Melena Z. Ryzik. "Boldface: Or Maybe One of Those Martha Stewart Ponchos." *New York Times*. September 7, 2005. Retrieved June 4, 2015, from http://www.nytimes.com.
Schwirtz, Michael. "Hoffman Killed by Toxic Mix of Drugs, Official Concludes." *New York Times*. February 28, 2014. Retrieved October 30, 2015, from http://www.nytimes.com.
Scott, A.O. "An Actor Who Made Unhappiness a Joy to Watch." *New York Times*. February 3, 2014. Retrieved October 14, 2015, from http://www.nytimes.com.
_____. "Big-Name Novelist, Small-Town Murders." *New York Times*. September 22, 2005. Retrieved June 1, 2015, from http://www.nytimes.com.
_____. "Estranged Bedfellows." *New York Times*. October 6, 2011. Retrieved August 19, 2015, from http://www.nytimes.com.
_____. "Film Festival Review: Love and the Single Misfit in a Topsy-Turvy World." *New York Times*. October 5, 2002. Retrieved May 2, 2015, from http://www.nytimes.com.
_____. "Film Review: A Prisoner of Grief Binges on a Deadly Diet of Sympathy." *New York Times*. December 30, 2002. Retrieved April 17, 2015, from http://www.nytimes.com.
_____. "Film Review: Confronting the Past Before Going to Prison." *New York Times*. December 19, 2002. Retrieved May 6, 2015, from http://www.nytimes.com.
_____. "Film Review: Lovers Striving for a Reunion, with a War in the Way." *New York Times*. December 25, 2003. Retrieved May 15, 2015, from http://www.nytimes.com.
_____. "Film Review: With Sympathy for the Devil, a Rock Writer Finds His Way." *New York Times*. September 13, 2000. Retrieved April 24, 2015, from http://www.nytimes.com.
_____. "Good-Time Charlie's Foreign Affairs." *New York Times*. December 21, 2007. Retrieved July 10, 2015, from http://www.nytimes.com.
_____. "In 'Strangers with Candy,' Amy Sedaris's Jerri Blank Is Streetwise and Starting Over." *New York Times*. June 28, 2006. Retrieved May 18, 2015, from http://www.nytimes.com.
_____. "Learning to Swim in the Deep End of Life's Pool." *New York Times*. September 16, 2010. Retrieved August 8, 2015, from http://www.nytimes.com.
_____. "The Punishment for Being Publicity-Shy." *New York Times*. September 5, 2013. Retrieved October 5, 2015, from http://www.nytimes.com.
_____. "Robbing a Mom and Pop Store, Too Close to Home." *New York Times*. October 26, 2007. Retrieved July 7, 2015, from http://www.nytimes.com.
_____. "There Will Be Megalomania." *New York Times*. September 13, 2002. Retrieved September 1, 2015, from http://www.nytimes.com.
Sedaris, Amy, and Stephen Colbert, and Paul Dinello. *Strangers with Candy* DVD Audio Commentary. Image/ThinkFilms.2006.
Seijas, Casey. "'Dark Knight' Exclusive: Michael Caine Says Johnny Depp Is the Riddler, Philip Seymour Hoffman Is the Penguin." *MTV*. September 8, 2008. Retrieved November 7, 2015, from http://www.splashpage.mtv.com.
_____. 'Dark Knight' Update: Philip Seymour Hoffman Responds To Casting Rumor, 'I Don't Know If I'd Be A Good Penguin.'" *MTV*. September 9, 2008. Retrieved November 7, 2015, from http://www.splashpage.mtv.com.
Serpe, Gina. "Philip Seymour Hoffman and Son Sport Adorable Matching Cheers at Knicks Game." *E!* January 4, 2013. Retrieved November 23, 2015, from http://www.au.eonline.com.
Shanley. John Patrick. *Doubt* DVD Audio Commentary. Lionsgate, 2011.
Shattuck, Kathryn. "What's on TV Saturday?" *New York Times*. August 9, 2014. Retrieved October 31, 2015, from http://www.nytimes.com.
Shepard, Richard. *I Knew It Was You: Rediscovering John Cazale* DVD Audio Commentary. Oscilloscope, 2010.
Slattery, John. *God's Pocket* DVD Audio Commentary. MPI Home Video, 2014.
Smith, Nigel. M. "'Bad Words' Star Kathryn Hahn on Being the Misfit and Working with the Late Philip Seymour Hoffman." *Indiewire*. March 12, 2014. Retrieved September 21, 2015, from http://www.indiewire.com.

Sneider, Jeff. "Jake Gyllenhaal, Amy Adams to Star in Director Philip Seymour Hoffman's 'Ezekiel Moss' the *Wrap*. January 31, 2014. Retrieved February 22, 2015, from http://www.thewrap.com.
Soloski, Alexis. "Rescued by Music Long Ago, He Sets His Life Story to Hip-Hop." *New York Times*. September 23, 2014. Retrieved November 1, 2015, from http://www.nytimes.com.
Sperb, Jason. *Blossoms and Blood: Postmodern Media Culture and the Films of Paul Thomas Anderson*. Austin, TX: University of Texas Press, 2013.
Stanley, Alessandra. "Alacrity on Parade, or the Lack Thereof." *New York Times*. June 20, 2005. Retrieved May 19, 2015, from http://www.nytimes.com.
_____. "Review: Showtime's 'Happyish' Is Funnyish." *New York Times*. April 23, 2015. Retrieved September 21, 2015, from http://www.nytimes.com.
Stasio, Marilyn. "Review: 'Death of a Salesman.'" *Variety*. March 15, 2012. Retrieved September 3, 2015, from http://www.variety.com.
_____. "Review: 'A Family for All Occasions.'" *Variety*. May 12, 2003. Retrieved September 14, 2015, from http://www.variety.com.
_____. "Review: 'Othello.'" *Variety*. September 28, 2009. Retrieved August 16, 2015, from http://www.variety.com.
Steinberg, Julie. "Philip Seymour Hoffman on His Directorial Debut 'Jack Goes Boating.'" *The Wall Street Journal*. September 17, 2010. Retrieved August 10, 2015, from http://www.blogs.wsj.com.
Stelter, Brian. "Countdown to a Writers' Strike." *New York Times*. October 29, 2007. Retrieved July 7, 2015, from http://www.nytimes.com.
_____. "'Family Guy,' 'Desperate Housewives' Feel Effects of Strike." *New York Times*. November 8, 2007. Retrieved July 8, 2015, from http://www.nytimes.com.
_____. "Strike Deadline Passes; WGA to Hold Member Meeting Tonight." *New York Times*. November 1, 2007. Retrieved July 7, 2015, from http://www.nytimes.com.
_____. "Strike News: Writer's Block Starts Monday." *New York Times*. November 2, 2007. Retrieved July 7, 2015, from http://www.nytimes.com.
_____. "Tick, Tick, Tick, Strike?" *New York Times*. October 31, 2007. Retrieved July 7, 2015, from http://www.nytimes.com.
_____. "TV Writers Edging Toward a Strike." *New York Times*. October 22, 2007. Retrieved July 7, 2015, from http://www.nytimes.com.
_____. "Writers Close to Setting Strike Date." *New York Times*. November 2, 2007. Retrieved July 7, 2015, from http://www.nytimes.com.
_____. "Writers Say They Have 'Tentative Deal'; Guild Leaders Call Strike a Success." *New York Times*. Februsry 9, 2008. Retrieved July 8, 2015, from http://www.nytimes.com.
Stephens, Niki. "George Clooney Eyes Chris Pine, Philip Seymour Hoffman, and Paul Giamatti for Farragut North." *JoBlo*. August 31, 2010. Retrieved November 14, 2015, from http://www.joblo.com.
Stern, Marlowe. "Philip Seymour Hoffman & Amy Ryan Talk Jack Goes Boating!" *Manhattan Movie Magazine*. September 16, 2010. Retrieved August 12, 2015, from http://www.manhattanmoviemag.com.
_____. "Philip Seymour Hoffman's Best Performances: 'Boogie Nights,' 'Capote,' and More." *The Daily Beast*. February 2, 2014. Retrieved March 8, 2015, from http://www.the dailybeast.com.
Sterritt, David. *Spike Lee's America*. Cambridge, UK: John Wiley & Sons, 2013.
Stevens, Andrea. "Next Stop, Gentrification, Everybody Out." *New York Times*. March 28, 2005. Retrieved May 18, 2015, from http://www.nytimes.com.
Stifel, Chris. Making Empire Falls. Home Box Office, 2005.
Stockman, Tom. "Wamg Interview: Yaron Zilberman—Director of a Late Quartet." *We Are Movie Geeks*. November 11, 2012. Retrieved September 13, 2015, from http://www.wearemoviegeeks.com.
Stokes, Melvyn. *American History Through Hollywood Film: From the Revolution to the 1960s*. London, New York: A& C Black, 2013.
Suskin, Steven. *Broadway Yearbook 2001–2002: A Relevant and Irreverent Record*. New York: Oxford University Press, 2003.
Suskind, Alex. "'A Most Wanted Man': Anton Corbijn on Philip Seymour Hoffman, 'Life,' Robert Pattinson & More." *Indiewire*. July 24, 2014. Retrieved October 4, 2015, from http://www.blogs.indiewire.com.
Svetkey, Benjamin. "Mark Wahlberg on Philip Seymour Hoffman: 'Fearless and Selfless.'" *The Hollywood Reporter*. February 5, 2014. Retrieved March 8, 2015, from http://www.hollywoodreporter.com.
Tartaglione, Nancy. "Philip Seymour Hoffman Project 'Ezekiel Moss' Will Not Be Sold in Berlin." *Deadline Hollywood*. February 2, 2014. Retrieved September 22, 2015, from http://www.deadline.com.
Tauber, Michelle, et al. "Philip Seymour Hoffman 1967–2014." *People*, vol. 8, no. 7, 2014: 58- 62.
Tedeschi, Bob. "E-Commerce Report. Searching the World, from Jersey City." New York Times. Retrieved June 20, 2015, from http://www.nytimes.com.
Telsch, Rafe. "Goyer Calls Shenanigans on Dark Knight Rumors." *CinemaBlend*. October 7, 2008. Retrieved November 8, 2015, from http://www.cinemablend.com.

Thielman, Sam. "Review: Unconditional." *Variety*. February 19, 2008. Retrieved July 25, 2015, from http://www.variety.com.

Thomas, Kevin. "Movie Review: 'Joey Breaker' Surprises with Substance Plus Laughs." *Los Angeles Times*. August 20, 1993. Retrieved December 29, 2014, from http://www.latimes.com.

Thomson, David. "Film: Without Them, Mr. Ripley Would Be a Nobody." *New York Times*. December 19, 1999. Retrieve March 29, 2015, from http://www.nytimes.com.

____. "Movie Review: 'Money for Nothing' a Comedy Worth Something." *Los Angeles Times*. September 10, 1993. Retrieved December 30, 2014, from http://www.latimes.com.

____. "The Sad Truth About Philip Seymour Hoffman." *New Republic*. March 22, 2014. Retrieved May 18, 2015, from http://www.newrepublic.com.

Tichler, Rosemary, and Barry Jay Kaplan. *Actors at Work*. New York: Faber and Faber, 2007.

Tinkham, Chris. "Philip Seymour Hoffman." *Under the Radar*. September 27, 2010. Retrieved August 12, 2015, from http://www.undertheradarmag.com.

Titze, Anne-Katrin. "Cate Blanchett Honoured." *Eye for Film*. October 7, 2013. Retrieved November 26, 2015, from http://www.eyeforfilm.co.uk

____. "First Time Fest Diary." *Eye for Film*. March 9, 2013. Retrieved November 23, 2015, from http://www.eyeforfilm.co.uk.

Tookey, Christopher. *Tookey's Turkeys: The Most Annoying 144 Films from the Last 25 Years*. Leicestershire, UK: Troubador Publishing Ltd, 2015.

Travers, Peter. "Almost Famous." *Rolling Stone*. September 13, 2000. Retrieved April 7, 2015, from http://www.rollingstone.com.

____. "Before the Devil Knows You're Dead." *Rolling Stone*. October 18, 2007. Retrieved July 7, 2015, from http://www.rollingstone.com.

____. "The Big Lebowski." *Rolling Stone*. March 6, 1998. Retrieved March 10, 2015, from http://www.rollingstone.com.

____. "Boogie Nights." *Rolling Stone*. October 10, 1997. Retrieved March 7, 2015, from http://www.rollingstone.com.

____. "Charlie Wilson's War." *Rolling Stone*. December 13, 2007. Retrieved July 10, 2015, from http://www.rollingstone.com.

____. "Cold Mountain." *Rolling Stone*. December 22, 2003. Retrieved May 22, 2015, from http://www.rollingstone.com.

____. "Doubt." *Rolling Stone*. December 11, 2008. Retrieved July 22, 2015, from http://www.rollingstone.com.

____. "The Hunger Games: Catching Fire." *Rolling Stone*. November 15, 2013. Retrieved September 14, 2015, from http://www.rollingstone.com.

____. "The Hunger Games: Mockingjay—Part 1." *Rolling Stone*. November 19, 2014. Retrieved September 21, 2015, from http://www.rollingstone.com.

____. "The Invention of Lying." *Rolling Stone*. September 14, 2009. Retrieved August 1, 2015, from http://www.rollingstone.com.

____. "Jack Goes Boating." *Rolling Stone*. September 15, 2010. Retrieved August 7, 2015, from http://www.rollingstone.com.

____. "A Late Quartet." *Rolling Stone*. November 1, 2012. Retrieved September 8, 2015, from http://www.rollingstone.com.

____. "Leap of Faith." *Rolling Stone*. December 18, 1992. Retrieved December 26, 2014, from http://www.rollingstone.com.

____. "Magnolia." *Rolling Stone*. February 27, 2001. Retrieved April 5, 2015, from http://www.rollingstone.com.

____. "The Master." *Rolling Stone*, September 10, 2012. Retrieved September 1, 2015, from http://www.rollingstone.com.

____. "Mission: Impossible III." *Rolling Stone*. May 5, 2006. Retrieved June 6, 2015, from http://www.rollingstone.com.

____. "A Most Wanted Man." *Rolling Stone*. July 24, 2014. Retrieved October 2, 2015, from http://www.rollingstone.com.

____. "Pirate Radio." *Rolling Stone*. November 12, 2009. Retrieved August 1, 2015, from http://www.rollingstone.com.

____. "Punch-Drunk Love." *Rolling Stone*. November 1, 2002. Retrieved May 2, 2015, from http://www.rollingstone.com.

____. "Red Dragon." *Rolling Stone*. October 4, 2002. Retrieved May 4, 2015, from http://www.nytimes.com.

____. "Salinger." *Rolling Stone*. September 6, 2013. Retrieved October 5, 2015, from http://www.rollingstone.com.

_____. "The Savages." *Rolling Stone*. December 13, 2007. Retrieved July 5, 2015, from http://www.rollingstone.com.

_____. "Synecdoche, New York." *Rolling Stone*. November 13, 2008. Retrieved July 14, 2015, from http://www.rollingstone.com.

_____. "25th Hour." *Rolling Stone*. January 10, 2003. Retrieved May 10, 2015, from http://www.rollingstone.com.

Travis, Ben. "John Le Carré: 'Philip Seymour Hoffman Was the Only American Actor Who Could Play George Smiley.'" *The Telegraph*. July 18, 2014. Retrieved October 4, 2015, from http://www.telegraph.co.uk.

Turner, Matthew. "Philip Seymour Hoffman Interview." *View London.Co.Uk*. Undated. Retrieved August 13, 2015, from http://www.viewlondon.co.uk.

Urbaniak, James. "What I Learned from Losing a Role to Philip Seymour Hoffman." *Slate: Browbeat*. February 3, 2014. Retrieved March 17, 2015, from http://www.slate.com.

Van Gelder, Lawrence. "Arts Briefing ... Footnotes." *New York Times*. February 18, 2004. Retrieved May 15, 2015, from http://www.nytimes.com.

_____. "This Week: Flight Time." *New York Times*. July 23, 2001. Retrieved April 17, 2015, from http://www.nytimes.com.

Van Syckle, Katie. "Beyond 'Mad Men': John Slattery and 'God's Pocket' Shine at Sundance." *Rolling Stone*. January 22, 2014. Retrieved September 23, 2015, from http://www.rollingstone.com.

Vary, Adam B. "Arts, Briefly ... Footnotes." *New York Times*. November 2, 2004. Retrieved May 16, 2015, from http://www.nytimes.com.

_____. "Arts, Briefly ... Theater News." *New York Times*. February 25, 2005. Retrieved May 16, 2015, from http://www.nytimes.com.

_____. "Arts, Briefly ... Warehouse of Dramas." *New York Times*. March 4, 2005. Retrieved May 16, 2015, from http://www.nytimes.com.

_____. "Bob Balaban Has No Idea How He Became a Brilliant Hollywood Character Actor." *BuzzFeed Entertainment*. March 5, 2014. Retrieved December 29, 2014, from http://www.buzzfeed.com.

Vaucher, Andrea R. "A Rare Success Story with Heroin at the Root." *New York Times*. August 24, 2004. Retrieved May 15, 2015, from http://www.nytimes.com.

Vest, Jason P. *Spike Lee: Finding the Story and Forcing the Issue*. Santa Barbara, CA: ABC-CLIO, 2014.

Voros, Drew. "Review: 'The Yearling.'" *Variety*. April 22, 1994. Retrieved March 1, 2015, from http://www.variety.com.

Wadler, Joy. "Boldface Names." *New York Times*. March 13, 2003. Retrieved May 15, 2015, from http://www.nytimes.com.

_____. "Boldface Names ... Just Don't Ask Us to Go Fishing." *New York Times*. September 29, 2004. Retrieved May 17, 2015, from http://www.nytimes.com.

_____. "Boldface Names ... We Must Try That Sometime with the Publisher." *New York Times*. February 19, 2004. Retrieved May 15, 2015, from http://www.nytimes.com.

_____, with Brescia Joe. "Boldface." *New York Times*. March 15, 2005. Retrieved May 16, 2015, from http://www.nytimes.com.

_____, with Campbell Robertson, and Kari Haskell. "Boldface Names." *New York Times*. October 2, 2003. Retrieved May 15, 2015, from http://www.nytimes.com.

_____, with Haskell, Karl. "Boldface Names ... They Will Make Some Great Heirlooms." *New York Times*. December 2, 2003. Retrieved May 15, 2015, from http://www.nytimes.com.

_____, with Jamie Wallis, and Melena Z. Ryzik. "Boldface Names." *New York Times*. October 7, 2003. Retrieved May 15, 2015, from http://www.nytimes.com.

_____, with Melena Z. Ryzik. "Boldface Names ... Thankfully, We Are Not That Sensitive." *New York Times*. February 24, 2015, from http://www.nytimes.com.

_____, with Paula Schwartz, and Melena Z. Ryzik. "Boldface Names ... Mr. Segue Man, Hit It!" *New York Times*. June 16, 2004. Retrieved May 15, 2015, from http://www.nytimes.com.

Wagner, Bruce. "Satire: Annals of the New New Groveling." *New York Times*. February 20, 1999. Retrieved April 10, 2015, from http://www.nytimes.com.

Webber, Stephanie. "Philip Seymour Hoffman's Diaries Reveal He Was Reportedly in a Love Triangle Before His Death." *US Weekly*. February 12, 2014. Retrieved November 27, 2015, from http://www.usmagazine.com.

Weber, Bruce. "Movies: Philip Seymour Hoffman, Actor of Depth, Dies at 46." *New York Times*. February 2, 2014. Retrieved December 21, 2014, from http://www.nytimes.com.

_____. "Spring Theater/Visions of America: An Unusual Case of Role Reversal." *New York Times*. February 27, 2000. Retreived March 19, 2015, from http://www.nytimes.com.

_____. "Theater Review: Hemingway Papafest for Paul Newman Charity. " *New York Times*. November 21, 2001. Retrieved April 24, 2015, from http://www.nytimes.com.

_____. "Theater Review: Throwing a Hissy Fit to Ease the Pain." *New York Times.* October 3, 2002. Retrieved May 3, 2015, from http://www.nytimes.com.
Wedding, Danny, and Ryan M. Niemiec. *Movies and Mental Illness: Using Films to Understand Psychopathology.* Boston, MA: Hogrefe Publishing, 2014.
Weiner, Jonah. "Fledgling Filmmaker Casts Against Type." *New York Times.* May 6, 2011. Retrieved August 18, 2015, from http://www.nytimes.com.
_____. "Solondz Nurtures His Indie Cred." *New York Times.* July 16, 2010. Retrieved March 24, 2015, from http://www.nytimes.com.
Weinraub, Bernard. "At the Movies: 'Boogie' Writer Back in Valley." *New York Times.* October 8, 1999. Retrieved March 23, 2015, from http://www.nytimes.com.
Weintraub, Steve 'Frosty.' "Philip Seymour Hoffman Interview—The Savages." *Collider.* November 28, 2007. Retrieved July 6, 2015, from http://www.collider.com.
Weiss, Glenn. *2003 Tony Awards.* Tony Award Productions/CBS, 2003.
_____. *2012 Tony Awards.* Tony Awards/White Cherry Entertainment, 2012.
Wells, Pete. "The Waiting Is the Hardest Part." *New York Times.* February 7, 2009. Retrieved August 14, 2015, from http://www.nytimes.com.
Wetta, Frank J., and Martin A. Novelli. *The Long Reconstruction: The Post-Civil War South in History, Film, and Memory.* Oxon, UK: Routledge, 2013.
White, James. "Steve Coogan Heads for Happyish." *Empire.* October 22, 2014. Retrieved September 22, 2015, from http://www.empireonline.com.
Whitty, Stephen. "The Talented Mr. Hoffman." *The Star-Ledger.* December 6, 2008, updated February 2, 2014. Retrieved December 22, 2014, from http://www.nj.com.
Wickman, Case. "'Catching Fire' Director Explains How He Snagged Philip Seymour Hoffman." *MTV News.* November 15, 2013. Retrieved September 19, 2015, from http://www.mtv.com.
Williams, Mary Elizabeth. "Why Didn't Philip Seymour Hoffman Leave Anything to His Children?" *Salon.* July 23, 2014. Retrieved October 27 2015, from http://www.salon.com.
Williams, Owen. "Philip Seymour Hoffman Joins Child 44." *Empire.* June 26, 2013. Retrieved September 10, 2015, from http://www.empireonline.com.
Willmore, Alison. "Showtime Releases Statement About Philip Seymour Hoffman's Passing." Indiewire. February 2, 2014. Retrieved September 17, 2015, from http://www.indiewire.com.
Wilson, Michael. "A Complicated Actor, Philip Seymour Hoffman, in His Last Days." *New York Times.* February 5, 2014. Retrieved October 16, 2015, from http://www.nytimes.com.
Wolf, Matt. "Theater: A First Play with an Unprintable Title: Call It a Hit." *New York Times.* January 25, 1998. Retrieved March 14, 2015, from http://www.nytimes.com.
Woodward, Adam. "Philip Seymour Hoffman." *Little White Lies.* September 11, 2011. Retrieved August 14, 2015, from http://www.littlewhitelies.co.uk.
Wright, Jessica. "Aaron Sorkin Reveals Chilling 'Overdose' Conversation with Philip Seymour Hoffman." *Sydney Morning Herald.* February 6, 2014. Retrieved July 11, 2015, from http://www.smh.com.au.
Yuan, Jada. "Sundance Three-Way: John Slattery, Christina Hendricks, and Philip Seymour Hoffman Talk God's Pocket." *Vulture.* Sundance 2014. Retrieved September 23, 2015, from http://www.vulture.com.
Zinoman, Jason. "Che at the Public Theater, but Not Just as You Pictured Him." *New York Times.* July 7, 2006. Retrieved July 11, 2015, from http://www.nytimes.com.
_____. "On Stage and Off ... Along the Way." *New York Times.* February 27, 2004. Retrieved May 15, 2015, from http://www.nytimes.com.
_____. "On Stage and Off ... Judas as Comedy." *New York Times.* March 12, 2004. Retrieved May 15, 2015, from http://www.nytimes.com.

Index

Page numbers in **_bold italics_** indicate pages with illustrations.

Abrams, J.J. 82, 84, 93–94
Adams, Amy 107, 108, 109, 126, 143, 144, 171, 177
Almost Famous 39–42, 59, 179
Along Came Polly 1, **_2_**, 3, 67–69, 73
Anderson, Jane 11, 28
Anderson, Paul Thomas 21, 23, 24, 27, 37, 38, 43, 47, 49, 55, 56, 57, 64, 85, 120, 128, 135, 142, 143, 144, 145, 146, 151, 154, 161, 168, 177
Arthur (TV series) 116, 119–120
Auslander, Shalom 163, 168, 175, 176, 182

Balaban, Bob 16, 17
Baldwin, Alec 18, 44, 67
Bates, Kathy 53, 55
Before the Devil Knows You're Dead 14, 94, **_95_**, 96, 106, 110, 114, 128, 140, 146
The Big Lebowski 26–27, 116, 129
Black, Jack 29, 40
Blanchett, Cate 37, 94, 116, 165, 177
Blank on Blank 182
The Boat That Rocked 111, **_112_**, 113–114, 115, 183
Bogosian, Eric 80, 87, 96–97, 177
Boogie Nights 3, 23–24, 40, 43, 45, 47, 62, 143, 164, 179
Brando, Marlon 16, 79
Bridges, Jeff 26, 131, 135

Capote **_2_**, 3, 10, 17, **_75_**, 76–80, 84–85, 86, 87, 88, 89, **_90_**, 103, 106, 110, 114, 122, 132, 138, 146, 156, 159, 174, 178, 179, 181
Capote, Truman 9, 39, 75, 76, 77, 78, 79, 85, 86, 87, 89, 100, 158
Celebrity Charades 82
Chaiklin, Rebecca 51, 52
Charlie Rose Show 49, 55, 63, 67, 78–79, 80, 96, 105, 109
Charlie Wilson's War 14, 97–99, 100, 106, 110, 114, 161, 162, 179
A Child's Garden of Poetry 142

Clarke, Gerald 75, 78
Clarkson, Patricia 74–75, 80
Clooney, George 1, 134, 139, 140, 141, 147, 174
Coen, Ethan 26–27, 81
Coen, Joel 26–27, 81, 177
Cold Mountain 64–66, 152
Coogan, Steve 183, 184
Cooper's Town Productions 3, 115, 116, 129, 141, 149, 155, 160, 161, 163, 171
Corbijn, Anton 147, 155, 156, 157, 171, 174
Crowe, Cameron 39, 40, 41, 42
Cruise, Tom 37, 38, 82, 83, 84
Culture (short) 27
Curtis, Richard 111, 113

Dafoe, Willem 155, 156, 158
The Daily Show with Jon Stewart 69, 73, 85, 121
Damon, Matt 35, 37
Davis, Hope 25, 102, 103
Davis, Viola 107, 109, 126
Death of a Salesman 7–8, 14, 102, 103, 116, 120, 136, 146, 148–149, 150, 154, 159, 161, 179
De Bont, Jan 21, 22
De Niro, Robert **_32_**, 33, 34, 129, 147, 159
Dennehy, Brian 67, 71, 136, 148, 177
The Directors: The Films of Anthony Minghella 37
Doubt 37, 101, 105–106, 107–108, **_109_**, 121, 126, 134, 174
Driver, Minnie 57, 58

Elliot, Adam 117, 118, 119
Empire Falls 81–82

Falls, Robert 67, 69
Farragut North 134, 136, 139; see also *The Ides of March*
Fiennes, Ralph 60, 61
The Fifteen Minute Hamlet 26
Film Trix 2004 73–74
Finney, Albert 94, 95, 96

Flawless **_2_**, **_32_**, 33–35, 36, 50
Fugit, Patrick 39, 41–42, 174
Futterman, Dan 8–9, 75, 78, 79, 85, 87, 88, 89

Gervais, Ricky 114, 115
The Getaway 18
Giamatti, Paul 139, 140
Glaudini, Bob 72, 100, 106, 115, 124, 141, 151, 160
God's Pocket 160, 161–163, 168, 184
Gosling, Ryan 139, 141
Guirgis, Stephen Adly 27, 42, 50, 51, 66, 73, 105, 110, 115, 127, 137, 141, 167, 179
Gyllenhaal, Jake 129, 171, 177

Hahn, Kathryn 163, 181
Hamburg, John 67, 68, 69
Hanks, Tom 97, 99, 100, 107
Hannah, John 115, 116
Happiness 3, 28, **_29_**, 30–31, 45, 116
Happyish (TV series) 4, 168, 175–176, 181, 182, 183, 184
Hard Eight 21, 23, 43, 47, 143
Hawke, Ethan 3, 14, 94, 95, 96, 137, 149, 159, 177, 179
Hendricks, Christina 161, 163, 168
Hoffman, Cooper 71, 114, 135, 159, 167, 173, 177, 178
Hoffman, Dustin 8, 120, 136, 148
Hoffman, Gordy 5, 6, 53, 54, 55, 85, 89, 173, 177
Hoffman, Tallulah 99, 114, 173
Hoffman, Willa 120, 173
The Hunger Games: Catching Fire 37, 151–152, **_153_**, 154, 160, 164
The Hunger Games: Mockingjay— Part 1 **_153_**, 163–165
The Hunger Games: Mockingjay— Part 2 165–166, 170, 174, 184

I Knew It Was You: Rediscovering John Cazale 126
The Ides of March **_139_**–141, 147, 152

Index

Ifans, Rhys 111, 113
In Cold Blood (novel) 75, 76
Infamous 3, 85, 86
Inside the Actors Studio (TV series) 34, 37, 38, 43, 48, 50
The Invention of Lying 114–115

Jack Goes Boating (film) 3, 115, 121–124, **125**, 126, 129, 134, 135, 136, 142, 160
Jack Goes Boating (play) 100, 104, 115
Jane, Thomas 23, 24–25
Janney, Allison 52, 59, 74
Jenkins, Tamara 90, 92, 93, 110
Joey Breaker 11, **15**, 16
Jones, Toby 3, 85

Katz, David Bar 149, 168, 170, 172, 178, 179
Kaufman, Charlie 81, 97, 99, 101, 102, 104–105
Keener, Catherine 76, 77, 85, 88, 102, 103, 105, 137, 138, 139
Kidman, Nicole 64, 66, 174

LAByrinth Theatre Company 20, 21, 25, 27, 42, 45, 50, 51, 66, 69, 71, 72, 73, 80, 96, 97, 100, 105, 106, 109, 110, 115, 116, 121, 124, 127, 128, 134, 135, 137, 141, 148, 151, 160, 162, 165, 174, 176, 179, 184
The Last Party 51, 52
The Last Party 2000 42, 51–52, 72, 73
Late Night with Conan O'Brien 69, 72, 86
A Late Quartet 137–139, 179
Law, Jude 35, 36, 64, 66, 174
Law & Order 10
Lawrence, Francis 151, 154, 163, 164, 165, 175
Lawrence, Jennifer 151, 163, 164, 165, 175
Leap of Faith 12–13
le Carré, John 147, 155, 156, 158
Ledger, Heath 88, 114, 126
Lee, Spike 62, 63, 64, 177
Leitch, Donovan 51, 52
Liberty! The American Revolution 27
Linney, Laura 90, 91, 92, 93, 110, 177
Long Day's Journey into Night 67, 69–70, 71, 99
Louiso, Todd 26, 53, 54, 55, 56, 72, 174
Love Liza 53–55, 88, 131
Lumet, Sidney 94, 95, 96, 99, 106, 110, 146

Macy, William H. 2, 44
Magnolia **2**, 37–38, 43, 50, 69, 84, 143, 164
Mamet, David 43, 44, 45, 53, 77
Martin, Steve 12, 13
Mary and Max 117–118, **119**, 136

The Master 1, 128, 131, 134, 135, 142–144, **145**, 146, 152, 154, 158, 159, 179
The Merchant of Venice 20, 121, 156
Miller, Arthur 6, 7, 136
Miller, Bennett 8–9, 75, 77, 78, 79, 80, 85, 86, 88, 89, 130, 132, 156
Minghella, Anthony 35, 36, 64, 65, 66
Mission Impossible III 3, 82, **83**, 84, 85, 90, 93, 94, 154
Mitchell, John Cameron 74–75
Money for Nothing 17–18
Moneyball 130–**131**, 132–133, 136, 143, 159
Montana 28
Moore, Julianne 23, 24, 37, 148, 163, 164–165, 166, 174–175, 177
A Most Wanted Man 147, 149, 155–156, **157**, 158, 168, 169, 176, 184
My Boyfriend's Back 16, **17**
My New Gun 11–12

Newman, Paul 19, 60, 81, 82
Next Stop Wonderland 25–26, 103
Nichols, Mike 14–15, 52, 59, 72, 97, 98–99, 120, 131, 135, 136, 146, 148, 149, 177, 183
Nobody's Fool 19–20
Norton, Edward 60, 62, 64, 183

O'Donnell, Mimi 42, 71, 86, 96, 99, 120, 121, 122, 124, 127, 136, 167, 171, 172, 173, 177, 178, 179, 183, 184
O'Neill, Eugene 9, 67, 71, 126
Ortiz, John 20, 51, 73, 96, 100–101, 121, 122, 124, 125–126, 127, 128, 175
Othello 121, 126–127, 128, 136
Owning Mahowny 57–59, 70, 74

Pacino, Al 13, 14, 120
Paltrow, Gwyneth 36, 37, 51
Paquin, Anna 59, 60, 62, 63, 177
Parker, Sarah Jessica 44, 45
The Party's Over see *The Last Party 2000*
Patch Adams 31–32, 45
Pendleton, Austin 9–10, 159, 184
Phoenix, Joaquin 88, 143, 144, 145, 146, 151, 177
Phoenix, River 1, 180
Pirate Radio see *The Boat That Rocked*
Pitt, Brad 1, 130, 132, 134, 139
Punch-Drunk Love 56–57, 143

Ratner, Brett 61, 62, 126, 174
Red Dragon **60**, 61–62, 63
Redgrave, Vanessa 67, 177
Reilly, John C. 21, 23, 24, 37, 43, 46, 47, 48, 49, 50, 56, 177, 183
Reynolds, Burt 23, 24
Riflemind 97, 106, 114, 115

Robards, Jason 37, 38, 69
Roberts, Julia 97, 98, 99
Rockwell, Sam 72, 75, 100
The Rosie O'Donnell Show 46, 47
Rubin-Vega, Daphne 100, 122, 123, 126
Ryan, Amy 121, 122, 125

Salerno, Shane 129–130
Salinger 129–130
The Savages 90–92, **93**, 96, 106, 110, 114
Scent of a Woman **13**, 14, 15, 16, 21, 26, 88
Schepisi, Fred 81–82
Schumacher, Joel 32, 33, 34, 35
The Seagull 37, 52, 59, 72, 97, 98, 138, 148
Sellars, Peter 20, 121, 128
Shanley, John Patrick 85, 101, 107, 108, 109, 110, 121, 126
Shepard, Sam 43, 48, 49
Simply Leon 90
Slattery, John 98, 160, 161, 162, 163, 168, 177
Solondz, Todd 28, 30, 116
Sorkin, Aaron 97, 99, 130, 132
Spielberg, Steven 110, 114
State and Main 3, 43, **44**, 45, 53, 58, 77
Stiller, Ben 67, 68, 69
Strangers with Candy 74
Streep, Meryl 1, 37, 52, 72, 101, 107, 108, 109, 120, 126, 131, 135, 148, 177
Sturridge, Tom 111, 113
Sutherland, Donald 152, 165
Synecdoche, New York 97, 99, 101, 102–103, **104**, 105, 115, 126, 138
Szuler 4, 10–11

The Talented Mr. Ripley 34, **35**, 36–37, 46, 50, 51, 62, 97
Tomei, Marisa 94, 95, 96, 139, 140, 177
Trending Down 163, 168; see also *Happyish*
Triple Bogey on a Par 5 Hole 11
True West 41, 43, 46–50, 56, 59, 135, 178
25th Hour 62–64
Twister 21–22, 40, 46

Upton, Andrew 94, 97, 106, 116, 177

Wahlberg, Mark 23, 24, 25, 62, 174
Walken, Christopher 52, 137, 138
Warchus, Matthew 43, 48, 178
What Sex Am I? 33, 34
When a Man Loves a Woman 19
Williams, Robin 31, 32
A World for Inclusion 120–121
Wright, Robin 155
Wright Penn, Robin 81, 82

The Yearling 18–19

www.ingramcontent.com/pod-product-compliance
Ingram Content Group UK Ltd.
Pitfield, Milton Keynes, MK11 3LW, UK
UKHW050529150426
5217IPUK00026B/1858